RUSSIA'S DEAD END

AN INSIDER'S TESTIMONY FROM GORBACHEV TO PUTIN

ANDREI A. KOVALEV

TRANSLATED BY STEVEN I. LEVINE | FOREWORD BY PETER REDDAWAY

onomist

"The publication of [*Russia's Dead End*] is a notable event. [Andrei Kovalev's] frank account and unsparing analysis of what he learned from his work at senior levels, from Gorbachev's perestroika to Putin's rule, have led him to the conclusion that 'after getting a taste of freedom, Russia has renounced it of its own free will.' . . . *Russia's Dead End* includes a number of pen portraits which ring true . . . and has a good deal to say about the inadequacies of the ruling group, past and present."—Andrew Wood, *International Affairs*

"Is the West fully aware of the dangers this huge, over-stretched nuclear power presents? How will Russia's leaders act and react in a critical situation which is almost bound to come about sooner or later? Not being an armchair alarmist, Kovalev leaves it to his readers to draw the appropriate conclusions from his narrative. If disaster happens, it will be the West's fault as well as the Kremlin's."—Martin Dewhirst, *Salisbury Review*

"Should be required reading for all American students interested in joining an intelligence service or a foreign-policy agency."—*Foreword Reviews*

"Andrei A. Kovalev has an insider's understanding of the Russian state and society. . . . *Russia's Dead End* is brilliantly written."—*Washington Book Review*

"A refreshing report from an insider."—*Kirkus Reviews*

"A fascinating read."—Robert Fantina, *New York Journal of Books*

"Andrei Kovalev has drawn on his remarkable career at the highest level of Russian politics from Gorbachev to Putin to give a picture of both successes and disappointments. This is a book written from the heart by a diplomat of acute intelligence. Kovalev rode the steed of Russian public affairs till his conscience told him to dismount, and this exceptional book explains his reasons."—Robert Service, emeritus professor of Russian history at St. Antony's College, Oxford University

"Andrei Kovalev loves Russia, a different Russia, an open and democratic one, where human rights are respected. His book is a must-read for those who want to understand the most recent history of Russia and who share his love and indignation over how the efforts to democratize his country were ruined by a small yet powerful corrupt clique."—Robert van Voren, professor of Soviet and post-Soviet studies, Vytautas Magnus University in Kaunas, Lithuania

Russia's Dead End

ARCTIC OCEAN

Arctic Circle

SAKHA

R U S S I A

FAR EAST

Lena

Sea of
Okhotsk

Sakhalin
Island

Kurile Islands

Northern
Territories

S I B E R I A

Krasnoyarsk

IRKUTSK

BURIATIA

Lake
Baikal

Khabarovsk

PRIMORSKII
KRAI

TUVA

Irkutsk

Sea of
Japan

MONGOLIA

NORTH
KOREA

JAPAN

SOUTH
KOREA

CHINA

Russia's Dead End

AN INSIDER'S TESTIMONY FROM GORBACHEV TO PUTIN

ANDREI A. KOVALEV

Translated by STEVEN I. LEVINE
Foreword by PETER REDDAWAY

Potomac Books

AN IMPRINT OF THE UNIVERSITY OF NEBRASKA PRESS

A two-volume Russian-language edition of this book was published
under the titles *Svidetel'stvo iz-za kulis rossiiskoi politiki I: Mozhno li delat'
dobra iz zla?* and *Svidetel'stvo iz-za kulis rossiiskoi politiki II: Ugroza dlia
sebia i okruzhaiushchikh* (Stuttgart: Ibidem-Verlag, 2012).

Library of Congress Cataloging-in-Publication Data
Names: Kovalev, A. A. (Andreï Anatol'evich), author.
Title: Russia's dead end: an insider's testimony from Gorbachev to
Putin / Andrei A. Kovalev; translated by Steven I. Levine; foreword
by Peter Reddaway.
Other titles: Svidetel'stvo iz-za kulis rossiïskoï politiki. English
Description: Lincoln: Potomac Books, an imprint of the University of
Nebraska Press, 2017. | "A two-volume Russian-language edition of this
book was published under the titles Svidetel'stvo iz-za kulis rossiiskoi
politiki I: Mozhno li delat' dobra iz zla?; and Svidetel'stvo iz-za kulis
rossiiskoi politiki II: Ugroza dlia sebia i okruzhaiushchikh (Stuttgart:
Ibidem-Verlag, 2012)"—Title page verso. | Includes bibliographical
references and index.
Identifiers: LCCN 2016037673
ISBN 9781612348933 (hardback: alkaline paper)
ISBN 9781640122338 (paper: alkaline paper)
ISBN 9781612349466 (epub)
ISBN 9781612349473 (mobi)
ISBN 9781612349480 (pdf)
Subjects: LCSH: Soviet Union—Politics and government—1985–1991.
| Russia (Federation)—Politics and government—1991– | Glasnost. |
Perestroïka. | Kovalev, A. A. (Andreï Anatol'evich) | Diplomats—Soviet
Union—Biography. | Presidents—Soviet Union—Staff—Biography. |
Political culture—Soviet Union—History. | Political culture—Russia
(Federation)—History. | Post-communism—Russia (Federation)—
History. | BISAC: BIOGRAPHY & AUTOBIOGRAPHY / Personal
Memoirs. | HISTORY / Europe / Russia & the Former Soviet Union.
Classification: LCC DK288 .K6913 2017 | DDC 947—dc23
LC record available at https://lccn.loc.gov/2016037673

Set in Minion Pro by Rachel Gould.

You might not be a poet
But it ought to give you pause
When you see a strip of light
Squeezing out between closed doors.

—ANDREI VOZNESENSKII

CONTENTS

FOREWORD

PETER REDDAWAY

Andrei Kovalev's powerful book argues that Russia's trajectory since 1985 has been circular. First, Mikhail Gorbachev and his colleagues carried out an improbable series of revolutionary reforms, taking their country all the way—as baseball fans would say—from home plate to first base and on to second. After a revolution did in fact occur and the Soviet Union fell apart, Boris Yeltsin presided over a Russia that stumbled back and forth on its way to third base, where he handed it over to Vladimir Putin. Then Putin quietly flooded the system with his colleagues from the secret police, thus infusing it with a Committee for State Security (KGB) mentality. In so doing, he took Russia back to a version of home plate, to a rootless, corrupt, authoritarian, de-ideologized version of the Soviet Union.

Regarding the future, Kovalev sees little likelihood of change in the near term. Domestic policy will continue to become gradually more authoritarian, and foreign policy will feature additional unpredictability and hostility toward the West and its allies. Further ahead, he fears, lie greater dangers, including the possibility of territorial fragmentation. But he hopes that eventually Russia will rebuild itself from the bottom up and join the world community. This monumental task will probably take three generations.

In short, Kovalev's book examines how and why, from 1985 to the present, Russia's domestic and foreign policies evolved in the ways they did. Only occasionally does it look at Western policy toward Russia. When it does, the author often chides the West for not evincing enough interest or generosity toward his homeland, or for showing a disturbing naïveté in appeasing hard-liners in the administrations of Yeltsin and, especially, Putin.

Although the book's initial primary audience was educated Russians, Westerners will be perfectly able to understand and benefit from its arguments. Kovalev's lively prose style and the inner freedom of his attractive personality are additional guarantees of this.

The book refers on occasion to the well-known Russian thinker Pyotr Chaadaev, who, starting in 1836, wrote a somewhat similar work, a series of "Philosophical Letters." In them he lamented his country's chronic backwardness and inability to govern itself. He saw its future as lying in an eventual reunion with European civilization. For his pains, Emperor Nicholas I declared him to be insane. However, after some minor official efforts to treat him for his nonexistent condition, Chaadaev continued to be active in Moscow's intellectual life. Now, 175 years later, Kovalev's diagnosis of Russia's condition evokes Chaadaev's. So does Kovalev's prescription for a cure.

As a former state official of the Union of Soviet Socialist Republics (USSR) and then Russia, Kovalev bases parts of his book on his personal experiences. This applies especially to the years 1986–91, when he was closely involved in the implementation of high-level foreign policy and then worked briefly for President Gorbachev. He also roots his analysis in his training as a historian with a PhD, in the work of Russia's most insightful commentators, and in the experiences of his many friends, including those of his diplomat father, Anatoly Kovalev, who retired as deputy head of the Ministry of Foreign Affairs in 1991.

During his thirty-year career, the author worked for the Institute for U.S. and Canadian Studies and the Diplomatic Academy (1977–85), the Soviet UNESCO (United Nations Educational, Scientific, and Cultural Organization) commission (1985–87), the ministry's Directorate for Humanitarian and Cultural Cooperation (1987–91), the USSR president's office (1991), the Russian mission to the UN's Geneva offices (1992–96), the Russian Security Council (1997–2001), the Russian mission to the European Community in Brussels (2001–4), and the Russian ombudsman for human rights (2004–7). Then, finding the Putin administration too politically oppressive, he moved to Belgium and settled in Brussels.

The first part of his book focuses mainly on the Gorbachev and

Yeltsin periods, the second part on the Putin era. Regarding Gorbachev's so-called perestroika—that is, "the transition from totalitarianism to democracy" in just a few years—the author rightly calls it "probably one of the most interesting, most confused, and most paradoxical periods in the whole history of humanity." Therefore, he goes on, "we should admit—as by no means everyone is ready to do—that each participant, and even observer, of those extraordinarily gripping and dramatic events possesses his own genuinely lived experience, which sometimes has nothing in common not only with what is conventionally called the truth, but even with simple plausibility. Yet they are all primary sources."

The result, Kovalev says, is that a lot of memoirs, journalistic accounts, and academic studies—either deliberately or through ignorance of aspects of what happened—present distorted pictures of events. He himself has tried to avoid this outcome by writing primarily about things that he did or witnessed. Thus, under Gorbachev he was involved in attempts to dismantle totalitarianism, and later, as a diplomat and a Security Council official, he witnessed its regeneration.

As Kovalev emphasizes, the launching of perestroika was far from predetermined. There were elements of sheer chance in Gorbachev's rising to the top and being able to push perestroika through with the strong support, initially, only of Alexander Yakovlev, Eduard Shevardnadze, and a rather small group of other officials. Since Shevardnadze was foreign minister, the Ministry of Foreign Affairs was put to vigorous use as an instrument of change. Meanwhile, most of the other ministries were much less keen on change, and some, like the Ministry of Health, surreptitiously sided with the reactionaries.

Among Soviet diplomats, Kovalev stresses, there were both progressives and conservatives. Shevardnadze mobilized the former, including Kovalev father and son, and tried—with decreasing success over time—to neutralize the latter.

The liberals had usually spent years living abroad. This made it easy for them to observe how far, contrary to Soviet propaganda, the USSR was lagging behind the advanced countries in many fields, notably human rights. Helpfully, the author presents at this point some insightful portraits of senior MINISTRY progressives such as his father, Shevardnadze, Anatoly Adamishin, Vladimir Petrovsky, and Alexei Glukhov. The author notes that the ministry's leadership was sometimes referred to as the "Shevardnadze-Kovalev team," a reflection of his father's personal authority and closeness to Shevardnadze.

How did it happen that Shevardnadze gave Andrei Kovalev important jobs? The key reason was that Kovalev had been the lead writer for an outstandingly successful speech that Gorbachev gave to the international forum "For a Non-nuclear World, for the Survival of Humankind" in February 1987. In this speech Gorbachev was the first Soviet leader to implicitly abandon Marxism and declare that human rights and values were universal. Thus, Kovalev, logically enough, was assigned to the ministry team whose charge was to ensure the massive domestic reforms that the speech effectively promised would be implemented. They involved bringing Soviet legislation into line with the international human rights covenants that the USSR under Brezhnev had signed. This was a major task, given the strong incentive the KGB-aligned leaders of, for example, Soviet psychiatry and the Russian Orthodox Church had to prevent anything more than cosmetic changes from being made to the existing laws.

Kovalev found himself dealing with precisely these people. Their fierce opposition meant that change could only be achieved in stages, over three or four years. Even then, some loopholes remained. It was a strange mission for diplomats to take on, moving domestic legislation in fields where they had no qualifications.

Kovalev's first meeting with the bosses of Soviet psychiatry provoked brazen denials of ethical abuse. Then, after he warned them that reform had been ordered from the top, they collectively walked out. His comment: "We met extraordinary resistance from the Ministry of Health." When asked to supply copies of existing regulations on the procedures for forcible hospitalization, ministry officials replied: "There are no regulations." Kovalev then made the same request in a private meeting with the USSR's chief psychiatrist Alexander Churkin. He got the same answer. However, by this time he had obtained the regulations from a source of his own. He had been shocked by what he read. The documents contained no significant safeguards of citizens' rights, and that made it easy for a relative or coworker or KGB officer to summon a doctor and have any individual, dissident or otherwise, forcibly interned in a mental hospital without reference to a court. The regulations had been signed by a deputy prime minister of health in 1984; however, in view of its unconstitutional and KGB-friendly provisions, it had been treated as a state secret. When Kovalev revealed this knowledge, Churkin sheepishly admitted the document's existence. Then he demanded to know: "How did you learn about it?"

To break down such resistance, Kovalev and his team collected evidence of different forms of abuse from dissidents, liberal lawyers, and a couple of secretly helpful psychiatrists; investigated lists of abuse victims that had been provided by Western governments and human rights groups; wrote interministerial documents that quoted from the liberal psychiatric laws of Vladimir Lenin's government; and offered the top psychiatric officials the carrot of diplomatic help to get the USSR readmitted to the World Psychiatric Association. This was attractive because in 1983 Soviet psychiatry had been pushed out of the association as punishment for using phony diagnoses to intern sane dissidents in mental institutions. Finally, in 1989 after most of these individuals had been released, Shevardnadze and Gorbachev forced a still-resistant Ministry of Health to go along with a lengthy inspection visit to the USSR by a large delegation of American psychiatrists. The group's charge was to investigate all aspects of the system of abuse. As a member of this delegation, I witnessed firsthand several attempts by ministry officials to disrupt the visit.[1]

On another topic, Kovalev and his team set about trying to get freedom of religious belief introduced in the USSR and appropriate legislation passed. Predictably, they encountered forms of determined resistance from the leaders of the Russian Orthodox Church that closely paralleled the unscrupulous blocking tactics of the psychiatrists. The Orthodox leaders were deeply frightened of freedom being given to, in particular, Roman Catholics, Protestants, and the Ukrainian Autocephalous Orthodox Church. These leaders would lose not only a significant proportion of their flock but also several thousand physical churches that had been taken from the other denominations as a result of Josef Stalin's bans and persecutions. Furthermore, their goal of having the Russian Orthodox Church reacquire its tsarist-era status as Russia's established national church would be seriously jeopardized.

Kovalev describes vividly his meetings with some of the leaders of the Russian Orthodox Church and other churches. He observed the predictable effects of their long-term collaboration with the KGB and was dismayed by "the complete absence of spirituality in my religious interlocutors." One of the Orthodox hierarchs, while wining and dining him, disturbed him with his worldliness and his enthusiasm over the murder of the dissident priest Alexander Men.

Gorbachev's fall from power in 1991 evoked Kovalev's regret but not surprise. From the spring of that year he had observed up close, from his seat outside Gorbachev's office, the rise of the conservative and reactionary opposition. He believes, as did Yakovlev, that Gorbachev's biggest mistake was to steadily emasculate the Communist Party. As its head, he should have maneuvered it into supporting and coleading his reforms until enough of a new system was in place. Then he could have gradually disengaged from it. Instead, by eroding and humiliating it, he provoked strong elements within it that, in alliance with their comrades in the KGB and the military, gradually created a hydra-headed opposition.

This opposition made its first major strike in the August 1991 coup. Although the revolt was overthrown in three days by the political resistance of Yeltsin, the Balts, and others, the hardliners never went away. As Kovalev persuasively argues, after the USSR's collapse, they regrouped around the Russian parliament and Yeltsin's crony and personal security chief, the former KGB officer Alexander Korzhakov. Then, even though in 1993 Yeltsin outlawed the parliament and used military force to kill or arrest those who resisted, and even though in 1996 he fired Korzhakov and two of his allies, after each of these occasions the hard-liners regrouped and once again advanced. Key landmarks for them were their successes in persuading Yeltsin in 1994 to invade Chechnya, in 1998 to appoint Putin as Federal Security Service (FSB) head and Yevgeny Primakov as prime minster, and in 1999 to elevate Putin to the premiership.

Kovalev had had misgivings about Yeltsin ever since his political rise in the late 1980s. He had noticed—along with virtues like Yeltsin's inclination to support personal freedoms and free media— his authoritarian personality, his excessive hunger for power, his love of anonymous denunciations of individuals, his readiness to lie when convenient, his toleration of slack and incompetent performance by his staff (a gross example being the work of the foreign policy adviser Sergei Prikhodko), and his drinking, which allowed his associates to manipulate his decisions easily when he had drunk too much alcohol. All this gave rise to contradictory behavior. Yeltsin would resist the hard-liners in both domestic and foreign policy but then suddenly give in to them. Moreover, when his popularity slumped, he created the oligarchs, bought their political support, and approved the crude manipulation of the 1996 election in order to get himself reelected as president. Meanwhile, under his rule the Russian intelligentsia felt unprotected. They were besieged from two sides. On the one hand, they were scared of any return to communism. On the other hand, they feared the further impoverishment of themselves and of Russia. Thus, they tended to abdicate their traditional independence and uncritically support the authorities.

From his job in the Security Council (1997–2001), Kovalev observed some revealing aspects of Yeltsin's dysfunctional administration. He depicts the council mostly through his sketches of five of the six heads of this body for whom he worked. (He was ill during most of Putin's brief tenure.) His first boss was the former speaker of the Duma Ivan Rybkin. Rybkin apparently liked the work of Kovalev's group in fending off the hawks in government who wanted to relaunch the war in Chechnya and their work in carefully planning the delivery of humanitarian aid to a region ravaged by two years of a destructive Russo-Chechen war.

Kovalev made a trip to Grozny to ensure that the convoy of trucks would receive safe passage. However, when all was set to go, some unknown intervention occurred, and Rybkin refused to sanction the operation. He gave no explanation. Evidently the business or other interests of some powerful individual or group would have been harmed if the aid, which represented a small token of Russia's atonement for the war, had been delivered.

Andrei Kokoshin came next, a rude and arrogant egocentric, according to Kovalev, who thought he didn't need help from his staff. He soon left but only after writing bad reports on the members of the staff—namely, individuals whom he had not used. Most of the president's orders to him had just piled up on his desk untouched. Kokoshin was interested only in issues of nuclear nonproliferation and export controls, the field for which Kovalev was the responsible official. But he did not consult with Kovalev, who, it happened, had uncovered a dangerous situation in which poverty had driven Russian scientists to sell classified information.

At this time also the scandalous case of Yevgeny Adamov, a senior Yeltsin official, came to light. He was widely suspected of commercially motivated crimes in the field of arms exports. Kovalev says that the evidence he found on this subject pointed to criminal activity. In 1998 he was appointed as Security Council representative on Prime Minister Primakov's commission of inquiry into the Adamov case and related issues. Kovalev writes that Adamov apparently had active links with well-known figures in the world of organized crime and that he had set up companies in the United States with a Russian émigré partner. Also, the impression grew in informed circles that the secret proliferation of nuclear materials might actually, de facto, be part of Kremlin policy. The commission's report, signed by Primakov, recommended that Adamov be fired. However, all this work came to nothing, because Adamov's partners included Yeltsin's daughter Tatyana Diachenko and other members of the president's political "family." Apparently these people barred any action.

In 2005, however, the Americans, who had long been on Adamov's trail, had the Swiss police arrest him. After a period in jail, he was turned over to the Russians rather than the Americans. He was tried and sentenced but, thanks to his high-level associates, was soon released.

The next head of the Security Council, a former KGB general called Nikolai Bordiuzha, was the only one of the six to leave with a positive reputation. Apparently honest, he also showed himself to be both focused and hardworking. His successor was Putin, who, on becoming prime minister four months later, passed the torch to his close associate Sergei Ivanov, who served from 1999 to 2001. Kovalev found Ivanov to be a remarkably superficial and hypocritical person, with deep prejudices and the cunning of a fox. He was also a narcissist who wore bright pink and blue shirts and ties to the office.

However, the most incompetent of the six was the last, a former police chief called Vladimir Rushailo. He knew nothing about international affairs and wasn't interested in them. At his first meeting with foreigners, he read out loud every word of his briefing paper, including the reference section at the end. He didn't realize that this section included some classified information. The unsuspecting Rushailo was happy with his performance—and the foreigners were even happier.

In 1999 Russia's mounting political chaos and bureaucratic paralysis, both aggravated by Yeltsin's deepening problems with alcohol, produced a situation that played into the hands of the already-prospering reactionaries. Hence occurred Yeltsin's calculated early resignation and the orchestrated election of Putin. This was followed by Putin's cleverly judged measures to "restore order" and by a gradual, mostly disguised trend toward reactionary policies over the next few years. From 2003, Kovalev argues, the reaction steadily discarded its disguise as being unnecessary, given that the Russian people actually supported or tolerated this reverse course.

Here Kovalev displays the insights of a social psychologist. It is difficult, he argues, for human beings to accept and adapt to large-scale change. In the late 1980s communist dogmas and idols were destroyed wholesale. For a time the people rejoiced that they could now express their resentments and hatreds of the communist regime, could exercise some choice, and could enjoy some personal freedoms.

But then Russia's status as a superpower vanished. And the economic disasters of the early 1990s struck most of the population. They had to struggle just to survive. They could do nothing to right the wrongs of communism. As time went by, they began to want relief from their sense of guilt and helplessness. They craved a freedom from responsibility, conscience, and choice and a protection from knowledge about the past. They consciously or unconsciously desired strong leadership and censorship of the media.

All this was highly convenient for Putin, who declared off the record in December 1999: "Order number one has been carried out. The FSB has successfully embedded itself in the government." Kovalev argues convincingly that this was probably the first real chance for the secret police to take power themselves. He dismisses, as do I, the theory that Yury Andropov had a chance to do so in 1982. He points out that in 1956 Andropov had his eyes opened by the Hungarian revolution, when he was Soviet ambassador to Budapest. Also, in 1975 he had supported Soviet acceptance of the human rights provisions of the Final Act of the Conference on Security and Cooperation in Europe. And he had backed the promotion of "within-system dissidents" like Fyodor Burlatsky and Georgy Arbatov. None of this indicated a man who favored a dictatorship run by the secret police.

Much of part 2 of Kovalev's book consists of his long cry of lamentation for the fate of his country under Putin. It is a terrifying and all-too-justified indictment. He goes to the heart of the matter by quoting Nikolai Nekrasov. In 1875 the poet said that Russia had endured harder times in the past but not times that were morally more despicable (*podlei*). This judgment, which Kovalev finds even more applicable to the present than to 1875, evokes another example of Putin's astounding good luck. His rule coincided with an unprecedented rise in the world prices for oil and gas. The resulting financial windfalls enabled the government to pay off its debts, fill the coffers of the treasury, and start spending serious money on remilitarization (much of it fortunately embezzled). Remilitarization was considered essential to the overarching project of "restoring Russia's greatness (*velichie*)."

Kovalev's succession of laments is a long one. The regime took control of the national TV channels and imposed upon them an effective censorship. Dissenters and members of the opposition were isolated in a small "information ghetto," where they could do little harm. The Kremlin dubbed Putin "the national leader" and photographed him in a wide variety of heroic roles and meetings with bikers, submariners, sportsmen, and entertainers. It promoted the Stalinist practice of having citizens voluntarily inform the authorities about suspicious or undesirable activities (*stukachestvo*). It organized and indoctrinated groups of young storm troopers, sometimes called Putinjugend, who have flexed their muscles on demonstrating dissidents and wayward foreign ambassadors. The Kremlin also sponsored the development of a "national ideology" (previously attempted in vain by Yeltsin), partly to make it easier to identify and target "enemies" among the population. Candidates for this status have included Caucasians, Central Asians, Islamists, and "political extremists" of various stripes, especially radical liberals and radical Russian nationalists. And it stepped up the amount of secret police eavesdropping on citizens' phone conversations and on various means of electronic communication.

The regime also set up a commission under President Medvedev to counter attempts to "falsify" history that put Russia in a bad light. And it tried to prevent the Organization for Security and Cooperation in Europe from passing a resolution condemning the Molotov-Ribbentrop Pact of 1939. The Kremlin also promoted the Russian Orthodox Church as being, in all but name, the country's established national church and plied it with both material and nonmaterial privileges. As a result, the church's leaders routinely bless the government in public and vote for its nominees in elections.

On the political side, Putin's regime eroded democratic institutions by abolishing the popular election of governors, banning the formation of blocs of parties, removing the line "against all" on election ballots, forbidding candidates to attack each other on television, narrowing the possibility of calling a referendum, reducing the minimum turnout needed for elections to be valid, and reintroducing the Soviet practices of falsifying election results and of requiring state employees to vote for the main government party. It also expanded the use of violence and murder against political opponents (Anna Politkovskaya, Alexander Litvinenko) and "inconvenient people" (Ivan Kiveledi, Roman Tsepov), and it waged massive violence and state terrorism in the North Caucasus, especially Chechnya, and in emergency situations like the Moscow theater and Beslan school tragedies.

In the field of illegal arms sales, the Kremlin protected practitioners of sales from exposure. When Kovalev worked in the Security Council, he saw documents that provoked his grave doubts as to whether the government was covertly proliferating nuclear materials.

Putin and his associates, by their example, caused corruption to become rampant in almost all spheres of life, and they encouraged xenophobia. They failed to discourage the highly dangerous practice of *dedovshchina*, or "systematic bullying" in the military. They pumped streams of money into an irretrievably demoralized army and a grossly inefficient weapons industry, with negligible results. They neglected the renewal of Russia's infrastructure and the building of badly needed new roads. Further, they allowed the education and health care sectors to provide declining levels of service to those people who could not afford to pay for privatized services.

The most serious broad problems, in Kovalev's view, are twofold: First, the authorities act as they wish, with no sense of being accountable to the law. Second, the population has been demoralized and rendered passive and manipulable by its political emasculation and its sense of helplessness in the face of police power and all-pervasive corruption.

In foreign policy, Kovalev sees the picture as equally gloomy. Through the regime's unearned sense of entitlement, Russia became "a danger to itself and those around it." Toward the West, Putin's administration was markedly more hostile than Yeltsin's was, but it still contrived on most occasions to mask the extent of this hostility. It also offered the West cooperation in certain limited spheres. Putin was astute to seize the opportunity presented by Al Qaeda's attack on the United States in September 2001. He promoted the convenient Russian line that extremist Muslim terrorism is a single, interconnected, worldwide phenomenon and that therefore the West should cooperate with the Kremlin in combating such terrorism inside Russia.

In the face of all this, Kovalev retains his hope that there are in fact some limits to the Putin regime's anti-Western policies. He argues, plausibly, that the Russian ruling class has deposited its capital in the West for safekeeping; therefore, it cannot afford to allow Putin to go too far.

As for Russia's neighbors in the Commonwealth of Independent States, Kovalev recounts the manifold ways in which the Kremlin has alienated them through its bullying, its political interference, and its use of such tools as gas supply blackmail, trade embargoes, encouragement of regional secession (contrary to Russia's traditional position), and, in the case of Georgia in 2008 and Ukraine in 2014, outright military force. As mentioned earlier, Kovalev rebukes the West for not opposing seriously enough the unrealistic but dangerous grandiosity of the Putin regime's foreign policy that obtains in regard both to the CIS and to the world at large. In some cases like that of Georgia, Kovalev sees the West's lack of concern as "amoral." More broadly, however, the West is indulging in a morally dubious Realpolitik that is likely to contain the seeds of danger for the West itself. It does not understand that, as Kovalev perceptively writes, Russia is currently led by individuals whose personalities display "a childish willfulness" (*infantilizm*). This willfulness comprises egocentricity, cruelty, hysteria, theatricality, irresponsibility, emotional immaturity, an imperviousness to reason, an inability to take account of the views and interests of others and to separate fantasy from reality, and a lack of concern for other people's suffering.

Kovalev sees Russia—with such an albatross of leadership around its neck—as having entered a second period of stagnation (*zastoi*). The first was under Brezhnev and his successors in the 1970s and the first half of the 1980s. Today the country's leaders are even more incompetent than were the Brezhnevite gerontocrats. They can tighten the screws, but they will continue to use terror only against individuals and small groups. They "simply won't be capable of engaging in mass repressions." These people have taken Russia into a dead end, and so far there is no sign of a new group of Gorbachevites waiting in the wings, preparing to extract it. Moreover, Russia is like "a disintegrating, delayed-action bomb." Thus, internal upheavals and/or territorial fragmentation are conceivable and even likely in due course. Eventual hope lies in an arduous and protracted rebuilding of its society and state from below.

Kovalev ends with some words from Chaadaev. His choice of quotation, like the theme of his eloquent book, shows how closely, across nearly two centuries, he and Chaadaev are in tune with each other. "It is permissible, I think," writes Chaadaev, "in the face of our tribulations, not to share the aspirations of the unbridled patriots who have brought our country to the edge of the abyss, and who believe they can muddle through by persisting in their illusions and not caring to notice the desperate situation that they themselves have created."

It would have been pleasant if Kovalev could have reached a less harsh conclusion. But, like Chaadaev, he believes that a cure can proceed only from a diagnosis that discerns correctly the core of the disease. In this book he offers an unflinching, perceptive, and compellingly written diagnosis.

PREFACE

In the twilight years of the Union of Soviet Socialist Republics, its then leader Mikhail Gorbachev and his colleagues made substantial contributions toward establishing democracy in their country. The infrastructure of Soviet totalitarianism was dismantled. The outlines of parliamentarianism, a multiparty system, the entire spectrum of civil and political rights, and authentic nongovernmental organizations appeared, and civil society began to take shape. But later it seemed, and soon became obvious, that things were regressing. In the Putin era one could only feel nostalgia for what, to borrow the words of Ivan Bunin, was the free atmosphere of the last two to three years of the USSR.[1] How had Russia's dismemberment of Georgia in 2008, its annexation of Crimea, its aggression against Ukraine, and the Kremlin's deliberate destruction of the entire system of international security become possible? In essence, this is the key question for the future not only of Russia but of the West and all humankind as well. After all, even a weakened Russia plays an extremely important role in the contemporary world.

It seems that some sort of evil fate is haunting Russia. Whatever happens, this evil fate turns against it and others. Russia's efforts to enhance national and international security lead to increased threat. Both the paternalism directed toward its own people as well as the neglect of their interests lead toward extinction. The state becomes degraded by force either of circumstances or of its own accord. Democracy fails to take root in Russia, for not only are reforms always implanted "from above," but with some sort of fatal inevitability, they also lead to disasters. In 1881 at the height of his liberal reforms Alexander II, the tsar who abolished serfdom, was assassinated by those who supposedly cared for the welfare of the people. This resulted in the counterreforms of Tsars Alexander III and Nicholas II, whose feckless policies led to the Bolshevik coup d'état. The brief interregnum between the fall of the monarchy and the Bolshevik putsch was even more significant. The provisional government was so full of good intentions that it turned out to be nonviable. Decades later, after Gorbachev's reforms began to be implemented, which did not happen until 1989, he formally retained power only until the end of 1991. Thereafter he became the most detested head of state in the history of Russia. The final collapse of the democratic transformation of Russia may definitively be dated to the autumn of 1993, when a constitutional crisis was resolved by force rather than through dialogue and compromise. Official and unofficial agents of the special services who came to power in 2000 under the collective pseudonym of Vladimir Putin exercised an inordinate influence over all aspects of Russian life.

What are the deep-rooted reasons why Russia represents a menace to itself and to those around it, and why has democracy remained alien to Russia? The overriding objective of this book is to attempt to provide at least preliminary answers to these questions.

Russia does not adhere to a normal conservatism that carefully preserves the best and discards that which is obsolete. By some strange sort of logic, in Russia conservatism has become a synonym for stagnation, the preservation of the existing order of things at any price. It is no accident that the concept of conservatism is absent from the political life and even from the everyday political vocabulary of contemporary Russia. Its camouflaged synonym is Putin's "stability." Evidently, the "national leader" has not read Aldous Huxley's *Brave New World*. However, there is another possibility: he read and admired Huxley's model of social organization.

It is extremely difficult to grasp what is going on in Russia and even more difficult to conceive of various possible future scenarios. This is especially true because the state constantly lies about both the present and the past, and it does everything in its power to withhold reliable information. But if there is no key that will open the doors to the repositories of truth that are securely bolted with both medieval and contemporary padlocks, it is both possible and necessary to pick these locks.

The author's testimony of how the Augean stables of Soviet totalitarianism were cleaned out during the period of Gorbachev's perestroika may serve as one pick with which to open these locks.[2]
Such testimony about bygone days provides a retrospective on the
more distant past and illuminates the present field of vision. The
second pick is the author's know-how, initially acquired in the
course of scholarly work, then via service in the Ministry of Foreign Affairs of the USSR and later the Russian Federation, in the
secretariat of President Gorbachev, and on the staff of the Security
Council of Russia. The combination of theoretical and practical
political work can lead to interesting results. Working in whatever
capacity in such institutions will yield nothing to the investiga-
tor in and of itself without freedom from dogma, stereotypes, and
preconceived analysis (*liberum examen*) of problems. When one
has worked on all sorts of issues ranging from international relations to domestic problems and human rights in both the USSR
and Russia, the picture that emerges is quite broad and multifac-
eted. Such a *liberum examen* thus constitutes the third pick. Using
these picks, I will try, first of all, to analyze the reasons why the
most profound democratic reformation in Russia, that initiated
by Mikhail Gorbachev, failed.

The epoch of the transformation of the USSR from totalitarianism to democracy during perestroika is perhaps one of the most
interesting, intricate, and paradoxical periods in the entire history
of humanity. There can hardly be any doubt about the significance
of dismantling a regime covering one-sixth of the earth's surface
that even the term *cannibalistic* describes inadequately. The intri-
cacies of this historical period are even more complicated. Every
participant or even observer of those fascinating and dramatic
events has his or her own perspective, which sometimes bears
no resemblance to what actually went on. And they are the primary sources . . .

The personal and other ambitions of some authors of memoirs, of researchers, and of journalists occasionally distort the historical mirrors to such an extent that quite soon after the events
it is often difficult to distinguish between the truth and its falsification. Sometimes, however, this is done unconsciously as a

result of an ignorance of what has transpired. But almost no one admits to such ignorance, and this gives rise to the Big Lie, so characteristic of Russia.

Well-intentioned authors should decide for themselves how to avoid purveying such falsification. One possible means is to write only about events in which one has personally participated or, at a minimum, of which one has direct knowledge. Without aspiring to "truth in the highest degree," such an approach allows me to sketch that part of history in which I was a participant. I was one of the reform-minded officials who attempted to create good out of evil in the USSR (to borrow a thought from one of Robert Penn Warren's characters, who considered that more good can be made from nothing). Such an approach also enables me to discuss the subsequent regeneration of evil after the collapse of the USSR.

The reader may derive a partly justified impression that I was not involved in some of the questions touched upon in this book. That would not be completely accurate. Taking part in insider politics entails possession of a broad spectrum of information; it is impossible to be fully engaged in policy formulation and implementation without knowing all facets of a problem. Needless to say, that is only possible if one does not function as an "answering machine" but takes a responsible attitude toward one's work—that is, pursuing not personal advantage but rather the interests of one's country. An important part of one's personal know-how is gained through the tons of official papers one has drafted and dozens of tons of such papers that one has read, as well as the exchanges of views in the hallways of power and, consequently, the sharing of information.

A fundamental misunderstanding exists concerning the decisive role of leaders such as presidents, prime ministers, ministers, and the like. That's not how things work. These personages are manipulated by their entourages. For example, in 1997–98, Ivan Rybkin, the secretary of the Security Council of the Russian Federation, and the staff he headed had a different, softer, and more balanced position regarding the enlargement of the North Atlantic Treaty Organization (NATO) than other ministries and departments did. I don't think that he was fully aware of what was going on, but it would have been wrong for me to pass up the opportunity to influence the Russian position on this matter. Unfortunately, my efforts were fruitless, but I can't go into details out of consideration for the safety of those colleagues who pretended they did not notice the game I was playing. After the government prohibited direct contact with foreigners and after it said that the West was "looking for our weak link," I had to admit my defeat. There are many similar examples in this book.

The second task is to reveal why, as early as the presidency of Boris Yeltsin, Russia took the path of revanchism and reaction. There are three aspects to this. Regarding the first, that of power, we need to try and understand why and how the Russian authorities adopted increasingly reactionary positions in both foreign and domestic politics beginning in the early years of the administration of Yeltsin, a man who was considered a democrat. The reasons that the Russian people followed this path constitute the second factor. Finally, the third aspect is why international society closed its eyes to the negative phenomena in Russia.

Closely connected to this is a third task: to try to imagine Russia's future as well as its shared future with the West. Here we need to address the question of whether the Cold War has actually ended and, if so, when and why. For many reasons the generally accepted view that it ended with the fall of the Berlin Wall is unconvincing.

Analyzing what is happening in and around Russia would be an entirely unproductive undertaking if one did not renounce myths and stereotypes. Unfortunately, an independent analysis of what is happening in contemporary Russia and of possible paths of development yields a cheerless conclusion. A new pernicious period of stagnation has begun in Russia, rife with the most dangerous consequences.

The fourth task consists of trying to define what is the starting point of contemporary Russian history. In the following text I argue that in many respects contemporary Russia began as a result of the August 1991 putsch.

While revising the text of my book for the English edition, I was struck by the many references to the special services.[3] Unfortunately, my own experience, as well as the analysis based on information about their activities, demonstrates without question the fatal role that existed under the leadership of the Communist Party of the Soviet Union (CPSU) and the Committee of State Security (KGB). After the collapse of the USSR, the CPSU and the KGB ceased to exist. But the monster—the security apparatus—survived and remained essentially the same as before. It may be named the Central Committee of State Security.

Although this book deals with the period when, in various capacities, I was a direct participant in or an informed observer of Soviet and Russian politics, by necessity it cannot strictly be limited to this time frame. To understand what was going on, it is sometimes necessary to refer in rather broad terms to the history of Russia. Moreover, many of the phenomena that originated in those years became evident only after I left government service and the homeland where I was born and had spent practically my entire life.

As testimony regarding the period from roughly 1985 to 2007, this book is based exclusively upon the facts and figures I relied on in my own work and that were known in the circles of power.

A final thought. The author and journalist Vladimir Giliarovskii pointedly remarked:

> Russia has two great curses.
> Below is the power of darkness
> While above is the darkness of power.

Squeezed between them is the realm of light, the realm of everything that is better in Russia and what the poet Andrei Voznesenskii spoke of in the verse cited in the epigraph of this book. Expanding the realm of light is objectively in the interest of everyone, in Russia itself and in the democracies, apart from those in the Kremlin, the Russian White House, the Lubyanka, and other Russian power structures who manipulate the power of darkness for the sake of the darkness of power. In what follows I devote primary attention to the search for a way to diminish the realm of darkness in Russian life.

The genre of this book—personal testimony—means that the reader should have some conception of just who the author is. Therefore, I must introduce myself. How can I do this most efficiently? Just who am I? Am I, according to Antoine de Saint-Exupéry, the sum of my human relations—my family, friends, acquaintances, enemies? Am I the sum of my knowledge gleaned from my own life and the countless number of books I have read? My experience, sometimes positive, sometimes negative? Poetry and literature that have moved me? Musical harmonies and art?

I think in the first place it should not be forgotten that we are all children of our parents and grandchildren of our grandfathers and grandmothers. My family was very different from others in our milieu. It was as if we lived in parallel worlds.

Generally speaking and in all seriousness, I am not sure just what "I" am. Therefore, for a start, I will follow the tried-and-true method worked out by personnel departments. I will fill out the standard columns of a questionnaire, although I will do this informally.

Personal Name, Family Name

I like my name Andrei. I am indebted to my father for it. When I was born as just another nameless creature, the process began of choosing a name for me. Father listened, but the names he wanted to give his son were not to the liking of others in the family. Then he said, "We will call him *Afrikan!*"

Panic ensued among the relatives. But father stood firm. *Afrikan* it would be . . .

"Perhaps, nevertheless, we will call him *Andriusha*," someone timidly suggested several days later.

"I still prefer *Afrikan*, but I think . . ."

And he thought for a long time until the others gave up. Then, as if reluctantly, he assented, . . . and his son was given the very name that he had wanted all along.

As for the family name, Kovalev, it sounds both very ordinary but is also a source of pride. I say very ordinary because there are lots of Kovalevs (just as there are lots of Kuznetsovs and Smiths). I am proud of it for two reasons. First, because it is my family's name. My own. Second, because of those who also bear the name.

It is under this name, Andrei Kovalev, that I have made my way through life. Sometimes I walk about, sometimes I run, sometimes I crawl, sometimes I sink into the swamp . . .

Patronymic

Anatol'evich. Because my father is Anatoly Kovalev, a well-known diplomat, politician, and poet in the 1960s through the 1980s who worked under a pseudonym as a journalist and screenwriter for documentary films. He also wrote the *Alphabet of Diplomacy*, which went through six editions.

Without the slightest doubt, I can say that he was the primary influence on me. He was a very solid and well-integrated man, but at first glance one might mistake him for a mass of contradictions. He was a diplomat with one of the most brilliant careers in the country, thus implying he had a fair measure of pragmatism, but at the same time he was an idealist and a romantic. He was one of the closest intimates of all the leaders of the USSR from Leonid Brezhnev (1964–82) to the last general secretary of the country, Mikhail Gorbachev (1985–91), with whom he was particularly close. At the same time, in his verses he barely concealed his opposition to the existing order and rulers during the era of stagnation (1964–85), and that was especially dangerous for a person of his position in Soviet society.

Actually there were no contradictions. He was simply a very gifted, hardworking, and stalwart person. This deserves at least a brief explanation.

The son of a colonel in the military medical service and the secretary of the director of the Bolshoi Theatre, Father grew up in the atmosphere of the Stalinist repressions. He never believed that his friends' parents who were arrested were "enemies of the people," and early on he understood everything about the Stalinist regime. In the xenophobic USSR, he had to know how to defend himself, including from physical aggression. Therefore, he took up boxing while a schoolboy. Like many of his peers, he was attracted to the especially apolitical game of chess and was en route to a good career in chess. But he chose instead to enter the Institute of International Relations (the present MGIMO) and the Literary Institute, and he studied at both simultaneously until he was warned that the KGB was interested in his verses.[4] He had to give up the Literary Institute.

He became the youngest department head in the Ministry of

Foreign Affairs, the youngest deputy minister, and the architect of the policy of détente. He fell into semi-disgrace, however, because of the Final Act of the Conference on Security and Cooperation in Europe (CSCE) and endured genuine persecution following the Soviet aggression against Afghanistan in 1979 and the USSR's turn toward confrontation with the West. He served as first deputy minister of foreign affairs under Gorbachev and was one of the architects of the new Soviet foreign policy. He preferred to work at his desk, solving real problems, rather than attend press conferences, diplomatic receptions, and other glittering gala events. He did not forsake his passion for poetry, which, first and foremost, reflects his political and civic positions.

In practice, to a high degree my professional development and my development as a human being occurred in this milieu.

What does a crisis of some sort—Caribbean, Mideast, Berlin—mean for any person, especially a child or an adolescent, wherever he might live?[5] Even more, a diplomatic document? In the best case, it is something deserving a few minutes of attention (if, of course, one isn't living in the area and is not directly affected by it). Everything was different for me. My father, gray from exhaustion, sometimes explained what was going on, sometimes was strikingly silent (as he was after the Prague Spring or the Soviet aggression against Afghanistan). News of the assassination of President John F. Kennedy burst into our home via a phone call from a family friend who had heard about it on the Voice of America. The ministry called after Father had already hurried out from our home. This is how the world in which I lived began to make sense to me, and politics became a natural environment, something like a way of life.

Toward what ends did Father employ his diplomatic mastery, his political influence, and his fighting character?

In 1965 after receiving an independent sphere of activity as director of the First European Department of the Ministry of Foreign Affairs of the USSR (France, Italy, Spain, Belgium, Switzerland, Portugal, Holland, the Vatican, and several small states), he immediately initiated a review of relations with these countries. France came first. The first tangible result of this work was the start of international détente, beginning in 1966, that arose from

President Charles de Gaulle's visit to the USSR. Parenthetically, I should say that the alternative to détente was an increase in international tension, threatening to lead to a large-scale war involving nuclear weapons. Father went down in history as a man dedicated to détente, from which he never retreated even though the Soviet leadership renounced it.

He made use of détente not only to overcome the threat of war and improve relations with the West but also to ameliorate the situation inside the USSR, particularly with regard to human rights. As far back as the 1970s, the heyday of the period of stagnation, Father was able to convince the USSR, quite uncharacteristically, to assume an obligation in the area of human rights, in particular with regard to the Final Act of the CSCE. In preparation for the conference, he succeeded in getting the Soviet Union to ratify the international human rights treaties.

His closeness to Brezhnev and Yury Andropov, to say nothing of Gorbachev, enabled Father to influence domestic policy as well.

The unique common denominator of his behavior was his critical attitude toward Josef Stalin. During this period one's attitude toward Stalin was a key indicator of one's political outlook. During the period of stagnation, serious efforts were made to rehabilitate Stalin. (Unfortunately, these efforts succeeded in the time of Putin.) This was a fundamental question of domestic and foreign policy since rehabilitating Stalin would inevitably signal an extreme hardening of Soviet policy in both foreign and domestic affairs, including transforming the Cold War into a "hot war." I could write a great deal about this, but I will confine myself to just one example, the question of whether—and if so, how—to punish Alexander Solzhenitsyn whose epic work *The Gulag Archipelago*, officially banned in the Soviet Union, had exposed Stalin's system of slave labor camps.

The then minister of foreign affairs and Politburo member Andrei Gromyko once asked Father about his attitude toward Solzhenitsyn. His immediate answer could not have pleased the minister: "I consider Solzhenitsyn a great Russian writer." That ended the conversation. KGB chairman Andropov also discussed the question of Solzhenitsyn with Father. "If, inevitably, something must be done about Solzhenitsyn," Father said to the all-powerful chief of the KGB, "my opinion is as follows: Do not bring him to trial and do not lay hands on him." But many wanted to do precisely that—that is, lay hands on him.

There was a follow-up to these conversations. Politburo member and chairman of the Soviet trade unions Alexander Shelepin, known as "Iron Shurik," flew into Geneva.[6] According to him, the Politburo had decided to put Solzhenitsyn on trial. In the evening, before flying out of Geneva, Shelepin invited Father to take a stroll around the delegation grounds and asked him if the head of the Soviet delegation to the negotiations could tell him he had no objection to putting Solzhenitsyn on trial. Father replied with a thunderous "No!" He spelled out his position in a coded message to Moscow so there would be no possibility of his words being distorted. Did it play a role in the subsequent fate of the great writer? Given that Solzhenitsyn was "only" exiled, one may conclude that the answer to this question is yes.

I also soon learned of another hardly insignificant episode that occurred during the second stage of the CSCE.

Father knew how to take risks and not only in calculating moves in chess. He was willing to wager everything when it came to his convictions and ideals. This is how he acted in bargaining for the principle of the inviolability of borders, so dear to Brezhnev's heart, in exchange for supporting the "third basket," which is dedicated to human rights, in the Final Act of the CSCE. The day before, he consulted with his wife—my mother—warning her of the risk that serious official troubles resulting from his support of the third basket might also affect the family. Not a single one of the delegation members failed to support his proposals. Moscow also gave its assent. The result was that the Final Act, which has long served as a foundational document of European politics, was signed and sealed, but Father and his convictions then fell out of favor, and he barely avoided being forced into retirement. He was unwilling to sacrifice his ideals. Mikhail Gorbachev, via the intercession of Alexander Yakovlev, restrained him from retiring. After Gorbachev came to power, Father became one of the chief architects of the new Soviet foreign policy, exerting invaluable influence on the democratic reformation of the country and propagating the idea of human rights and democratic standards. Of course, it was not by chance that Gorbachev later entrusted Father with representing him in Stockholm when the president of the USSR was awarded the Nobel Peace Prize.

It would hardly do to call the atmosphere in which we lived normal. We knew that we were always being followed and that not only was our telephone tapped but our whole apartment was bugged as well.

The following occurred . . .

Father, tense and literally ashen, came home and informed Mother and me that we should be extremely cautious and say nothing unnecessary. (As if he were unaware that we didn't know this!) Strange, fantastic words were spoken: "I am under arrest. This is very serious. Act accordingly." The conversation was over. Confused, we went off to our own rooms. Obviously, Father was in a terrible mood.

Later, I learned the following, which I quote from Father's memoirs.

In early April 1973, I got a call from Brezhnev's office saying that he was inviting me and several other colleagues to his dacha outside of Moscow. . . . Something unusual was afoot. It turned out that Brezhnev had invited several persons: [Andrei] Alexandrov, [Anatoly] Blatov, [Georgy] Arbatov, [Anatoly] Chernyaev, me, and, I think also Nikolai Shishlin.

In Brezhnev's small, second-floor office he started the conversation in a roundabout way, in a sort of confessional tone. The leitmotif of the conversation was the feeling of deepening solitude which, in the words of Leonid Ilyich, was increasingly evident around him. As persons experienced in these matters and accustomed to the general secretary's mode of expression, we had no particular difficulty in deciphering that what he was getting at were changes he was contemplating in the leadership, in the Politburo. But he did not speak directly about this or of anything concrete. He ended the conversation in a peculiar way; he picked up the telephone and spoke to Andropov.[7]

"Yurii," Brezhnev said, "I have with me the following persons." He ticked off our names. "From now on consider them under arrest and don't lose sight of them." Addressing us, Brezhnev asked, "Did you hear what I said? Well, let's go to tea. Viktoriia Petrovna is inviting us."

What a charming situation. In effect it was an invitation to a family tea with the leader of a superpower while simultaneously under a peculiar form of arrest and the looming threat of punishment.

Often a man is known by the friends he keeps. In Father's case, a list of several of his main enemies is more revealing: Mikhail Suslov, a Politburo member and number 2 on the Central Committee of the Communist Party of the Soviet Union and, consequently, of the USSR during the Brezhnev era; Nikolai Podgorny, the chairman of the Presidium of the Supreme Soviet of the USSR; Viktor Grishin, a member of the Politburo and first secretary of the Moscow Municipal Committee of the CPSU; Shelepin, a member of the Politburo of the CPSU, who was joined at a certain point by his immediate superior, Minister of Foreign Affairs Gromyko; Yegor Ligachev, a member of the Politburo and number 2 in the country during the era of perestroika; and Vladimir Kriuchkov, the KGB boss during the same period. Of course, this list is far from including even all of Father's distinguished enemies.

During perestroika Father was able to come fully into his own. He was one of the inspirers and authors of Gorbachev's January 1986 proposal for the complete elimination of nuclear weapons, of the concept of a common European home, and of a nuclear-free and nonviolent world. He was an unconditional supporter of German reunification and played an important role in averting a military clash between the USSR and NATO at the time the Berlin Wall came down. He was a champion of the decolonization of the Eastern and Central European countries, he was responsible for the reduction of military confrontation in Europe, and he discovered evidence confirming the existence of the secret protocols of the Molotov-Ribbentrop Pact. This is far from a complete list of his accomplishments. In sum, he was a poet and philosopher of diplomacy.

Date and Place of Birth

The very fact of my forthcoming appearance on earth was problematic for a long time. My grandfather Professor Nikolai Zavalishin, a two-star general of military medical services, was in disgrace toward the end of Stalin's rule. On the day the tyrant died, on Stalin's desk lay a blacklist headed by my grandfather's name. Had Stalin signed it, Grandfather would have been liquidated. Afterward, in the best case, the members of the family of "the enemy of the people" would have become prisoners of the GULAG and I would not have been born in October 1953.

Even though my place of birth, Moscow, may be where one would expect me to have been born, I was actually supposed to be born in Berlin. Father was working there at the time on the staff of the Supreme Commissar Vladimir Semenov. Sensing what would happen in 1953, he sent Mother to Moscow.[8]

It was never clear why my peers befriended me, whether because they liked me or from work obligations. I confess I made more than one mistake. The worst was that of idealizing people, thinking them better than they were. However, I have one excuse: I was deceived by the worst kind of people; there were none worse than they. And from a desire for self-preservation I alienated worthy persons. Mea culpa.

I understood early in life that in order to survive in the USSR one had to put on an act, to seem to be someone other than who you really were. Fyodor Tyutchev's well-known maxim—"Keep quiet, keep a low profile, don't reveal yourself"—became practically the dominant mode of life for many decades.[9]

Nationality

First, let me explain that in Russian the word *nationality* has a different meaning than in other languages, where nationality is a synonym for citizenship. In Russia and in the Russian language, it means one's ethnicity. Therefore, speaking in Russian, I am Russian. This means a lot. But at the same time it means nothing. Why?

Russia, and before that the USSR, consists of numerous and extremely differentiated strata of peoples who have practically no contact with each other and speak various languages, but everyone knows Russian. That said, the Russian they speak differs greatly depending on their education and social position. The Russian of the highbrow intellectuals is strikingly different from the Russian of the so-called plain folk. Many workers and peasants speak an extremely coarse and vulgar patois. In style and vocabulary one can even distinguish between schoolteachers and university lecturers.

I was reproached from childhood for being a cosmopolitan. This was a terrible word in those years. Stalin's campaign against "rootless cosmopolitans" was still fresh in people's minds. (Moreover, Jews were the primary target, although not everyone understood this.) What provoked these reproaches? Very simply, from an early age I preferred Mozart, Bach, Beethoven, Haydn, Brahms, and other West European composers to Tchaikovsky and other Russian composers. I was more taken with reading Balzac than, say, Turgenev.

Moreover, when I was fifteen years old, I read and took to heart the profound words of Charles de Montesquieu: "If I knew of something that could serve France, but would harm Europe, or if I knew something that could serve Europe, but harm humankind, I would consider this a crime . . . because I am necessarily a man, and only accidentally French."

In sum, I offer to the reader, completely free of any other considerations, my testimony regarding my personal experiences in the USSR and Russia from 1985 to 2007. It is the testimony of an active participant in the attempt to bring about a democratic reformation of my country, the testimony of a journey from hope to despair regarding the future of my country.

It is the testimony of an author whom the KGB, despite all its efforts, was unable to break and a story of how the post-Soviet authorities succeeded in getting me to emigrate from my own country. This occurred not only because I realized the complete impossibility of exercising any influence on what was going on in Russia but also because of the applause of my fellow countrymen and many Western politicians, political scientists, and journalists for what, from the start, was the criminal regime of Vladimir Putin.

This book testifies to the failure of democratic and liberal values in an enormous country. Russia possesses not only suicidal tendencies but also an immense potential and, most important, a determination to suppress, and possibly even destroy, all those who disagree with its imperial will. Putin's statement in 2015 about his readiness to employ nuclear weapons during the criminal annexation of Crimea demonstrates this point.

I hope that my personal testimony will enable readers to sharpen their view regarding Russia's recent past and to overcome what in my opinion is an inappropriate, starry-eyed idealism regarding what is taking place in the country of my birth.

ACKNOWLEDGMENTS

First of all, I would like to express my gratitude to those who made the writing of this book possible. I am speaking of my father, Anatoly Kovalev, who taught me how to analyze what is going on realistically and skeptically and, most important, without losing one's human feelings when it comes to politics even when this may harm one's career. And, of course, I am speaking, too, of my wife, Olga, who has always supported me in what, according to prevailing Russian concepts, were my most "extravagant" escapades and who helped me a great deal in preparing this book for publication.

The publication of this book would not have been possible without the active and all-around support of Peter B. Reddaway. In turn, I am obliged to Robert van Voren for renewing my acquaintance with him. Robert van Voren became interested in the manuscript at a time when it totally contradicted all the generally accepted myths and stereotypes about what was transpiring in and around Russia. I must also acknowledge my debt to Andreas Umland who decided to publish this book in Russian in his series Soviet and Post-Soviet Politics and Society.

I would like to express my sincere thanks to Potomac Books editor Tom Swanson and to Maggie Boyles, Sabrina Stellrecht, and everyone else at the University of Nebraska Press for all they did to bring this book to publication. I owe a debt of gratitude to Vicki Chamlee who did a stellar job of copyediting. She went well beyond the call of duty to transform the translation of my manuscript into a readable and accurate text.

The translation and preparation for publication of the English edition became a genuine and satisfying adventure. In the literal sense of the words, Steven I. Levine, who agreed to translate the manuscript into English, brought selflessness, enthusiasm, and passion to the task. In overcoming difficulties in translation, including at times Russian realia that have no equivalents in other languages, Peter B. Reddaway and Martin Dewhirst provided enormous help with their thoughtful critiques, invaluable comments, and painstaking work.

Moreover, in accordance with the advice of my literary agent Peter W. Bernstein, who found a most suitable publisher for this work despite the abundance of Russia books in the marketplace, Steven I. Levine performed the task of somewhat abridging and restructuring the manuscript for publication.

I am grateful to Francis Greene and Peter Reddaway for their willingness to provide generous financial support toward the translation, which, however, proved unnecessary due to Steven I. Levine's selflessness.

Finally, I want to express my most sincere gratitude to everyone, including those persons not specifically mentioned here, who helped me destroy the stereotypes, widely disseminated in Russia as well as in the West, regarding the supposed domination of self-interest and egoism in human affairs.

Russia's Dead End

Introduction

The twists and turns of Russian politics are cause for wonder. Mikhail Gorbachev, the last president of the USSR, nurtured by the communist totalitarian system that elevated him to the summit of power in 1985, is the one who pulled it down. Another communist who also occupied high positions in the party hierarchy of the USSR and who supposedly metamorphosed into a democrat, Boris Yeltsin, became the first president of post-Soviet Russia. He, in turn, virtually bequeathed power to retired KGB officer Vladimir Putin, who throughout the post-Yeltsin period consistently and methodically uprooted the shoots of democracy. Putin viewed the democratic reforms undertaken in the twilight years of the Soviet Union as a foul legacy, and he pronounced the demise of the USSR the greatest geopolitical catastrophe of the twentieth century.

In 1983 President Ronald Reagan characterized Russia, then called the Union of Soviet Socialist Republics, as an "evil empire." This definition shocked even those Russian patriots who loathed the Soviet Union. Only later was Reagan's truth acknowledged. It was this president who via diplomatic means made a substantial contribution to the transformation of the USSR into a democratic and lawful state. Of course, it was possible only because Mikhail Gorbachev was pursuing the very same goal.

Evil empire is an accurate description of the USSR. It really was an empire that disseminated its messianic evil throughout the occupied territories of Central and Eastern Europe and the "socialist-oriented," Third World developing countries. Yet the basic features characteristic of the Soviet state system did not take root in these places, nor could they since they contradicted human nature itself.

For centuries Russia was an empire founded on universal servitude. After the Bolshevik coup of 1917, it was a dictatorship of a systematic ideology, Marxism-Leninism. The ideological dictatorship not only embraced all the new territories but also strived to implant its philosophy of servitude in other countries.

Nevertheless, the definition of evil as the complete opposite of good was not applicable to the USSR. In the post-Stalin period it was not applicable even to those in power, as witnessed by the fact that the liberalization of the country during Gorbachev's perestroika "descended from on high"—that is, it came from a higher authority, decreed and implemented by those whom we may call dissidents within the system. This concept requires explanation. The within-system dissidents were an extremely small but very influential category of Soviet functionaries. Liberated from the normal logic of the system, they were not supportive of the status quo in the Soviet Union. They were often influential and highly placed; consequently, they prospered by Soviet standards. Outwardly their lives appeared normal: they enjoyed the use of official black automobiles, official means of communication, virtually free annual leaves in rest homes from which ordinary people were barred, and medical care accessible only to the chosen few. Without any formal arrangements or publicity, but in full knowledge of what they were doing, they did what they thought was right, using their positions and influence to change the Soviet system. They took fundamental risks in doing so. Russia is greatly indebted to them for the collapse of Soviet totalitarianism.

There is a simple and logical explanation for the appearance of such within-system dissidents at all levels of the Soviet hierarchy. The system co-opted the most qualified and talented personnel. Naturally, these persons had been brought up to respect communist dogmas, but these dogmas were by no means monolithic. For example, the writings of the young Karl Marx and Friedrich Engels were not at all like the works of their later years. Vladimir Lenin spoke and wrote so voluminously that one could find absolutely contradictory pronouncements of his on practically any topic if one wished to engage in such an exercise. I myself buttressed arguments concerning the need for a variety of democratic reforms with citations from Marx, Engels, and Lenin, our revered "Founding Fathers." I kept mum with regard to other, diametrically opposed citations.

Even in their inner selves, however, it was impossible for those inside the system of Soviet power to be totally free of its dogmas. One's upbringing and education, which differed little from hypnosis; one's lifestyle; one's circle of acquaintances—all these inevitably had an influence. There was also the obligatory dinning into one's head of Marxism-Leninism, the daily exaltation of socialism, which was sometimes elevated to an absolute lie—the Big Lie. We should not forget that neither the genuine dissidents nor the within-system dissidents rejected the system itself in those times.[1] My own upbringing, education, and experience speak to this point.

After Gorbachev came to power and preparations for democratic reforms began, it seemed to the within-system dissidents that overcoming the inertia of evil and, transforming the USSR into a normal democratic system, was within reach. Instead, the attempt to liquidate evil in the USSR during perestroika wound up destroying the country.

During President Yeltsin's administration (1991–99), Russian authorities already began to adopt thinly disguised revanchist positions, first with respect to Latvia, Lithuania, and Estonia; then toward the war in former Yugoslavia; and later with respect to other issues. The changes brought about by Gorbachev's "Democratic Reformation"—to use leading reformer Alexander Yakovlev's term—including withdrawing Soviet troops from Afghanistan, ending the Cold War, slowing the arms race, terminating support of terrorism and other "anti-imperialist" (that is, anti-Western) forces were now judged to be evidence of failures. Moreover, according to a twisted sort of logic, the source of all of Russia's real and imaginary disasters was said to be democracy, which had never actually existed in Russia. What began was not simply a retreat but rather a headlong flight away from the shoots of democracy and a return to the Cold War and the attempts to impose one's will on others without considering their interests or the interests of other countries. No later than the year 2000, a consistent assault began at home against human rights and democratic freedoms along with a restoration of the dictatorship that the outward show of free elections and democratic institutions could not conceal. The revival of Soviet-style Russian imperialism proceeded full steam ahead, including the proliferation of images of the enemy and the psychology of defending a besieged fortress. To a lesser degree, attempts were also undertaken to remilitarize the country.

There is no shortage of explanations for why Russia has again chosen a road to nowhere. Many writers have sought to explicate why there has been an unprecedented backlash in Russian politics after the year 2000 and why there has been an explosion of political murders, persecutions, and punishments of nonconformists under the present system of Putinocracy. What follows is one such explanation.

There is probably nothing more painful than breaking long-standing habits and stereotypes, whether it is the consumption of narcotics or the habits of thought and action. In the past thirty years the people of Russia have experienced at least two such traumatic breaks. The first was a rejection of the Marxist-Leninist dogmas on which the generation of the Soviet "builders of communism" was raised; they witnessed the dethroning of the gods, goddesses, icons, and other "sacred objects" during the Gorbachev Reformation. Many Russians viewed support for the Velvet Revolution in Eastern Europe in 1989, to say nothing of the reunification of Germany the following year, as a "surrender of the fruits of victory" in the Second World War. Likewise, they perceived the USSR's real steps toward disarmament and its support of Iraqi-occupied Kuwait and Operation Desert Storm as tantamount to abandoning one's foreign policy positions and "capitulating to imperialism."

This break, however, primarily affected the elite. The second break, the dissolution of the USSR on Christmas Day 1991, was very difficult to bear for the majority of the population who was simultaneously impoverished by the depreciation of the currency. After the start of Yeltsin's economic reforms in the early 1990s, those persons who considered themselves members of the elite felt disoriented. To be sure, it was the very same Moscow, the very same Kremlin. But objectively the country and the population had shrunk, and Russia's economic, foreign policy, and military potential had changed as had the entire system of international relations. The Soviet imperial monster had fragmented into fifteen states, and the Third World countries with a "socialist orientation" and other "progressive forces" were left without a guide and fell into the abyss. Russians, who had been accustomed to superpower status, found all of this very hard to swallow.

Objectively speaking, Russia was given a unique opportunity to become a normal country. The short-term democratic gains of perestroika could have developed into a new qualitative breakthrough not only on a national but also on a civilizational level. This, however, did not happen. The people who came to power in Russia were incapable of positive thinking, of discarding stereotypes, of reconsidering reality. Yeltsin's team, which took over in 1992, was a strange mixture of theoreticians of democracy and mid-ranking Soviet functionaries who had ascended not only the many steps in their official careers but also the levels of their own incompetence. In addition, frequently a significant number of them were disguised *siloviki*.

With its ambiguity, untranslatability, and widespread diffusion, the concept of *siloviki*, which came into general usage during the Yeltsin period, requires some explanation. In part the concept derives from the Soviet expression "power ministries and departments," which traditionally meant the Ministry of Defense and the Ministry of Internal Affairs, as well as the Committee for State Security (KGB). In addition, on account of its influence, the Ministry of Foreign Affairs was included, although its power consisted only in the importance of the questions with which it dealt, its knowledge, and its ability to conduct negotiations and, if desired, to find mutually beneficial compromises.

In the post-Soviet period, the number of power ministries and departments significantly increased. To the traditional *siloviki*— that is, the Ministries of Defense, Internal Affairs, Justice, and Foreign Affairs and the Federal Security Service (FSB, as the direct heir of the KGB)—was added the Ministry of Emergency Situations, which had its own troops; the Foreign Intelligence Service (previously the First Division of the KGB); the Investigations Committee; the Federal Guards Service (formerly the Ninth Division of the KGB); the Federal Courier Service; the Federal Service for Financial Monitoring; the Chief Directorate for Special Programs of the Russian President; the Administrative Directorate of the President of the Russian Federation; and the Federal Narcotics Control Service which, however, was dissolved in April 2016, and whose duties were transferred to the Ministry of Internal Affairs. Some also include the General Procuratorate among the *siloviki*. Because *siloviki* are defined not only by power (for example, their possession of troops or repressive function) but also by their direct subordination to the head of state, it would be no exaggeration to say that one of the main *siloviki* is the Presidential Administration (especially if following the Constitution), an institution that also supports the staff of the Security Council. Apart from tradition, it is precisely according to this logic that the Ministry of Internal Affairs belongs among the *siloviki*.

Sometimes the *siloviki* are automatically assumed to be "hawks." Of course, this is not without foundation. For example, the Ministry of Internal Affairs—a department that is very hospitable to hawks—has always had an entire nesting site for hawks, but there are also "doves" in the Ministry of Defense and in other "military" departments.

This is one of the reasons that the word *siloviki* is untranslatable. Another, no less important reason is that there is no analogous situation to that in which many *siloviki* are effectively outside the sphere of legislative action, to say nothing of any sort of control, and report only to the head of state. Even during Soviet times, the power ministries and departments were subordinate, at a minimum, to the Politburo. It seems that this is precisely why the concept of *siloviki* is impossible to translate.

The unwillingness and inability of Russian authorities to understand and acknowledge the changes in Russia's place and role in world affairs, and their lack of any vision of the new possibilities, inevitably led to serious consequences, including withdrawal symptoms from dictatorship at home and abroad. The Kremlin and the elite experienced a real break, like that of the most inveterate drug addict.

A win turned into a loss. At a fork in the road, instead of choosing the uncertain but hopeful path toward a better and democratic future, Russia's new leaders turned back and toward the phantom glory and repressive authoritarianism of the Soviet past with dire consequences for their country and the world.

Working in the USSR Ministry of Foreign Affairs in the late 1980s on assignments that included the elimination of punitive psychiatry, I constantly ran across physicians' diagnoses asserting that one or another patient "represented a danger to himself and those around him." As a member of a working group drafting a law governing psychiatry, I always posed the question, just what sort of *danger* is indicated? Then I thought to apply this term to my own country. Could anyone really doubt that the USSR, which had destroyed millions of its own people for the sake of some abstract "radiant future" and had been seriously preparing for nuclear suicide, really represented a danger to itself and the rest of the world? Under Gorbachev it seemed that this danger could be overcome. On the one hand, power had ceased to be a refuge for the superannuated; instead, the authorities were trying to heal the country. On the other hand, power had not yet entered into the stage of "fiddling while Rome burned." Its collapse into the infantilism of the Putin-Medvedev era was entirely unforeseen.

This infantilism was no less dangerous than the senility of Leonid Brezhnev and Konstantin Chernenko, who preceded Gorbachev in power. Why do I use the term *infantilism*? Egocentrism and an unwillingness and inability to consider others are characteristic of infantilism. So, too, is hysteria, one of whose distinctive features is a pronounced tendency to engage in theatrics and an urge to focus attention on oneself. Such demonstrations are very typical of the Kremlin under Putin. In particular, they manifest themselves in an ostentatious eagerness to confront the West and to engage in a new cold war. The thinking of hysterical persons is based on emotion; reasonable arguments and facts have little meaning for them. Their hysteria also affects those around them. This, in turn, plays into the hands of those in power, since hysterical people are very open to suggestion and easily manipulated. Given their inability to distinguish between reality and their own fantasies, infantile adults typically live in an imagined world. Infantile leaders such as Putin are always playing games—not with lead soldiers but with human lives. They care nothing about suffering inflicted on others.

Psychiatrists are familiar with the peculiar psychological disorder of "shared psychotic disorder" (known as folie à deux [madness of two])—that is, when a healthy person develops the delusional symptoms of another individual, and the affected person can be more dangerous than the transmitter. Similarly, the Kremlin cynically infects those around it with the phantoms of benefits and power. Meanwhile, via a process of autosuggestion, it convinces itself this is how things really are. The Russian people are easily convinced that they have been constantly humiliated by quasi-democracy, by the decolonization of countries in Eastern and Central Europe that have been occupied as a result of the Second World War, and, finally, by the normalization of relations with the West.

The Kremlin is quite effective in palming off these false notions on the people, who readily embrace them. One of the main goals in so doing is to divert the attention of those habitually deceived persons, humiliated by their impoverishment, toward problems other than their own. This tactic is a throwback to Soviet times, when a large part of the population subordinated its own real interests to the sham interests of the state. Following the collapse of the USSR, the Kremlin's conceptual shell game succeeded quite well because it had been skillfully prepared and facilitated by the influx of petrodollars when prices were high, making it easier for many ordinary Russians to identify their own interests with the interests of those in power.

For many Russians, carefully fabricated myths trumped their own well-being. The ephemeral and mindless dreams of "restoring the greatness of the USSR" pushed them to support such criminal adventures as those in Chechnya, in Georgia, and in Ukraine.

Russian society, destroyed by the Bolsheviks, had been atomized into a mere collection of people lacking in social solidarity. In the post-Soviet period, through the efforts of its masters, it became an illusory electorate.

In Vladimir Nabokov's novel *Invitation to a Beheading*, the condemned man must become friends with his own executioner. This is precisely what the communist regime—beloved by many of its slaves—succeeded in achieving. Putin's regime has also managed this quite well. In Nabokov's novel, the condemned man, understanding the savagery and unreality of the world around him, rebels against it, pulls it down, and thereby abrogates his own execution. In Russia, unfortunately, this has not happened. To be sure, a protest movement has begun, and people come out on the streets from time to time to defend their own dignity. But this movement, and every one of its participants, has been ill-served by the so-called democratic leaders. Many of the condemned Russian dissidents have become reconciled to their fates.

The regime in Russia since the year 2000 is usually identified with Vladimir Putin. This is a mistake that has cost both Russia and its foreign partners dearly. When, after two consecutive terms in office, Putin entrusted Dmitry Medvedev with safeguarding his presidential chair between 2008 and 2012, many in Russia as well as abroad believed that changes for the better were imminent. In fact, Putin had merely carried out another successful special operation. Medvedev secured the support of Russian liberal idealists, and the West waited, in vain as it happened, for Medvedev to implement his wonderful promises. The main point was lost from view. It was not a question of personalities. No matter how painful it is to admit, albeit with several caveats, *the special services had really come to power for the long term. And they will never share this power with anyone nor give it up voluntarily.*

Russia is sick. Its illness is complex and psychosomatic in character. This presents itself, among other ways, as manic-depressive psychosis accompanied by acute megalomania, persecution complex, and kleptomania, all compounded by dystrophy given the objectively declining economy. The latter is true despite what was an intermittently satisfactory financial situation, at least until the imposition of increasingly tough Western sanctions in 2014. An obvious manifestation of this diagnosis is that Russia's military organization has been in a state of accelerating disintegration since the Yeltsin era. The inadequate remilitarization of the country or at least the appearance of this, beginning under Putin, does not contradict this reality.

Social psychologists assert that persons who have spent considerable time in places where they were deprived of their freedom, such as prisons and mental institutions, are often drawn back to such places after they are liberated. There everything is clear: they are clothed, shod, fed, given drink, sent to sleep according to a strict regimen, and awakened in the morning. But in freedom everything is different. "Yesterday I was given freedom, what shall I do with it?" Vladimir Vysotsky, Russia's great bard of the 1970s, declaimed this prophetic question.

How many times has Russia *willingly* rushed into bondage, mistaking it for freedom and democracy, thinking that it would bring happiness to itself and to those near and far? It did so without realizing that such a condition was freedom from responsibility, freedom from conscience, freedom from choice, freedom from individuality, from one's own opinions. For the Russian people, crippled by those in power and imbued with false values, this condition was their only choice. It is the choice of those for whom fear of the authorities is virtually embedded in their DNA, the choice of a generation educated in a single way of thinking, without alternatives, bled white by the aftereffects of "class struggle" and of the Leninist-Stalinist concentration camps. This is also the only possible choice for many of the younger successors of that generation.

Russia was also affected by kleptomania, when one steals not only from others but also from oneself, from one's own future. This phenomenon began in 1917, when the Bolsheviks, an unscrupulous gang of thieves and persons who were not only poverty-stricken materially but also spiritually destitute, came to power. Since that time the thieving has not stopped. It acquired a special, truly Bolshevik scope during the period of privatization in the 1990s when the entire country was pillaged. Since that time the thievery has changed; there is no less robbery, but it is of a different sort. Corruption reigns everywhere at a level, according to Transparency International, that puts Russia in the same category as Azerbaijan, Guyana, and Sierra Leone.[2] Meanwhile, the number of billionaires is growing in this impoverished country.

Russia is sick, a disgrace that was already nurtured by Josef Stalin and by Nazism. Of course, at present, entire nations are not seeing their people deported as the Chechens and others were in Stalin's time. But it is a fact that the ultranationalist society Pamyat' and Vladimir Zhirinovsky's Liberal Democratic Party of Russia were organized on the initiative and with the participation of the Central Committee of the Communist Party of the Soviet Union and the KGB. To this day, Russian Nazism, initially encouraged by the Soviet authorities, is cared for and cultivated by the state.

The communist regime brainwashed an inert people. It did so by means of mass executions, concentration camps of the GULAG, and mind-numbing and morally destitute propaganda. Sadomasochistic perversions became the norm of life in Russia, where the state mocked the people, and they in turn were delighted by their humiliation.

This almost worst-case development of events in Russia was brought about by a series of maneuvers at various levels. Among them we must single out psychological factors, which, in Russia, play a disproportionately large role, especially because of the high degree of suggestibility and the ease with which the majority of the population can be manipulated. Russians lacked the opportunity to acquire an instinct for freedom and an immunity from attempts to oppress them. The ruling authorities make very effective use of this, especially with respect to compromising freedom and liberalism.

Such an outcome was facilitated by the fact that although mass repression ended with Stalin's death in 1953, the mechanism for suppressing dissenting thought had been preserved and even perfected. Thus, Russia slid into a state of socioeconomic and political decay that not even Gorbachev's benevolent therapy and Yeltsin's cruel measures were unable to halt. The remission of Russia's diseases was short lived. That the majority of the population joyfully accepts Putin's repudiation of democracy unequivocally confirms the seriousness of the state of national affairs.

Revanchism has already brought Russia catastrophes from the early twentieth century to the present. For example, after its defeat in the Russo-Japanese War (1904–5), and against the background of serious setbacks on the front during the First World War, the Bolshevik reaction triumphed. The defeat of Moscow's decade-long intervention in Afghanistan, marked by the withdrawal of Soviet troops in 1989, led to the genocide of Russia's own citizens in Chechnya. More recently, Russia's annexation of Crimea in March 2014 and its de facto military intervention in Ukraine have catalyzed a stiffening Western response. There is no reason to suppose that revanchism, which germinated under Yeltsin and flowered luxuriantly under Putin, will turn out well for anyone.

Traditionally, the reality of what Russia actually is, has nothing in common with how both Russians and foreigners alike perceive it. Russia's rulers have perfected the art of lying and hypocrisy to achieve their own objectives. One of the most vivid modern examples is the myth that the Bolshevik coup and everything that followed from it, including the Stalinist genocide of Russia's own people, were done for the sake of the people themselves. Not only were they proclaimed to be free and happy, but they came to believe it themselves. Prevaricating, cruel tyrants were often immensely popular, while those leaders who tried to improve the lives of the people and who spoke the truth were hated. A prime example is Gorbachev, who liquidated the system of totalitarianism and came close to destroying the nation's slave mentality. Rather than being honored, many considered him a "traitor to Russia's interests."

Gorbachev and the very tight circle of his comrades in arms—notably Eduard Shevardnadze, Alexander Yakovlev, and a few others—performed the dirty work of cleaning out the Augean stables of totalitarianism. But Gorbachev made so many mistakes that he was unable to hold onto power.

Something akin to a law of nature appears to operate in Russia. It not only dooms the infrequent and short-lived attempts at liberal reforms and sensible domestic and foreign policy to failure, but each reaction to such attempts also throws the country so far into reverse that it seems as if the people had been inoculated against freedom. The situation in Russia today looks very gloomy. The Russian authorities beat people, throw them into prisons and camps, and ruin them and exterminate undesirables. They liquidate freedom of the media, preserving only its facade, and eliminate judicial independence, parliamentarianism, and other elements of democracy. Yet some Western politicians and scholars continue to pretend that everything is really not so bad.

Pragmatism is surely necessary in politics, but it cannot be the only motive for government action. Western policies based solely on ensuring the delivery of Russian oil and gas are unworthy of the West. Ignoring flagrant and massive violations of the entire spectrum of human rights in Russia, its rapidly progressing slide toward totalitarianism, and the reality of new threats to international security such as Russia's actions in Ukraine are equally unworthy.

Russia forfeited its future by choosing as its president in 2000 a mumbling, stammering, knock-kneed, brow-furrowing ex-KGB agent who speaks the language of the gutter and values power above everything else. He is prepared to do anything to preserve this power. He attained the summit of baseness and cynicism thanks, in part, to the indulgence, until very recently, of his foreign partners.

Scarcely had he come to power when Putin began to establish a "dictatorship of the mediocre over the imbeciles."[3] He had no problem with mediocrity, either his own or that of his close associates. It was harder to fool that part of the population who had already acquired a certain taste for freedom of the media and, consequently, for having opinions of their own. He worked on this problem from his first day in power and dealt with it brilliantly.

The intentions and moral direction of Putin and his associates became crystal clear after the murder in October 2006 of the popular journalist Anna Politkovskaya, who had courageously opposed the Kremlin. Almost no one doubted this act bore the fingerprints of the hand of power—whether of Moscow or of the Chechen capital Grozny was not important. Even more sinister was the poisoning in London one month later of the former lieutenant colonel of the FSB Alexander Litvinenko by means of the rare radioactive substance polonium-210. This murder was so shocking that suspicion arose that it might have involved some sort of bizarre ritual; otherwise, the use of polonium was difficult to explain. Moscow concocted a number of fantastic explanations including, for example, that Litvinenko had committed suicide in order "to annoy Putin."

From time immemorial, Russians have been brought up to possess a slave psychology. Serfdom was only done away with in 1861. But serfdom under the tsarist regime was quite humane compared to the social order established under the communist dictatorship. The slave-communal psychology is also firmly embedded in the heads of those in power, not only from their upbringing, but also from what they imbibed as they accumulated power. Power in Russia is traditionally identified with various blessings and perquisites unobtainable by "ordinary mortals." Their recipients become dependent on these privileges.

It is a cliché to extol the long-suffering nature of Russians. This is actually a reflection of their powerlessness and their habit of fulfilling the "will of those on high," whether it is the department head, the municipal head, or the head of the country. A belief in the "good Little Father Tsar" is virtually the foundation of the national mentality.

This mentality is the source of the complete misunderstanding of what democracy is. One cannot speak of democracy when both the people and the authorities neither know how nor desire to implement existing legislation. There can be no democracy in a nation whose politics rest upon lies. Of course, in politics a certain degree of hypocrisy and verbal trickery is inevitable. But the political cynicism in Russia, a country where democracy has supposedly triumphed, is off the charts.

Another component of Russian political culture that is likewise incompatible with democracy is the authorities' view of citizens as virtual bond slaves, serfs, or their own property. For its part much of the population views power as something holy, unshakable, virtually ordained by God.

These are certainly bitter words, yet I begin from the premise that Russia is a great nation. It has given to the world many geniuses who have been noted for their steadfastness and heroism. Unfortunately, Russia is a nation that has been crippled by its rulers.

Summing up, Russia, like the former Soviet Union, again presents a danger to itself and to those around it. Russia has become transformed into a degraded and absolutely disorganized power. The anarchy, constantly growing xenophobia (in the broad sense of the term), terrorism, and much else that have persisted for many years at all levels and in all spheres of activity in Russia embody not only significant dangers for the region but also for civilized society itself. Many of these dangers are now too obvious to ignore any longer.

One must give one's due to the Soviet leaders, beginning with Lenin. They implanted the shoots of discord and hatred throughout the world. It was they, too, who created much of the infrastructure, including international terrorism. Therefore, it is impossible to understand and deal with contemporary Russia and the international problems arising from its policies if one ignores the history of the communist monster and its successor. It is precisely this history that the following chapters explore.

Chapter 1 focuses on the unexpected role of the Soviet Foreign Ministry under Eduard Shevardnadze in leading the struggle for democratic reforms inside the USSR during perestroika. Chapter 2 examines the fateful coup d'état against Soviet president Gorbachev in August 1991 and the paradoxical achievement of its goals even though the coup itself failed. Central to these events was the rise of the secret services to a position of paramount power. Chapter 3 probes the roots of Russia's tragedy by exploring the psychology of servitude that began centuries ago during the imperial era and well served the totalitarian regime that the Bolsheviks instituted in 1917. Gorbachev's attempt from above to institute democratic reform encountered widespread resistance from below and culminated in the breakup of the USSR and the rise to power of Boris Yeltsin, an easily manipulated product of the old system that had little inkling of democracy.

Chapter 4 enters the corridors of power to discuss the decision makers and decision-making process of Russia under Yeltsin and Putin. It describes the disintegration of the Russian foreign policy establishment and the compromised state of Russia's intellectual elite. Chapter 5 focuses on the rise of the secret services, whose embodiment is Vladimir Putin and whose presence is ubiquitous. To replace Marxism-Leninism, the new leaders have propounded the Russian national idea—a toxic mixture of autocracy, Russian Orthodoxy, and the supposed superior virtues of the Russian people. Chapter 6 details the methods by which Putin and his associates methodically destroyed the fledgling institutions of democracy begun during perestroika. Their techniques included violence, lies, suppression of dissent, and phony spy scares. Chapter 7 argues that Russia, nostalgic for the superpower position it occupied in the Cold War, has reverted to a policy of revanchism, expansion, and militarism that poses a threat to its neighbors as well as to itself. Rather than confronting Putin, until the Kremlin annexed Crimea and launched a proxy war in eastern Ukraine, Western powers turned a blind eye both to Russia's domestic repression and to its foreign adventurism. Finally, the conclusion asserts that only the eventual emergence of an authentic Russian elite imbued with liberal and democratic values can break the hold on power of the current criminal authorities whose grip is secured by a hypnotized and subservient public.

Diplomacy and Democratic Reforms

It is hard to imagine. In the Ministry of *Foreign* Affairs in the capital of what, in the second half of the 1980s, is still the totalitarian Soviet Union, a number of ministry officials are working openly to destroy the totalitarian foundations of the state. This was the same ministry headed during the Cold War by the grim-faced Andrei Gromyko, widely known in the West as "Mister No" from the results of his negotiations and almost automatic rejection of all Western proposals. Yet the story is true. It was the Ministry of *Foreign* Affairs that initiated and pushed through almost all of the democratic changes in the Soviet Union during the tenure of Mikhail Gorbachev, the last president of the Union of Soviet Socialist Republics.

Why did part of the *foreign* policy establishment of the USSR seek to destroy the totalitarian regime and establish democracy and a state ruled by law in a country devoid of legitimacy and justice? The answer reflects the rather well-organized confusion of the era of change that began with Gorbachev's accession to power in March 1985. The new leadership of the ministry demanded it.

From their service abroad, many Soviet diplomats were familiar with a world outside their own country that was entirely different. More than many others in the USSR, they had a better and clearer understanding of not only the need to promote the democratic reformation of society but also how to achieve it. To give one prominent example, Gorbachev's close associate Alexander Yakovlev, generally recognized as the chief ideologist of perestroika, had spent many years on diplomatic assignment in Canada.

The Foreign Ministry and Foreign Minister Eduard Shevardnadze were meant for each other. A unique synthesis existed in the ministry between those officials who had mastered the science and art of diplomacy and Shevardnadze, Gorbachev's minister of foreign affairs, who possessed political will and was intimately acquainted with every facet of Soviet life. Prior to becoming the leader of the Soviet Republic of Georgia (1972–85), he had headed Georgia's Ministry of Internal Affairs.

Of course, Shevardnadze did not act on his own. First, appropriate conditions had to be created for the Foreign Ministry to become active in the field of human rights, an area that had been clearly outside its domain. According to a resolution the Foreign Ministry proposed at the Twenty-Seventh Congress of the Communist Party of the Soviet Union (CPSU), in February–March 1986, humanitarian affairs was designated one of the foundations of international security. This empowered the Foreign Ministry to address human rights issues inside the USSR that had previously been out of bounds not only for the diplomatic service but also for all other government departments apart from the punitive ministries, which punished those who even dared to speak of human rights.

Soon a Directorate for Humanitarian and Cultural Cooperation was established in the Foreign Ministry. Its main task was to resolve a broad range of questions in the field of human rights. It was far from obvious, however, how to undertake the task of cleaning up one's own home, sweeping out all the accumulated dirt and trash.

Shevardnadze's appointment as minister of foreign affairs triggered an intense allergic reaction among many ministry officials. After the simple and predictable Andrei Gromyko, Shevardnadze was an enigma, especially to officials who were unfamiliar with the complex issue of human rights or simply clueless as to what was going on around them. For almost a year Shevardnadze sized up the ministry and made no changes among its leading personnel. Only just prior to the explosion of the nuclear reactor at Chernobyl on April 26, 1986, did he replace his first deputies. Instead of the hawkish Georgy Kornienko and Viktor Mal'tsev, he appointed Anatoly Kovalev and Yuly Vorontsov to these positions. Then Kovalev's closest associates, Anatoly Adamishin and Vladimir Petrovsky, also became deputies to the minister.

Starting from the top down, I shall provide brief sketches of those persons to whom Russia is indebted for what was good and democratic in its recent past.

I can only judge Eduard Shevardnadze, whom both well-wishers and adversaries referred to as the Silver Fox, on the basis of what I know personally. There have always been too many lies and too much slander surrounding him, born of misunderstanding and hatred. Yet there can be no doubt that he made an invaluable contribution to the establishment of democracy in Russia. He and Alexander Yakovlev were the main authors of the democratic reforms.

During perestroika, this lively, charming, energetic, gray-haired man was as greatly respected by the supporters of democratic reforms as he was hated by their opponents. His name is linked to the end of the arms race, the Velvet Revolutions in Eastern Europe, the end of the Cold War, and the Soviet Union's entry on the path of establishing democracy and observing human rights at home. His enemies accused him of abandoning the foreign policy positions of the USSR and of weakening the country's military potential. His supporters admired the courage with which he jettisoned moldy dogmas and facilitated the USSR's rapprochement with civilized, democratic countries. He was always in the thick of contentious matters and seemed to attract them to himself.

His first deputy (and my father) was Anatoly Kovalev. Shevardnadze did not deal with a single important foreign or domestic policy issue without consulting him. Possibly this was because of my father's closeness to Gorbachev; possibly it was because of the foreign minister's empathy and trust in him. As far back as the height of the period of stagnation in the 1970s when Leonid Brezhnev was in power, Kovalev was instrumental in having the USSR assume unprecedented obligations with regard to human rights by signing the Final Act of the Helsinki Conference on Security and Cooperation in Europe (CSCE). He was close to all the Soviet leaders, starting with Brezhnev, and was especially close to Gorbachev, to whom he had direct access. Kovalev's other persona was that of a poet. He embodied a paradoxical combination of idealism grounded in what, for those times and for people in his profession, was an unusual belief in common sense together with a

combative personality. He was a cunning chess master who calculated diplomatic moves many turns in advance. In his youth he
had boxed and played soccer and many other sports. This synthesis of creativity and combativeness enabled him to be effective in
both the foreign and domestic policy arenas.

Yet he was hampered by a tendency to idealize his like-minded
political associates, and he was excessively loyal toward Shevardnadze and Gorbachev. His combativeness helped when he was
pushing forward some good initiatives but not when he failed to
realize there was no chance for success. Still it was thanks to Shevardnadze and Kovalev that the Foreign Ministry succeeded in getting the Twenty-Seventh Congress of the CPSU to include human
rights on the agenda of international security policy.

The deputy minister of foreign affairs of the USSR Anatoly
Adamishin was a liberal even down to the smallest details. Clever
and intelligent, he was a very modest man who achieved much
more for democracy and liberalism than all the inveterate demagogues put together. He liked to compare himself to a medieval
battering ram in the service of Shevardnadze and Kovalev. This is a
striking metaphor, of course, but if he was a battering ram, he was
by no means a medieval one. Adamishin acted too intelligently,
too resourcefully, and with too much talent for this comparison
to be valid. This slim and resourceful diplomat was distinguished
by his outstanding boldness and exceptional human decency.

Vladimir Petrovsky replaced Anatoly Adamishin as the custo-
dian of human rights and democratic standards after Adamishin's
departure to serve as ambassador to Rome. Even after Eduard Shevardnadze's retirement in December 1990, Petrovsky continued
to work actively on human rights and did everything he could to
ensure the successful convening of the Moscow Conference on
the Human Dimension of the CSCE (September–October 1991).

Under Shevardnadze the Foreign Ministry's activity in the field
of human rights may provisionally be divided into three basic components. First was freeing political and religious prisoners from
their places of confinement including psychiatric hospitals. Second was resolving the problem of the so-called refuseniks—that
is, persons who were refused permission to emigrate. The third

was "bringing Soviet legislation and the implementation of Soviet laws into accord with the international obligations of the USSR." (This was my basic brief.) Translating the bureaucratic jargon into ordinary language, it turned out that during my government service in the Foreign Ministry, my assignment was to promote the democratization of the country. Thus, I had to deal with activities that according to existing legislation were illegal and punishable by imprisonment.

In transforming the Soviet Union into a law-based state, the international human rights standards that had been formulated in the Universal Declaration of Human Rights, which was proclaimed by the United Nations in 1948, and other such documents served as a kind of "absolute weapon." The declaration was a reliable guidepost that had been tested by others and was *protected* from ideological crusaders. An emphasis on international standards provided a legal foundation for our dialogue on human rights with Western countries, with the United States in the first instance. Soviet diplomats stopped avoiding discussions with Western colleagues regarding human rights violations in the USSR. We ourselves often added names from our own information to the lists Western diplomats gave us of prisoners of conscience, psychiatric prisoners, and refuseniks before we sent the lists on to the relevant ministries and departments to confirm the grievances presented to us. Fortunately, no one thought to compare these enhanced lists with the original lists; otherwise, there would have been an incredible scandal.

When we were accused of allowing foreign interference in our domestic affairs, we always had this naive response at hand: "We are simply cooperating in the implementation of universal human rights standards!" It may sound paradoxical, but without the critical input and pressure from our foreign partners, it would have been extremely difficult, if not impossible, to resolve many problems of democratization in the USSR. Richard Schifter, the U.S. assistant secretary of state for human rights and humanitarian affairs, played a special role in this regard. Western representatives often acted as intermediaries between the Soviet authorities and Soviet dissidents. At the time there was no simpler path for dialogue.

The Foreign Ministry had another powerful means of exerting

pressure on opponents of liberal reform—the Vienna conference of states represented in the CSCE (1986–89). The USSR had succeeded in persuading the Vienna meeting to hold a human rights conference in Moscow. By this means the Foreign Ministry provoked our Western colleagues to push more actively for the Soviet Union to respect human rights. We needed them to do this. The West introduced the proposals that we needed, the Soviet delegation in Vienna requested Moscow's approval, and the Foreign Ministry secured the agreement of the "relevant ministries and departments," which mistakenly supposed they would not have to fulfill their promises. The delegation in Vienna received the go-ahead from Moscow, and these same ministries and departments had no alternative but to fulfill their own promises.

The Foreign Ministry also took advantage of other opportunities to resolve human rights problems. Mikhail Gorbachev's speech at the UN on December 7, 1988, would provide what we thought was a unique opportunity to deal a crushing blow to the obstructionists. I was in the office of my boss Alexei Glukhov when Anatoly Kovalev, the first deputy minister, called on his secure line and instructed him to prepare a specific section of the speech.[1] (Gorbachev and Shevardnadze were not in Moscow at the time; Kovalev was acting on his own initiative and later reported on this issue to a session of the Politburo.) I was assigned the task of preparing a first draft that both Glukhov and Kovalev Sr. subsequently revised. Standing at the rostrum of the UN and barely containing his sincere jubilation, Gorbachev would shortly make his sensational announcement, "There are no persons in prison [in the USSR] for their political and religious beliefs." The previously unrevealed background to these words was rather dramatic.

A text that openly contradicted the status quo in the USSR had been prepared in the Ministry of Foreign Affairs of the USSR. Its purpose was to transform that status quo. A memorandum containing specific instructions to the ministries and departments was immediately drafted in the Central Committee of the CPSU regarding measures that needed to be taken to ensure that the imminent declaration would accord with the actual situation. It was approved in record time. Just a few days remained until the speech. I heard that during this time no one in the Procuracy and the KGB slept at all. By December 7 all the dissidents known to the Foreign Ministry had completed their passage through the purgatory of the Main Directorate for Corrective Labor Camps (GULAG) and the psychiatric prisons. Gorbachev could now make his speech at the UN with a clear conscience.

We took advantage of Gorbachev's talks with "appropriate" Western interlocutors to release as many political and religious prisoners as possible and to grant refuseniks permission to emigrate. I don't know whether Gorbachev himself ever discussed any of these lists; most likely such questions were resolved at a lower level. But his talks provided an excellent opportunity to resolve existing problems.

Naturally, dialogue also took place in other arenas. One such example was connected to Pope John Paul II's desire to visit the USSR on the thousandth anniversary of the baptism of Rus', or when Grand Prince Vladimir had accepted Orthodox Christianity in Kiev in 988 CE. Although Shevardnadze tried his best to facilitate the proposed visit, he failed. The Central Committee of the CPSU, the KGB, and the Russian Orthodox Church—all opposed the visit. Unfortunately, they prevailed. The great pontiff was unable to realize his dream of visiting Russia. Neither the USSR during perestroika nor its successor, the Russian Federation, passed the test of real democracy and real freedom of conscience.

Although the diplomatic instruments of the Foreign Ministry were fully employed in the democratic reform of the country, they were obviously insufficient to cleanse the country from the accumulated layers of dust and filth of totalitarianism and to air out the ideological mustiness, the atmosphere of fear, and the other unpleasant odors. That demanded action at a higher political level, especially since the democratic trio of Gorbachev, Shevardnadze, and Yakovlev was opposed by most of the other leaders. Had Shevardnadze only been the minister of foreign affairs, and not concurrently part of the top leadership as a member of the all-powerful Politburo, many of the democratic reforms in the USSR and Russia would have been impossible. In every possible way we took maximum advantage of the minister's political clout. The Silver

Fox not only encouraged our efforts but even pushed us toward even greater activity. As a member of the Politburo, Shevardnadze initiated legislation removing political and religious articles from the Criminal Code, introduced religious freedom, established the right to freely exit and reenter the country, put an end to punitive psychiatry in the USSR, and pursued other measures.

Every day draft proposals piled up and were dispatched by special messenger to Politburo members for their views before the Central Committee took any decisions. Shevardnadze assigned Adamishin to deal with those concerning democracy and human rights. Adamishin, in turn, often called upon me. I must give Shevardnadze his due, for he never failed to respond when asked. And, of course, my thanks to Adamishin who initiated all of this.

We ourselves were not slackers. Vladimir Lenin himself and other "Founding Fathers" unwittingly provided invaluable assistance. At the time almost no one knew what "Leninist norms" really meant, but they were considered virtually sacred. The citation of Lenin's sayings, particularly if they were buttressed by quotations from Karl Marx and Friedrich Engels, produced a virtually surefire, literally hypnotic effect on the most hidebound dogmatists and reactionaries. We undertook veritable "excavations" of appropriate quotations of Lenin, Marx, and Engels, as well as of legislation passed under Lenin. There was no use to which we did not put them! This included the need to abolish the death penalty, which Lenin had spoken about passionately prior to his seizure of power and his resorting to mass extermination. We cited him regarding the inadmissibility of censorship, the need to guarantee freedom of conscience, the right of exit and reentry, the option of an alternative military service, the necessity of rectifying the practice of psychiatry, and even the abolition of residence permits. We juggled quotations and used everything we could find to facilitate the establishment of democracy in our country.

To deal with human rights we needed to master informal thinking. For example, a message arrives from the United States that a hundred rabbis want to visit a cemetery in Ukraine, but they are denied visas. Phone calls back and forth to the Council on Religious Affairs and other "relevant ministries and agencies" get us nowhere. On Glukhov's secure government line, I phone the chairman of the executive committee of the town that the rabbis wish to visit and ask what is the problem. It turns out that the cemetery has been destroyed, there are no fences, the monuments are in ruins. I threaten him with an international scandal. The cemetery is restored, and the rabbis receive permission to pay their respects to their ancestors.

In another episode, the KGB intercepts a letter from a desperate woman in Ukraine to the secretary-general of the UN saying that she has been living for many years in a small room in a communal apartment with her husband, two children, and relatives—I don't remember if it was a sister or a brother—and her or his family. The local authorities will not rehouse them or give them a new apartment. A photograph attached to the letter shows how they slept side by side on the dining table and under it. Glukhov gives me permission to call on the secure line, and I scare the living daylights out of the swindling chairman of the local executive committee by raising the specter of an international scandal. In just over a week, the poor devils have resolved a housing problem that had been festering for many years.

The democratization of society was Shevardnadze's "special interest." Much of what was done during perestroika was on his initiative. A real conveyor belt was in operation. Not infrequently those who had nothing to do with our ministry's actions and actually did everything they could to obstruct them were credited with what we had achieved. The former chief of the Visas and Permissions Division of the Ministry of Internal Affairs of the USSR Rudolf Kuznetsov insisted that it was he who had initiated and worked on the law regarding exit and reentry. The former chief psychiatrist of the Ministry of Health Alexander Churkin claimed credit as the principal reformer of Soviet psychiatry. What can one say to this? Neither on Judgment Day nor in an earthly court do such persons have any credibility.

Taking Stock

Soon after the establishment of the Directorate for Humanitarian and Cultural Cooperation, Shevardnadze "authorized" his staff to inform him of human rights problems. There was a healthy dose of make-believe in this. After all, as already noted, it was the minister himself who had initiated the work of the Foreign Ministry on human rights. This is largely because from his experience in Georgia he was very familiar with the actual state of affairs in this sphere. Following his instructions, work began on drawing up an inventory of the USSR's international obligations regarding human rights, on juxtaposing them with current legislation and practice, and on drafting proposals to align Soviet legislation with the USSR's international obligations.

The phrase *taking stock* has a dry bureaucratic connotation, conjuring up an association with bookkeeping, yet precisely this phrase best describes the task of diagnosing the worst maladies of Soviet society and looking for ways to cure them. Taking stock of the dark side contradicted the elementary instinct of self-preservation, since what we were doing, from a strictly legal point of view, was a crime against the state. According to the spirit and the letter of the existing laws, that is how what we were doing to heal the country had to be interpreted. Leaving aside the legal perspective, the picture is no less depressing, since our activities impinged upon the interests of too many powerful persons. Soviet citizens had lost years of their lives in the GULAG simply for criticizing the totalitarian system.

Taking stock revealed rather strange things. First, not a single ministry or department knew what obligations the USSR had undertaken with respect to international treaties on human rights. Until the start of perestroika, the Foreign Ministry had shown no interest in this either, even though, according to the existing laws, it was supposed to monitor the USSR's fulfillment of its treaty obligations. No one had even thought of undertaking such work, and no scholars were officially studying human rights issues.

My investigation revealed that according to the International Bill of Human Rights alone, the USSR had more than sixty obligations. Even from a formal, legislative point of view, let alone with regard to prevailing practices, it had violated international law with regard to every one of them. The picture that emerged was appalling. In the hands of the Foreign Ministry liberals, stocktaking became a powerful weapon. We produced what looked like a thick, three-column bookkeeping ledger. On the left side were the obligations of the USSR, in the center were the relevant statutes of the existing legislation, and, finally, on the right were our proposals. They referred, for example, to the abolition of the death penalty, the abolition of residence permits, the deletion of political and religious articles from the Criminal Code, the adoption of laws guaranteeing the right to depart from and reenter the country, the freedom of conscience, the freedom of the press, the rights of persons suffering from psychiatric disorders, and so forth. There were also proposals to introduce alternative service for conscientious objectors, to revise laws relating to criminal procedures, and much else. All these proposals became major components of the work of our ministry.

When the inventory was being drawn up, one of the points that we emphasized, even though we had to venture beyond the International Bill of Human Rights, was our failure to implement our obligations under the Final Act of the CSCE concerning the right of persons to know what their rights and obligations are and to act in accordance with them. In the pre-perestroika era the people were ignorant of their rights. This served the interests of the authorities. The Constitution of the USSR, which contained many beautiful words about human rights, was displayed in shops everywhere, but if you referred to it in court, you could be silenced or banished from the courtroom. It was also impossible to procure copies of the Labor Code, the Criminal Code, or the Criminal Procedural Code. Their print run was artificially restricted. Nor was it a simple matter to access them in a library. It became abundantly clear in the process of taking stock that one of the basic problems was the existence of all sorts of quasi-legal regulations. Each ministry and department could create its own "norms" and adopt its own secret guidelines for those who implemented them. In other words, it was not only the Constitution but also many laws that went enforced. It was practically impossible to protest the actions of an official.

I was shocked to learn that the Ministry of Justice and the Ministry of Internal Affairs lacked even basic knowledge of which directives regulated residence permits, of how many there were, or even of their sequence. It turned out that some of these directives had been in force from the earliest postrevolutionary years. The authorities had simply forgotten to annul them. Surrealistic situations arose in which a passport officer was operating according to some ancient directives that everyone else had forgotten about and no one else possessed. To the question of why a residence permit had been refused, she would reply, "It can't be done. There are directives."

Representatives of the Ministry of Justice, the Ministry of Internal Affairs, and the Procurator General laughed at the news that in Vienna we had undertaken the obligation to publish and make easily accessible all of these quasi-legal regulations and directives that affected human rights. Later, however, they had to rescind these unpublished directives.

The brilliant Soviet writer Fazil Iskander compared the relationship between the state and Soviet citizens to that between a boa constrictor and the rabbits it swallowed. The boa constrictor was chiefly concerned that the rabbit not jump out of the boa's jaws. But on one occasion it did happen. One boa constrictor told what had occurred: "This was one of the darkest days of our history. It was not clear what the escaped rabbit would say about our internal system. How would the other rabbits respond to his words?" To ensure that nothing like this happened again, the snakes decided "to restrict the freedom of rabbits inside boa constrictors." From then on rabbits inside the belly of a boa constrictor were allowed to move in only one direction.

According to its authors, the introduction in 1932 of an internal passport regime and a system of residence permits was supposed to solve certain problems connected, in particular, with agricultural collectivization, one of the key economic programs of Stalinism. The internal passport regime served as an instrument for controlling population movements. Thus, certain categories of persons were simply not issued internal passports. This primarily affected peasants, who were forbidden to move from their state farms and collective farms.

Shevardnadze supported our efforts to eliminate residence permits, and after the conclusion of the Vienna meeting of the CSCE member states, our work on this issue emerged from "underground" onto the interdepartmental level. We made little progress. There were several reasons for the disappointing results, chief among them the position of the Moscow authorities who apparently wielded a permanent veto on rescinding the institution of residence permits.

"Movement in just one direction" and "conduct inside the boa constrictor" constituted an iron curtain that, among other things, forbade Soviet citizens from leaving and returning to the country freely. Drafting a law on departure and reentry became one of the core missions of our ministry. In the USSR, going abroad or not returning from abroad was viewed as an anti-Soviet action punishable under the Criminal Code. "Non-returnees" were even "given the honor" of a mention in Article 64 of the Criminal Code under "Betrayal of the Motherland." Persons whom the authorities considered undesirable were subjected to illegal expulsion from the USSR and stripped of their Soviet citizenship. Contrary to the law, persons leaving the USSR on Israeli visas were likewise deprived of their citizenship.

The most common grounds for refusing permission to go abroad were considerations of secrecy. On that basis refuseniks could be detained for decades. One's closest relatives also possessed a virtual "right of veto" on one's emigration. You could have been prohibited from traveling abroad simply because your apartment faced a secret establishment and you might have seen or photographed those working inside. Those Soviet citizens who went to live abroad permanently were forbidden to return, even to visit their relatives. With the beginning of perestroika the number of refusals to travel abroad for permanent residence was sharply curtailed. The application procedure for temporary travel abroad on private business also was greatly simplified.

I was involved from the beginning in drafting the law on the freedom of exit and reentry but, unfortunately, was no longer involved when it was finally enacted. This was because unlike Glukhov, Yury Reshetov, who had become the head of the division, reacted very irritably when our unit came into conflict with other ministries. Kuznetsov, who then headed the Visas and Permissions Division of the Ministry of Internal Affairs and for some reason was viewed as a democrat after the disintegration of the USSR, very clearly expressed his views regarding the position of the Foreign Ministry and my own stance when he began yelling at me during an interministerial conference at the Ministry of Justice: "Do you want to be assigned to felling timber?"[2]

"That's a good idea. Clean air, a healthy way of life. And a civilized bunch of men headed by my minister whose instructions I am now carrying out."

A break was declared. Kuznetsov immediately approached me to apologize and claimed it was a joke. After this it became easier to reach agreements with him and his office.

The struggle over adopting this law not only was torpedoed by certain departments but was also used by other departments to resolve their own problems—to the benefit of the former. The Ministry of Transportation suddenly and categorically opposed the law. It could not guarantee its implementation. Not only would it need to increase the amount of its rolling stock but it would also need to develop new railway lines. The national airline Aeroflot was alarmed, for it had too few aircraft. Nor did the Ministry of Finance remain on the sidelines. "Where will we be able to get enough hard currency?" they asked. The unanimous conclusion of those opposed to the law was they needed more time to take the necessary "preparatory measures." Naturally, when the law was nevertheless adopted, to be implemented in phases, no one moved a finger to facilitate its implementation.

As with other bills, I considered it imperative not merely to declare a right but also to bolster it with an appropriate implementation mechanism. The government bill, adopted on the first reading, incorporated many provisions of prime importance.

It contained a provision stating that persons beginning work in fields where, for reasons of security, travel was restricted would have to be informed of this in advance. It was envisioned that such restrictions would be established directly at the place of employment. An upper limit of five years that departments could not exceed was set on the period of restrictions on travel. This term could be extended only in exceptional cases by a Commission on

Citizenship of the Presidium of the Supreme Soviet of the USSR. Yet another key feature of the law was the opportunity to appeal to this selfsame commission a decision to refuse permission for permanent residence abroad. Everyone feared this feature like fire. Often it simply sufficed to inquire what were the grounds for refusing an exit visa to a certain refusenik for the department itself to rescind the refusal. A judicial complaint was anticipated in controversial cases where the obligations had not been fulfilled regarding persons who wanted to travel abroad. This feature also removed another of the sore points regarding the problem of exit and reentry. Thus, for the first time since the Bolshevik coup of 1917, the right of Soviet citizens to leave and return to the country was secured.

After our division had just been established, the "traditional" drafters of laws such as officials in the Ministry of Justice and the Procuracy tried to keep from us the bills that were being drafted. As a case in point, one of my colleagues simply stole the text of one of the drafts and enabled us to intervene in a timely fashion. Officials from other ministries simply could not understand what business it was of the Foreign Ministry. Once they figured it out, they tried to hide what was going on and exclude us from the working groups.

The main thrust of our efforts was to reform legislation regarding criminal activity. The Criminal Code of the Russian Soviet Federated Socialist Republic (RSFSR), the "model to emulate" for the other republics of the USSR, was critically important in the mechanism for maintaining power. Before examining the content of this remarkable document, let us make a historical-juridical excursion. As far back as 1922, the Criminal Code of the RSFSR contained such articles pertaining to "propaganda and agitation directed at helping the world bourgeoisie" and "the preparation and preservation with the intent to disseminate and the dissemination of agitational literature for counterrevolutionary purposes, false rumors or unproven information that could provoke panic in society, arouse distrust toward the authorities or discredit them." The most curious was "in the absence of proof of the counterrevolutionary character of the aforesaid actions," punishment may merely be mitigated. The notorious Article 58-10 of the Stalinist Criminal Code, "Anti-Soviet Agitation and Propaganda," came later, but its path was already well prepared. After Josef Stalin's death, smoothly and with only a few changes, it metamorphosed into Article 70 of the Criminal Code of the RSFSR and was in force even during the period of perestroika.

Glasnost, or "transparency," was a crime according to this article, and it was not treated as a simple one but as especially dangerous. The "anti-Soviet agitation and propaganda," as cited in Article 70 of the Criminal Code of the RSFSR, referred to particularly dangerous crimes against the state. The text of this article was formulated in such an all-encompassing manner that it is worth quoting the target it describes in its entirety: "Agitation or propaganda conducted with the aim of undermining or weakening Soviet power or the commission of specific particularly dangerous crimes against the state, the oral dissemination toward the same ends of libelous thoughts that defame the Soviet state and social order, as well as the dissemination or preparation or possession of literature of such content toward these same ends."

This article accompanied the less severe Article 190-1, which defined a crime against state authority as "the systematic dissemination in oral form of knowingly false fabrications that defame the Soviet state and social order as well as preparation or dissemination in written, printed or other form of works of like content." This article enabled the authorities to hold persons criminally liable, for example, for an anecdote or entries in a diary. Anyone who spoke or, even more to the point, anyone who wrote—unless, of course, they exercised extreme caution—would find themselves "under the sword of Damocles" of these two articles. Naturally, we drew parallels between the Criminal Code in force in the Brezhnev era and the Stalinist one, carefully hushing up the fact that the former scarcely differed from the "sacred Leninist norms."

On April 8, 1989, the Presidium of the Supreme Soviet of the USSR adopted a decree that altered the wording of Article 70. It replaced the former deliberate vagueness of this article with a clear judicial formula containing two fundamentally important criteria. The first specified that the statements covered by the article must be of public character. The second concerned the article's focus on calls to change the state and social order, and it removed wording that violated the Constitution of the USSR. An important change was also introduced into the literature section of the article stating that only the preparation *with intent to disseminate* such materials, as well as their dissemination, was prohibited and not, as heretofore, private notes. At the same time, the Supreme Soviet of the RSFSR revoked Article 190-1 of the Criminal Code of the RSFSR. Thus, the juridical foundation for battling dissent by means of the Criminal Code was removed.

I am especially proud of the changes regarding the political articles of the Criminal Code and, in particular, the new wording of Article 70. My draft was adopted with the exception of one or two clarifying words. The wording occurred to me while I was taking a bath before work, and I dictated it to my wife so I would not forget. The reactionaries, however, took short-term revenge, making it a criminal offense to insult or discredit organs of the state, responsible officials, and, what was most surprising, public organizations and their public media. The notorious Article 11 lasted only until the Congress of People's Deputies of the USSR met in the following year (1990).

However, even the changes introduced into the Criminal Code were insufficient for glasnost and for securing freedom of thought and of the mass media. The most blatant example was the Chernobyl nuclear catastrophe of April 1986, for according to the laws then in force, it could not even be mentioned since the location of atomic energy plants was strictly secret. Secrecy, one of the major props of the regime, was founded on lies and fear. We succeeded in tackling this "sacred object" by a multifactor approach, emphasizing its enormous cost, drafting the law on exit and entry, and pointing out the absurdity of the list of what was considered secret information. Finally, the leadership of the ministry understood the need to ease the regime of secrecy.

Paradoxically, the struggle against the institution of censorship, the state organ in Russia that traditionally embodied the suppression of freedom of speech, culminated in a comparatively easy victory. The partisans of perestroika and glasnost still had to wage a long battle, to be sure, although in what were already objectively different conditions.

But let us return to the Criminal Code then in effect, starting with Article 64, "Betrayal of the Motherland," which best illustrates its distinctive character. It immediately becomes clear that this article refers to a "flight abroad or refusal to return from outside the borders of the USSR." There is probably no need to explain that "non-returnees" generally enjoyed the internationally recognized right to leave their own country. What follows in this article appears at first glance to be even more "criminal": "rendering assistance to a foreign state in conducting activities that are hostile to the USSR." If one extracts the meaning from these ominous words, it becomes clear, especially in the context of the subsequent political articles of the RSFSR Criminal Code, that any professional activity abroad—for example, work connected to journalism or to Sovietology—could be subsumed under this article. Punishment could be as severe as the death penalty plus confiscation of property.

A strange amalgam existed. Proclaimed rights and freedoms were joined with criminal responsibility, thus ensuring the rights would not be exercised. An article in the Criminal Code about parasitism turned the right to work on its head. The right to preserve health was distorted by the Ministry of Health into a license for arbitrary conduct on the part of physicians, while the right to housing in response to the phenomenon of homelessness was twisted by an article about vagrancy and residence permits. The right to enjoy the achievements of culture was nullified by the persecution of its best representatives and bans against their works; thus, the freedom of scientific, technical, and artistic creativity existed only in the private domain. Further, the right to suggest improvements to state organs and public organizations and to criticize their defects was twisted around by Articles 70 and 190-1 of the Criminal Code. A bold person who took the risk of making use of this right hazarded a trip to a psychiatric hospital for "urgent consultations."

I have already spoken of freedom of speech and of the press. The freedom of assembly, of meetings, and of street marches and demonstrations was "implemented" exclusively so the toiling masses could show their support for the policies of the CPSU and the Soviet government. Otherwise, the exercise of this right was equated with hooliganism or stirring up the public. Freedom of conscience was achieved to a considerable degree by the religious articles of the Criminal Code of the RSFSR. The inviolability of the person and of one's dwelling was included in the Constitution just to observe the niceties. And Article 56, which proclaimed that "the personal life of citizens, privacy of correspondence, of telephone conversations, and telegraphic communications is protected by law," was simply a mockery.

Throughout most of perestroika, a fierce battle was fought over the abolition of the death penalty, a measure we insisted on. Almost all the nonspecialists opposed its abolition. They were actively supported by the mass media. Nevertheless, the Ministry of Foreign Affairs did not surrender. A compromise was reached. The list of capital crimes was drastically cut. Specifically, economic crimes were taken off the list.

The lion's share of this work was mainly directed toward restoring what had long been uprooted from Soviet life—that is, the right of persons to be themselves. Without taking a risk, it was impossible to hold opinions that contradicted the official ideology on major questions or the official point of view on current events, to move from one apartment to another without permission from the authorities, to "break loose from the collective," and so forth. Each person had to be just like everyone else.

Andrei Sakharov, in writing about the need of human society for intellectual freedom, included the right to receive and disseminate information, the freedom of "unprejudiced and fearless discussion," and the freedom from "the pressure of authorities and prejudices." In his opinion, "this three-fold freedom of thought is the only guarantee against infecting the people with massive myths that, in the hands of perfidious, hypocritical demagogues can easily turn into a bloody dictatorship. This is the sole guarantee for implementing a scientific-democratic approach to politics, economics, and culture." He defined the threat to intellectual freedom as follows: "It is a threat to the independence and value of the human personality, a threat to the meaning of human life."

After Gorbachev came to power, a turning point occurred in society, and the country's leadership regarding all questions concerning its worldview centered on freedom.

An integral component of the ruling political cult was a dogmatic, belligerent, and ignorant type of atheism. To a large extent the education of the "New Man" was built upon this principle. The main reason for persecuting even the most harmless dissent was a strict political-ideological prescription for the "moral-political unity of society." In other words, translating from Soviet newspeak to normal language, it eliminated any convictions that were not included in the directives from on high. This, naturally, included all religious teachings. In the best of cases, believers and, even more to the point, churchgoers were merely tolerated, but they were seen as second-class persons for whom the doors of the GULAG and the psychiatric hospitals were always open.

While taking our bearings from international standards, we realized that we could not automatically transfer foreign experience and the provisions of the relevant international rights documents to Soviet soil. For example, in the sphere of freedom of conscience, the existence in the country of various confessions, denominations, interpretations, and tendencies was a reality that contained significant moral potential, but if handled incautiously it was rife with new and serious problems that would be difficult to resolve.

Not infrequently stocktaking occurred under the pressure of circumstances. During the years of perestroika, extremists fired shots first in one region of the country and then in another. Each time it was a disaster. A majority of cases were provoked by the neo-Stalinists for whom force was an instrument of their political game. People's lives and welfare were small change in their struggle to achieve their political and other ambitions.

The sharp interethnic conflict in Nagorno-Karabakh, the predominantly ethnic Armenian enclave within Azerbaijan, was the raison d'être for devising a legal framework for a state of emergency. About a year before its adoption, I was included in an interministerial group to draft a directive for what was then still the Presidium of the Supreme Soviet of the USSR. Considering the events that followed, I do not presume to say whether this effort was the beginning of an attempt to resolve the problems facing the country posed by those who resorted to force, especially since there are grounds for supposing that the events in Nagorno-Karabakh were one of the provocations that opponents of reform initiated.

I had not expected such an assignment at all. I learned that I would have to deal with it only when I was hastily summoned to the initial meeting, which was held in the hall of the collegium of the Ministry of Justice. It was a typical meeting. Literally right after it began one of the generals in attendance took the floor and argued in favor of handing all power to the military during a state of emergency. Speaking on behalf of the Ministry of Foreign Affairs, I took the initiative to neutralize this danger. To be honest, I had no right to do so at the time.

Subsequently, by then fully authorized to defend the ministry's position, I succeeded first of all in ensuring that the draft bill fully conformed to the USSR's international obligations. Another extremely important feature was strengthening the draft edict to include a detailed regulatory mechanism for declaring and implementing a state of emergency and thus preclude any arbitrary, unjustifiable restrictions on human rights.

The circumstances of the disturbances in Tbilisi (April 1989), when Soviet troops attacked and killed nineteen unarmed Georgian demonstrators, resulted in particularly strong pressure. Hot on the heels of these events we proposed strictly regulating any resort to force. Naturally, despite the minister's support, the law enforcement departments blocked this proposal. An enormous amount of work to elucidate what special means had been employed "to restore order," including nerve gas, ended in failure. Officials in the Ministry of Internal Affairs and the Procuracy who had passed highly classified internal instructions and other documents to me had put themselves at risk to no avail.

All our work to promote order in the sphere of human rights took place amid the ongoing bitter political struggle. The period when the Central Committee exercised absolute power was particularly complicated and protracted. Everything became much simpler after the creation of the Congress of People's Deputies of the USSR (March 1989) and the election of Mikhail Gorbachev, who systematically deprived the party and the Central Committee staff of power.

In general, pushing things to a decision point was a science in itself. Notwithstanding the myth of a monolithic Soviet state and Communist Party structure, the state and party bureaucracies were actually extremely heterogeneous. A paradoxical situation often arose in which diametrically opposed decisions were forthcoming from one and the same ministry, department, or office of the Central Committee. All one needed to know was which buttons to push and what questions to submit to precisely which persons in order to achieve a positive outcome.

In the USSR the presumption of innocence was proclaimed in principle but disregarded in practice. This naturally promoted a sense of personal insecurity. In reality a presumption of guilt existed, and it tilted any criminal investigation and legal proceedings in favor of the prosecution. For example, defense attorneys were allowed to participate in a criminal case not from the time of detention but only after the conclusion of the preliminary investigation. The presumption of innocence, stipulated in the UN International Treaty on Civil and Political Rights guaranteeing the right not to be compelled to give evidence against oneself or to confess guilt, was honored in the breach.

Nonjudicial forms of persecution were widely employed. Among them Andrei Sakharov listed dismissal from work, obstacles to receiving an education, exile abroad, conditions that compelled persons to emigrate, and revocation of citizenship for Soviet citizens who were abroad.

In drafting the acts relating to human rights, we always insisted firmly on openness. Stereotypical disputes often arose. "This cannot be published." "That means it can't be adopted."

Paradoxically, depriving the CPSU Central Committee and its apparatus of its plenary powers for a certain period significantly complicated our work. Many opponents of change hastened to take advantage of the breakdown of the mechanism for making and implementing decisions. We were deprived of the effective assistance that liberal staff members from the Central Committee had previously rendered. However, opposition from the reactionaries in this same organ of power now ceased. Unfortunately, the power that the party reactionaries lost was more than compensated for by that of the reactionaries from the state bureaucracy.

Freedom of Religion

The fate of religious freedom in Russia was no better than that of freedom of speech. Prior to the Bolshevik coup, Russian Orthodoxy was the state religion; soon after the coup all religions were in effect virtually tabooed and placed under the strictest control by the secret police. Many Russian Orthodox priests, including the upper ranks of the church hierarchy, were simply KGB officers in cassocks. During Gorbachev's reformation, however, an initially successful attempt was undertaken to promote religious freedom and normalize church-state relations.

The early work on rectifying this situation typified the romantic period of perestroika. Clearly there was a problem, and how to deal with it was also fairly clear. Nonetheless, for a long time nothing happened. To be sure, the USSR managed to celebrate the thousandth anniversary of the baptism of Rus' and publish a massive edition of the Bible, a natural decision that seemed hardly worth noting. But before then even possessing a Bible made one criminally liable.

That we failed to secure permission for Pope John Paul II to take part in celebrating the millennium of the baptism of Rus' is still a matter of shame. The KGB, the Russian Orthodox Church, and those members of the Central Committee of the CPSU who supported the reactionary Yegor Ligachev, then number 2 in the hierarchy, were adamantly opposed. Following the disintegration of the USSR, their replacements hardly differed from them and perhaps were even worse. During the Soviet period there was not such open hostility, such hysteria, and other dubious mental displays toward the Vatican as what came afterward.

The core issue we faced during perestroika was what to do about legislation codifying the lack of religious freedom in the USSR. This issue became so prominent that from the depths of the law enforcement establishment, draft legislation emerged that would have permanently consigned the church—already slavishly dependent on the state—to something like a ghetto. The Ministry of Foreign Affairs exercised its veto and sent a note to the Central Committee of the CPSU demonstrating the need to pass a democratic law on freedom of conscience in conformity with the USSR's international obligations. As in other cases, we grounded the international obligations of the USSR in what was then called Leninist norms, which we sharply contrasted with Stalinist ones. The classics of Marxism-Leninism spoke eloquently of religion. Therefore, even in "materialist" and "atheistic" Russia, their words imparted a kind of truly mystical significance.

When we began working on the issue of freedom of religion, existing restrictions limited the teaching of religious beliefs. Churches and religious societies had no right to own property, including buildings and liturgical objects. Thus, the door was wide open to arbitrary official actions. The position of religious groups and organizations was minutely regulated by the state; in force were numerous prohibitions and restrictions affecting believers and religious associations. The only books permitted in places of worship were those required by the ministers. People were denied the Bible, the Koran, and, consequently, access to their own history and culture. The approach to believers, who were treated as a special class of citizens, reflected the bonfires of the Inquisition and ideological racism.

Shevardnadze established a working group in the Foreign Ministry under the leadership of Deputy Minister Vladimir Petrovsky to deal with the whole set of church-state problems. Along with Deputy Chief of the Directorate of International Organizations V. Sidorov, we were supposed to establish contacts with the leadership of the Russian Orthodox Church and other denominations. Parenthetically, it should be noted that this work too was illegal. Without exception, all contacts with religious leaders were supposed to take place exclusively through the Council on Religious Affairs. In practice, this meant it was inconceivable. If any government official, no matter what rank, wanted to explain something to members of the clergy or reach agreement on some matter, he or she had to address the Council on Religious Affairs. If this body approved, council officials would contact someone from the clergy and, at their own discretion, communicate the response. Under such conditions true dialogue was impossible. Thus, the Foreign Ministry broke with the existing practice and established direct contacts with religious leaders.

Making personal acquaintance with the hierarchy of the Russian Orthodox Church was an interesting experience. For example, I paid a visit with my then direct superior, Yury Reshetov, to Metropolitan Yuvenaly to inform him of the results of the Vienna meeting of the CSCE member states. I naively supposed that the Orthodox Church would be very satisfied with the agreements under which Russian Orthodoxy, like other religions, would receive unprecedented freedom in our country. Was I ever wrong! We entered Yuvenaly's rooms in the Novodevichy Monastery, where the metropolitan was reading the text of the document in *Izvestiia*. He saw us and instead of saying hello, he flung down the paper: "So now we have to recognize the Uniates?"[3]

Reshetov was dumbfounded. Taking a deep breath, I coolly confirmed this supposition and said something about what the Russian Orthodox Church would receive. I did not fail to make spiteful mention of the separation of church and state and the equality of all religions before the law.

With that our conversation concluded. This was my second meeting with Yuvenaly. The first time, when I went to see him with Sidorov, he had been extremely pleasant and impressed us as an inspirational and well-educated person.

Realizing it was useless to speak with Yuvenaly, we paid a visit to Filaret (of Minsk), who proved to be rather different. Convincingly, he cursed at length the obtuseness, sluggishness, and alcoholism of those who should be "removing" obstacles to the Uniates. Filaret's joie de vivre was more becoming than that of his higher-ranking colleague. Parenthetically, I should note that at different times both of them were involved in external church relations.

Their successor, Metropolitan Kirill, who later became patriarch, was cut from different cloth. He was a consummate diplomat and master of protocol. At the time, he was already no less ambitious than Yuvenaly, who had pretensions to the patriarchate. Kirill thought that any Russian should become Orthodox, and if the person didn't like the church, then he or she could leave it. His was an enlightened position. The closest contact I made was with Metropolitan Pitirim. He was an interesting conversationalist, a very worldly man. To observe Lent with him was unbelievably tasty.

Naturally, there were also meetings with religious leaders from other denominations. At one of them we heard: "How good that you have finally come. Now we shall know what to do."

These contacts convinced me of the *complete* absence of spirituality on the part of my religious interlocutors. My experiences also persuaded me to form my own opinions about church-state relations and intra-church problems.

The working group drafting a new Soviet law on freedom of conscience assembled in a house belonging to the Council on Religious Affairs and then in the Supreme Soviet of the USSR. The positions of the group's participants were clear and diametrically opposed. An overwhelming majority were strongly opposed to any liberalization in this sphere. What passions raged during the drafting of the bill! The ideological fanatics even tried to prohibit the churches from engaging in charitable activities by including provisions in the draft that, for example, would have made it impossible for them to open hospitals.

Passage of the Law on Freedom of Conscience and of Religious Organizations on October 1, 1990, not only thoroughly liquidated the old order but also established a new political and legal framework that guaranteed the sovereignty of the individual in questions of faith and in relation to religion. Until the law was adopted, directives from the Council on Religious Affairs were in force that categorically forbade "the registration of religious societies and groups of Jehovah's Witnesses, Pentecostals, True Gospel Orthodox, Orthodox Christian, the True Orthodox Church, Adventist Reformers, and Murashkovites."[4] But the list was not comprehensive, since it contained an "etc." at the end. Thus, the directives prohibited just about any religious group.

The new law precluded such arbitrariness. It specifically stipulated that documents defining religious teachings and deciding other internal matters of religious organizations were not subject to registration. Government departments of religious affairs no longer possessed plenary powers and could no longer interfere in the internal affairs of religious organizations. As far as the law enforcement organs were concerned, holding religious beliefs could no longer in and of itself be seen as a violation of the law.

Naturally, the process of drafting and passing the law did not occur in a vacuum. The Council on Religious Affairs estimated that at the beginning of 1991, there were about 70 million believers in the USSR belonging to almost fifty different denominations, sects, and tendencies. The situation became even more strained with regard to intra-church affairs. Centrifugal tendencies became sharply evident. In October 1990 the Ukrainian Orthodox Church separated from the Moscow Patriarchate. Mutual reproaches flew back and forth between the Moscow Patriarchate and all those who disagreed with it.

The Moscow Patriarchate believed that it was one thing if the Ukrainian Orthodox Church became autonomous in the course of normal intra-church development, but it viewed the establishment of a Ukrainian Autocephalous Orthodox Church as an entirely different matter. The Autocephalous Church specifically accused the Russian Orthodox Church of having failed to maintain control of the situation in western Ukraine and of "having retreated without giving battle in the face of Catholic pressure." Similar processes occurred in Moldova. The Moscow Patriarchate, with no less passion, reproached the Kiev ecclesiastical hierarchy for its inertia and for its inability to cope with the evolving situation.

Relations between the Moscow Patriarchate and the Russian Orthodox Church Abroad became strained. However, they had never enjoyed cordial relations. The Moscow Patriarchate was considerably agitated when the Russian Orthodox Church Abroad established its first legal parish in the Vladimir district in 1990.

Hints of normalizing relations between the Russian Orthodox Church and the Vatican and the dialogue that had commenced between them, as well as the strengthened position of Catholicism in various regions of the country, caused the so-called patriotic wing of the Russian Orthodox Church to attack the church leadership and accuse it of complicity in the "Catholicization" of Russia. Similar accusations were leveled at Gorbachev, especially after his conversation with John Paul II in the Vatican in 1989. The agents of darkness and regression accused Gorbachev of "plotting with the Vatican."

Problems relating to the Ukrainian Greek Catholics (Uniates), who were dominant in some districts of western Ukraine, proved especially complicated for both the government and the Moscow Patriarchate. According to official data the Uniate Church had four million to five million followers. Naturally the faithful demanded that both the government and the Russian Orthodox Church grant full juridical recognition to the Ukrainian Greek Catholic Church and restore it as an autonomous religious organization.

In a number of western districts of the USSR, the Uniates became a symbol of personal freedom and national consciousness. It was useless and harmful to struggle against them. At sessions of the interdepartmental working group drafting a bill on freedom of conscience, we were told of occasions when the police received reports that a Uniate service was taking place literally two steps behind a police station. A military detail would be dispatched to the scene. It would return and report that no service was taking place. The original complainant would insist that it was and that even the singing was audible! He would be told that no one else but him had heard any singing, that he was imagining things, that he needed to rest up, otherwise . . . The complainant had no recourse but to return home.

The hierarchy of the Russian Orthodox Church complained about both the inaction of the authorities as well as the severe shortage of Orthodox priests capable of conducting services in Ukrainian and of religious literature printed in Ukrainian. They asserted that the Vatican was skillfully and actively filling this vacuum in order to "implant" Catholicism in the USSR. The redistribution of church property was far from the last item on the Moscow Patriarchate's list of complaints. It did not want to lose what it had received, while the Greek Catholics tried to recover what they had lost. Unfortunately, for too long the government failed to distinguish its own position from that of the church. The process of registering the Uniate communities only began in mid-1990 after a considerable delay.

The new patriarch Aleksei II, who was well acquainted with the activity of the USSR Foreign Ministry in defense of the rights of believers and religious organizations, attended the final meeting of the parliamentary commission drafting the law. I refused the blessing of this KGB agent even though he may have been only a "former" agent. Regrettably, this law was not in force for long. The RSFSR parliament began feverish attempts to draft its own law. It is a curious fact that those members of our commission who had been unable to persuade the commission of the Supreme Soviet of the USSR to adopt their own aggressively atheist and KGB-type approaches later joined the RSFSR parliamentary commission.

I must confess that while I was involved in helping to resolve these religious problems, because of my own naïveté, I failed to realize that religion could be a commercial enterprise. The churchmen themselves were not so naive. They were well aware of this potential.

A Page from the Book of Sorrows

In the winter of 1986–87, a classified radio transcript summarizing foreign radio broadcasts into the USSR that was intended for the Soviet leadership's use revealed the political abuse of psychiatry in the Soviet Union. Eduard Shevardnadze instructed us to report to him promptly on this matter. From that evening serious efforts began to reform Soviet psychiatry, work in which I was engaged for several years. Frankly none of us suspected the scale of the tragedy or the depth and complexity of the problems confronting us. We possessed only moral reference points. By acquiring information we were able to adopt a position but not to analyze the problem comprehensively and devise appropriate and, most important, realistic proposals. Everything had been done to conceal the truth from outsiders' eyes. Although they knew more than we did, the guardians of the law were in roughly the same position. Yet the main point soon became obvious: A healthy person who landed in a psychiatric hospital could be deprived of his or her will with a single jab in the arm. A second jab and the person would go mad. Practically no one who underwent such "treatment" emerged healthy.

Among the main preoccupations of our Western partners concerned with human rights in the USSR were their lists of the prisoners of Soviet psychiatry. These lists contained the names of about three hundred persons who had been placed under psychiatric treatment for political reasons and often held criminally accountable under political and religious articles of the Criminal Code. Some among them had never had any connection to politics.

For many years, in response to widespread accusations about politically motivated psychiatric abuse, Soviet psychiatrists either maintained a proud silence or alleged that they were being libeled. As a result, in 1983 they were actually expelled from the World Psychiatric Association.

By rebuffing any sort of criticism as slander or libel, Soviet psychiatry showed that it had been gravely ill itself for many years. The psychiatrists were adept at diagnosing their patients' inability to critically assess their own actions as a symptom of their illness; however, the psychiatrists failed to observe this in themselves. To be fair I must note that it was not the psychiatrists themselves who were responsible for introducing the belief in their own infallibility. They were simply the executors of a political and religious line that came from above.

The criticism from the West was shocking. In essence it maintained that in the USSR, healthy people were placed in psychiatric hospitals because of their political and religious convictions. Our Western interlocutors handed the Soviet authorities lists of psychiatric prisoners who, after the start of Gorbachev's perestroika, for the first time became objects of intense scrutiny by the Soviet Ministry of Foreign Affairs.

Establishing the dictatorship of comprehensive ideology in the USSR had both moral as well as juridical consequences. The political and religious articles of the Criminal Code, along with the bizarre system of psychiatric diagnosis devised by Academician Andrei Snezhnevsky, who propounded the notion of sluggish schizophrenia, facilitated the transformation of nonstandard political or religious convictions into a criminal matter and then a psychiatric diagnosis. Even worse was the subsequent arbitrary action via extrajudicial compulsory hospitalization. The pretext was so-called hospitalization for emergency reasons on account of urgent symptoms. The abuse of psychiatry intensified after the Prague Spring of 1968 and the 1975 signing of the Final Act of the Conference on Security and Cooperation in Europe, which provided a powerful impetus for defending human rights in the USSR.

In organizational terms, the suppression of dissenters was done in two ways. The first, more complicated way involved applying the political and religious articles of the Criminal Code, followed by compulsory treatment in special hospitals run by the Ministry of Internal Affairs. This system worked flawlessly. A person held criminally accountable could be transferred to judicial-psychiatric specialists at any stage of the investigation or by a court. Normally, however, such matters did not reach a court. Moreover, supposedly out of "humanitarian considerations," defendants who were tried were not brought to court. Many of them never even saw a lawyer face-to-face.

Why were such violations of criminal procedural laws necessary? In some cases even the elastic wording of the Criminal Code allowing persons to be judged for expressing thoughts to a spouse or to friends, or for writing thoughts in a diary, for example, did not suffice to hold persons criminally accountable. That's where expert opinion came in. The psychiatric instruments of combating dissent were honed to perfection. Psychiatrists were free to act as arbitrarily as they pleased. The arbitrariness of some encouraged the arbitrariness of others. One's neighbors, one's boss, or anyone at all could demand that someone be isolated in a psychiatric hospital because of "urgent symptoms."[5] This was the second method of uprooting "heresy" from the "monolithic Soviet society" and suppressing dissenters.

Battling this monster was difficult. To initiate action, my father, then first deputy foreign minister of the USSR, spoke with Prime Minister Nikolai Ryzhkov, who was surprised and indignant upon learning of the scale and methods of psychiatric abuse for non-medical ends. Ryzhkov asked my father if there was anything on paper. After receiving information I had prepared, he vented his anger at a Politburo meeting according to those present. However, psychiatric repression was so deeply entrenched that even the clear and firm position of Gorbachev, the prime minister, the minister of foreign affairs, and Yakovlev sufficed only to provide a legal basis for the investigatory work that was under way. Moreover, this legal basis was quite shaky. According to the existing rules, everything that transpired at Politburo meetings was strictly confidential. I was not supposed to know about it, let alone refer to it.

Initially the task seemed fairly mundane: figure out what was going on, draft proposals to amend the normative documents, and submit them to the Politburo for the signatures of Shevardnadze and the minister of health. Obstacles arose almost at once. First was the unprecedented opposition we encountered from the Ministry of Health. Naturally we wanted to study the existing protocols. Unexpectedly, the bureaucrats in the ministry told us, "There are no protocols." We knew that there were. There had to be. Moreover, we had our own set, copies that had come into our hands via means like something from the plot of a detective story.

At my first meeting with Alexander Churkin, the chief psychiatrist of the Ministry of Health of the USSR, I referred to these protocols, using a pretext I had prepared in advance: "I need to report to the leadership the measures we need to take for the USSR to rejoin the World Psychiatric Association."

This pretext was invented so that the feudal lords and inquisitors of Soviet psychiatry would all agree to the reformation of their domains. Specifically, there were questions about the protocols governing psychiatric examinations.

"There are no such protocols," Churkin flared.

I took out my notebook and flipped through it to the proper page. "Well, how could there not be, Alexander Alexandrovich? Their full title is 'Protocols Concerning the Initial Medical Examination of Citizens to Determine Their Mental Health.' First Deputy Minister of Health [Oleg] Shchepin approved them on 26 June 1984."

"There is such a protocol," Churkin acknowledged grudgingly, almost interrogatively. He knew he was trapped. "But how do you know about it?"

"We have our own ways of getting the information we need."

The psychiatrists had much to hide. According to this document, anyone could be subjected to a compulsory psychiatric examination if one's conduct "aroused suspicion that he manifested severe psychiatric disturbances that threatened the life and safety of the person in question or those around him." A special provision stipulated the right of responsible officials, relatives, and neighbors to send for a psychiatrist. Moreover, "individuals who disrupt the work of institutions, enterprises, and so forth by absurd actions, innumerable letters containing absurd contents, as well as groundless demands may be examined by a physician-psychiatrist directly in these institutions." Therefore, practically any person distinguished from the mass by unusual thoughts or eccentricity, or by insisting on his or her rights, could ultimately be hospitalized against his or her will by deploying the medical terminology "for emergency reasons."

Together with our judicial "investigations," we conducted others as well. From every possible source we added names that had not appeared on the original list of victims of punitive psychiatry presented to the Soviet delegation in Vienna. We circulated these revised lists to all departments so they could initiate possible reviews of the fate of the persons named therein. I say "possible" because among those on the lists there turned out to be persons—criminals—who really were suffering from psychiatric illnesses. Sometimes, to be sure, we were deceived in this regard. In the overwhelming majority of cases, the physicians concluded that the victims of punitive psychiatry, whose names appeared on the lists, could be discharged from psychiatric hospitals or transferred from the special hospitals of the Ministry of Internal Affairs to regular hospitals.

The breakthrough came during preparations for Gorbachev's first visit to the United States. Included among the numerous materials was an official document listing the names of persons who had been discharged from psychiatric hospitals and those who would be discharged prior to the start of the visit. The lists had been compiled with the help of psychiatrists after they had reexamined these patients.

Nevertheless, at the last moment someone somewhere reneged on his word. The mechanism of releasing dissenters from the psychiatric torture chambers was stuck in neutral gear. We needed to adopt harsh measures to convince the psychiatrists and the concerned ministries and departments that there could be serious consequences if the general secretary of the Central Committee of the CPSU engaged in misinformation. Of course, we exaggerated somewhat, but they snapped to at once. The conclusion I drew was crystal clear: "Do what you want to, but keep your promises. Otherwise, we shall all pay the price."

It was obvious that a good law was needed to bring order into psychiatry. We possessed a powerful weapon in the initial stage of perestroika in the form of a Leninist-era resolution (directive) from People's Commissar of Justice Pēteris Stučka, published in *Izvestiia*, that governed the examination of those suffering from mental illnesses. This directive was presented to Shevardnadze, who fully grasped the lethal power of "Leninist norms" for the Soviet psychiatric inquisition. A whirlwind of activity began to push through a Politburo resolution on the need for a law regulating all aspects of psychiatric care. Unfortunately, the Ministry of Health, allied to the punitive organs, came out on top in the struggle with the Foreign Ministry. Thus, on January 5, 1988, the Presidium of the Supreme Soviet of the USSR issued a decree authorizing compromise regulations governing the provision of psychiatric care. Although it had been drafted on Shevardnadze's initiative, in the key memorandum to the Central Committee we had been able to exert influence only at the stage of formal balloting by Politburo members.

Despite the decree's shortcomings, it contained many positive elements. Most important of all, it was the first legislative, rather than bureaucratic, effort to regulate the provision of psychiatric care. It established strict time frames for examining and reexamining patients who had been involuntarily placed in psychiatric hospitals. The decree provided not only administrative but also judicial as well as prosecutorial control over the actions of psychiatrists. Unfortunately, the mechanism of such control was not specified and, therefore, could not function. The special psychiatric hospitals that had been operated by the Ministry of the Interior were to be transferred to the public health services, but this decision, too, was also sabotaged at the last possible moment. One of the excuses given was that the salaries of personnel in the special hospitals were higher than those working in ordinary hospitals. The decree also established the principle of criminal culpability for placing a "person undoubtedly known to be healthy" in a psychiatric hospital. Since it was impossible to say that someone was "undoubtedly" known to be healthy, this was a masterful—and completely useless—formulation.

The decree also contained a provision broad enough to cover almost any abuse: "Persons committing actions that gave sufficient grounds for supposing that they suffered from psychiatric disorders, and who infringed upon public order or the rules of socialist communal life . . . can be subjected to an initial psychiatric examination without their agreement, or the agreement of their relatives or legal representatives." It would be impossible to think of a vaguer and more expansive formula for any sort of arbitrary action than the notorious "rules of socialist communal life," since they could be interpreted in a completely capricious fashion. In sum, the positive elements were practically nullified by the absence of an enforcement mechanism and by the traditionally elastic formulations. At the same time, the decree was significant since it actually did facilitate the further reform of psychiatry.

Even with the full support of Shevardnadze, nothing could have been accomplished at that time without the close cooperation of reform-minded personnel in the offices of the Central Committee of the CPSU. The section on human rights, whose work was overseen by Alexander Yakovlev, took up these issues. It was undoubtedly because of the incontestable authority of the all-powerful party apparatus that the psychiatrists began to cooperate with the Ministry of Foreign Affairs.

Later, when things took a dangerous turn, Deputy Minister Adamishin relayed instructions from Shevardnadze that I should act entirely on my own so that no one in the Central Committee bureaucracy or the Foreign Ministry, including my own immediate supervisor Yury Reshetov, would know what I was working on or how. Soon Shevardnadze sent his own special messenger to transmit his order to take possession of all the rough drafts of the papers I had presented to him the previous day. His instructions were that from then on, without exception, I should give him all the papers dealing with psychiatry without first having them officially stamped, in order to leave no paper trail, and transmit them only to the then de facto head of the secretariat of the ministry, the future foreign minister Igor Ivanov. If necessary, I should inform him orally as to who else was in the know and from where the information came.

I am not joking in speaking of the danger. The attempts by various persons to intimidate, including by psychiatric methods—manipulation, intimidation, and provocation—especially by the KGB, were merely a trifle though certainly unpleasant. The major provocation was undertaken on the eve of a visit of American psychiatrists to the USSR. We had initiated this visit based on domestic political considerations; we needed powerful pressure from abroad to spur new efforts toward restructuring psychiatry. The main objective was to gain approval from above to draft an effective law strictly regulating all aspects of psychiatric care that would prevent new abuses by the white-coated guardians of ideological purity. No less important was freeing the maximum number of political and religious prisoners from the psychiatric torture chambers. To secure permission from the Soviet psychiatric "generals," we informed them that without a successful visit, restoring Soviet membership in the World Psychiatric Association would be impossible.

The first meeting to prepare for the visit of American psychiatrists took place on November 9–12, 1988, in Moscow. It was agreed in advance that the preparations for the visit and the visit itself would take place under the aegis of the Soviet Ministry of Foreign Affairs and the U.S. Department of State. Accordingly, I was appointed to head the Soviet delegation, and my American counterpart was Ambassador Robert Farrand. The American side presented a document outlining conditions it considered necessary for the delegation to conduct its work successfully. Initially, the document seemed unacceptable.

The American delegation had a particular objective in mind—to ascertain whether perestroika was occurring in Soviet psychiatry and whether the preconditions for the abuse of psychiatry for nonmedical purposes still existed. The American specialists drafted a work plan in accordance with this objective. We were presented with a list of forty-eight persons; of those, they wanted to examine fifteen who were hospitalized and twelve who had been discharged from hospital. This plan was eventually carried out.

I will not conjecture about the difficulties the American specialists faced. One thing was clear: the results of their inquiries had to be 100 percent reliable according to criteria applicable in the United States. But implementing the political will of both sides during the initial phase of cooperation depended both on correctly interpreting the intentions of one's counterparts and on purely technical aspects.

The success of the negotiations was facilitated by the acknowledgment, literally on the eve of their start, by Alexander Churkin, the chief psychiatrist of the Ministry of Health of the USSR, that there were cases of "hyper-diagnosis" and "unjustifiably lengthy periods of compulsory psychiatric treatment." However, as he himself admitted to me, he fabricated the number of such cases, so the number bore no resemblance to reality. It should not be forgotten that the system Soviet psychiatrists devised for diagnosing psychological illnesses could satisfy the most refined taste of the most demanding politicians—that is, demanding of others, not of themselves! In this context, the word *hyper-diagnosis* has a distinctly ominous sound.

Just as the "medical" contingent of the Soviet delegation was headed by Churkin, on the American side this function was fulfilled by one of the leading American authorities in the field of judicial psychiatry, Dr. Loren Roth. Thanks very much to his efforts, a Soviet-American dialogue in the field of psychiatry resumed, and a new impetus was given for reforming Soviet psychiatry. I viewed Dr. Roth as both passionate about his work and trustworthy. When we exchanged views during a critical moment when just the two of us were together, and Dr. Roth virtually confirmed my suppositions concerning the goals and possible results of the visit, I began to feel I was now on solid ground rather than just relying upon my own questionable conjectures.

Naturally, the major divergence between the Americans and

us was political. I was granted considerable freedom of maneuver with just one, although very important, caveat: under no circumstances was the Americans' visit to lead to inspections, but since there actually were calls for inspections, they had to be on a mutual basis. Reshetov and the Soviet psychiatrists anticipated that they would discover political prisoners in American psychiatric hospitals. For form's sake, I had to go along with this demand for a while.

Robert Farrand stuck to an extremely inflexible position: there was to be no reciprocal visits. "How can there be mutuality when you have political abuses of psychiatry and we do not?" he inquired. When it seemed that we had already agreed to and decided everything, and the members of the Soviet and American delegations began to rise from the table to exchange handshakes and warm congratulations, I felt compelled to take the floor and, summing up the results of the negotiations, emphasize that the visit would take place on the basis of mutuality. Otherwise, responsibility for aborting the visit would lie with the State Department. I knew that the next day, during Secretary of State George Shultz's visit, I was supposed to meet with Assistant Secretary of State for Human Rights Richard Schifter. I had no doubt that this intelligent and subtle diplomat would take a different stance than that of his subordinate, and that, in fact, is what happened.

The most interesting part of this episode began when everything was finally agreed to and it was time to carry out the obligations we had undertaken. Complications arose partly because we only had oral understandings regarding certain technical aspects of the visit. I had blocked the signing of any sort of document, even an informal one. Everyone—including the leaders of the Ministry of Health, the Ministry of Internal Affairs, and the KGB—would have had to sign off on it, and that was manifestly impossible. It was the source of many disagreements. Frankly, some things had simply been forgotten. No one in our delegation had written anything down, and it was simply beyond my capacity to record everything. Basic problems arose, however, through the fault of the "generals" of Soviet psychiatry and of Soviet medicine as a whole. The patients who most interested the American psychiatrists had undergone psychiatric examination in the Serbsky Institute of Forensic Psychiatry, but a stamp of secrecy had been affixed to their medical histories. The examinations had been conducted by academicians and distinguished professors, and the medical records contained monstrous things. For example, the hospital had refused to discharge one patient until he renounced the religious beliefs for which he had been hospitalized. Wanting to conceal this fact, everyone decided to stonewall.

With the Americans, we had drawn up a carefully planned schedule in preparation for the visit, including, with the patients' consent, handing over to the American psychiatrists photocopies of the medical records of the patients' illnesses to examine. The patients' records were declassified and given to me for safekeeping. The time came and passed for delivering these records to the Americans, but despite my insistent reminders, permission from the Ministry of Health was not forthcoming. Finally, the telephone rang, and Vladimir Yegorov, who was in charge of psychiatry and narcotics in the Ministry of Health, happily informed me that a decision had been reached on handing over the records. I told him that I would quickly summon a representative from the U.S. Embassy.

Before I was able to hand over the medical records, the phone rang again. The very same Yegorov, this time speaking in an entirely different and official tone, declared, "This morning a meeting of all the leaders of the ministry took place at which a final decision was taken not to hand over the medical records to anyone." I asked whether he himself had been at the meeting. He replied affirmatively. In other words, I had deliberately been given false information in order to settle accounts and thereby demonstratively sabotage the visit. Naturally, the Ministry of Health was well aware that anyone responsible would be held criminally liable for the unauthorized transfer of this sort of information.

Such a denouement heralded not only the aborting of the visit and the end of perestroika in psychiatry but also the victory of the darkest forces over any changes. Shevardnadze saved the situation by phoning Minister of Health Yevgeny Chazov and asking him to do everything he could to ensure the success of the visit. Nevertheless, I was told by an eyewitness that on the eve of the visit, the Soviet Union's chief "physician" screamed, "Kovalev is selling out the honor and dignity of the Motherland!" I suppose that everyone has his or her own idea of what constitutes honor and dignity.

Now the Ministry of Health had nowhere to turn, so it resorted to technical measures. I was told all the photocopiers in the ministry were broken, so they couldn't give me, and consequently the Americans, any photocopies of the records. Naturally, the same story was forthcoming from the Serbsky Institute and the Vartanian Mental Health Center. Then a fire broke out in Gennady Milëkhin's office, where the medical records were stored. Fortunately, by some miracle, the medical records survived intact. Ultimately, they had to be photocopied in the Ministry of Foreign Affairs.

The Americans, of course, sensed that preparations for the visit were encountering significant difficulties. Therefore, in December Robert Farrand and Loren Roth came to Moscow on a one-day visit for negotiations that lasted far into the night. Once again there was a real possibility that the visit would fall through. Churkin resorted to shouting. Several times I had to instruct the interpreter not to interpret what our psychiatrists were saying and to declare breaks so they could calm down. Farrand, who knew Russian, saw and understood what was going on. At one point the self-possessed but emotional Loren Roth said that further negotiations were senseless. Nevertheless, around 4:00 a.m. we managed to reach an agreement. In addition to everything else, the KGB did not want to permit former Soviet psychiatrists who had emigrated to the United States, and whom the American delegation needed as interpreters, to come back into the USSR. However, we succeeded in solving this problem, too.

The "disappearance" of patients and other absurdities continued until only hours remained to decide the fate of the visit. Sitting in his office at the Serbsky Institute, Milëkhin and his team and I searched for one of the "missing" patients until 4:00 a.m. We were repeatedly informed that he had been taken from one hospital but not delivered to another. We located him only via the chief medical officer of the hospital to which this patient had actually been brought. We probably spoiled the mood of the chief medical officer as we tracked him down at his mistress's place. The fate of the visit depended upon whether, at the last moment, we would be able to fulfill our promises to present this patient to the American psychiatrists.

Because of these and similar difficulties, whether the visit would actually take place was not finally settled until just before the scheduled arrival of the lead group of the American delegation.

The "front line" during both the period of preparation and the actual visit did not run according to national or political principles. The division was between those who stood for common sense and those who opposed it. One must give due to the dogmatists on both sides who stuck to their guns no matter what. There were negotiations within negotiations (or negotiations squared), when dialogue was taking place not only with one's foreign interlocutors but also—and mainly—with one's domestic interlocutors. Nevertheless, the visit finally did take place from February 26 to March 12, 1989. The work of the delegation and its conclusions are spelled out in detail in various reports on the visit. Therefore, I will not retell it here.

We had agreed with the Americans that prior to publishing the report they would send us the text so we could append our comments for inclusion in the published report. When these comments were ready, I was ill, and they were delivered to the U.S. Embassy without me. After returning to work and hearing of this, I was horrified when I read the document and the accompanying notes written by the head of my directorate Reshetov. The medical part of the commentaries was written in an exceedingly confrontational and, to put it bluntly, rude manner. It took a long while to persuade Reshetov to replace this outrage with a new text, but he finally agreed. We revised the draft with the help of specialists who had not been involved in the first version. But it had already been sent off to the U.S. Embassy in Moscow! The representative from the American Embassy, whom I had summoned, asked me to repeat over and over again that the previous version was void, and we asked the Americans to ignore it. Soon after the visit Soviet membership in the World Psychiatric Association was restored, making what, to be honest, had been my unauthorized promise to Churkin and his fellow psychiatrists come true.

Immediately after the visit was concluded, a motion was tabled in the Central Committee of the CPSU containing a draft resolution substantiating the need to adopt a human rights law that reformed psychiatry. By now neither the medical personnel nor the jurists could object.

Powerful resistance arose from a rather unexpected quarter. When the Central Committee's resolution was already well on its way, so to speak, Politburo member Viktor Chebrikov entered a dissenting opinion about it. I drafted Shevardnadze's reply to this bureaucratic gibberish. The minister signed it and went on leave. After a while I was summoned to the secretariat of the ministry and shown a new document by Chebrikov on the same theme. Its tone was hostile, so I decided to draft an appropriate response: "Why not draft and adopt the law since both the Ministry of Health and the Ministry of Justice were convinced of its necessity, as were leading jurists, including Academician [Vladimir] Kudriavtsev?" The draft was sent to Shevardnadze in the south, and despite his customary sense of propriety, he signed this barefaced insult. Chebrikov no longer had a leg to stand on, and the resolution was finally adopted.

This led to a whirlwind of activity to draft the law. When the draft was ready and approved by the relevant ministries and departments, I proposed discussing it with A. Sebentsov, a member of the Legislative Committee of the Supreme Soviet of the USSR. I knew him very well from working on the law about freedom of conscience.

The first session of the working group of the Supreme Soviet met in October 1990, literally on the eve of my departure for Geneva for the agreement on "The Protection of Persons with Mental Illness and the Improvement of Mental Health Care." I believed that the principles should be adopted in a form that could be used to maximum effect in our internal battles. The draft of the law gave me sufficient freedom of maneuver, and I made a plan.

On assignment in Geneva in November 1990, and without Moscow's sanction, I approved the principles in the name of the USSR. I did so, first of all, because they were necessary. Second, I could justify the liberties I took from the law approved by the relevant Soviet government departments on the grounds that it was in the spirit of the law if not its letter. Moreover, I categorically objected to sending the contents of the agreements that had been reached by coded telegram to Moscow, because this might torpedo the compromise that had been worked out. A telegram would inevitably fall into the hands of the Ministry of Health as well as other "interested ministries and departments," and Chazov and his friends—punitive psychiatrists and law enforcement officials—would do everything they could to disavow my actions. If that happened, the reform of Soviet psychiatry would return to square one. In public life, maximum access to information is essential for society to regulate itself, for civil society to flourish, and for the state to be grounded in law. Bureaucratic and, in many cases, political struggle is quite another matter. To achieve outcomes that are crucial both to society and every individual within it, sometimes one must assume responsibility oneself. But this is possible only if you are fully confident that you are acting correctly and are ready to take what may be a considerable risk.

During the period of perestroika, we succeeded by political means to stop the psychiatric *oprichnina*.[6] Could such people reemerge? Unfortunately, yes.

The Moscow Conference

On January 19, 1989, immediately after the conclusion of the Vienna conference of the CSCE, I was summoned to work late at night by Yury Deriabin, chief of the CSCE Division of the Ministry of Foreign Affairs. His office was crowded with colleagues who were preparing a draft resolution on the results of the Vienna document for the higher-ups. I was needed to take responsibility for the domestic portion. The draft was so detailed that I realized only that it contained all the points I considered important. It seemed that my rather tepid approval was somewhat upsetting to the assembled throng.

Soon a Politburo resolution appeared in which literally nothing remained of this preliminary draft. All the points that had been carefully spelled out were replaced by a single sentence saying that the relevant provisions of the Vienna agreement applied directly to the territory of the USSR. Of course, there was a large dose of juridical demagoguery in this, but from a political point of view, the approach was risk free. There was no point in disputing the decision of the higher-ups. We were still in Soviet times. It turned out that my father was the one who had thought up and formulated this cunning approach that left no out for the reactionaries.

Nowadays the Moscow Conference on the Human Dimension of the CSCE has been forgotten. At the time, however, on the one hand, it was an important element in the internal Soviet political struggle, and, on the other hand, it occasioned a dialogue between Soviet leaders and their foreign colleagues on a wide range of issues. For the Western leaders the crux of the matter was whether they could trust Gorbachev and whether perestroika was just another attempt to deceive them. For the USSR the Moscow conference was an opportunity to promote democratic reform.

The idea of convening the Moscow conference was first broached at a session of the Politburo in October 1986 as members were approving the directives for the Soviet delegation to the Vienna conference of the CSCE. The key point of the directives was a proposal to assemble a conference on humanitarian questions. On his way to the session, Anatoly Kovalev, who had to report on this question, conceived the idea of holding it in Moscow.

Thus, from the beginning, the Moscow conference, which originally was proposed as the Moscow Humanitarian Conference, became a focus of my work. The decisive moment came when the Politburo stated that its preparation was a government priority, but to emphasize its importance it was often referred to as a political priority, and respective proposals to the higher-ups were often couched in terms of their utility in convening the conference. Under these banners the deletion of political and religious articles from the Criminal Code was carried out, as well as the liquidation of punitive psychiatry, the introduction of religious freedom, and practically all the other reforms.

In the fall of 1990 I wrote a concept paper for the Moscow conference, naturally not as a draft document, but as a point of departure for subsequent discussions with representatives of the member states. Then, as we prepared to hold talks, two events burst upon us—in December news of Shevardnadze's resignation, which benefited the plotters preparing the coup of 1991, and in January the tragedy in Vilnius.[7] Those officials opposed to convening the Moscow conference were ecstatic.

The efforts of the Foreign Ministry to establish democracy and human rights in the USSR were grinding to a halt, not to be resumed. The new minister of foreign affairs Alexander Bessmert-nykh sought revenge for the humiliation he had endured because of his opposition to democracy and common sense. He had a simple attitude toward human rights issues. Somehow a miracle occurred, however, as Yegor Ligachev had earlier issued an order to prepare a memorandum and draft resolution on psychiatry for the Central Committee. My best recollection is that this was in December 1988, after Gorbachev had already flown to New York to deliver his speech at the UN. Since everything was top secret when it concerned the United States, I had to coordinate the drafts of the documents with the Foreign Ministry's America hands and then forward them to Shevardnadze, not by the ordinary route through Adamishin, but via Bessmertnykh.

Quickly glancing through the papers, he said, "I'm not going to report such crap to Shevardnadze."

Placing the papers in a folder, I replied, "Shevardnadze estab-lished a department for what you are pleased to call this 'crap.' And, as you know, this job was undertaken on orders from Ligachev."

I left his office.

Soon Adamishin's secretariat hunted me down. He was not there. Deputy Director of the USA and Canada Division Viktor Sukho-drev, who was better known as the interpreter for Brezhnev and other Soviet leaders and who had been present at my encounter with Bessmertnykh, was there instead.

"Bessmertnykh will sign everything. Just don't show your face. Wait in a corner where he won't see you if he comes out of his office."

Perhaps because of the position taken by the minister of for-eign affairs, rumors circulated both within the Moscow diplomatic corps and in several other capitals that Moscow was no longer interested in hosting the conference.

Many people associate the shootings of Lithuanian "separatists" in Vilnius with Gorbachev's policies. As a result, many angry voices began to condemn the awarding of the Nobel Peace Prize to him, and loud protests occurred against holding the European-wide con-ference on human rights in Moscow. The majority of Soviet human rights defenders felt this way. Doubts, some of them absurd, circulated abroad. The following was said in one of the European capitals: "We cannot participate in a conference on human rights that will take place in the Hall of Columns where Nikolai Bukharin was put on trial."[8]

With Shevardnadze's resignation, the situation in the Ministry of Foreign Affairs became difficult. The reactionaries emerged from the woodwork. It was obvious that the liberal leaders of the ministry were losing influence. Echoes of the Cold War became increasingly evident in Soviet diplomacy. People like me went around looking battered and bruised. Those now in charge in the ministry attacked us for liberalism in domestic affairs and for trying to pursue a commonsense policy abroad. Soviet diplomats were isolated at CSCE forums and voiced indefensible views.

As almost his final order in the Foreign Ministry, Shevardnadze appointed me to head a section, endowing me with the authority of a deputy head of a directorate. My understaffed department was tasked with preparations for the Moscow meeting of the CSCE Conference on the Human Dimensions of the CSCE. I was ridiculed almost everywhere I went. "So is your conference ready to roll?"

I received an invitation from Andrei Kozyrev, who by then had been appointed foreign minister of the Russian Federation, and weighed my response. It was not clear how things would turn out regarding the invitation I had received to work for Gorbachev. It seemed to me, mistakenly as was later evident, that working in the Kremlin I would have greater opportunities to influence the situation. In any case, I decided to leave the Foreign Ministry. Meanwhile, I cooperated closely with Kozyrev's closest colleague, Andrei Kolosovskii, and with Vyacheslav Bakhmin, with whom I had established the most cordial relations. I met with dissidents—I have particularly warm memories of Larisa Bogoraz—and managed to resolve the question of holding a Moscow-based meeting of the International Helsinki Federation for Human Rights and to have visas issued to persons of whom the punitive organs disapproved.

Problems piled up one after the other. In its best tradition, the USSR Procuracy held that those guilty of the event in Vilnius were the victims themselves. For reasons that became fully understandable only after the August 1991 coup, Soviet troops continued to hold the television center in Vilnius. Joint patrols by the militia and the army were ordered. Tensions in Nagorno-Karabakh flared.

The duo of Vladimir Kriuchkov and Boris Pugo did nothing to improve the lot of prisoners. Pamyat', the hypernationalist organization created by the KGB and encouraged from above, grew increasingly out of control, and the anti-Semitism that it whipped up took on threatening proportions.

Nevertheless, in early 1991, consultations began in our department with representatives from the Moscow embassies of CSCE member states. We presented foreign diplomats with our vision of what the Moscow document might look like based on the ideas we had been developing. Concretely, the following partial text was proposed: "The participating states will be guided by international laws on human rights, conducting their policies in accordance with the highest ideals of morality and humanism. Confirming their adherence to the principle of non-interference in the internal affairs of other states, the participating states declare that this principle cannot serve as a basis for limiting human rights or for restricting the free flow of information, including information regarding human rights. They likewise affirm the primary importance of cooperation contained in the Final Act of the Conference on Security and Cooperation in Europe for further progress in observing human rights."

Efforts to implement these measures domestically—that is, the democratization of the Soviet Union—proceeded in parallel. The USSR's failure by this time to carry out a series of obligations it had already assumed made it significantly more difficult to convene the Moscow conference. A particularly pointed question concerned the approval of the second reading of the USSR law "On Departure from the USSR and Reentry into the USSR of Citizens of the USSR." The matter of restoring Soviet citizenship to all those who had been unlawfully deprived of it was of prime importance. Nor was the obligation fulfilled to publish within one year after the conclusion of the Vienna conference, and make easily accessible, all laws and regulations governing travel within state borders. Moreover, a cunning trap existed: there was some risk that the documents would be legalized *after* their actual publication.

The question of the USSR's participation in the UN's Optional Protocol to the International Treaty on Civil and Political Rights was unresolved until the last moment. We succeeded in gaining the Supreme Soviet's ratification of the act of adherence to the protocol at its session in the spring of 1991. All the reservations of the USSR regarding the International Convention on Ending All Forms of Racial Discrimination and the Convention against Torture and Other Cruel, Inhumane, and Humiliating Forms of Treatment and Punishment had to be removed, and the procedures envisaged in Article 41 of the International Treaty on Civil and Political Rights had to be recognized.

We succeeded in securing a decision to draft a law guaranteeing the right of Soviet citizens to freedom of travel and to choose their place of residence within the borders of the territory of the USSR. It became clear that a step-by-step approach to removing the previous restrictions was warranted. I saw this, however, as an unjustified concession to the old-style ministries on the part of the Foreign Ministry. We even succeeded in including a point in the presidential directive about the need to draft a law that "envisaged punishing persons guilty of committing torture and other cruel, inhumane, and humiliating acts."

The sharpest struggle developed around the preparation and promulgation of so-called parallel measures undertaken by public organizations.

Immediately after the collapse of the August 1991 coup against Gorbachev, the question arose of what to do about the Moscow conference—that is, whether to convene it on schedule or to delay it. Many influential and previously uncompromising supporters of the conference believed that it would be impossible to convene the conference in post-coup Moscow. Specifically, everyone was afraid that another group of anti-Gorbachev plotters within the State Emergency Committee would take over. There were no doubts concerning their existence.[9]

It became increasingly difficult to defend the expediency, and even the necessity, of holding the conference on schedule. Anatoly Chernyaev, Gorbachev's assistant, informed the president of who was for it and who was against it and why. There was dissension within his closest circle and likewise in the Ministry of Foreign

Affairs. Our family was also split on this matter. My father, who was the greatest authority on European affairs, believed that the conference had to be postponed. We called each other several times each day, presenting new arguments to each other. I heard that Gorbachev was very amused when he was shown the list of supporters and opponents of holding the conference at the appointed time, and my father and I were in diametrically opposite columns. (At that time I was working in Gorbachev's secretariat, which I discuss in chapter 2.) At the critical moment apparently there were more votes against. Nevertheless, the president decided in favor of going ahead.

Just before the opening of the conference, the Committee of European Foreign Ministers admitted three newly independent states: Latvia, Lithuania, and Estonia. For these states it spelled the end of the shameful 1939 agreements between Joachim von Ribbentrop and Vyacheslav Molotov.

Many were struck both by the fact that Sergei Kovalev, a leading human rights defender, was appointed cochairman of the Soviet delegation and by the tone of his speeches. One of the Western diplomats shared his impressions with me. "I always have the feeling that an earthquake will occur on the spot, the ceiling will collapse, and the KGB will burst into the room and arrest Mr. Kovalev in this very hall. The democratic breakthrough in your country cannot but shake things up."

On October 4 the chairman's gavel came down, signifying adoption of the Moscow document. This was the culmination of Gorbachev's perestroika. Gorbachev and his associates envisioned that the Moscow conference would clear away obstructions in the USSR's adherence to internationally recognized standards of human rights. That the international and domestic triumph of Gorbachev and his associates in the field of human rights was the *final* success of his policy of reforming society along liberal lines was perhaps inevitable.

While engaged in this work I did not ponder the abstract philosophical aspect of the possibility of transforming evil into its opposite. Unfortunately, neither did many other people. We destroyed a man-made hell and tried to replace it with a new, humane, and democratic reality. It seems to me that, on the whole, the operation to excise the malignant growth in human civilization went well. But had we understood from the outset that the cancer could not transform itself into healthy cells, we would have acted much more effectively.

To decree democracy and human rights from above, something unprecedented in history, was no simple matter. Nor was it a manifestation of totalitarianism.

2

The August 1991 Coup

The Breaking Point

There is an unusual entry in my personal file: *Released from position on the staff of the President of the USSR due to the staff's disbandment.* This entry appeared in December 1991 as the logical consequence of processes that converged in the August coup d'état and contributed greatly to the disintegration of the USSR.

The coup was an authentic breaking point in Russian history. Let us recall its context. Everyone knew that the vast country was falling apart, that the existing government was unable to rule this gigantic territory inhabited by so many different ethnicities with their many national characteristics, traditions, and faiths. Various reasons were suggested. Supporters of reform viewed the Soviet regime as completely nonviable; orthodox communists blamed all the disasters on Mikhail Gorbachev's reforms.

The economic collapse was already so obvious at the beginning of perestroika that even the Twenty-Seventh Congress of the CPSU, packed with reactionaries, supported some liberalization of the Soviet economy. Between 1986 and 1988, measures were adopted that permitted individual labor activity and the formation of cooperatives to produce and sell everyday consumer goods. These measures were insufficient, however, and constant shortages developed, including shortages of food and other daily necessities.

Everyone sensed that the existing order was changing. In the territory of the USSR Gorbachev aimed to establish a democratic government based upon law. His actions threatened the sacrosanct power of the *nomenklatura*, or the "privileged elite" of the Soviet Union, and transforming the state structure of the USSR meant that many of the country's leaders would be replaced. In the State Committee on the State of Emergency (hereafter State Emergency

Committee), the formal name for those leading the coup against Gorbachev, some members saw their actions as a simple matter of self-preservation.

At the time of the coup I was working on President Gorbachev's staff. I came by that position somewhat accidentally as the result of an earlier assignment when Gorbachev happened to take notice of me. In the early fall of 1986, I had been summoned by Deputy Minister Anatoly Adamishin, who assigned a difficult speechwriting task to three colleagues and me: devise a new policy and embody it in a speech that Gorbachev would deliver at the international forum For a Nuclear-Free World, for the Survival of Humanity. My schedule alone allowed me to focus wholly on the assignment. I took up paper and pen and wrote down thoughts that were quite heretical for that time. Gorbachev liked the draft and wanted to know who had written it. That was the background to the invitation I received early in the fall of 1990 to join the president's staff. (For a long time, KGB chief Vladimir Kriuchkov personally blocked my transfer to the staff, and it was not until the following summer that progress was made.)

Not long before the planned signing of a new union treaty for the USSR, Gorbachev left Moscow to vacation in the Crimean resort town of Foros on the Black Sea. Almost all of his colleagues also went on holiday. I remained in Moscow, since several questions connected to the upcoming Moscow conference remained to be resolved, and the president's speech had to be drafted. On the Thursday before the coup, I sent a draft of the speech along with some other materials to Foros. (The couriers who took them there were arrested on the orders of the plotters.)

A day earlier I had spoken with Anatoly Chernyaev on a secure phone from Gorbachev's reception room. He wanted to know if the speech would be ready on time. I was interested in something else. Would they intervene to clean up the political mess resulting both from the actions of self-styled anonymous "national saviors" and from Gorbachev's "turn to the right" in such matters as political appointments? Despite Chernyaev's vacillations, we were able to reach agreement on the main points; moreover, in the best tradition, we decided to present the proposal to the president without submitting it for anyone else's approval. (To be sure, I simply ignored Chernyaev's instruction to contact Politburo member and Secretary of the Central Committee Alexander Dzasokhov, an unpleasant man whom I did not trust.)

I spent the three days of the coup just steps from its epicenter, in Gorbachev's suite of offices on the third, or presidential, floor of the Kremlin. The floor was almost empty since my colleagues were on vacation. The plotters were meeting one floor below in the office of the prime minister.

On the first day of the coup my name was deleted from the list of officials on the president's staff. On the third day of the coup, August 21, several colleagues from Gorbachev's press office showed up, headed by my longtime acquaintance Vitaly Ignatenko, then Gorbachev's press secretary. He whispered to me that I should leave the Kremlin immediately since the cannons located in the Tainicheskii garden were aimed at our building, and he expected an imminent attack via our floor and the arrest of the State Emergency Committee. I don't know whether the cannons were really there, but no one stormed the building and, as far as I know, no one intended to.

I witnessed many strange things during and after the coup. For example, why did the plotters not arrest the leaders of the democratic reforms, including Alexander Yakovlev, Eduard Shevardnadze, and Boris Yeltsin? Why wasn't the Russian White House attacked? Why did Gorbachev's colleagues, including those vacationing in the Crimea, all return to Moscow simultaneously, but none of them thought to visit the president either to try to help him or, at the least, to ascertain if he really was under arrest? How were the plotters able to hold a press conference with the participation of Yevgeny Primakov, Vadim Bakatin, Arkady Vol'sky, Georgy Shakhnazarov, and Ignatenko? (Let us note that two of them soon headed the special services, and it is quite likely that some others were in league with the plotters as well.) Why on August 21 did they allow the Supreme Soviet of the Russian Soviet Federated Socialist Republic to convene a session that inevitably would condemn the coup? How could the plotters have allowed a delegation of the Supreme Soviet of Russia, headed by Vice President of the RSFSR Alexander Rutskoi and Prime Minister Ivan Silaev, to fly to Foros where Gorbachev was being held?

On August 22, the morning after the coup collapsed, I encountered a strange phenomenon right after showing up for work. Standing near the elevator I was waiting for was an anxious colleague from the Kremlin commandant's office, listening to a loudly squawking walkie-talkie. At first I paid no attention to him. Soon shouts could be heard from both the walkie-talkie and above: "They're bringing him! They're bringing him!" Apologetically, the guard asked me to wait in the corridor and closed the door behind me after I complied. Literally a minute later he invited me back to the elevator and explained what had just happened.

The evening before, all the plotters had been arrested, apart from Gennady Yanaev, who somehow had managed to hide. In the morning he was found drunk and asleep in his own office. Naturally, the KGB could not "lose" Yanaev, who, prior to the coup, was the second-ranking person in the state and the man whom the State Emergency Committee had proclaimed president. What was the point of this game?

Many of the stranger aspects of the coup could be explained by the fact that the members of the new "Soviet leadership" were heavy drinkers. Officials in the Kremlin guard told me that Kriuchkov and Oleg Baklanov were the only ones who had stayed sober. However, a "but" is in order here: The plotters were not really acting on their own; the most powerful agencies in the USSR were behind them, including the KGB, the Ministry of Defense, and the Ministry of Internal Affairs. Why did they fail to act when a political decision had been taken? For example, after the State Emergency Committee documents were published, no additional orders from on high were needed to block the appearance of any additional information that would have discredited the plotters. Nonetheless, such information appeared even on television's Channel One.

Either the entire coercive apparatus was dysfunctional, which is difficult to believe, or one must admit another possibility—the assertion that the coup failed may not be entirely accurate. To put it mildly, the peculiar aspects of those August days may actually have been part of some sort of plot hatched by the plotters or, more likely, at least by the second level down of the State Emergency Committee. Much was said about this at the time and then, implausibly, quickly "forgotten."

The plotters quickly covered their traces, including physically eliminating persons in the know. On August 22 Minister of Internal Affairs Boris Pugo supposedly committed suicide after first shooting his wife. The public sobbed sentimentally. On August 24 Marshal Sergei Akhromeyev, Gorbachev's military adviser, is alleged to have hanged himself. The public was hysterical: what a worthy, honest, and respected man he was! Almost nobody asked why a military man, who possessed his own weapon, did not shoot but rather hanged himself and succeeded only on the second attempt. On August 26 Nikolai Kruchina, who managed the finances of the Central Committee of the CPSU, either fell from the balcony of his fifth-floor apartment, committed suicide, or, most likely, was killed.

On every level the political life of the country was convulsed in hysteria. Those who say otherwise were either out of the loop or determined to distort the truth. All things considered, there were persons, including well-known "democrats," who knew what would unfold and how it would all end.

After the coup failed, a strange, almost unnatural emptiness prevailed in the presidential quarters of the Kremlin. Only a few officials of the president's secretariat remained on the job. After Gorbachev's return to Moscow, none of my colleagues, either from the foreign affairs group headed by Anatoly Chernyaev or from other subdivisions of the president's secretariat, deigned to return from leave and go back to work. Therefore, I was at everyone's beck and call and involved in everything that the boss did, from discharging the duties of secretary, including answering phone calls, to making decisions on matters that were obviously far from my areas of competence, including what and what not to report to the president, whom to let in to see him, and so forth. There was also a dearth of technical support personnel. Gorbachev's secretaries had to run up and down the endless Kremlin corridors so often that by the second day after the coup they changed from wearing shoes to wearing slippers.

There was good reason for the strained, high-tension atmosphere during the first days following the coup amid fears of revenge by the closest associates of the State Emergency Committee. The coup seemed like a bad comic operetta, with the plotters being incredibly inept, but many powerful persons who had remained in the shadows were implicated in the attempted coup. Thus, Gorbachev's personal guards would not allow even persons with the highest-level official security badges to access "the summit," as they called the president's offices. After all, the plotters had been in possession of such badges. Therefore, the guards checked people against lists. When, for the first time after the coup, I had to report something urgently to Gorbachev, I wrote a short note to Chernyaev, who was with the president at the time, and took it to the president's reception room. The secretary obviously panicked, as I had not met him before, and without my knowing it he pressed the alarm signal. Guards immediately stormed into the reception room. It was quite a spectacle. I never thought that so many weapons would be pointed at me.

That day, August 25, was a family holiday to celebrate the birthday of my twins, who were turning three years old. So I hurried home from work as quickly as possible. It also happened to be the evening when my father was discharged from the Kuntsevo Central Clinic, which served the Kremlin and was where he had been treated for a stomach ulcer.

My father returned home after his solitary hospitalization feeling happy and in a good mood. Like all of Gorbachev's close associates, he had gone on leave with him at the same time and underwent treatment at Barvikha, an elite sanatorium outside Moscow for high-level government officials. It combined a splendid park, rather comfortable accommodations, and vulgar luxury with good medical treatment.

Soon after his arrival in Barvikha, his sworn enemy, Yegor Ligachev—the former second-ranking member of the CPSU and, consequently, of the USSR, who had been forced to retire—showed up there. At once, as my father put it, "a rather strange swarm" gathered around Ligachev. Official automobiles and well-known people visited him. Father had stopped frequenting the dining hall to avoid running into Ligachev and his visitors. My father had told me this shortly before the coup.

I went to see him on the second day of the coup. Naturally, we started talking at once about what was going on. My father ushered me into the corridor, where we naively tried to avoid being over-heard, and told me that in the room adjacent to his he had seen some sort of equipment being brought in. Then a man entered the room whom, long before these events, Vladimir Kriuchkov, the then head of the KGB, had pointed out to my father as "our secret weapon, our Otto Skorzeny."[1]

Soon after my trip to Barvikha, my father's physician took him out into the street, farther away from potential snoopers, and said, "Anatoly Gavrilovich, you're in danger here. If you have no objections, I'll immediately write a note saying it's urgent that you be transferred to a hospital." The doctor was not concerned about a danger to my father's health but about a murderer equipped with a deadly apparatus in the neighboring room. The transfer took place.

Then came the holiday. Father and I were political animals, so right after congratulating the twins on their birthday, our conversation turned to the latest events and speculation about the future. I quoted something from our beloved Boris Pasternak, whom we both considered the best Russian poet. At first I thought my father's reaction was a bad joke. "Why quote Pasternak?" he said with uncharacteristic excitement and a dismissive wave of his hand. "Now Dolmatovsky—there's a real poet!"[2] These words were completely ridiculous. Yevgeny Dolmatovsky was never considered a real poet any more than I was.

When the conversation turned to what was going on, again I was unable to fully grasp my father's reaction and assessment. I then asked my wife to remove all the alcoholic drinks. In a state of apparent euphoria, of unnaturally heightened excitation, he predicted all the very worst things that would happen to the country and its people. For the first time in his life, he seemed to be disavowing himself and his convictions. I could not believe this was occurring naturally. Father was behaving so strangely that I was forced to tell him I would not return him to the hospital. He would not accept this. How could his son not allow him to regain his health?

"It's very simple. I'll call the chief Kremlin doctor, Dmitry Shcher-batkin, and explain the situation to him," I said.

"That's impossible! It's too dangerous! It'll be the ruin of you."

"If you don't want to, don't go back to the hospital," I said.

"I can't do that. I promised I would return."

After a couple of torturous hours, his speech and the expression in his eyes returned to normal. He finally agreed that he had been "in a strange state," and soon he said he understood why. It turned out that the attending physician had prescribed some sort of water and brought it to him in an unlabeled bottle stoppered with a twist of paper. The nurse whispered that she didn't know what it was and that if she were him she wouldn't drink it. Father had paid no attention to what she said until this evening. He returned to the hospital, and, little by little, so as to give the impression he was drinking it, he began pouring the suspicious liquid down the sink. He sounded all right on the phone and resumed working. An official phone was installed in his room, and papers were brought to him from the ministry. Colleagues came to consult with him or to make decisions. His downward slide was halted.

In early 1992, however, he suffered a stroke. The entire right side of his body was paralyzed, and he was unable to speak. An incomprehensible mumbling was all he could manage. What happened next may strain credulity. The emergency physician dispatched from the Kremlin clinic first looked closely at Father's medical file, which was begun when he was still in his old post in the USSR rather than in Russia; then the doctor took a cursory look at the patient himself—paralyzed, his face distorted, unable to speak. "Everything is okay; it's just a matter of age," the doctor said. The clinic wouldn't even respond to a second call. This occurred on Saturday morning. He was not hospitalized until Monday. He soon recovered, but right there in the hospital something else happened, and he again lost the use of his right arm and his speech problem recurred.

Was the refusal to hospitalize him and the repeat incident just a matter of chance? There can be no definitive answer to this question. The medical records of the Kremlin clinic are actually classified and, moreover, subject to falsification. Records there were not kept in the generally used thick, bound notebooks but in loose-leaf binders from which pages could be removed at any time and others inserted. The physicians provided no reasonable explanation for this practice.

I was able to guess what happened and how from my knowledge of punitive psychiatry and my acquaintance with many psychiatrists. From my successful battle against the abuse of psychiatry, a psychiatrist I knew gave me a letter from physicians at one of the psychiatric hospitals in Leningrad. It said the following: A secret, shielded bunker had been constructed in this hospital. People randomly taken off the street were placed in it; their heads were shaved, and electrodes with antennas were connected to their brains. Then, under the direction of Academician Natalia Bekhtereva, they were subjected to the action of some sort of apparatus that had been installed in this place but to which none of the physicians in the hospital had access. After the "patients" were no longer needed, the antennas were removed, and they were simply let go in the city, with some of them in a truly lamentable condition.

Naturally, I tried to make sense of this letter. But the information was too dangerous to share even with people I knew and trusted. Therefore, I showed the letter only to my father. Several days later he passed along a request from Shevardnadze to forget about it, since too many powerful forces, including military and space medicine people, were involved. It was impossible to ignore this request from such a fearless and influential figure in our country.

Knowing all this and observing my father's condition, I realized that he had most likely been subjected to similar inhuman experiments. Obviously, only Kriuchkov, the KGB chief, whose relations with my father had seriously deteriorated, could have given such an order. But on whose initiative, it was difficult to say, since father had too many powerful enemies.

But most revealing is the following. What I have just described happened on August 25, when the coup had apparently failed. Why then did the mechanism set in motion by the plotters, who were already under arrest, continue to function? Was this not evidence that the defeat of the State Emergency Committee was merely window dressing, a diversionary maneuver? Working in the Kremlin,

I heard echoes of what was going on in the KGB. I knew how its new head, Vadim Bakatin, was carrying on and how in the Lubyanka they turned pale at his tirades, which carried through his ultra-soundproofed, closed office door. Against this background, the fact that after the coup the KGB-controlled and directed Kremlin clinic continued the course it had initiated prior to the coup appears rather ominous.

In addition, I had long been accumulating questions about the Kremlin clinic, including with respect to my father. As soon as his role in top-level decision making sharply increased after Gorbachev's advent to power and he became one of Gorbachev's most trusted colleagues, the physicians began dishing out preposterous advice to him. For example, they said, "Anatoly Gavrilovich, you work so hard that you absolutely must get a good rest during the afternoon. After lunch you must have a nap, and to do this take a sleeping pill." A physician would not proffer such advice. No genuine physician would insist that his patient take two powerful sleeping pills every day (the second at night). Moreover, the Fourth Main Department of the Ministry of Health of the USSR—the Kremlin clinic—as knowledgeable people asserted, was headed by a general from the Ninth Department of the KGB who was personally involved in everything pertaining to the most influential patients and their doctors' prescriptions. Everyone knew it was simply impossible for my father to take an afternoon nap. After he dined and took his sleeping pill, the phone would ring almost at once, with either Shevardnadze, Yakovlev, more rarely Gorbachev, or some other top-ranking official calling. Yet the physicians insisted, "You must sleep after lunch, especially since you work so late. You have a room to rest in and every opportunity to sleep with the aid of a sleeping pill."

I never understood why he followed this advice. Perhaps he did so because he was just so fatigued. We regularly quarreled over his abuse of sleeping pills. I was convinced they would damage his brain. But for the time being, Father stubbornly stuck to his guns. Without additional intervention, a collapse such as he experienced could not have occurred under hospital conditions during the several days when we did not see each other.

The facts about psychiatric abuse for nonmedical purposes were widely known. Punitive medicine as such was met with silence, perhaps from a dearth of information. But it was indubitably a reality in Russia, where there were too many mysterious deaths, heart attacks, and strokes.

Unfortunately, there can be no answer to the question of why my father "deserved the honor" of being an object of special operations. All one can say fairly confidently is that they did not want to kill him. It would have been extremely easy to do so, but they simply wanted to take him out of action and to do so in a way that would compromise whatever he was doing.

Professional hitmen do not eliminate people without reason, not even simply for revenge. They always act pragmatically, pursuing one or another concrete objective. Not infrequently it is to eliminate inconvenient witnesses who possess dangerous information that could interfere with their plans. Could that be why from the beginning, Anatoly Kovalev did not believe the coup had failed? Judging from the subsequent course of events, perhaps he was right.

To answer the question of what exactly happened in Russia in August 1991, we must make a clear distinction between what lay on the surface and what was carefully concealed behind "seven seals." On the surface, the outcome of the coup was the defeat of the party-*nomenklatura* reactionaries, the victory of democracy in the USSR, and the collapse of the Soviet empire. Most likely this is an overly simplified approach. I think that much of what has been occurring in post-Soviet Russia, including the advent to power of the special services, is largely an echo of those events.

It *seems* as if the coup set in motion a revolutionary course of events. But in what was essentially a ludicrous parody of the taking of the Bastille, the plotters' seizure of a block of buildings of the Central Committee of the CPSU changed nothing. The CPSU was already then in its death throes, shorn of its power, and without any discernible support in society.

The desire to destroy and overthrow had gained the upper hand.

Such actions as pulling down monuments, renaming streets, and completely negating the past had already occurred in 1917 and later. After the August 1991 coup, Russia once again overflowed with hatred. There is something almost mystical about the repetition of events in its history. Russia was increasingly overwhelmed by slogan mongering. The words *freedom* and *democracy* were sometimes used appropriately and sometimes not. A struggle to redistribute power and reapportion the perquisites that accompanied it got under way. Everyone claimed to be a democrat.

The people as a whole were sidelined from deciding the future of the country. To appease them, they were given, in confused verbiage, declarations of sovereignty that, most importantly, had been formulated in different circumstances. Boris Yeltsin gathered all power into his own hands by issuing one decree after another. A creeping coup d'état was in progress. All the extremist forces present in what was then still Soviet society converged to overthrow the president of the USSR.

Staraya Square, where, by an irony of fate, the Yeltsin government had installed itself in the headquarters of the Central Committee of the CPSU, again began to determine Russia's fate. The leader of Ukraine Leonid Kravchuk took advantage of his premature support of the coup and skillfully played on Ukrainian nationalism. The other republics, including Russia, fanned the flames of their own nationalism, forgetting that all of them were multiethnic in nature. Personal hatred of Gorbachev, who was blamed for every ill, became the main motivating force of postcoup events. A redistribution of power commenced, with the fifteen republics receiving the lion's share. All of this, however, explains neither the August events nor what followed. If one tries to probe more deeply, one is driven to the conclusion that the real objectives of the coup are best explained by its aftermath.

The *first outcome* of the coup, in chronological order, was the banning of the CPSU in August 1991. I would not want to exaggerate the significance of this action. Communist ideology had collapsed by then. Moreover, the Communist Party itself soon revived and was operating in an altered guise. Two other elements deserve greater attention: (1) It was then that President Gorbachev began to lose power, and (2) the opportunity to ascertain reliably the fate of the party's financial assets vanished.

The *second outcome* was the decision to dissolve the Congress of People's Deputies, which was the only legitimately elected nation-wide organ of power at the time. This was done spontaneously without preparation or prior consideration of its consequences. I am positive about this because on the eve of the congress I was burning the midnight oil, preparing for it, and not only many drafts and proposals regarding it passed through my hands but also documents already approved by Gorbachev, including the text of his speech and the draft resolutions of the congress. I left the Kremlin after Gorbachev, so that most likely it was someone who had the prepared drafts of all the documents in his possession who convinced Gorbachev even later to take this mistaken decision to abolish the Congress of People's Deputies. (Colleagues told me it was Nursultan Nazarbaev, first secretary of the Kazakh Communist Party.) However, Gorbachev himself was psychologically prepared to make such a decision. He was afraid of the congress. I don't know how Gorbachev could deprive both the country and himself of this, the only legal, nationally elected support.

The *third outcome* was President Gorbachev's departure from power and the end of liberal reforms, thus achieving one of the main goals of the coup. Here it should be noted that at the time of the coup, neither the reactionaries nor those who called themselves democrats accepted Gorbachev. Reactionary elements in the KGB and the CPSU, as well as Yeltsin, especially hated him.

Yeltsin's tendency to be easily manipulated is well known. Wasn't this why he remained untouched during the August coup and why, after it ended, the leadership of Russia was immediately penetrated by agents of the special services?

The *fourth outcome* was the breakup of the USSR, which may not have been among the aims of the plotters. Yet it served the interests, including the material interests, of very many of them. I should note that, objectively speaking, the Soviet empire was ungovernable for several reasons. Among them were the accumulated mistakes committed by leaders over decades, the sheer size of the empire, and its interethnic, economic, and other problems.

Therefore, its breakup was unavoidable. It is also possible that this was an entirely anticipated result of the coup.

The *fifth outcome* was the introduction of "economic freedoms" in Russia and the redistribution of property that ultimately led to the emergence of the so-called oligarchs and the massive, almost criminal impoverishment of the people. Most of what was previously "public property" likely wound up in the hands of entities that belonged to the CPSU and the KGB. I say more about this later.

Finally, the *sixth outcome* was what initially appeared to be the weakening of a disbanded KGB, on the basis of which intelligence, counterintelligence, government courier, guard, and border patrol services were created. In reality, the exact opposite occurred. What happened was the special services were elevated to an unprecedented degree in world history as the monster replicated itself. The special services—whose personnel began to seize key positions in politics, the economy, the mass media, and other spheres of public life—achieved genuine, all-around power after the collapse of the USSR.

The special services did not undergo some sort of diabolical transformation. Simply their members had incomparably more opportunities to take advantage of the unfolding situation. The KGB was doing its usual work of recruiting and inserting agents everywhere it could, including in Yeltsin's retinue, in parliament, in leading positions in government institutions, among the reformers and entrepreneurs, and in the mass media. Moreover, the KGB was changing. On the one hand, it began to merge with the power structure, and on the other hand, it allied with business and organized crime. Virtually omnipotent and controlled by nobody, the special services had unparalleled opportunities for unlimited expansion of their influence.

We should pay close attention to the following information from Yury Shchekochikhin, an investigative journalist and parliamentary deputy who died suddenly in 2003 under circumstances suggesting he was poisoned to shut him up. He did not identify his source due to security considerations. According to his information, in 1989–91, groups—namely, the "Patriots of State Security" (also called Patriots SS)—began to form spontaneously and were organized as secret associations resembling clandestine militarized units. Basically, the Patriots ss comprised former and current operatives of the special and militarized services of Russia and the members of the Commonwealth of Independent States who considered themselves the true patriots and servants of the state. The organizational formation and descent deep underground of these basic Patriots ss units were completed after the 1991 coup in which many such "patriots" took part. The chaos then reigning in the security system facilitated their development into influential organizations with strict discipline and a tight structure that was adapted to undertake effective underground activity over many years.[3] The list of persons with whom Shchekochikhin's source was acquainted from working in the clandestine structure of the KGB and other "patriotic" organizations, and whom he knew from their line of activity, is extremely interesting. It includes the future president of Russia Vladimir Putin, the well-known journalist Evgeny Kiselev, future oligarchs Vladimir Potanin and Alexander Lebedev, and many other prominent political figures and political operatives. If one accepts the accuracy of this information, the picture is terrifying. *An unknown secret organization*, even coming from what is undoubtedly an incomplete list, *seized the commanding heights in the political sphere, the economy, the media, the banking system, and the criminal world.*

By the early 1990s the contours, and some of the representatives, of what basically constituted a new elite in the USSR were extremely clear. The members of this elite believed that they enjoyed the freedom that had been bestowed upon them—that is, a license and freedom to receive personal benefits. Naturally, entrepreneurs and those with the greatest opportunities for enrichment became members of what was then still a covert elite. Traditionally, the ones who had this opportunity were highly placed bureaucrats in the sector of the real economy; party big shots, including people from the Komsomol (Communist Youth League) and the trade unions; and, of course, the KGB, which controlled every aspect of life. A symbiosis developed between pseudo-democratic demagogy and the cynicism and mercilessness of a part of the ruling class linked to the goal of achieving their own aims.

In August 1991 an extremely curious document came into the hands of the paper *Moskovskie novosti* (Moscow news):

Personal Pledge to the CPSU

I ____, a member of the CPSU since____, party membership No. ____, hereby confirm my conscious and voluntary decision to become a trusted agent of the party and to carry out assignments from the party in any position and under any circumstances without disclosing my membership in the institution of trusted agents. I swear to preserve and carefully utilize in the interests of the party the financial and material means entrusted to me, and I guarantee to return them at the very first request. I acknowledge that everything I earn as a result of economic activity using party funds is the property of the party, and I guarantee to turn such earnings over at any time and any place. I swear to maintain strict confidentiality of the information entrusted to me and to carry out the instructions of the party conveyed to me by authorized persons.

 Signature of member of the CPSU ____
 Signature of the persons undertaking the obligation.[4]

According to the *Moskovskie novosti* the Central Committee of the CPSU and the KGB were engaged in this activity. KGB Col. Leonid Veselovskii was transferred to work in the Administrative Department of the CPSU Central Committee. In his report to the KGB dated July 9, 1991, Veselovskii wrote that he was transferred to meet the "urgent need of the leadership of the Administrative Department of the Central Committee to establish a subdivision capable of coordinating the economic activities and economic structures of the party under changing conditions . . . SU."

His report continued, "The means of generating income for party coffers that are not reflected in the financial documents must be used to acquire anonymous shares, stocks in individual companies, enterprises and banks, on one hand to ensure a stable income independent of the party's future position and, on the other hand, so that these shares can be sold on the stock exchange at any time and the capital subsequently invested in other areas with the aim of concealing the party's participation while preserving its control." To implement this plan, he proposed "organizing a timely selection of particularly trustworthy persons who would be tasked with carrying out specific points of the program, not excluding the possibility of establishing a category of secret party members who would guarantee the program's viability under any circumstances during this extraordinary period." He also proposed establishing, with the help of the KGB, a network of stock companies abroad in which the brokers would be trustworthy persons, a list of whom should be drawn up immediately. Then in banks of the countries where these stock companies would be based, accounts should be established in the names of the stockbrokers and funds deposited in these accounts. The next step would be to establish joint ventures on the territory of the USSR.

According to the article, it was precisely through initiatives by the KGB colonel that, in the spring of 1991, Soviet millionaires to whom the CPSU entrusted 400 million rubles appeared on the scene simultaneously.[5] These plans basically meshed with the project for market reforms that envisaged restricting political and civic freedoms—including freedom of speech, the right to strike, and so forth—that Anatoly Chubais, one of the most influential and resilient persons in post-Soviet Russia, proposed to Gorbachev in March 1990.[6] The concept outlined therein of isolating the government from the interests of various social groups can hardly be deemed democratic. Summing up the preceding information, it turns out that at least many, if not all, of the conditions created in the late Soviet and early post-Soviet periods, and perhaps later as well, came about as the result of joint action between the KGB and the CPSU aimed at conserving and increasing the funds of the CPSU. Those in possession of these fortunes are incredibly highly paid managers of these assets and perform an extremely delicate function.

If one accepts this version as plausible, even correct, then two fundamental questions arise. The first and foremost is, to whom do these assets now belong? To the Communist Party of the Russian Federation (CPRF)? It is possible though unlikely. The oligarchs do not curry favor with the Communist Party and its leader

Gennady Zyuganov; rather, they do so with the executive branch of power, the Kremlin above all.

The second question is, whose responsibility is it to ensure that the "trustworthy persons" of the now defunct CPSU carry out their obligations? At least formally, the CPRF is quite unable to do this. But the transfer of the assets of the CPSU to "trustworthy persons" took place jointly with the KGB and, one may reasonably suppose, under its aegis. Thus, one cannot exclude the possibility that what happened around the time the CPSU was banned, and then reborn as the CPRF, was the division of property or its redistribution between the communists and the special services.

I should add, even though I have already spoken about this and have more to say, that it was right after the coup that the KGB itself and its agents became flush with power.

Let us return to the August coup. I should note that a traditional, fundamentalist Soviet elite, exemplified in the State Emergency Committee, existed in the USSR. This traditional elite differed from the unusual aggressiveness of the emerging new elite, which is often closely linked with the old elite and dependent on it. (It would be a mistake, however, to lump together these two elites, despite the dependence of the new elite on the old, since only a very small number of the old elite became members of the new ruling elite.) The liberal reformers, who might provisionally be called Gorbachevites or supporters of perestroika, found themselves between the hammer and the anvil. They did everything in their power to liquidate totalitarianism, but they could not stomach the irresponsible egotistical radicalism characteristic of much of the new elite. As a result of Gorbachev's own initiatives, by this time very little depended upon him and his supporters because the old mechanism of supreme power—the Central Committee of the CPSU—was stripped of its plenary powers and a new mechanism had not been created.

One could reasonably suppose that this new elite was the real puppet master of the August 1991 events. It succeeded in transforming the theatrical and highly stylized violent seizure of power into a creeping coup d'état that led to the redistribution of power and property. Such an assumption explains why the plotters pretended to be so weak and powerless and lacking the resolve to conclude what they had begun. Sadly, however, the coup was widely supported in society. Much is explained if one assumes that the new elite used the coup to achieve its own aims. For example, this would explain why the State Emergency Committee did almost nothing to hold onto the power it had seized, its refusal to attack the Russian White House, and the swift withdrawal of troops from Moscow.

This hypothesis is worth considering and not only with regard to Russia since something similar may well have occurred in other Soviet republics. Moreover, it explains the convergence in Russia of business with power and the special services that lead to the monstrous penetration of all socially significant spheres of Russian life by agents of the special services, among them ministers, deputies, journalists, politicians, and many, many others.

Even this quick retrospective look at the results of the August 1991 coup and the events that followed confirms that despite its apparent failure, the puppet masters behind the scenes undoubtedly succeeded in their criminal activities. Apart from the destruction of the USSR, they achieved both the official goals of the coup as well as those that were carefully concealed. This is why August 1991 became the point of departure for contemporary Russian history. The scriptwriters for this production, as well as the lighting specialists, the makeup artists, and the costume designers—all deserve high marks for their professionalism.

Anna Akhmatova, one of Russia's finest poets, said, "One cannot live in the Kremlin." I would add that one also cannot work there; it is a place inhabited by specters, according to the definition of the Marquis de Custine, the discerning French aristocrat who wrote about his travels in Russia in 1839. With extremely rare exceptions the entire presidential wing consists of immense, luxurious offices with adjacent visitors' waiting rooms of similar proportions. In addition, there is an office for one's assistant. And, of course, a break room for the chief to rest in. There are four-room deluxe suites. But there is simply nowhere to work. While the degree of luxury for the chief was over the top, Chernyaev's deputy, Karen

Brutents, worked in his break room. Five advisers, including me, were crammed together in the assistants' cubbyhole, which was meant to accommodate one person and was equipped with one desk and one city phone and one official telephone. Accordingly, one not only had to read but also to write on one's knees or, in the best case, on a little table for visitors on which there was no room to spread out papers. The single desk was assigned to whomever had the most urgent and important task. Looking around from inside this palatial administrative cubbyhole, one wondered how any work at all could be done there.

Contrary to legend, working in the Kremlin was remarkable for the complete absence of any perquisites and privileges. I recall that store shelves in Moscow were empty; even bread and milk were difficult to find. A rationing system existed, but in order to convert your coupon into goods, you had to find a store where they had what you needed and then wait in line, often for hours. Administrative officials in the Office of the President were occasionally able to buy a kind of absolutely inedible mystery chicken—my wife and I have never seen anything like that before or since—a dozen eggs (that was a real treat), and a kilogram of noodles. Once, however, we were given a unique opportunity to ride to a vegetable supply depot and buy potatoes by the sackful. For those times this was a real bonus. Our neighbors in the elite apartment house—senior scholars, famous artists, high-ranking civil servants—surreptitiously took potatoes from the sack that was placed on the staircase landing. My wife and I pretended not to notice.

A sojourn inside the Kremlin walls might seriously distort one's vision if one was unaware of the danger. I am thinking not only of the president and highly placed officials but also about myself and people like me.

Working in Gorbachev's secretariat during this period was often a theater of the absurd. The country was collapsing, not least because of the president's inaction. Instead of working on solving real problems, he was receiving foreigners and often repeating himself. The president assigned us to draft talking points for his conversations, various speeches, and personal messages. He wasted a lot of time on these. Everything that was really important and that his guests might have found interesting was either not included or deleted before reaching the president. Every attempt to exert influence ran into a brick wall. For example, I remember proposing to Anatoly Chernyaev that in my new post I should maintain my contacts with Soviet human rights advocates and democrats. Looking daggers at me, he responded, "Don't forget that everything you do here reflects upon the president."

Many other proposals were similarly rejected. My work often boiled down to meaningless verbiage. Even the hard-won decision to have Shevardnadze take part in the Rome meeting of the Council of the North Atlantic Treaty Organization, which was supposed to elevate relations with that organization, was not implemented. Shevardnadze plunged into domestic political struggles. Contrary to his memoirs, in which he writes that his main goal was to secure the independence of Georgia, he tried his utmost to prevent the disintegration of the Soviet Union. Incidentally, this was one of the few occasions when the Office of the President showed some initiative. Often our work with respect to policymaking and taking concrete positions on important matters was not well coordinated with the Ministry of Foreign Affairs and other ministries and departments. In other words, Gorbachev did not utilize the potential inherent in his foreign policy to guide events into what he considered the proper channel. There was a surprising lack of clarity as well as an unfortunate tenuousness with regard to essential matters in his conversations with, and personal messages to, foreign interlocutors. The situation was no better with regard to other issues where, too, everything drowned in verbiage and in meetings that, likewise, were dedicated to yet more verbiage.

Working with my immediate boss, Chernyaev, was no simple matter. His previous experience had taken its toll. (Chernyaev was a party functionary who had been involved in the "international communist and workers' movement." Even in his personal diaries he put "human rights" in quotation marks, and he had no use for Alexander Solzhenitsyn, Andrei Sakharov, or "anti-Sovietism" in general.) Sometimes it seemed as though we spoke different languages. Incidentally, the majority of officials in Gorbachev's secretariat came from the Central Committee. Perhaps there was nothing terrible about this, since there are decent people everywhere, as well as dogmatists, freethinkers, and reactionaries. Unfortunately, their prior experience left its mark.

Thus, after the battle to hold the Moscow Conference on Human Dimension of the Conference on Security and Cooperation in Europe (discussed in chapter 1), Chernyaev assembled in his office the officials of his small group—five advisers, including me, and Brutents, who, as the lone deputy assistant to the president, had a unique status. Just one issue was on the agenda: blocking the inclusion in the final document of a sentence stating that respect for human rights transcended the domestic authority of the state. I had drafted the offending sentence while I was still working in the Foreign Ministry and could not let it be buried so easily. Unfortunately, I was overcome with emotion. After my very pointed remarks that this discussion betrayed an utter lack of understanding of human rights and an unwillingness to accept democratic changes in the country, the meeting broke up. The following evening Chernyaev passed along Gorbachev's order to me that I should "be at the conference so that everything would work out well." I suspect that my outburst played a role in this.

The result was that the Moscow conference document contained language initiated by the Ministry of Foreign Affairs that had been adopted by consensus and that was binding upon all states: "The participating states emphasize that questions relating to human rights, basic freedoms, democracy, and the supremacy of law are international in character. . . . They categorically and resolutely declare that the obligations undertaken by them in the area of assessing human rights by the CSCE are questions of direct and legal interest for all participating states and are not exclusively domestic matters of the governments concerned."

Despite some difficulties in my relationship with Chernyaev, I had an excellent opportunity to observe from the inside what was going on. For example, I remember the following fleeting episode in the first days after the coup that attested to the tense and incandescent atmosphere. The Kremlin was still practically empty. I ran into Yevgeny Primakov in the corridor. We were walking along and talking about some trifling matter. Suddenly his eyes narrowed. He stared down the dimly lit corridor and, instinctively trying to hide, dashed to the right into the bay of the door to Yakovlev's future office. Without stopping to think, I followed him since, against the background of endless conversations about the second-level membership of the State Emergency Committee, I saw a group of military men coming toward us. It turned out that they were new officers whom Marshal Yevgeny Shaposhnikov had just presented to the president.

Overall there was not a bad atmosphere in and around Gorbachev's secretariat. (I will not speak about all of the president's staff, since I had almost no contact with the protocol, housekeeping, and other auxiliary services.) A characteristic feature: when at the height of the regular nightly crush of work and Gorbachev's secretary brought in papers to his assistant Georgy Shakhnazarov, Shakhnazarov would treat her to a shot of cognac to keep her going and would say that everyone who was still on the job should drop in and see him. The only instance of arrogance I encountered was with Vadim Medvedev.[7] I had already approached the entrance to the building when I was stopped by his guard lest I disturb his boss, who was promenading up and down. It was just the opposite with Alexander Yakovlev. I was waiting for the two-person elevator when Yakovlev and his bodyguard approached. Naturally, I stepped slightly aside to let them go first. The ideologist of perestroika insisted that I ride with them despite my objections about overcrowding. Incidentally, whenever I saw him, Yakovlev was a font of benevolence and wisdom. However, I had little contact with him. And one reservation: naturally, Yakovlev and Medvedev were not colleagues in the secretariat—they had much loftier positions—but at least we were "together in the same boat" with Yakovlev and his circle. These observations may be trifles, but they are rather revealing. How we got along with each other in the secretariat and the Office of the President was largely determined by just how few of us were involved. Not infrequently, however, the outwardly comradely relations masked something entirely different, including an abundance of KGB agents, unequal relations, intellectual differences, variations in how well grounded different people were, and so on. Most of these factors are typical among colleagues everywhere.

Only in the president's milieu could the chairman of the KGB walk up and ask, "Gentlemen, I trust you won't object if I join you? I will not inconvenience you?" (This was Vadim Bakatin.) It was only in such a setting that encounters with the most well-known persons in the country, those not belonging to the "royal party," were of no great interest and speaking with them no big deal. Working in such places implied confidentiality. Certainly it was only there that, literally in the space of a few minutes, one could ask the head of state any question one liked or express one's own opinion.

Unfortunately, at work, one sometimes encountered dirt that had been brought into politics by the Central Committee and the KGB, but at least for me these instances were exceptional. I can think of only two such occasions, both connected with Vladimir Zhirinovsky, the leader of the right-wing nationalist Liberal Democratic Party of Russia. During the rather brief interval between the August coup and the breakup of the USSR, I had to deal with him twice, though fortunately not face-to-face. The first time was when an extremely distressed colleague dropped in on me in the Kremlin. Public opinion polls had revealed Zhirinovsky's enormous popularity. Publishing his standing in the polls would have shown an already overwrought public just how much support he enjoyed. It would inevitably have further swelled the number of his supporters. Therefore, without hesitation I crossed out the real figure and substituted one that was much lower. Surprisingly, this ersatz figure survived without any significant changes many years after the collapse of the USSR.

Was this unseemly? Of course. Undemocratic? Undoubtedly. Many other unflattering definitions of what I did are appropriate, and I would agree with them. But at least I had an absolutely clear justification in this crisis situation, soon after the coup. Why did Zhirinovsky, who must have noted the obvious forgery in the published public opinion poll, not protest this forgery? It is easy to imagine him, brows knit and lips pursed, shocked at his own standing in the polls. "And just where did this figure come from?" he asks. "From the Kremlin," his colleague says guiltily, shrugging his shoulders. So why didn't this self-proclaimed guardian of Russia's national interests, who dreamed of washing his boots in the Indian Ocean, settle accounts with a petty Kremlin bureaucrat? He would have been right to do so. Yet he swallowed the lie as the scoundrel he was. Knowing the history of Zhirinovsky and his Liberal Democratic Party of Russia, I was all but certain the matter would end here. Under any regime, the devil created by the Central Committee of the KGB must know his place.

The second involved an almost personal encounter. I was drinking coffee in the buffet of the Moscow Conference on Assessing Human Dimension of the CSCE when I heard strange noises and hysterical shouts in the foyer. Going out to take a look, I saw Zhirinovsky, shouting, "Germans to the buses, to Sheremetevo, to Germany! Jews to the buses, to Sheremetevo, to Israel! Catholics to the buses, to Sheremetevo, to the Vatican!" I glanced around. Although such public outbursts were not allowed according to the conference rules, the officials of the executive secretariat did not react to what was going on. When I ordered that the guard be summoned to throw Zhirinovsky out, several of the executive secretariat colleagues did not agree with what I felt was the only possible course of action.

In the Kremlin the implications of Yeltsin's seizure of power after the August 1991 coup were felt constantly and everywhere. For example, after yet another change in the agency that controlled the Kremlin guards—first it was the KGB, then it was the Presidential Guard Service of the USSR—under Yeltsin they came under the control of the Russian special services. Gorbachev's guards only had authority over the presidential suite of offices. Once I stayed late at work, and upon leaving, I handed over the key to Chernyaev's office. I lingered a bit, and when I was already out on the street, I heard through the still partly open door a guard speaking to someone on the telephone, "Comrade Kovalev has left." Most likely someone was interested in the contents of the desks and the safes.

The official telephones were tapped so blatantly and with such poor technology that it was often impossible to talk because of the interference and noises. Not infrequently it became necessary to redial and talk on the unsecured municipal line.

Gorbachev's loss of power was due in large measure to his own gross errors. Returning to Moscow after his confinement in Foros during the coup, instead of going to the Russian White House, the seat of Russia's parliament, as soon as his plane landed or, at the least, the next morning, he spent the whole day consulting with his confidants. In the evening he held an uninspired press conference in which he affirmed his loyalty to "the socialist choice." Almost no one grasped that he was speaking of social democracy and not of Soviet-style socialism. When he went to the Russian parliament the next day, this mistake played a fatal role, and Gorbachev was humiliated in the eyes of the entire country, including those who blamed him for the ban on the CPSU, an action that was forced upon him.

By this time, Gorbachev had lost his political instincts, his feeling for the historical process. I think it was due in large measure to his circle of confidants, who deliberately misguided him and from whom he often received distorted information. In this regard, Valery Boldin is a prominent example. Boldin, who served as Gorbachev's assistant starting in 1981, became the director of the General Office of the Central Committee and head of the president's staff. He detested his boss and his reforms and wrote about this openly in his book *Collapse of the Pedestal.*[8] Most of the information that Gorbachev, a reformer, received first passed through the sieve of his trusted and powerful confidant, whose reactionary character the president apparently never realized. Naturally, Gorbachev also received information from those who had direct access to him. But after Shevardnadze and Yakovlev were thrown off his team, the future plotters—KGB boss Vladimir Kriuchkov, Minister of Internal Affairs Boris Pugo, Minister of Defense Dmitry Yazov, and others of their ilk—had a virtual monopoly when it came to informing the president. This is probably why Gorbachev was so nonchalant regarding information about preparations for the coup d'état.

Often, for some reason, those in daily contact with Gorbachev were afraid to give him critical information. I became firmly convinced of this when I learned from a reliable source that the communists planned to organize massive disturbances and explosions at one or more of the nuclear reactors located in the capital on the Lenin Days in January 1992. I immediately went to Chernyaev who, as it turned out, already knew about this plot and was afraid to tell Gorbachev. But he agreed to pass along this information in my name. Once informed, Gorbachev phoned Yeltsin, who several minutes later phoned him back to say that he had already issued all the necessary orders. Why Chernyaev was so timid remains a mystery to me. Even stranger was that the special services did not inform either Gorbachev or Yeltsin about this matter. They must have been cognizant of the source of my information, a person who was known as a successful, highly placed official in one of the totally harmless departments and was an officer in the KGB's active reserve, as I was well aware.

Moreover, Gorbachev's personal bodyguard, who carried out orders from his immediate superior, KGB boss Kriuchkov, "pumped" Gorbachev full of antidemocratic information in the car on the way to work. Thus, Gorbachev arrived at work already ill disposed toward his own democratic reforms and toward the democratic leaders.

Too often Gorbachev was a poor judge of people. For example, he befriended the behind-the-scenes plotter Anatoly Lukyanov and completely trusted the minister of defense Dmitry Yazov, who was also a plotter, to say nothing of the aforementioned Boldin. That the entire top leadership of the country came out against the president speaks for itself.

Gorbachev spoke of Alexander Yakovlev as follows, "He is a good strategist but a rotten tactician." (Gorbachev actually used a stronger word.) Experience revealed that Yakovlev, not Gorbachev, was right.

I recall the following episode.

The morning after the tragic events in Vilnius in January 1991, Gorbachev telephoned my father, whose friendship with many Balts, as well as his sympathies toward Latvia, Lithuania, and Estonia, the president knew very well. "Do you know what this National Salvation Committee is and who is in it?" he asked.

Of course, like much else, Gorbachev's bewildered, helpless question to his deputy foreign minister demonstrated not only that he had not given the criminal order to attack demonstrators but also that he was also not in control of the situation. In other words, the opponents of democratic reforms manipulated Gorbachev and played their dirty and criminal political games behind his back, while his supporters, for wholly understandable reasons given the Soviet mentality, were afraid to oppose them. Gorbachev became such an object of manipulation that, if one believes Ignatenko, when the president decided to go to Lithuania after the events of January 1991, he let himself be talked out of this undoubtedly correct step by his own bodyguards—namely, the KGB.

In another example, in 1990 Gorbachev, after entrusting my father with receiving his Nobel Peace Prize on his behalf, met with him shortly before his departure for the awards ceremony. As he escorted him to the elevator, the president said in the corridor, "Bear in mind that I am now executing a necessary shift to the right. I will end this with the Nobel lecture." Apparently, the president realized that his cabinet was listening in. This practice was confirmed when once, speaking on the telephone with my father, Gorbachev said that he heard some sort of noises in the receiver and would call back, which he did a few minutes later, saying that he had reprimanded Kriuchkov and had warned him not to allow this anymore.

Still one more observation on how the highest level of power functioned: in some situations the secretary in Gorbachev's reception room could actually decide the fate of the country, since it was up to him who could speak to the president and who could not. Sometimes the secretaries and trusted stenographers were better informed and more influential than the ministers. Let us not forget where the loyalties of many of them lay, as well as the loyalties of the waiters and many other service personnel from the KGB.

Working in the secretariat of the head of state, one could learn and understand a lot. It held an abundance of the most delicate and sensitive information and not always only what you needed to know in order to discharge your direct responsibilities. You could understand even more if you were in the very thick of the "political soup," closely associating with the reformers who were intimates of Gorbachev's and working together with them on a daily basis. In the final analysis, grasping this truth leads me to conclude that in the dramatic break in Russia's history that occurred in 1991, there is too much that cannot be explained simplistically by using obvious words and reasons. It would be just as premature to repeat the mistakes of the vain politicians of that era and jump to any conclusions.

3

Anatomy of a Lost Decade, 1992–2000

Between 1986 and 1993, from the launch of Mikhail Gorbachev's democratic reformation through the initial period of Boris Yeltsin's tenure as the first president of post-Soviet Russia, Russia found itself at a fork in the road. One choice was the well-worn totalitarian and imperial path; the other was that of transforming Russia into a normal country, a home for people wanting to live normal lives. Unfortunately, Russia's choice of one of the worst possible paths forward was partly conditioned by history and partly foisted upon it by the new Russian elite. Why did perestroika—Gorbachev's democratic reformation—fail? Why did Russia slide toward a new type of reactionary politics accompanied by a totally unjustified foreign policy of revanchism?

The fall of a colossus such as the USSR is always an impressive spectacle even if observed from a distance, a safe distance that provides a panoramic view. But may one really speak of safety when the clay feet of ideology and violence crumbled in a country bristling with nuclear weapons and potential ecological time bombs?

For those buried under the wreckage, the spectacle was not something to be contemplated from any distance, safe or otherwise. They lacked both the time and the moral strength to ponder what until recently had been the reality of the USSR, what lessons to draw from its collapse, and what consequences might follow.

Gorbachev's perestroika and the Yeltsin period that followed evoked a strong reaction comparable to that of the Bolshevik coup after the overthrow of tsarism and the establishment of a weak provisional government. One of the main consequences of Yeltsin's presidency was that he created the opportunity for *a slow-motion coup d'état in which members of the special services seized key posi-*

tions in the country—that is, *to the revolution of the Chekists.* Thus, in 2000 Russia was being run by the special services in the guise of Vladimir Putin.

The entire Soviet period of Russian history, when punitive state institutions played an extraordinarily important role in politics, prepared the ground for this outcome. The influence of the special services receded after Josef Stalin's death, but the KGB continued to exert an inordinate impact on Soviet politics and the lives of Soviet citizens. The special services also retained their covert influence on even the most highly placed Soviet officials. If the Communist Party of the Soviet Union was the law, then the KGB was above the law. Not a single law could be adopted and implemented without its agreement. The CPSU, which, in the pre-perestroika era, lauded itself as "the mind, the honor, and the conscience of our epoch," became dependent on its own instrument of repression and coercion. The tail began to wag the dog.

The situation only began to change during perestroika. The dismantling of the totalitarian system implied the inevitable transformation of the KGB into a normal special service. Even the KGB's notorious Fifth Department, concerned with ideology and political investigations, was supposedly abolished. In its stead a department to defend the constitutional order was established. But what transpired was merely a change of the signboard; in essence nothing really changed. Under attack, the totalitarian system desperately fought to survive even prior to the first attempt at revenge during the 1991 coup.

A Trap for Democracy

The Soviet totalitarian system established after the Bolshevik coup of 1917 was so all embracing that it functioned like an unknown law of public life. Moreover, just like the Phoenix bird, it was capable of arising from the ashes. It would be a simplification to conceive of the totalitarian system as a straightforward aggregation of punitive and other coercive institutions and the punishment of dissenters. The reality was much more complicated. For example, Alexander Yakovlev, the theoretician of perestroika, accurately wrote, "I apply the definition of 'punitive' to the entire system, for all of the organs of power were punitive—the special services, the army, the party, the Young Communist League (YCL), the trade unions, even the Junior YCL organizations."[1] I should add that KGB agents had penetrated the entire state apparatus as well as the so-called Soviet public organizations and cultural associations.

Not only did Gorbachev's change of political direction—the demolition of totalitarianism—fail to gain the support of the overwhelming majority of the population, but also most of the Russian political elite likewise gave it the cold shoulder. Despite their dissatisfaction with the period of so-called stagnation, during the rule of Leonid Brezhnev (1964–82) and his fleeting successors Yury Andropov and Konstantin Chernenko, most people were not ready for even half-hearted democratic reforms. Therefore, these reforms, although real, remained unimplemented.

The only ones to support Gorbachev's reforms were liberal Soviet intellectuals and other dissenters who were then able to say and write what they pleased. Because of their extremely small numbers and fragmentation, however, they enjoyed a degree of influence very briefly and only when Gorbachev gave them some support. Within the Soviet bureaucracy anti-reformist and reactionary moods prevailed. This was inevitable, given the traditions and mentality implanted in the nation from the time of Vladimir Lenin and Stalin—that is, if one can even refer to the multiethnic and multifaith conglomerate that inhabited the USSR as a nation. At the very least, everyone else was indifferent to the reforms or did not embrace them for a variety of objective reasons, including a decline in their standard of living. In sum, only a tiny portion of the population embraced the reforms as necessary.

The overwhelming majority of the peoples of the USSR were committed communists of the Leninist-Stalinist school who either did not believe that abuses of power occurred or, worse, who actively supported such abuses by engaging in denunciations and other inhumane behavior. As a matter of reflexive self-preservation, after the repressions had ended, those who had discarded Stalinism expunged this terrible period of history from their minds, especially after Nikita Khrushchev's superficial and half-hearted condemnation of Stalin in 1956. The USSR had fallen into the trap of selective and restricted truth. The abuses of Lenin and his henchmen continued either to be idealized or ignored. Stalin was viewed as a leading statesman who had merely "carried things too far." The collectivization of agriculture that had destroyed Russia as a great agricultural power; industrialization, which had been accomplished by an unpaid prisoner labor force; and victory in the Second World War, achieved by the people despite their mediocre commander in chief—all were presented as the tyrant's personal achievements. In the collective consciousness of the people, Stalin's "individual shortcomings" and "occasional excesses" evidently took a backseat to these "magnificent accomplishments." As happens so often in Russian history, lies triumphed over historical truth and common sense.

At the start of perestroika the generation in power had grown up in Stalin's lifetime and admired him. Most successful persons lived according to his "precepts," fostering evil. Everyone knew that under Stalin the "organs of state security," which had swelled like cancerous tumors with their innumerable agents, were omniscient. Writers, poets, journalists, scholars, and YCL and Communist Party activists, as well as what some called "simple people," pursued their callings in this environment. From time to time they all received tangible benefits from their baseness: Some achieved advancement in their careers, others boasted of publications and undeserved fame, still others gained improvements in their living conditions, and their children received a suitable education. The swarm of informants, the legions of handlers from the "organs," and the local executioners were not conscious of their own crimes, let alone willing to acknowledge them. These people were the ones who, during the Gorbachev reforms era, were from thirty to forty years old, forming the generation upon which great hopes were placed.

The process of creating "a Soviet person" comprised several stages. It began with kindergarten and school, then the Junior YCL and YCL organizations, followed by the GULAG and everything that belonged to it, including the "law enforcement organs," the courts, and, in the times of Lenin and Stalin, the extrajudicial organs. Just what did the valiant secret police teach those who had the misfortune to make their acquaintance on political and other grounds? The first lesson was that force decides everything. The second lesson was the impunity they possessed and the utility of lying. The investigators lied, often inventing accusations and "extending" sentences and not just for "politicals" but for ordinary criminals as well. Those under investigation also lied, slandering both themselves and totally innocent people in the hope of easing their own lot. The third lesson was the absence of justice. Judges handed out sentences to please the investigators or other authorities; the extrajudicial organs did not even bother with formalities.

The great Russian writer Alexander Solzhenitsyn was entirely correct in comparing the GULAG to a metastasizing cancerous tumor. The incremental growth of the system of concentration camps and a concomitant increase in the number of victims led to far-reaching consequences. Among the most serious was the wide dissemination of camp "culture" throughout all strata of the Soviet and, later, the Russian population. The "organs of law and order" used torture, fear, and humiliation to "educate" the prisoners. Common criminals who were "socially close" to the authorities were also sent into the camps, and they inflicted their ways upon others, primarily the "enemies of the people"—that is, the political prisoners. This practice also became state policy.

Inhuman living conditions and excessive work norms that, if unfulfilled, led to a reduction in the already scanty prisoners' rations, which were insufficient to maintain their strength, made elementary physical survival the chief goal of the prisoners. Many of the morally steadfast perished. Other prisoners survived by jettisoning anything that smacked of humanity, including decency, conscience, and morality. It was they who disseminated camp culture among the rest of the population. Millions passed through the GULAG and raised children and grandchildren. Their influence spread into morals, habits, and language.

Vladimir Bukovsky, a leading Soviet dissident who exposed the abuses of punitive psychiatry, wrote that according to the most conservative calculations, the number of prisoners in the GULAG at any one time was not less than 2.5 million persons, constituting 1 percent of the population, and they served an average term of approximately five years. The rate of recidivism was no more than 20–25 percent. Thus, according to Bukovsky, almost a third of the country passed through the camps.[2]

It is revealing that the romanticism of criminality occupies an important place in contemporary Russian culture. At the core of this "romanticism" is a senseless cruelty, a complete disrespect for human life, and a rejection of everything humane, leading to absolute legal nihilism. In turn, these victims of the regime, partly through their descendants, constructed the guillotine for democracy in contemporary Russia. But there existed another very large stratum of the population that comprised torturers, executioners, guards, judges, and prosecutors. None of them received any punishment whatsoever for their terrible crimes, which were not subject to any statutes of limitation. No one was even condemned from a moral point of view. These butchers and sadists, just like their henchmen, walked away with heads held high and likewise raised their children and grandchildren.

There was yet another category of people who poisoned democracy and Russia's normal development—namely, the legions of informers who condemned their victims to inhuman tortures or death. Informers were motivated by numerous reasons: many from "ideological considerations"; others for the sake of their careers, for the receipt of some sort of benefits, for the elimination of a more successful rival in love—there are too many to list—but mostly from selfish motives.

Here let us recall the prophetic words from *The GULAG Archipelago* by Alexander Solzhenitsyn: "The young learn that baseness is never punished on this earth, but always brings rewards. How bleak and terrible it is to live in such a country!" This applied to all of the unpunished butchers of the Stalinist regime.

Moreover, in accordance with a secret OGPU circular from February 1923, the following were condemned to physical extermination:

Political parties and organizations:

1) All former members of pre-revolutionary political parties; 2) All former members of monarchist associations and organizations; 3) All former members of the Union of Independent Landholders, as well as the Union of Independent Farmers during the period of the

independent Central Parliament (Rada) in Ukraine; 4) All former members of the old aristocracy and nobility; 5) All former members of youth organizations (Boy Scouts and others); 6) All nationalists of whatever stripe.

Officials of tsarist institutions:

1) All officials of the former Ministry of Internal Affairs; all officials of the guards, the police, and the gendarmes, all secret agents of the guards and the police, all ranks of the border guards, and so forth; 2) All officials of the former Ministry of Justice: all members of the circuit courts, judges, prosecutors of all ranks, Justices of the Peace, judicial investigators, officers of the court, heads of rural courts, and so forth; 3) All officers and junior officers of the tsarist army and navy without exception.

Covert enemies of the Soviet regime:

1) All officers, junior officers, and rank-and-file soldiers of the White army [anticommunist forces], irregular White Guard detachments, Petlyura units, various rebellious subunits and bands that are actively fighting against Soviet power. Persons who have been amnestied by Soviet authorities are not exempted. 2) All civil officials of the central and local organs and departments of the White Guard government, of the army of the Central Rada, the Hetman administration, and so forth; 3) All religious figures, bishops, Orthodox and Catholic priests, rabbis, deacons, monks, choirmasters, church elders and so forth; 4) All former merchants, owners of shops and stalls as well as "NEP men"; 5) All former landowners, large-scale tenants, and rich peasants who in the past utilized hired labor. All former owners of industrial enterprises and workshops; 6) All persons whose close relatives occupy an illegal position or are continuing armed resistance to the Soviet regime in the ranks of anti-Soviet bands; 7) All foreigners regardless of nationality; 8) All persons having relatives or acquaintances abroad; 9) All members of religious sects and communities (especially Baptists); 10) All scholars and specialists of the old school, especially those whose political orientation is not known to this day; 11) All persons who were earlier suspected or convicted of contraband, espionage, etc.[3]

Any commentary on this comprehensive list would be superfluous.

The foundation of Soviet and Russian totalitarianism is slavery, with deep historical, psychological, and philosophical roots. Pyotr Chaadaev, the nineteenth-century philosopher-critic of Russian society and culture who urged that Russia should orient itself toward Western European civilization, noted the "inverse action of religion" in Russia. The Roman clergy, he noted, provided an example by freeing their own slaves, but the Russian people descended into slavery only after becoming Christian.[4] After seizing power, the Bolsheviks palmed off a new form of the worst kind of slavery under the guise of freedom. It enabled them not only to restore serfdom, which had been abolished by the tsar in 1861, but also to extend it to the entire population.

As a weapon to achieve this qualitatively new level of enslavement, the Soviet government made use of the innate reflex toward freedom discovered by the Nobel laureate Academician Ivan Pavlov, a reflex that was suppressed by hunger and other means of deprivation. Pavlov believed that the combined effects of terror and hunger would transform the freedom reflex into a reflex toward slavish submissiveness. In Soviet Russia words substituted for reality and elicited reflexive obedience. Soviet power, according to Pavlov, created animal-like relations among people such as what exists in the jungle among beasts.[5]

This discovery by a leading physiologist came at an opportune moment for Soviet power and, much later, for the Putin regime. "Utilizing such ancient and dependable mechanisms as semi-starvation and inescapable poverty, permanent terror and forced, stupefying labor, the [Communist] party tirelessly hammered down simple Soviet people in the country it had conquered," writes V. D. Topolyanskii. "Millions of prisoners in the socialist zone were required to jettison their innate tendency toward independent thinking, renounce the outmoded habits of personal responsibility toward succeeding generations that the Bolsheviks perceived as harmful, forget feelings of personal dignity, and be imbued with sensations of permanent happiness in life-long slavery."[6]

There is something "magical" about slavery—not just for the slaveholders but for the slaves as well. It is simpler for the slaveholders. They find it convenient not to have to deal with real persons but with a species of obedient bio-mechanisms. With regard to the slaves, if slavery implies certain conditions—for example, a comprehensible goal that is within reach, the absence of responsibility, or even a degree of comfort—then the slaves may be content. (Even the Stalinist underlings were slaves, although they lived not badly by the standards of that time and place.) Many of them simply don't notice the circumstances in which they live; they misperceive their normal condition as freedom. This is the sort of slavery that Russians chose for themselves. Perhaps it is why in reality they have known nothing else for practically their entire history.

Another dimension of Russia's de facto thralldom is feigned piety. A striving to appear "better" in the eyes of public opinion—in other words, a sanctimoniousness—long ago became a way of life for the conformist majority. The Bolsheviks found the prevailing spiritual and intellectual slavery very much to their liking as they built on the Russian people's habituation to what, in comparison to that of the Bolsheviks, was the moderate savagery and petty tyranny of tsarist power. Stalin and his ilk proclaimed a new state religion and established a historically unprecedented slave-owning theocratic state.

The doctrine of the Bolshevik religion combined traditional elements of Russian Orthodoxy and paganism. Elements borrowed from these antecedents included, among others, idolatry— flagrant examples of which were the public exhibition of Lenin's mummy and the countless portraits and statues of the "Founding Fathers"—and the practice of sacrifices. The latter involved both human sacrifices—for example, in the show trials and in the GULAG—and financial sacrifices in the form of party and trade union dues and of the obligatory purchase under Stalin of state bonds and, later, of lottery tickets.

These new dogmas, which were universally disseminated throughout the USSR, required that complete control be established over the physical and spiritual lives of its citizens, who were forced to follow these dogmas. Soviet authorities effectively used varied means to achieve this goal.

The Soviet slaveholding system mandated that everything without exception belonged to the state, including intellect, qualifications, and knowledge. It was the basis for the suppression of individual sovereignty and the elimination of even its outward appearance. For example, unless applicants possessed a workbook and references, no personnel department had the right to hire them. References had to be signed by the so-called triangle: the enterprise or institutional leader (the shop, department, etc.), the party organizer, and the trade union organizer. Even brilliant specialists were unable to secure a good job if they had bad references or, even worse, no references at all. There was no alternative for procuring employment. This requisite was the first element of the system in which Soviet citizens, like serfs, were dependent upon the state.

A second element was the state monopoly on housing. Along with the system of internal passports, it enabled the state to dictate to its citizens where to live and work. In essence, Stalin's introduction of internal passports, and a system of passes for controlling people's travel and changes in their place of residence, strengthened serfdom via legislation. It would be difficult to conceive of a more effective policy for controlling the people.

The Soviet slaveholding system paid special attention to educating the "new person." The measures employed included massive hypnosis of the subjects of the communist empire and liquidation of "vestiges of the past," including the maniacal destruction of Russian science, medicine, and culture, as well as quotidian culture, or the "old way of life." Those who embodied this culture were isolated from society in concentration camps; the luckier ones were expelled abroad.

The Iron Curtain was an effective barrier against the emergence of any kind of heresy. Soviet citizens were prohibited from going abroad, the circulation of foreign newspapers and magazines was banned, and Western radio stations broadcasting in Russian were jammed. Censorship and secrecy were the most effective prophylactics. Soviet people could know very little about the world around them—only that which the state permitted and only according to the interpretation that the state deemed necessary.

The coercive measures employed differed greatly depending on the specific goal. For example, those persons wishing to secure what, from the time of the Bolshevik coup, were the minimum benefits that constituted "well-being" had to cozy up to the authorities or, even better, join the *nomenklatura*, the privileged elite of Soviet society. The state's establishment early in the Soviet era of special retail stores where one could purchase foodstuffs unavailable elsewhere at subsidized prices, and the retention of these special stores until the end of the communist regime, clearly demonstrated the unbreakable connection in Soviet thinking between one's social position and the opportunity to obtain quality foodstuffs and other "benefits and privileges." To obtain the level of supply ordained from "above," those who enjoyed access had to play by the "rules of the game," and they included membership in the Communist Party of the Soviet Union.

Those who ignored the rules of the game were severely punished. The most egregious example of this was the persecution of Boris Pasternak after publication abroad of his book *Doctor Zhivago* in 1957 and his receipt of the Nobel Prize for Literature in 1958. The Stalinist tradition of public reprisals against dissenters long survived the dictator's death in 1953. Another level of "coercive means" was the elaborately devised, differentiated, and diverse mechanisms of punishment and reeducation for various kinds of "heretics" to teach them and others a lesson.

The system of punishment, including the notorious GULAG, was the most effective means of all. Punishing criminals and struggling against "heretics" were far from the only, or even the primary, goals of this monstrosity. According to the great criminals who came to power for the long term in November 1917, the concentration camps, as they were openly called at the time, were meant to achieve very concrete economic tasks. Soviet-style state capitalism, or the planned economy, required universal compulsion to labor. The scheme was grounded in the colonization of unassimilated territories using prisoners' labor. What a truly revolutionary approach! That is why the GULAG was supplied with an inexhaustible influx of prisoners, who were viewed as a slave labor force. Economic considerations were obviously among the reasons for the abnormally long prison sentences in the USSR.

Another extremely effective mechanism of punishment was punitive psychiatry, which I have already discussed at length.

The army was in an especially difficult position in Soviet slave-holding society. Military personnel were excluded from the purview even of the existing legislation. Battalions' constructing generals' dachas or "objects of the national economy" and soldiers' harvesting crops—all amounted to slavery under the name of "honorary rights and duties." The officers were also slaves. While the soldiers could again become relatively free after serving their compulsory two years, the officers could not escape military slavery until they retired after completing their term of service.

Were there any free individuals in the USSR? No. But the prisoner in the GULAG and a member of the party-state *nomenklatura*, for example, experienced different kinds and degrees of servitude.

Paradoxically, those with the least spiritual and material needs may be considered the freest. How may we compare the freedom of hereditary alcoholics (of which, regrettably, there is no small number in Russia), whose only interest in life is their bottles, with the freedom of a scholar, a writer, or an artist? Even the highest-ranking Soviet officials were slaves to Marxist-Leninist-Stalinist dogmas, to the Iron Curtain, to political investigations, to the benefits extended to them in connection with their duties.

From this perspective, the *nomenklatura* is quite an interesting phenomenon. To reach this level one had to ascend the lengthy party-bureaucratic career ladder. For the overwhelming majority this was impossible without immersing themselves in the dogmas of the communist quasi-religion—in the spirit of hypocrisy and sanctimoniousness—or, at the very least, adapting to it. The slave thus becomes a slaveholder yet remains in a state of slavery (and even the members of the highest-ranking Soviet leadership were in such a position). What could be more unnatural and more dangerous? Let us not forget that we are speaking of the very people who ran the country or held responsible positions during perestroika and of their successors.

The mild democratic reformation that was perestroika was doomed to defeat because it was *top down*, carried out by a narrow circle of the leadership. Moreover, to a significant degree the reformers themselves were dogmatic and set themselves unrealizable goals, including the humanization of the Soviet regime by relying on the CPSU. To no lesser degree perestroika could not be implemented successfully due to the absolute power of the repressive organs, the CPSU and the KGB, in the first place. Even though they were the most odious manifestations of the Soviet totalitarian system, though, they were far from monolithic.

Here I should emphasize that perestroika alienated many people because it coincided with the start of the antialcohol campaign.[7] Also, it proclaimed many incomprehensible slogans such as "Acceleration," put forward vague goals and tasks, and instituted glasnost, or "transparency," which unmasked the sins of the past as well as of contemporary Soviet life.

The political struggle over the "democratization of Soviet society" unfolded primarily at the ideological level. Was "socialist democracy" a good thing? Was free enterprise compatible with Soviet-style socialism? Was a multiparty system permissible in "monolithic" Soviet society? Could a "formal approach" to human rights be adopted in the USSR? Could the USSR provide freedom of choice to the "people's democracies" (Eastern bloc countries) and reach agreement with the "imperialists"—for example, on problems of disarmament—and cooperate with them to neutralize Iraqi aggression against Kuwait? These were the questions that engaged people. It was basically at this level that the struggle between dogmatism and common sense was waged.

The fall of the Berlin Wall symbolized the end of the Cold War, but as subsequent events showed, it did not write finis to it. The politicians who came to power in Russia after the fall of the USSR, starting at the top with Boris Yeltsin, were insufficiently competent and inadequately prepared for the challenges they faced. Consequently, they were unable to work for the interests of the nation either in foreign or domestic policy. This occurred in large measure because of the glaring gap between the pro-Western aspirations of the liberals in Yeltsin's entourage and the constantly growing mood of revenge in society and in the state apparatus. This mood characterized not only the military and the special services but also significant numbers of diplomats, politicians, and economists.

Yeltsin, as well as most of his democratically inclined associates, had only a very remote understanding of Western values. This was to be expected considering their life experience, education, and upbringing in Soviet times. Naturally, on the crest of the political struggles of the 1980s, when a man who until quite recently had been the first secretary of the Sverdlovsk regional Communist Party organization was *thrust* into the national leadership of the democratic opposition, some things had to be explained to him. One must give Yeltsin his due: he did grasp some of what he was told but not enough for a deep understanding of what was going on in Russia and abroad. The liberal system of coordinates was quite unfamiliar to him. An important question is, *who* exactly prepared Yeltsin for the role of democratic leader? Even if one dismisses any conspiracy theories, even if the persons who pulled his strings were progressive, they were still *Soviets* with the characteristic aberration of political outlook that label implies.

The special services, including agents who had penetrated every layer of society, also played an important role in Yeltsin's ascent. Such agents are in a very distinct category. The overwhelming majority of them do whatever they consider necessary in discharging their specific functions or while awaiting new instructions. This is why many of them are not merely successful but also brilliant, especially since they are assisted by one of the most powerful special services of all times and places. When they get a new set of orders, they don't ask whether it is from a committed democrat, a liberal, a state official, or a communist. Under Gorbachev and Yeltsin, these "sleeper agents" objectively did quite a bit of good. Then they were awakened. Those who had only recently stood on the barricades of democracy, either literally or figuratively, and even helped to build them now began to destroy them even more effectively.

In his memoirs, Alexander Korzhakov, the former chief of the Presidential Guard, which later was elevated to an independent ministerial-level department—the Presidential Security Service— made a strikingly frank acknowledgment of the role of special service agents in contemporary Russia. As a man who knew very many agents, he wrote, "If a miracle occurred and a list appeared in the press just of those agents whom citizens knew by sight, a political crisis would occur in the country. To the questions of who our leaders are, who is governing us, the straightforward answer would be—agents of the special services."[8] The fundamental sources and vectors of influence upon Yeltsin are clear. What is not at all clear, however, is why this scandalous confirmation by such a well-informed source remained practically unnoticed. Perhaps from squeamishness? Not very likely. Perhaps from the new ruling ideology of "political correctness" that, in the name of decency, permitted one to close one's eyes to the most scandalous things, especially when it was advantageous to do so?

Speaking of Yeltsin's presidency, it should be pointed out that at least in his outward action, the "early" Yeltsin appeared different from the "later" Yeltsin. His authoritarian ways, initially clearly visible only within the halls of power, were illuminated during the political crisis of September–October 1993, pitting Yeltsin's executive authority against a legislature dominated by his opponents. This confrontation culminated in Yeltsin's order to shell the Supreme Soviet on October 3, resulting in numerous casualties. This action unambiguously signaled a retreat from democracy. It was partly to be expected with the popularity of communists and fascist nationalists in Russia, on the one hand, and the unwillingness of Yeltsin and his circle to give up power, on the other. One may confidently mark the beginning of the authoritarian period in post-Soviet Russia from this date. One also should not lose sight of the fact that the members of the new Russian elite, upon which Yeltsin was extremely dependent and whose foundation was agents of the special services, would never have relinquished their power and wealth. For the time being, Yeltsin was the guarantor of that power and wealth.

The outcome of the ill-considered cascade of privatization that commenced from the start of Yeltsin's rule was the rise of a kleptocracy. (However, it is also possible that the kleptocrats skillfully carried out privatization in their own interest.) Along with the new secret police, with which it frequently overlapped, the kleptocracy squeezed out the very persons who had brought Yeltsin to power—namely, the democratic leaders of the late 1980s and early 1990s. The kleptocrats attempted to fashion a *democratic leader out of yesterday's party hack*. By December 1992 the liberal government of Premier Yegor Gaidar had ceased to exist. After the shelling of the Supreme Soviet in October 1993, democratic leaders continued to be eliminated from Yeltsin's entourage and to lose influence. Deprived of his democratic entourage and constantly in need of guidance (or support) because of his incompetence, Yeltsin fell under the influence of the *siloviki* and the nouveaux riches, who had no interest in promoting democracy in Russia. All they needed (and what they still need) was the semblance of democracy. Still Yeltsin evidently had absorbed a lesson or two from his tutors during his transformation into an ambiguous symbol of Russian democracy. For example, there were no serious assaults on freedom of the mass media during his administration. During this period, however, gross and massive violations of human rights began, first with respect to Chechnya. The First Chechen War started on December 11, 1994, and was not concluded until the fall of 1996. During the war the entire spectrum of rights, including the right to life, was destroyed for the inhabitants of this republic. From the outset, political rights were effectively suppressed by Yeltsin's authoritarianism.

During Yeltsin's term the symbiosis of all levels of power, business, and the criminal world occurred. This was particularly dangerous, given the criminalization of the law enforcement organs that were boldly penetrating the highest levels of state power. They succeeded in doing this in the late Yeltsin era. Corruption at every level became the basic feature of Russian power. Everything was for sale. In Yeltsin's first term, government officials already began selling their services to business. A few words from the "appropriate" minister conveyed to a particular firm cost tens of thousands or even hundreds of thousands of dollars. Press secretaries sold the rights to interview their bosses. Even deputies' inquiries had their price. Corruption penetrated medicine, education (including secondary education), and all aspects of life. However, the full-scale flowering of corruption came after 2000.

Under the distinct influence of the special services, Yeltsin and his entourage viewed Russia as a Russian Orthodox country and consequently interpreted religious freedom narrowly as freedom for Russian Orthodoxy alone. Right after the collapse of the USSR, this led to denying the rights of those who were not Orthodox.

Yeltsin's most egregious mistake was underestimating the human factor in pursuing his reforms. The Russian people, hoping to better their conditions quickly, endured massive impoverishment and lost all their savings early in Yeltsin's rule. His entire presidency was marked by flagrant and massive destruction of a wide range of socioeconomic rights, with wages withheld over many months. The manipulation of election results also began during Yeltsin's presidency. By the time Putin came to power, people were already so accustomed to such manipulation that they no longer reacted negatively. What developed in Russia under Yeltsin was a system of rule that may be called authoritarian kleptocracy, which transformed bandit capitalism into oligarchic capitalism—that is, a system fully controlled by, or at least entirely dependent upon, a narrow circle of persons who ran the country.

The ruination of minds, which the Soviet writer Mikhail Bulgakov called Russia's main disaster after the Bolshevik coup d'état, brought about the further disintegration of the country. In turn, it provoked a crisis of Yeltsinocracy and the further powerful onset of revenge and reaction.

Fortress Destroyed

A strange fate befell Russia in the twentieth century. From the time of Lenin, the country prepared to fight the whole world. Initially Russia was supposed to be the launching pad for the "world proletarian revolution." Later on even more confusing reasons were offered. The entire history of the USSR until Gorbachev's reforms was directed toward achieving impractical goals. Naturally this led inexorably to collapse. The senseless arms race not only sucked dry the material resources of the USSR but also its intellectual resources. The normal development of nonmilitary production became impossible.

In trying to make the USSR an impregnable fortress, the Soviet leadership destroyed it. The decisive loss in the Cold War during the years of stagnation (1964–85) set the stage for the USSR's repudiation of traditional, Soviet aggressive messianism during the Gorbachev era. Orthodox communists viewed this sensible adjustment in Soviet foreign policy as a retreat from "Leninist norms" and as a surrender to the "imperialists."

After the breakup of the USSR, Gorbachev's thorough and rational approach to changing the Soviet role and position in the international system devolved under Yeltsin to the absence of any real foreign or domestic policy. This led to the complete loss of Russia's international positions and maximum economic and financial weakening. By 2000 a country that had been built as a fortress had collapsed into ruins.

Russia's downward slide in the world economy demonstrates this point. Between 1992 and 1997, its GDP decreased by almost 40 percent, industrial production by almost 50 percent, and agriculture by 35 percent. By the latter date Russian production constituted just 2 percent of world production, and Russia's per capita GDP ranked forty-fifth in the world.

Russia's dependence on foreign markets increased. The share of imports in consumer goods reached 50 percent, and many Russian products practically vanished from the domestic market. Imports of equipment grew as the capacity of the domestic machine-building industry declined. An economic model emerged based on the export of energy and raw material resources and the import of machines, equipment, foodstuffs, and consumer goods.

Financial stabilization was officially proclaimed as the main economic goal of all Russian governments from 1992 to August 1998. This meant overcoming a high rate of inflation and shrinking the budget deficit. To accomplish this, the money supply was squeezed to the maximum possible extent, budgetary expenditures and the budget deficit were curtailed, and the latter was covered with the help of so-called noninflationary sources: domestic short- and long-term treasury bills and state bonds and foreign loans.[9]

Russian authorities declared these goals achieved in 1998.[10] However, this had been accomplished by squeezing the money supply to the limit, making it impossible for production to function normally. On January 1, 1992, the money supply in Russia constituted 66 percent of GDP; by the beginning of 1998 it had dropped to 14 percent and continued to contract mostly with the help of non-cash methods—that is, the working assets of enterprises.

The lack of an adequate money supply required for normal commodity-production exchange led to complete disorder in the monetary payments system. By September 1, 1998, creditors' loans amounted to the enormous sum of 2.3 trillion rubles, or close to 85 percent of annual GDP. Approximately 70 percent of the transactions between enterprises were carried out through barter or via quasi-monetary means. The contraction of the money supply and the crisis in payments created artificial limits on demand and accelerated the decline in production.

The high profitability of short- and long-term treasury bills and federal loan bonds, and the opportunity for banks to reap large profits from dealing in them and in currency transactions and from manipulating budgetary funds, led to a complete separation between the financial system and the real economy. Financial resources were concentrated in the financial markets, while the real economy was practically bled white. These developments constantly reduced the tax base and made it more difficult to fulfill the revenue side of the budget, thereby requiring even greater curtailment of expenditures and the supplementary contraction of the money supply. Budgets were not met even in sequestered form. The entire chain repeated itself over and over again in a vicious circle.

A second vicious circle came about in connection with the growth of internal and external government debt. The domestic debt in treasury bills and state bonds as of October 1, 1998, constituted 387.1 billion rubles. Moreover, the redemption of previously issued treasury bills and state bonds required the increasing issuance of new series. The funds needed to service the external debt also grew. To pay off the old debts, more and more new credits were needed.

The decision by the government and the Bank of Russia on August 17, 1998, to depreciate the ruble drastically demonstrated the need to find a way out of the existing situation. A devaluation of the ruble was implemented to reduce the budgetary deficit via inflation and to increase revenues. To emerge from under the curtain of debt, a default was declared.

Naturally, these decisions failed to yield positive results. In fact, the negative results were overwhelming. In August inflation stood at 3.7 percent and in September at 38.4 percent. The major banks that had invested their assets in frozen treasury bills were now on the brink of bankruptcy; the interbank credit and currency markets stopped functioning. Payments ceased. Russia forfeited the confidence of foreign creditors and became utterly dependent on the decisions of international financial organizations for the provision of credits. At the very least, Russia became dependent on ineffectively utilized financial assistance from the West.

The threat of further devaluation of the ruble remained, presaging renewed inflation. There were enormous hard currency savings (according to expert estimates, from $40 billion to $60 billion, which far exceeded all potential foreign credits and investments). At an exchange rate of 15–18 rubles to the dollar, this equaled 600 billion to 900 billion rubles, a sum that was one and a half to two times greater than the budget revenues approved by the State Duma. The total value of government debt relative to GDP exceeded 138 percent. The ratio of external debt to GDP exceeded 110 percent.

The level of imports of new industrial machinery and equipment was eight to ten times lower than what was needed simply to replace obsolete and depreciated working stock. By this time, fully two-thirds of the basic working stock was outmoded. Even in the most successful export-oriented branches, the share of new equipment had decreased by two to three times compared to 1990.

The technological level and physical condition of the majority of main and branch enterprises in the fuel and energy sector not only failed to meet contemporary standards but in many cases also failed to meet safety and environmental protection standards. More than half the equipment in the coal industry had exceeded its designed working life as had 30 percent of gas pumping units. There was more than 50 percent amortization in over half of oil-field equipment and more than a third in the gas industry. In oil refining the amortization on assets exceeded 80 percent, and it was projected that in the near future half of the capacity of all the electric power stations in the country would have to go off-line. By this time more than half the main oil pipelines had been in service for more than twenty-five years. As many as half the atomic power stations needed refurbishing.

Russia's transport system was also antiquated. The rate of replacing rolling stock was reduced, leading to a sharp growth in the average age of the equipment, which was increasingly in poor condition. A large fraction had been in use beyond its designed service life, resulting in a drastic decline in safety and an increase in transportation costs. Losses in the merchant marine fleet and the destruction of the Arctic transportation system were a very real possibility.

The economic crisis caused serious social problems. People's disposable real income was 40 percent lower than before the reforms of 1991. The gap between rich and poor increased dramatically, exacerbating social tensions.

Meanwhile, there was also an ecological crisis. Serious and even very serious ecological problems existed on almost a fifth of Russian territory. More than 60 percent of the urban population breathed unhealthy air containing various toxic substances in concentrations far exceeding maximum permissible levels. Approximately 40 million Russians breathed air with more than ten times the maximum permissible concentration of toxic substances. The regions of Moscow, Samar, Sverdlovsk, Irkutsk, and Kemerovo and the Krasnoyarsk and Khabarovsk territories were the worst offenders in this regard.

The Don, Terek, and Ural Rivers were dead. The waters in the Volga, Oka, Kama, Don, Ural, Tom, Irtysh, and Moscow Rivers were no longer potable. About half of the water draining into these rivers was polluted. Water purification systems could not cope with the toxic substances. Almost 70 percent of the Russian population consumed polluted drinking water.

Virtually no enterprises in Russia employed nonpolluting technology. An insignificant portion, less than one-fifth, of waste products was utilized and rendered harmless; the remainder piled up. Almost 1.5 billion tons of toxic and dangerous tailings, including mercury, chrome, and organic chlorides, poisoned the soil, causing irreversible degradation of the natural environment in an area of more than 2.47 million acres. Technological waste from urban industries was spread over distances of hundreds of miles (for example, 125 miles in the Moscow region). In the greater part of Russia's European territory, soil pollution as the result of leaching of lead meant that people in numerous cities were exposed to lead pollution at more than ten times permissible levels. Across the length and breadth of Russia the soil was polluted with other heavy metals and arsenic.

Russia represented a flagrant example of just how dangerous progress is in the hands of irresponsible politicians. If nuclear blackmail was no longer a reality internationally, then inside Russia the nuclear factor operated powerfully and continuously without any deterrents. Even leaving aside the nuclear power plant meltdown at Chernobyl in April 1986, when radioactive contamination affected a wide area with a population of some 4 million people, the situation regarding nuclear power plants was intolerable. As a result of radioactive pollution from catastrophes and accidents between 1956 and 1967 and irresponsible attitudes toward nuclear waste, Russia was unquestionably the worst offender in the world. Most of the spent nuclear fuel was stored in on-site storage tanks, posing a threat to the safety of persons living in the vicinity of the nuclear power plants. Almost all nuclear power plants were located in densely populated European Russia, and about a million persons were exposed to dangers from them. It will take a century and a half to reprocess the spent nuclear fuel. This fact didn't bother the authorities who, going back to the Soviet era, welcomed spent nuclear fuel and nuclear materials from other countries for reprocessing.

There was even more to the man-made hell in Russia. More than thirty-five hundred chemical works processed an incalculable amount of dangerous substances such as chlorine, ammonia, hydrochloric acid, and others. They often utilized antiquated and outmoded equipment, posing a threat of poisoning some 116,000 square miles with a population of about 54 million people. More than half the population of Russia was exposed to an elevated risk of technological and natural catastrophes due to poor management in combination with natural conditions. Almost 70 percent of accidents were caused by fires, explosions, and open gas and oil gushers, creating dire environmental consequences. Every year more than five hundred large-scale oil and gas pipeline ruptures occurred. As a result of the leakage of petroleum products, almost all the rivers in northwest Siberia, many other rivers, and the southern part of the Barents Sea were polluted with oil. Yet Russian authorities steadily reduced aggregate expenditures on environmental protection. In 1997 they were 60 percent less than in 1992 and constituted just 0.04 percent of total budgetary expenditures.

Economic and financial ruin combined with the horrendous state of the environment produced catastrophic consequences for the nation's health. Over a six-year period (1990–96), the incidence of diseases such as tuberculosis increased 1.9 times, syphilis 49 times, drug addiction 6.5 times, and alcoholic psychosis 4.2 times. Deterioration in the health of pregnant women (for example, over six years the rate of anemia among them almost doubled) led to an increase of illness among newborns (1990, 14.8 percent; 1996, 31.3 percent among the total number) as well as to premature births. Twenty percent of preschool children suffered from chronic illnesses. By the time they graduated from high school only 15 percent of children could be considered healthy.

In several industrially developed districts, up to 40 percent of illnesses were caused by the harmful effects of air, water, and soil pollution; poor-quality foodstuffs and raw materials; production processes; and general conditions of life. The high levels of bacteria and viruses in drinking water caused acute intestinal infections and viral hepatitis A. The constant consumption of drinking water containing high levels of natural and man-made chemical pollutants contributed to the elevated incidence of illnesses.

Genetic damage is one of the dangerous consequences of environmental pollution. Studies of the frequency of genetic defects among urban residents exposed to varying levels of air, drinking water, and food pollution demonstrated that the degree of damage was linked to the overall level of environmental pollution by mutagenic and carcinogenic substances.

In Russia, 60,000 out of 1.2 million–1.3 million children born annually suffered from developmental birth defects and congenital illnesses. One of every four of these babies was seriously ill. Some died soon after birth; many others were invalids from childhood. About 15 percent of the population suffered from congenitally predisposed diseases such as diabetes, bronchial asthma, hypertension, psoriasis, and other illnesses. In 1999, deaths exceeded births by almost 1.7 times. Premature mortality also remained high. In the 1990s the working life for men decreased by five years and for women by one year.

In the face of this situation the authorities simply ignored the breakdown of public health and deteriorating conditions in society. They also did virtually nothing about chronic late payment of wages.

In October 1999 50 million persons, or more than 33 percent of the population, had incomes below the minimum living wage, as compared to 35 million people, or less than 25 percent, just one year earlier. In 1999 the wealthiest 10 percent of the population enjoyed incomes more than fourteen times greater than the poorest 10 percent. The difference in rates of savings was even greater: the wealthiest 20 percent of the population (by income) had 80 percent of all savings, while the poorest 20 percent had only about 1 percent. Minimum income guarantees were woefully inadequate, or less than 10 percent of what constituted a subsistence wage for the working population. The paltry measures taken to alleviate the financial crisis of 1998 were mostly cosmetic and manifestly insufficient.

Objective as well as subjective factors were responsible for this state of affairs. In a step for which no preparations had been made, the union republics with a high degree of specialization departed from what had formerly been an economically integrated USSR, inevitably destroying the economic ties among them and leading to the breakdown of industry in the territory of the former USSR. Subjectively, massive privatization, also implemented without preparation, frequently led to the irrational utilization of Russia's economic potential.

The failure of the Belovezhe Accords (1991) to regulate even a single real issue in relations among the post-Soviet states predetermined that the Commonwealth of Independent States (CIS) would be stillborn. The most contentious problems were the status of Crimea, which Khrushchev had given to Ukraine in 1954; the ownership of the Black Sea fleet; and the status of the Russian-speaking people in the post-Soviet states. Putin would subsequently tackle all these issues unilaterally.

The situation was exacerbated by the growth of anti-Russian sentiment in the CIS that was provoked in large measure by Boris Yeltsin himself and his team. This sentiment initially arose during the struggle for sovereignty of the Soviet republics, during which an aggressive form of nationalism was ignited. It later grew due to gross errors committed in Russia's relations with the newly independent states. Among them were Moscow's anti-Georgian policy, largely the result of Yeltsin's personal antipathy toward Georgian president Eduard Shevardnadze; Moscow's support of the Abkhazian separatists; its meddling in the Armenian-Azerbaijani conflict over Nagorno-Karabakh; and its position regarding the Trans-Dniester region of Moldova.

There were no agreed-upon borders with other states of the CIS; thus, their external boundaries with Russia simultaneously became Russia's borders. The problem was compounded by Russia's dependence upon events within the CIS. The lack of reliable state borders made it difficult for Russia to deal with cross-border crime and turned Russia into a convenient staging ground for contraband, including narcotics, and facilitated illegal migration into Russia and, through transiting its territory, to third countries.

Moscow was troubled by the massive and largely uncontrolled migration of Chinese into the depopulated Far East and several districts of Siberia as Chinese citizens began to dominate several spheres of economic activity in the Far East. Moscow seriously feared changes in the demographic composition of the population in several border regions. According to various statistics, between 400,000 to 2 million Chinese were living illegally in the Far East region of the Russian Federation. Officials in Moscow were deeply concerned that the number of Chinese in the Far East would come to exceed that of the Russian population. Their concern stemmed from the fact that about 9 million people lived along Russia's Siberian and Far Eastern border with China, while more than 100 million Chinese lived in the adjacent regions of China. Given China's overwhelming population and the Russian authorities' inability either to stop the massive migration of Chinese or to guide it into a positive channel, Moscow saw this influx as a serious threat to national security that might lead to Chinese military aggression against Russia under the pretext of defending the Chinese population.

The *disintegration of all aspects of the nation's military establishment*, however, is what struck terror into the hearts of the masters of the Kremlin. It never occurred to them that the military in its previous form was quite unnecessary. But the significant diminution of defense potential, the sharp curtailment of the armed forces, and the loss of some of the most important elements of defense industry and of defense-related science, along with the reduction of the state's overall operational readiness and its decreased capacity for military mobilization, were viewed as nothing short of a catastrophe. Objectively speaking, there really were several grounds for worry. Among them were an unsecured border, air and missile defense systems riddled with holes, and diminished air force and naval efficiency. They are just several general instances, but things were bad throughout the military establishment. No one had even thought of undertaking a fundamental reassessment of military-political doctrine.

Russian political and military leaders reacted very badly to the changes in Russia's military capabilities compared to those of Soviet times. Moscow ascribed its own mistakes and miscalculations, to say nothing of the objective tendencies of the evolving world situation, to the self-dissolution of the Warsaw Pact and the loss of its influence in Eastern Europe that had already occurred in Soviet times.[11] Complaints about the sharp shift in the balance of forces in Europe accompanied assertions that changes had occurred in the substance and trends of the disarmament process, resulting in the need to review relevant treaties and agreements. Moscow was particularly troubled by the strengthening and expansion of the North Atlantic Treaty Organization (NATO) and the eastward advancement of its infrastructure.

The expansion of NATO is a special page in the history of Russian politics. As the Cold War ended during perestroika, the USSR and NATO were on the threshold of establishing a relationship of partnership and cooperation. The breakthrough was supposed to occur at the Rome meeting of the NATO Council on November 7, 1991, that Soviet minister of foreign affairs Eduard Shevardnadze was going to attend.[12] He was unable to do so, however, because of the domestic political situation.[13]

The West's negative reaction to Russian president Yeltsin's statement in December 1991 that Russia desired to become a member of NATO offended the Kremlin.[14] However, cooperation continued, if only formally, until the appointment of Yevgeny Primakov as minister of foreign affairs in 1996. He poisoned the attitude of the Kremlin, parliament, and the previously neutral public toward NATO. From then on, the position Russia adopted toward NATO's enlargement was irrational and illogical.[15]

Overall a paradoxical situation developed regarding national security. While remaining a mighty nuclear power, Russia virtually lost its nonnuclear defensive capability. With good reason both the Russian military leadership and the Kremlin concluded that the effectiveness of the army and its ability to guarantee the security of the borders were practically nil. From the start Russia's military reform was doomed to failure, primarily because of the yawning gap between the military-political ambitions of the country's leadership and part of the Russian population, on the one hand, and Russia's economic resources, on the other.

From the outset there was no way to achieve the postulated missions. The half-hearted character of the decisions that were adopted foreordained the growth of negative tendencies in the military establishment. It acquired greater airs than it had boasted in Soviet times and became an independent threat to the security of Russia as well as that of other states. In this context it suffices to recall the bombastic talk about the need to raise the army's fighting spirit by achieving military victory in Chechnya. The situation in the army merited special attention. Russia's disdain of the USSR's former allies in Central and Eastern Europe caused Moscow to underestimate their interests and influence. Viewing these countries as unfriendly, Moscow itself largely provoked the consequences that were inimical to its own interests. It was absurd virtually to ignore the states that were candidates for entry into NATO while, at the same time, trying to prevent NATO's expansion.

From within the Kremlin's walls Russia's overall situation appeared catastrophic. Japan had claims on the Kuril Islands. China was engaging in demographic and economic expansion in Russia. The Russo-Mongolian border was uneasy. Relations with neighboring Georgia were tense. As for Chechnya, although it was a part of Russia, since it was close to Turkey, the border there had particularly symbolic value. Kaliningrad, the former East Prussian Königsberg that was annexed to the USSR after World War II and is a Russian exclave wedged between Poland and Lithuania, experienced significant difficulties, and doubts arose as to whether it would remain part of Russian territory. Despite many attempts to break the stalemate on resolving the extremely serious problems of the Kaliningrad region, the authorities firmly refused to do anything at all. Their arguments were more than slightly peculiar and contradictory. On the one hand, they said that "the European Union will give us everything themselves." On the other hand, they asserted that the Kaliningrad region was an internal matter and that no Europeans had any business sticking their noses into it. Objectively speaking, however, Western help was badly needed to resolve such problems as organized crime, drug addiction, AIDS, and prostitution, the indicators of which were literally off the charts in this region.

In addition to these objective difficulties, for Russia, a no less important consequence of the Soviet Union's collapse was the loss of its global influence. The traditional Soviet mentality was unable to cope with this. However paradoxical it might seem, surveys of public opinion showed that superpower status was more important to people than their own well-being.

Given both objective reasons and the mentality of Moscow politicians, between 1992 and 2000 Russian foreign and domestic policy became unpredictable. The Kremlin and the Ministry of Foreign Affairs were unable to come to terms with the loss of a superpower role, the enlargement of NATO in 1999, and the loss of Russia's former sphere of influence. Missing from view were objective trends in international relations as well as the leaders' own mistakes and miscalculations.

Russia's real and imagined vulnerability, the generations-long psychology of a besieged fortress, the great power syndrome combined with the basically false thesis that the fall of the USSR and what followed were due to the nation's defeat in the Cold War—all taken together led to the kindling of revanchist feelings. The democratic reforms that had recently been undertaken were blamed for all the ills that had befallen Russia. Of course, the attempts to observe democratic standards and human rights during perestroika were facilitated by revelations regarding the many contradictions and conflicts in the USSR, with interethnic ones in the first instance. What disappeared from the view of those bent on revenge was the inconvenient truth that all the nation's disasters were due to domestic, not foreign, reasons. The pernicious consequences of self-destruction were basically ascribed to the external adversary. This position was extremely convenient and accorded with Russian traditions since it enabled the authorities to disclaim responsibility. Instead of rethinking the new realities, they rattled their sabers and shifted responsibility onto an external threat. The processes that led toward the disintegration of the country, however, deserve special consideration.

Tendencies toward Disintegration

By the turn of the twenty-first century, serious grounds existed for supposing that Russia might disintegrate. This situation arose partly from Boris Yeltsin's 1990 preelection populist slogan "Take as much sovereignty as you want!" Bashkortostan, Buriatia, Tuva, Sakha (Yakutia), and Komi—all constituent republics of the Russian Federation—responded to this appeal in one way or another by behaving like sovereign states.

Some members of the Russian Federation appropriated for themselves Russia's sovereign rights. Some of the contemporary symptoms pointing toward the disintegration of the country included the following:

- the priority of republic legislation over federal laws,

- the right to nullify laws and other normative acts of Russia on the territory of a republic if they contradicted the laws of that particular republic (Sakha [Yakutia], Bashkortostan, Tuva, Komai, and Tatarstan) or the sovereign rights and interests of a member of the Russian Federation (Dagestan),

- the right to declare a state of emergency (Buriatia, Komi, Tuva, Bashkortostan, Kalmykia, Karelia, North Ossetia, and Ingushetia),

- the right to impose martial law (Republic of Tuva),

- the republic laws about military service (Bashkortostan, Sakha (Yakutia), and Tuva),

- the procedures for establishing territorial military and other detachments (Sakha [Yakutia]),

- the need to secure permission from a member of the federation before deploying military units on its territory (North Ossetia),

- the right to regard as its exclusive property all natural resources on its territory (Ingushetia, Sakha [Yakutia], and Tuva), and

- the right to proclaim its own territory as a zone free of weapons of mass destruction (Tatarstan, Sakha [Yakutia], and Tuva).[16]

Moreover, in Ingushetia, Kalmykia, Tatarstan, Bashkortostan, Tuva, and the Kabardino-Balkar Republic, the republic constitutions were viewed as the fundamental law with juridical supremacy over the Russian Constitution. Analogous norms were contained in the statutes of the Khanty-Mansiiskii Autonomous District and Irkutsk region.

A paradoxical situation developed regarding the budget. Thus, the tax advantages conferred upon them by the federal authorities meant that compared to the other members of the federation, Tatarstan, Bashkortostan, and Sakha (Yakutia) transferred to the federal budget only half the taxes they collected.

The disintegration of Russia was also facilitated by the fact that the constitutions (statutes) and legislation of many of the members of the Russian Federation contained numerous provisions violating constitutional rights and freedoms that were linked to the particular status of the inhabitants. Restrictions were placed upon their citizens' freedom of movement and choice of place of residence.[17]

The regions were increasingly less oriented toward financial assistance from the federal center. A vivid example of this was the declaration by Kirsan Iliumzhinov, president of the Republic of Kalmykia, on November 17, 1998, concerning the possibility that Kalmykia might unilaterally alter its status to associate membership in the Russian Federation (providing that its budget not be included in the federal budget) or that Kalmykia might withdraw altogether from membership in the Russian Federation. Karelia counted on help from Finland, which, according to the Kremlin, was interested in recovering the Karelian territories it had lost in the Second World War. The Southern Kuril Islands, Sakhalin, and the Maritime Province hoped for financial assistance from Japan and reoriented themselves toward the countries of the Asia-Pacific region, thereby creating the preconditions for regional sentiments to develop into separatist ones.

Along with the decrease in the regions' financial dependency on the center was a noticeable diminution of Moscow's importance as the focus of centripetal forces. But what perhaps troubled Moscow most was the desire of many military units deployed in the member states of the federation to be subject to local leadership rather than to the federal center.

The North Caucasus

The political and historical illiteracy of the Kremlin masters and their inability to assess the consequences of their own decisions, combined with the country's and the region's objective difficulties, brought about an extremely complicated situation in the North Caucasus. The economic situation there during the Yeltsin era was marked by a fall in production; deterioration in the financial condition of industrial enterprises, almost half of which operated at a loss; and a decline in agriculture. These factors promoted the growth of separatist sentiments in the North Caucasus. Moscow complained about the extremely tense situation in Chechnya that was destabilizing the sociopolitical situation in the entire region, especially in Dagestan, the border districts of the Stavropol region of southern Russia, and Ingushetia.

The problem of Chechnya typified the state of affairs in Russia primarily because it was mostly artificial. The First Chechen War (1994–96) was one of the most terrible and senseless crimes of the bloody twentieth century.

In the prologue to the war, first the Chechens did essentially just what Yeltsin advocated when he was battling for the post of chairman of the Supreme Soviet of the Russian Soviet Federated Socialist Republic in 1990: they took as much sovereignty as they wanted. The second act of the prologue to the Chechen tragedy was when Yeltsin brought air force general Dzhokhar Dudaev to power in Chechnya. The last act was the transfer to Chechnya of a large part of the gigantic Soviet army arsenal located on its territory.

There are many versions of how the war in Chechnya began. The standard one points to Chechnya's quest for independence and acquisition of sovereignty.[18] Among the reasons for the First Chechen War that deserve to be considered are the so-called oil factor, the supposed financial machinations of Russian and Chechen bureaucrats in which someone ditched or dumped somebody else, and even "the need to restore the army's fighting spirit after Afghanistan."[19]

Obviously, one should not overlook the purely political elements. President Yeltsin, who was seriously ill, had become unpopular. The events of October 1993—the clash between Yeltsin and the Russian parliament—clearly demonstrated the shakiness of his rule. Its end would have brought catastrophe down upon his closest associates (including what Yeltsin himself referred to as his "family") and the corrupt members of his government. The war in Chechnya might have been devised as a means of strengthening Yeltsin's power, perhaps as an excuse for introducing a state of emergency, for gradually extending it to other parts of the country, and postponing the 1996 presidential election. One should not forget that war is a lucrative business, especially when it is fought on one's own territory, and consequently entails rebuilding what was destroyed or its equivalent.

The attempt by the Russian special services to overthrow Dzhokhar Dudaev in October–November 1994 failed. Russian minister of defense Pavel Grachev then promised to seize the Chechen capital, Grozny, quickly and without losses. With the "war party" ascendant in Moscow, in December the Kremlin launched a large-scale war on its own territory against its own citizens that led to the genocide of the Chechens, one of multiethnic Russia's nationalities.

The results of the First Chechen War were tragic. Gen. Alexander Lebed estimated the number of dead as 80,000 to 100,000. Most of the victims were civilians. In the battle for Grozny alone (December 1994 to February 1995), 23,000 to 25,000 people died. Of these casualties, 18,700 were killed as a result of Russian bombing and artillery strikes.

An extremely complicated situation arose as a result of the First Chechen War. Russia itself seized Chechnya and categorically opposed its departure from the federation, but Chechnya could be retained as part of Russia only via large-scale reconstruction of the republic. In addition to Russia's having insufficient resources, reconstruction failed because of thievery in both Moscow and Grozny. The goal of retaining Chechnya within Russia should have entailed according it either a special status or an undefined status within the Russian Federation such as was envisioned by the Khasavyurt Agreement.[20]

Considering Stalinist and other crimes against the freedom-loving republic, the second and more humanitarian option—namely, letting Chechnya go[21]—was unacceptable to the Kremlin both on ideological grounds and, above all, in order to prevent a chain reaction leading to the disintegration of Russia. However, maintaining the relations that developed after the end of the First Chechen War at the time actually facilitated the process of disintegration.

The third option, the one that eventually triumphed, if only nominally and temporarily, was isolating Chechnya within the boundaries of Russia and creating a kind of Chechen ghetto behind barbed wire. This decision was not implemented straight away because of its expense and the lack of the requisite means to do so.[22]

Public opinion on both sides of the conflict, decisively influenced by Moscow's official propaganda, was extremely hostile.[23] For a long time, law enforcement agencies "found" so-called Chechen imprints on every major terrorist act. Two derogatory terms were employed to designate the peoples inhabiting the Caucasus—

namely, *persons of Caucasian ethnicity*, a phrase used in official documents even though there was no such ethnicity, and *blacks* (from the hair and eye color of a majority of the people from the Caucasus). The unspeakable cruelty of Russian troops both during and after military engagements inevitably incited hatred on the part of the Chechens.

The situation grew much worse after Vladimir Putin's appointment as Russian prime minister on August 10, 1999, and President Yeltsin's announcement that Putin was to be his successor. Two days earlier, Chechen fighters led by Shamil Basaev and Khattab had crossed the border into Dagestan and occupied four Dagestani settlements but were forced to return to Chechen territory. On September 4–6, the incursion into Dagestan was repeated. This served as the pretext for the beginning of Russian military actions against Chechnya, including the bombardment of Chechen territory.[24]

That same month, apartment houses were blown up in Moscow and Volgodonsk.[25] The total number of victims of terrorist acts for just the period from August 31 to September 16, 1999, was more than 530 persons, of whom 292 were killed.[26] Thus began the Second Chechen War, which the Kremlin hypocritically referred to as an antiterrorist operation.[27]

Chechnya became an extremely large irritant in relations between Russia and Georgia. Among other reasons it was because of the situation in the Pankisi Gorge, a part of Georgia that was not controlled by Tbilisi and that, according to Moscow, provided a sanctuary for Chechen fighters.

The situation in Dagestan, neighboring Chechnya on the east, was extremely unstable. The complicated situation was brought about by the weakness of the authorities as well as interethnic contradictions, criminal depredations, especially along the border with Chechnya, and a host of other reasons.

Things were also difficult in the Stavropol territory of southern Russia, where the sociopolitical situation was greatly complicated by its proximity to the Chechen Republic from whose territory there were constant incursions by Chechen fighters who ran off with cattle and matériel. The situation along the "border" with Chechnya periodically heated up. Not infrequently there were instances of discrimination on the basis of nationality in the Krasnodar territory. Local authorities took decisions aimed at depriving national minorities of the right to education and access to medical care as well as depriving them of the right to possess residence permits, to register marriages, and so forth.

The Kremlin's Chechen folly reflected the mentality of the Russian authorities who were panic-stricken in the face of Islam. Yeltsin's verdict was simple: cut off Islamic fundamentalism. In early May 1997 I received a directive from the highest level to draft appropriate "measures and proposals." Not without difficulty, I succeeded in transforming the assignment by drafting a document compatible with freedom of religion. Nothing came of it, however, despite the fact that Yeltsin liked the draft.

The Chechen War, in tandem with the Russian leadership's gross errors and miscalculations regarding interreligious and nationality policy, exacerbated the problem of Islam. As often happened, the authorities in Moscow confused cause with effect and attempted to present the spread of "several tendencies of Islam" as the prime reason for many of the problems in Russia. They concocted a thesis claiming that the Islamic factor had been turned into a weapon in the struggle for spheres of influence among the leading world powers and that Islamic extremism was deliberately being channeled into Russia so that it would be concentrated there and not spread to the United States and Western Europe. In other words, the Americans and the West Europeans were supposedly seeking to turn Islamic extremism against Russia to protect themselves from it.

Meanwhile, it was true that certain forces in Russia made use of the revival of Islam in Russia as an effective means of political struggle. The nationalist leaders of several member republics of the Russian Federation played the card of political extremism rallying under the banner of Islam. Given the Kremlin's persistent stereotype of the Caucasus as a "single entity," it claimed that all the contiguous states and territories would be affected. The authorities were extremely fearful that the developing sociopolitical and economic situation would facilitate the spread of pan-Islamism, an aggressive form of Islamic fundamentalism, including Wahhabism, which Moscow accused of being responsible for all the troubles.[28] Moscow blamed the spread of Wahhabism in the republics of the North Caucasus and other regions of Russia for the flourishing of radical nationalist organizations and the exacerbation of interethnic and interreligious relations. Given the spread of Islam in the central districts of Russia, Tatarstan, Bashkortostan, and Kalmykia, and the flourishing of Islam in Siberia and the Far East, the Kremlin was frightened that Russia might break up along the "arc of Islam."

In this way the Kremlin identified an enemy in the form of Islam. Next came the reflex action of looking for guilty parties to blame for what in reality were self-inflicted disasters. Another tradition of Russian "political culture" also surfaced—the habit of viewing everything that differed from the familiar (and for the Kremlin that meant only Russian Orthodoxy) as alien or, worse than alien, actually hostile.

While noting that the "Islamic problem," as the Kremlin perceived it, was an artificial construct, one must acknowledge that, in part, it had an objective dimension largely rooted in Soviet history. By assisting the "revolutionary," "friendly," and "anti-imperialist" Islamists, as well as Islamist terrorist regimes and organizations in the struggle against "world imperialism"; by sustaining them financially; and by training their fighters on its own territory, the USSR had flung a boomerang that was bound to return upon itself. Likewise, the Soviet Union's aggression against Afghanistan was repaid with the antagonism of part of the Islamic world. The de facto prohibition of Islam in the USSR provoked the creation of underground, informal Muslim structures, which, in a number of cases, became radicalized.

After the end of the Soviet dictatorship, Islam firmly occupied second place among religions in Russia in terms of its number of adherents and its geographical range.[29] In addition to its religious and ideological role, Islam provided a national-religious identity for part of the population, a banner for national liberation struggles, and a means of contending for power in the traditionally Islamic, newly independent states and nationalities in other countries of the CIS as well as in Russia itself.

At this time a majority of the population in Dagestan was religious; 60 percent held deep religious convictions and actively propagated Islam. The number of followers of Wahhabism swelled. According to Moscow, a characteristic of the Dagestani Wahhabites is their manifest hatred of Russia and of adherents of what had been the traditional sect of Islam in Dagestan who were seen as "accomplices of Moscow." Moscow also said that the Wahhabites maintained close relations with the Chechen rebels. The *siloviki* and their supporters claimed that the ultimate goal of the radically inclined leaders of the Wahhabites was to transform Dagestan into an Islamic state with the help of powerful external support and the Chechens.

The authorities viewed the spread of Wahhabism in the republics of the North Caucasus and other regions of Russia as a serious threat that might significantly spur the activity of national radical organizations and further exacerbate interethnic and interreligious relations. Characteristically, Moscow blamed the spread of Islamic extremism in Russia on the Arab countries, the United States, and Western Europe, all of which supposedly were striving to confine Islamic extremism to Russia, thereby weakening Russia and facilitating its "guided disintegration." In this connection, Russia's own mistakes and miscalculations were either minimized or entirely ignored.

The Arctic and Siberia

The Arctic region, which, in addition to the sea waters, includes wide swathes of territory on the mainland and the islands of the northern Arctic Ocean totaling more than 1.16 million square miles, is one of the richest and most vulnerable parts of Russia. To illustrate the significance of the Arctic territories for Russia, it is enough to point out that in 1996 they were responsible for 11 percent of the national income and 22 percent of its exports while containing only 1 percent of the population.

However, the government's life support system and supply of goods and provisions that previously existed were destroyed and a new system not put in its place. All kinds of expeditions and scientific activity were sharply curtailed. State support was withdrawn from the fleet of atomic-powered icebreakers and the infra-structure of the Northern Sea Route. The result was that by the year 2000, the society and economy of the Arctic, eastern Siberia, and the Far East were in crisis. An entire economic system was destroyed, and a mass exodus of qualified specialists occurred. Many enterprises were shut down. In most regions in the north, the construction industry virtually collapsed. In many cases trans-portation costs constituted at least half the price of products. The peoples of the north, each of the many numerically small ethnic-ities, were in a particularly disastrous situation. In several regions there was a very real danger of an ecological catastrophe.

The uncontrolled outflow of people, specialists above all, from the Arctic to the central regions of Russia triggered by the closure of enterprises and airports and the disbandment of military units led to the destruction of the existing infrastructure, the growth of social tensions, and the upsurge of criminality in the region. With enterprises shuttered, including factories in "one-factory" towns, entire population centers were liquidated. In the period starting from 1991, the population of the Far North District and adminis-tratively equivalent localities shrunk by more than a million per-sons. Because savings had been devalued and moving costs were high, pensioners, invalids, and those who had become unemployed by force of circumstances were unable to leave and turned into virtual hostages. More than 200,000 persons wanted to leave in the year 2000. Meanwhile, an estimated 380 settlements housing more than 200,000 persons were to be closed by the end of 2000.

Moscow's impotence impelled the leaders of several republics within the Russian Federation to seek to resolve the old and new economic and sociopolitical problems more autonomously and independently of the center. They also sought to play a more sig-nificant role in both domestic and international affairs in their own regions.

Meanwhile, there was an increase in the activity of various ethnic groups and popular movements of Far Northern peoples as they formulated ideas of national and regional separatism and posited the goal of achieving sovereignty within Russia. The sharpest inter-ethnic friction occurred in several districts of the Sakha (Yakutia) Republic, particularly in the Allaikhovskii District, where the leaders of the Evenki community began dividing up the property of state farms and demanded that the best arable land and pasture be allotted to the native inhabitants. The actions of the local authorities in Yakutia aimed at limiting and restricting the rights of various segments of the population led to a significant exodus of the Russian-speaking population of the region. Starting in 1992, every year on average more than 2,000 persons left the northern districts of Yakutia.

This trend fundamentally changed the ethnic composition of most of the industrial centers of Russia's Far North and was among the reasons for shuttering a number of major industrial enterprises. The human and intellectual potential of Russia's northern regions suffered significantly, given the absence of a broad system of training and retraining specialists.

Preserving the numerically small indigenous peoples of the Far North remained a pressing problem. Industrial expansion in several northern regions made the survival of these peoples problematic. The broad-scale development of natural resources in Russia's northern territories drastically undermined the foundations of the traditional economy, as large areas of reindeer pasture and hunting grounds (more than 49.4 million acres) were declared off-limits and many rivers were ruined. The widespread reduction of their natural habitat and degradation of the conditions needed to pursue their traditional economic activities and their way of life could lead to the disappearance of individual tribes.

It was against this background that the Chinese expansion referred to earlier caused anxieties in Moscow. In long-range perspective, Moscow feared the danger of China's claims to 579,000 square miles of the Far East and Siberia that it considered historically its own.

The Region of Kaliningrad

The dissolution of the USSR highlighted the problem of the Kaliningrad region, which is located between Poland and Lithuania on the southeastern shore of the Baltic Sea and separated from the rest of Russia. It had a population of 941,000 according to the

2010 census and an area of 5,800 square miles, or around the size of Connecticut. The region's special significance derives from its location in the center of Europe as part of the Baltic Sea zone and its proximity to economically and militarily powerful European countries. The Kaliningrad region possesses an advantageous geographical position at the intersection of the main freight routes from the East to the Northwest. The transportation corridors that cross the region link Russia with Western Europe via the shortest route. Moreover, Kaliningrad contains Russia's only year-round, ice-free port complex on the Baltic Sea.

From Moscow's perspective the military-strategic significance of the Kaliningrad region was much greater than its economic importance since it vastly expanded Russia's ability to protect its western borders from the sea and anchored Russia's naval presence on the Baltic. The loss of the Kaliningrad region as a military-strategic zone, an economic center, and an important transportation hub would inevitably signify Russia's retreat from the Baltic Sea.

From the establishment of the Kaliningrad region in 1946 on part of the former East Prussia, it was basically used for military purposes. Therefore, the regional economy was wholly financed from the state budget and oriented toward imported raw materials. After the breakup of the USSR, the region was placed in an extremely difficult position because of the virtually complete loss of its productive enterprises' ties with Russian enterprises. Its contacts with suppliers of raw materials and goods were significantly weakened. On top of this, a sharp decrease in military orders occurred, there was a lack of funds to convert production facilities to civilian purposes, and state support for the fishing industry was cut off. The rupture of traditional economic relations with the noncontiguous regions of the former USSR led to a deeper recession in the region's economy than that in Russia overall and seriously impacted social stability.

Realizing that it was impossible to provide broad-scale financial assistance to the Kaliningrad region, Moscow decided to establish a free economic zone in its territory. At the same time, the regional administration received supplementary authority to manage regional development. These steps contributed to the criminalization of the local organs of power. Moreover, regional authorities were granted additional financial powers, in particular the right to retain in the local budget a higher share of tax revenues than regions in central Russia, of hard currency receipts from the sale of regional export quotas, of Ministry of Finance tax credits, and of receipts from the sale of auctioned quotas for imported goods within the framework of the federal earmark program.

After the breakup of the USSR, the Kaliningrad region changed from an exporter of agricultural products to a major importer, importing up to 85 percent of its foodstuffs. The grain harvest shrank by more than 50 percent, 90 percent of potatoes and vegetables were grown by the local population, the machine and tractor stations decreased by a factor of three, and by the year 2000, 80 percent of them were obsolete. Experts calculated that in order to provide the minimal consumption needs of the regional population, $30 million worth of foodstuffs had to be imported annually.

Real income and consumer buying power decreased, and the percentage of persons with incomes below subsistence level increased. According to the State Committee for Statistics, 42 percent of the population lived below the poverty level in 1999. According to a sociological survey conducted on March 13–15, 2000, 66.6 percent of respondents rated their material position as "poor." At the end of 1999, the unemployment rate in the Kaliningrad region was 13.8 percent of the working population, significantly higher than in Russia overall. If one included hidden unemployment, then the figure would be much higher. The death rate regularly exceeded the birth rate. In 1998 it was 163 percent; in 1999 it was 180 percent (13,617 deaths versus 7,549 births). The problems of youths were exacerbated by an epidemic of drug abuse, the spread of AIDS, and an ever-increasing rate of prostitution. This list far from exhausts the problems in this area.

Thus, the Kaliningrad region was in a terrible state. Moscow did virtually nothing to improve the situation. Kaliningrad's privileged economic status was revoked for good reason. Instead of serving as an instrument for regional economic development, it had turned into a powerful stimulus for the growth of corruption and organized crime. The practically coerced change of governors

Moscow initiated did not improve things. This was not surprising, since Moscow paid little heed to the problems in the region, and when issues were brought to its attention, it limited itself (in line with Soviet tradition) to words and administrative measures.

Russia's position regarding numerous West European proposals to help it solve the problem of the Kaliningrad region was extremely irrational. Moscow said it was a domestic problem of the Russian Federation and would be dealt with by itself. Meanwhile, the Kaliningrad region continued to collapse.

Naturally, given certain conditions, Russia will manage to preserve its territorial integrity. Yet hypothetical disintegration scenarios could assume many forms. The following are the most plausible.

The first candidate for independence from Russia is Chechnya, followed by other republics of the North Caucasus. In this case, one cannot exclude the possibility that the country will break up along the line of the "Islamic arc."

There is a considerable chance the Kaliningrad region may secede from Russia, especially since a change toward greater cooperation with the European Union would confer significant economic and social benefits.

Another candidate for secession from Russia is St. Petersburg and the Leningrad region. This is the most self-sufficient entity with a developed economy, science, education, and culture, and it possesses an outlet on the Baltic Sea and a port infrastructure.

Although not viable under current conditions, the trans-Ural region, well-endowed with useful mineral and other natural resources, given the right sort of investments might objectively be interested in changing its status. One cannot predict what course events may take here, given the possible competition of potential investors in the region, the Chinese factor, and many other circumstances.

The transfer of the Northern Territories (the Kuril Islands) to Japan is only a matter of time; such is the historical and political logic.

If the Kremlin continues to place its bets on the "vertical of power" structure rather than on resolving real problems, Russia may wind up not only without the North Caucasus, Siberia, and the Far East but quite possibly without part of its European territory.

The Year 2000 Problem

Thus, in the year 2000, Russia approached an imminent national catastrophe. The federal authorities had virtually lost all control over the situation.

Something else, however, was troubling the deities in Moscow: what would happen to them personally as a result of Yeltsin's inevitable departure from power? The coming change of president in accordance with the Constitution was dubbed "the year 2000 problem."

The question of who would be the future power holders greatly exacerbated the financial and political crisis of 1998. In this context it needs to be emphasized that—contrary to the assertions of the Russian authorities as well as of widely regarded opinion makers—*political, not economic, reasons were the foundation of the negative phenomena occurring in Russia.* The economic difficulties that the country was experiencing were among the consequences *of Russia's failure since 1992 to devise genuine foreign and domestic policies.* As a result, the traditional Soviet dualism—that is, the disparity between political declarations and actual goals and plans—continued to prevail and was rife with unforeseeable consequences. Overall, the desire of the executive authorities to guarantee their own personal security played the decisive role in determining their actions in the course of events.

The upcoming election campaign of the "party of power" was significantly complicated by the fact that prior to Vladimir Putin's launching the Second Chechen War, there were no favored figures within the president's retinue or in high government posts. The "patriotic" path breaker in the wider arena of Russian politics was the KGB protégé Vladimir Zhirinovsky, founder of the grossly misnamed Liberal Democratic Party. Putin, who was much more cunning, followed the path blazed by the flamboyant Zhirinovsky and Gen. Alexander Lebed, who had run for president in 1996. Putin himself practically gushed an ostentatious form of "patriotism."

The victory in the 1999 parliamentary elections of a newborn movement whose only slogan was unconditional support for Vladimir Putin, and his victory in the presidential election of 2000, sounded the death knell of democracy. The persons who came to power were irreconcilable enemies of democracy, human rights, and the application of humane principles to Russia's domestic and foreign policies.

Besieged, badly managed fortresses will fall, sometimes from the unwise expenditure of resources and from epidemics, filth, and other problems brought about by the siege. This can occur even if the siege exists only in the minds of the powers that be. Many of Russia's problems were occasioned precisely by this imaginary siege. The country's resources were wasted on senseless military pseudo reforms and on the appearance of supporting national security (a component of which was a "financial stability" that led to collapse) as viewed by the authorities rather than on constructing a space within the country in which one could live normally.

It is difficult to imagine another country where the leaders treated their people, their own earth, and their own natural wealth in such a barbarous fashion.

The destruction of a people is senseless and pointless as well as an extremely rare event in world history. It is usually associated with tyrants such as Adolf Hitler, Stalin, or Pol Pot. What occurred first in the USSR and then in Russia is so senseless and so protracted that it constitutes one of the greatest puzzles in history. Russia's tragedy reflects the inherently odious features of Russian power, power that is burdened by the vices of stunted intellectual and moral development and is confident of its absoluteness and its impunity. The crimes that brought Russia to the blind alley in which it found itself in the year 2000 were committed by very different kinds of persons, from orthodox communists to the quasi-democrats under the early Yeltsin. These leaders were responsible for Russia's degradation at the time Boris Yeltsin betrayed democracy by handing the reins of power to his appointed successor, Vladimir Putin.

4

How the System Really Works

The core of the enigmatic Russian soul sometimes appears to be located in the Kremlin. Of course, in Russia as elsewhere the real action of politics and diplomacy takes place behind closed doors, and the outcomes of the often painstaking and intensive struggles become known to the wider public as official foreign and domestic policy. The following anecdote from the early Yeltsin era, when there were very specific ways of doing things, affords a look behind those closed doors. It was a time when incompetence, irresponsibility, seeking personal advantages, and drunkenness on the job, especially in the Kremlin, were typical features of working life. They surprised nobody. This episode speaks to the level of qualifications of one high-level Kremlin official—Sergei Prikhodko—and, for that matter, almost all of the Kremlin administration.

Once, when I was filling in for my boss, who was away on assignment, I had to reach an agreement urgently on some question with Sergei Prikhodko, Yeltsin's assistant and chief of his foreign policy staff. (In May 2013 he became the vice premier and head of the government bureaucracy.) Someone who was very close to Prikhodko worked in our department at the time, so I requested that he stop a government official who, for unknown reasons, was doing his best to block all our initiatives regarding the matter in question, the nature of which is not relevant here.

"Andrei, I simply can't!" my colleague literally howled.

I replied that it was absolutely imperative, explained to him why, and asked him why he sounded so despairing. I was dismayed by his answer.

"You know, when I go to see Sergei Eduardovich [Prikhodko],

I take two bottles of whiskey with me. I drink the first bottle with his assistants. The second with him. And today I've already been there twice! Do you really want me to go there again?"

All I could say was, "I'm sorry. It has to be done. There's no other way."

"Well, then I won't come back to work today," he said hopelessly.

"Okay, if anyone asks, I'll say you're in the Kremlin. But call me and let me know how it went."

"I won't be able to," he shook his head despairingly. "You'll know the results tomorrow, okay?"

"The boss wants it today."

"Then you can say right away that Prikhodko agrees."

"Really?"

"I always keep my word, as you know . . . although perhaps I need to take another bottle as a guarantee."

As this anecdote suggests, after the August 1991 coup, Russia's government and diplomatic service began to disintegrate. During the acute political struggles between reformers and reactionaries preceding the coup, a paradoxical alliance had formed between the hard-line communists and many democrats. The former rejected the reforms outright, while the latter were dissatisfied with the depth and speed of progress. In the run-up to the coup, the CPSU and the KGB closely cooperated in redistributing property and forming a new elite. If one accepts this as a fact, and I do, it is logical to suppose that after the breakup of the USSR this cooperation continued in one form or another. The catastrophic results of Russia's "liberal" economic reforms indirectly confirm this.

It is worth heeding the words of Andrei Illarionov, a respected economist and former adviser to Putin who is now a senior fellow at the Cato Institute in Washington DC: "In our view what happened was the nomenklatura revenge of the Soviet bureaucracy and special services." Illarionov characterizes the economic reforms of the early 1990s as a "bureaucratic-nomenklatura type." He believes they were directed toward providing "exceptionally favorable conditions in the new economic and political system for the nomenklatura bureaucracy left over from the Soviet Union." Moreover, he is convinced that all the mistaken decisions of the

Russian authorities were made "for the benefit of the nomenklatura, including the special services," who wanted "to receive the property inherited from the USSR. In order to achieve this goal it was necessary to destroy their real and potential economic and political competitors, and thereby secure the economic and political instruments of power, including the means of coercion, to defend their new property and new position."[1] Naturally, it would have been more accurate had Illarionov made it clear that really only an infinitesimal part of the Soviet *nomenklatura* participated in the redivision of property.

Yet his valuable testimony indirectly indicates that the purposeful destruction of the Soviet Union's ruling mechanisms was inevitable. By devoting themselves wholly to self-enrichment, a tiny fraction of the *nomenklatura* and the ruling apparatus succeeded in landing on its feet. They did so in the name of "the public" by, among other things, seizing control of the mechanisms that governed their own activities. In other words, a small number of the old guard adapted to the new rules of the game and then adopted these rules as their own. Toward the end of the Soviet period, for example, I know of one very highly placed official who would perform no government service unless he personally received 1,000 percent per hour of his nominal salary.

Moreover, in the late Soviet period the system of decision making was able to neutralize plans for the suicidal, pseudo-liberal economic reform. It was already functioning without the previous obligatory assent of the KGB and the Central Committee of the CPSU, as well as personal connections among various state officials. Finally, as a result of Gorbachev's perestroika, the stagnant but resilient Stalinist administrative command system had become moribund and outside the control of the special services, which were playing the key role in shaping post-Soviet Russia. Of course, the special services, accustomed to total power, were loath to accept this situation and strove to restore, and even enhance, their role. Their ideal was a Stalinist model of governance, and they painstakingly began to reconstruct it at the first opportunity. In sum, the institutions of government had to be destroyed in order not to interfere with the total makeover of Russia.

The decisions made by Russian leaders, like those made by their Soviet predecessors, are often bewildering. To grasp their meaning, not infrequently one must resort to ingenious and improbable explanations such as extremely far-fetched plots, perfidy, and so forth. In reality, nothing is as it seems, and nothing works the way it appears to work. In making decisions, the authorities almost never proceed from the actual state of affairs for several reasons. The first, even in the best of circumstances, is the pervasiveness of half-truths or lies embedded within most of the information upon which national policies are based. Again, there are several reasons for such misinformation. Officials at every level of decision making who report up the chain of command almost always take into consideration just what their superiors want of them; therefore, the leadership receives information that almost invariably is distorted and sometimes even unrecognizable. Add to this the fact that personal ambitions of the reporting officials almost never coincide with national interests and that their well-being and sometimes their careers depend upon the content of their reports. Thus, accurate information, which rarely reaches the desks of the leadership, is not deemed credible. Accumulated lies trump everything else.

Under Yeltsin the practice of manipulating Russia's top leadership reached unprecedented heights. He made decisions intended to please those who had most recently had his ear. Among those with easiest access to him were such odious figures as his daughter Tatiana Diachenko; his chief bodyguard Alexander Korzhakov; the tennis coach Shamil Tarpishchev, whom Yeltsin had appointed minister of sport; and other members of his "family." Lubricated by whatever amount of alcohol was needed to do the trick, he made decisions that served the interests of his advisers.

It is a truism that everywhere power seeks to preserve itself. However, in Russia preservation became virtually its primary motive. For example, when Yeltsin, who loved to emphasize that he was the "guarantor" of the Constitution, was threatened with impeachment, he did not even consider the possibility of leaving his position. Instead of following the basic law, he was preparing to arrest the parliamentary deputies.

Beginning with the Yeltsin era, among the Russian authorities who were suffering from their own growing inferiority complex, the acquisitive reflex overrode all others. To the rulers in Moscow, all of Russia's wealth, let alone their own personal wealth, was too little. Corruption and the pillaging of their own country were far from being the only indicators of their greed. While I was serving on the Security Council staff, I saw how my colleagues dreamed of arranging large-scale arms sales to whomsoever they pleased, apart from countries such as Poland that were unsympathetic to the Kremlin. Well aware of American concerns about Russia's observance of a nuclear missile nonproliferation agreement, I was unconvinced of the accuracy of the information we were providing our foreign colleagues. Moreover, when I received relevant material from the ministries and departments that I was supposed to redraft into documents for the country's leadership, I had more questions about this material than did my foreign interlocutors.

Russian authorities usually do not understand the mentality and, consequently, the motivations and objectives of their foreign partners. It is worth noting that the Russian tradition includes the practice of exploiting official positions for self-enrichment or other personal benefits. (It is a curious fact that bribery was legalized by Ivan the Terrible, whose boyars [high-ranking noblemen] did not receive salaries but supported themselves by means of requisitions from the local population. This mode of payment for their services was officially called feeding.) The lack of control over the officials, on the one hand, and the ruin and poverty of the country, on the other, inevitably led to pervasive corruption and other extremely serious consequences.

An important element in the decision-making mechanism is the state apparatus itself. Despite the many obvious defects of the Soviet Union, its system of processing documents greatly hindered making decisions that obviously contradicted the national interest; however, this same system equally inhibited making necessary decisions. In a nutshell, without exception all the leaders of the relevant ministries and departments had to indicate their approval of whatever measures were under consideration. Often reservations entered by one or another government ministry or department sufficed to block the adoption of pernicious measures or, at least, to mitigate their consequences. After the breakup of the USSR, the situation changed drastically. For various reasons the overwhelming majority of the most competent officials found themselves out of government. Ministries and departments were now headed by persons known to be mediocrities. These officials repeatedly leapfrogged above their level of competence to positions of leadership. The system of securing agreement was abolished, but no other filters were introduced.

The most paradoxical feature was that although it seemed the bureaucracy was dependent on those in power, at the same time it actually bossed them about. For one thing any decision might remain unimplemented if the bureaucracy chose to drag its feet. Also decisions might be ill justified but sent upward to high-level officials who, suffering from a lack of time and competence, were unable to judge them correctly. Even worse a decision that had not been adopted might be passed off as one that had been, while a resolution that actually had been adopted might not be registered and, thus, deemed invalid. To illustrate these points, I share some observations about what went on in the inner sanctum of power during the Yeltsin era and the early Putin period.

Let us consider the Russian position on one of the key aspects of the country's defensive posture—namely, the treaty on antiballistic missile defense. For various reasons the treaty was coming apart at the seams, yet in accordance with its unfortunate tradition of spinning the truth, the Foreign Ministry gleefully reported that everything was going splendidly and that no changes were necessary in the position Moscow had adopted many years earlier. Noting a certain surrealism in this attitude, we prepared changes in the position, coordinated them with the military, and sent the proposals to the president. We received neither an answer nor an acknowledgment. We called Sergei Prikhodko to learn the fate of our proposal; his deputy, Alexander Manzhosin, who in 2007 would head the Presidential Foreign Policy Directorate, responded. His answer was worthy of Kafka.

"You know," said this worthy, who had important responsibilities in the area of foreign policy on behalf of the president, "*we don't understand anything about this,* and so we're leaving it just like the Foreign Ministry proposed."

What an admission! The deputy head of the Foreign Policy Directorate declares, without a trace of embarrassment, that neither his boss nor he and his colleagues understand anything—and don't want to understand anything—about a crucial question of Russia's foreign policy.

The same work ethic prevailing among officials in the Security Council foreshadowed their response to threats. Their standard approach was that their work should be measured by the magnitude of the threat they discerned. To curry favor with the Presidential Administration, several departments felt it practically their duty to pass along information that exaggerated the threats. Given the preponderance of precisely such information, it was sometimes difficult and, for some officials, impossible to maintain a balanced approach in the Security Council. However, this does not mean that no balanced and useful work was going on there.

After Andrei Kokoshin became secretary of the Security Council, we became fully engaged with the problem of the nonproliferation of weapons of mass destruction and the means of obtaining them. We must give the Americans their due: they correctly identified Minister of Atomic Energy Yevgeny Adamov as the person responsible for violating the nonproliferation agreement. It was only in 1999 that the effort to expose him bore fruit. (His subordinates and those who had anything to do with him were terrified of the man they referred to as "Stalin from Ordynka Street."[2]) Only with great difficulty did we manage to receive reliable information about Adamov's illegal activities. Yevgeny Primakov, who was then the prime minister, appointed an official commission to investigate the activity of this blatantly criminal minister. Armed with the results of the commission's labors, Primakov signed a memorandum to President Yeltsin that we had drafted spelling out Adamov's official misdemeanors and proposing that he be dismissed from his post given his illegal business dealings in nuclear technology.

If everything had gone properly, Adamov's dismissal would have been only the overture to what should have followed. He should have been held criminally accountable, and, most important of all, the many opportunities for trade in nuclear secrets would have been exposed and order returned to export controls. However, *nothing of the sort occurred*. Although an attempt was made to block the commission's report and to withhold it from Yeltsin—most likely by Tatiana Diachenko, who was close to Adamov—this resistance was somehow overcome. But the report to Yeltsin had no effect. It was as if Adamov, to put it mildly, had not committed any of the official offenses that violated written and unwritten laws, as we had demonstrated. It was as if the prime minister had not spelled out the blatant outrages to the president. It was as if his memorandum and our protocol were nothing more than a bad joke that was best quickly forgotten or ignored. However, there was one consequence of our work: V. Malkevich, who then headed the Russian Federal Service on Currency and Export Control (VEK) was dismissed from his post, and Putin disbanded the service. The upshot of this failure to implement the commission's findings was that suspicion naturally arose that the *proliferation* of nuclear missile technology was a carefully concealed government policy.

The story of Adamov and nuclear affairs was quite typical of contemporary Russia. The double standards of Russian politics were revealed in all their glory. Lip service was paid to the notion that national security was the primary concern, but in reality the authorities took no interest in the fact that an actual threat was being created. Is this some sort of schizophrenia? Some sort of perverse kleptomania when you steal the right to your own security?

I will not try to judge the reliability of the rumors and reports in the mass media concerning Adamov's links with the criminal world. Their very appearance, however, speaks volumes. It was also a matter of considerable curiosity to learn that Adamov was supposedly the only member of a foreign government to possess a Social Security card in the United States and, according to the same information, to direct an American company. However, addressing these questions was not within the competency of the government commission. They should be the province of the services responsible for ensuring state security. Without parading their connection and through their own channels, these same services should refute information appearing in the press if it does not correspond to the truth.

During the period I served on the Security Council, Ivan Rybkin, Andrei Kokoshin, Nikolai Bordiuzha, Vladimir Putin, Sergei Ivanov, and Vladimir Rushailo rotated through the position of secretary. Rushailo left the most vivid impression. The first shock was when in his initial meeting with foreign interlocutors Rushailo read verbatim a set of talking points we had drafted for him to use. Its reference section, which was for his eyes alone, contained extremely sensitive information that should not have been revealed to his interlocutor under any circumstances. However, droning on with the same intonation, Rushailo continued, "Eyes only—current situation . . ." And he read it out loud to the end. He was very satisfied with the discussion. His interlocutors were even more so. My colleagues and I decided that the less he knew the better, and as far as we were able, we stopped providing him "sensitive" information.

A few words about the other secretaries—except for Putin, as I was ill when he served in that position—are in order. Rybkin, as far as I know, restrained the Russian hawks from resuming the slaughter in Chechnya. At least that is what I saw and heard. During his tenure, my like-minded colleagues and I worked toward that end, and he not only refrained from hindering us but even helped a little.

Under Rybkin I spent a lot of time working on Chechnya. In addition to the daily work flow, I tried to create a mechanism for extending foreign humanitarian assistance to this long-suffering republic. To work out a concrete plan, I spent several days in Grozny in September 1997. Only there was it possible to understand every detail about how to secure the safety of the personnel from international humanitarian organizations, on the one hand, and guarantee that aid got through to those intended, on the other. Leaving aside my other impressions, I will say a few words about the humanitarian situation in Chechnya at that time.

My Chechen interlocutors said that since August 1996, or for more than a year, not a single pill or any other pharmaceutical supplies had reached them. The problem of childhood nutrition was extremely acute. Production facilities in Chechnya had been totally destroyed, and Moscow had done nothing to remedy the situation, getting away with making formal replies. Through its embassy the Russian Foreign Ministry was blocking all efforts from abroad to supply humanitarian aid to Chechnya.

The infrastructure of secondary and higher education, as well as of public health, was also destroyed. As of September 1, 1997, poverty kept one of every five children from attending school. Parents lacked the funds to clothe, shoe, feed, or send their children to boarding schools. The epidemiological situation was extremely worrisome. Experts predicted that in a year to a year and a half, one out of every three residents of Chechnya would be infected with tuberculosis. Under any scenario, containing the epidemic within the boundaries of the republic would be impossible. The situation was fraught with the danger that other serious epidemics might also occur.

To initiate wide-scale international action, all Rybkin had to do was sign a single letter (albeit to many addresses). But he was not too lazy to cross out every letter, which was very unusual. I was unable to receive an explanation regarding such an unexpected finale to something that he had earlier agreed to. From then on I began to withdraw from the problem of Chechnya.

As a self-sufficient egocentric, Kokoshin initially believed he could manage without a staff. For some reason he smugly announced this publicly, but he was soon convinced otherwise. After his dismissal he inflicted official punishments on entirely innocent officials for failing to implement the president's directives, which they had not even seen. Kokoshin simply piled the presidential papers onto his desk, where they remained without any action being taken. He was interested only in nonproliferation and export controls. His rudeness to his subordinates was legendary.

Bordiuzha was the most capable of the secretaries of the Security Council for whom I worked. He impressed me as an honest, energetic man, who worked hard with only a short break for a nap. Consequently, he often fell into a somnambulistic state. Sergei Ivanov struck even people who had been around a while with his superficiality, hypocrisy, and prejudices. Every feature of his face radiated self-infatuation and fox-like cunning, his speech was vacuous, and he dressed garishly.

Living in a hall of distorting mirrors that reflected false information, residual dogmas, and ideological clichés; not forgetting their personal interests for a single second; and being manipulated by their subordinates, the Kremlin bosses were incapable of adequately responding to the sum total of Russia's domestic and foreign problems, which they themselves often created with their mistaken decisions. Sergei Dovlatov thought that hell is within us.[3] It is difficult not to agree. But Russian satirical writings (and drawings) on the model of Francisco Goya's *Los caprichos* show how easy it is to create a man-made hell in just a short time.

The Woes of Diplomacy

The Russian diplomatic service also disintegrated. After the Bolshevik coup d'état, it began to acquire genuine professionalism only when Stalinist repressions came to an end in 1953. This service is an extremely complex and sensitive mechanism that not only involves vertical and horizontal coordination within the Foreign Ministry in Moscow and between the ministry and its overseas representatives but also among different generations of diplomats. Here I am referring to the Russian diplomatic school from the prerevolutionary period that trained generations of diplomats and was destroyed by the Bolshevik putsch. Under Stalin it could not be revived because of the repressions. Therefore, a diplomatic academy could not really become an effective establishment until after 1953. I do not mean to suggest that in the interim there were no leading figures in Soviet diplomacy; in fact, just such persons founded the diplomatic school.

The art of diplomacy merits separate treatment since it represents a universal system of sophisticated sensors of a country's position in the international arena and the resolution of problems. Diplomats abroad naturally operate within the framework of instructions received from the Foreign Ministry. Ideally these representatives act as sensory organs of the governments they represent in the countries to which they are accredited, and they participate in the making of policy.

At the start of perestroika the USSR Ministry of Foreign Affairs was largely staffed with more or less qualified personnel. It contained several schools of thought and was able to fulfill a wide variety of assignments, from achieving mutually acceptable agreements to conducting a policy of sharp confrontation, from manifesting every sort of dogmatism to cooperating with foreign countries. After the fall of the USSR, however, not only was the leadership of all its departments changed but also many of the best-trained and qualified officials left the ministry.

Loathsomeness and desolation—both material and intellectual-moral—reigned after the merger of the Russian and USSR Ministries of Foreign Affairs. The daily routine of foreign policy, constituting the larger and basic part of the work, fell into a deplorable state. For all the negative aspects of the Soviet system that were overcome only toward the end of Gorbachev's rule, that system appeared almost ideal compared to the "early" Yeltsin era when incompetence and dissipation characterized the foreign service.

Important issues were left virtually unstudied. Basically, the inertia of Soviet approaches prevailed. In fact, no matter how paradoxical it may seem, sometimes the approaches were more reactionary than during Gorbachev's perestroika. The reactionaries in Yeltsin's entourage were taking their revenge. Yeltsin himself made off-the-cuff remarks and then took childish offense when his Western partners failed to understand him.

When the Russian Ministry of Foreign Affairs absorbed the USSR Ministry of Foreign Affairs, it felt like an occupation. To be sure, at times it went off without a hitch as in the department where I worked. In the process of reorganization that naturally occurred, the dismissal of some officials often turned into an internecine struggle for survival, settling of personal accounts, and attempts to secure one's own "warm seat" via unscrupulous means.[4] Only a handful of leaders in the USSR Foreign Ministry refrained from taking part in these unscrupulous games. A majority of the new leaders of Russian foreign policy and diplomacy either lacked any practical work experience or had skipped several rungs on the career ladder and lacked the requisite experience. In many cases this led to a dearth of sufficient professionalism or to the acme of servility. The result was that they made ill-considered and contradictory decisions, and documents—including secret, presidential, and other decisions and instructions—vanished into thin air. Some of those in leadership positions ran off to consult with foreign embassies on domestic as well as international problems and openly rustled their papers there. Corruption flowered luxuriantly. Hardly bothering to conceal it, diplomats received rewards from firms for lobbying on their behalf and for other services. The mechanism for foreign policy decision making went out of kilter. Minister of Foreign Affairs Andrei Kozyrev was subordinate to the incompetent, narcissistic, and peculiar Gennady Burbulis, who held the post of state secretary.

To escape the avalanche of not only unnecessary but sometimes harmful and nerve-wracking work on a pitiful salary, which was inadequate even to buy food, I accepted a lengthy overseas assignment in Geneva.

High-level work at the Foreign Ministry headquarters performed under normal circumstances produces constant intellectual and nervous stress. Diplomatic service abroad is entirely different. First, in the majority of Russian overseas diplomatic postings, there is usually nothing that can really be called work. Basically, one spends one's workday in the leisurely and rather boring perusal of newspapers and in reading mostly vacuous ciphered telegrams that are worth neither writing nor reading. (This is after reviewing the huge piles of paper from Moscow; many of the "top" papers require prompt and, sometimes, not at all obvious responses.) Of course, occasionally there are bursts of activity, but most of the art of being a Russian diplomat abroad consists of doing nothing while appearing to be extremely busy.

The complete, literally slavish dependence upon the leading members of the diplomatic corps explains a great deal, including the atmosphere of subservience. Diplomats in any normal country receive a salary and decide on their own how to spend it, but in the Russian diplomatic service, everything is different. There is a small salary along with an apartment, car, and furniture provided by the diplomatic representative office. Russian diplomats cannot choose where to live, what to drive, or how to furnish their homes.

Such paternalism may be partly justified considering a certain pathological greediness exhibited by some holders of Russian diplomatic passports. For example, in New York the parents of one child skimped so much on food that the local authorities were forced to intervene. Some were eating canned cat and dog food. Some were living practically in darkness since they had to pay for electricity from their own pockets; some closed off almost all their rooms in winter so as not to have to heat them and huddled in only a single room. And just look at how many of them dressed! That provided the best evidence of how the concept of a proper life was an abstraction for very many of them. The real question is quite different: why should the system depend upon such people?

After the collapse of the USSR, almost all my colleagues had an extremely distorted notion of diplomacy. They were unfamiliar with the definition of diplomacy as a science and an art, as the application of mind and tact. They did not realize that a diplomat should study a problem, understand what his country's interests were with regard to that problem, work out appropriate recommendations to the government, and, if they were accepted, make every effort to implement them.

The main criteria for assessing the work of diplomats in foreign postings as well as the diplomats themselves are the quality rather than the quantity of their dispatches and, even more, the effectiveness of their work. In the case of Russian diplomats, hardly anyone was bothered that almost all their cables were copied from the press and that many of them bore only a distant resemblance to reality. The record breaker in this connection was Mikhail Fradkov, a future prime minister and later chief of the Foreign Intelligence Service, who was then the ambassador to the European Union. This worthy insisted that every diplomat must write no fewer than four telegrams per week. His directive produced a veritable paper blizzard rather than useful information. Most of the dispatches were copied from the local media; the telegrams contradicted each other, relayed unverified information, and unsubstantiated interpretations and commentaries. Quantity was the name of the game.

Another peculiarity of the diplomatic service was that nobody ever knew who was really who. For example, a chauffeur or a workman might turn out to be a high-ranking officer of the spe-

cial services, a diplomatic courier, or even one of the top political leaders, as occurred with the chargé d'affaires in Lithuania on
the eve of World War II.

Groveling in front of and being completely dependent on one's
superior and lacking any sort of real work led to absolute idleness
and to lying. (What could you do when you had to demonstrate
nonexistent work?) It also led to such a disastrous state of affairs
in the Russian foreign diplomatic service that it was tantamount
to an epidemic of alcoholism.

When I arrived in Geneva, Fradkov was already working there.
Geneva became the launching pad for a dizzying career. From
senior counselor he catapulted to deputy minister of foreign trade,
then minister, deputy secretary of the Security Council, head of
the tax police, Russian representative to the European Union with
the rank of federal minister, prime minister, and then chief of the
Foreign Intelligence Service.

During Fradkov's service as Russia's permanent representative
in Brussels, he demanded unquestioning submission to the most
unrealizable and extravagant directives. His favorite response,
which he literally squeezed out of his subordinates, was the military response: "Yes, sir!" He permitted no one to doubt his infallibility. On one occasion one of the most obsequious diplomats dared
to doubt the practicality of an outlandishly extravagant directive:

"Mikhail Yefimovich, and what if it doesn't work out?"

"How could that be? Not work out?" roared the special representative of the president with the rank of federal minister. "That would
be betrayal of the M-m-motherland! Just watch what you're saying!"

He really loved to repeat, "Better watch your step! Don't get out
of line! . . . There should be a paper for everything so that every
trace of our work is preserved!"

Here is a significant brushstroke in his portrait and perhaps in
his schemes for power. Judging from several indicators, Fradkov
already knew that he would soon be appointed prime minister. He
let us know that Putin frequently called him on his mobile phone.
What striking hypocrisy! In order to maintain security—the unsecured building of the permanent representative was totally open
to eavesdropping—he forbade anyone to carry mobile phones.

His own telephone rang in the single secured facility ("the sub-marine"), which he never allowed anyone else to enter.

Rudeness bordering on outright boorishness was inbred in him. He was pathologically disrespectful toward others. He suffered from both mediocrity and a Napoleon complex. He viewed everyone else as members of the common herd, dirt, and at best the hoi polloi. To an unprecedented degree he promoted a culture of informers in the mission that astounded even those who had seen everything from Soviet times. (Speaking of everyone, I include clandestine officers of the special services who were working under diplomatic cover.) His style of behavior was redolent of the Soviet past and familiar to anyone who has lived in the USSR.

While working in Geneva I had occasion to encounter a number of other more or less well-known persons. The strongest impression was produced by Minister of Emergency Situations Sergei Shoigu, whose brief sojourn in Geneva illustrates many of the special features of the Russian foreign diplomatic service. Permanent Representative to the UN Office Yevgeny Makeyev, who really disliked me—a feeling I reciprocated—was terribly apprehensive about Shoigu's arrival. In addition to requesting that I draft various memoranda and reference materials, he ordered me to prepare a critical dossier on Shoigu and his ministry in order to have arguments at hand in case the minister criticized him.

As soon as Shoigu arrived, Makeyev handed him this analysis of the errors and omissions of the Ministry of Emergency Situations, along with public accusations printed in the press, and said, "Andrei Anatol'evich has prepared this for your arrival." Naturally Shoigu immediately hated me and barred me from all of his meetings, heedless that others were simply not up to speed on the problems. Therefore, I played no role at all in preparations for his major assignment during this mission, a discussion with UN High Commissioner for Refugees Sadako Ogata.

During that meeting various facts and figures arose, but these facts and figures were erroneous. The discussion almost produced a major scandal. Returning from the discussion, Shoigu asked a classic Russian question: who among the Russian diplomats was guilty of Ogata's not having been briefed for her discussion with him? (Needless to say, Ogata had been splendidly briefed but by her own colleagues; Russian diplomats had nothing to do with it, nor could they have had.) The immediate response, however, was: "Kovalev." "Get rid of him," Shoigu commanded in his usual style.

In the evening an event was held at the Office of the Permanent Representative that, as usual, I did not attend. Later I was told that the chauffeur of our mission, who was sitting right behind Shoigu, clapped him on the shoulder and invited him into the sauna. Shoigu thus declined an invitation to dine with the ambassador, saying, "I have already agreed to visit the sauna with your chauffeur." The chauffeur was no ordinary person; he was an officer of the special services who had gone to Geneva to take a breather. In his capacity as a chauffeur, he performed his basic duties, including engaging in numerous intrigues. And the chauffeur said to the minister, "Don't touch Kovalev." Shoigu listened to him as the chauffeur was appointed to a high-ranking position in his ministry.

Later Shoigu demanded that his colleagues urgently procure cash to pay officials of his ministry who had worked in the former Yugoslavia. This was done, not without difficulty. Immediately afterward he sent a fax, which he personally signed, saying that his colleagues should receive a piddling share of the money due them. One can only guess where the rest of it went.

Incidentally, it should be noted that Sergei Shoigu holds the record for the longest tenure as the head of a state organ in Russia, having headed the Ministry of Emergency Situations from 1991 through all the successive governments until 2012. For a short time, he shifted to be governor of the Moscow Region and then became minister of defense in November 2012. Shoigu was undoubtedly a fitting symbol and sign of the period that Russia was going through. He rescued everyone and everything, including Russian history, from "falsification" as the prime mover in initiatives to produce the "definitive" official version of Russia's past.[5] In 1996 he directed Yeltsin's election campaign in the Russian Federation, then he actively supported Putin on his path to becoming the president. In 2000 he headed the Unity Party upon whose foundation its successor, United Russia, was subsequently established.

No one dared speak ill of Shoigu—not about his corruption, his extreme personal moral deficiency, or his being a petty tyrant. This silence reflected his basic strength: Everyone feared him. Everyone fawned upon him.

With rare exceptions I took no pleasure at all in associating with other well-known persons in Russia. I was absolutely stunned by my namesake Valentin Kovalev, who fancied himself the leading jurist in the country because of his position as minister of justice. Later he became notorious for misappropriating state funds and for corruption. He flew to Geneva escorted by a number of desperadoes who were listed as his assistants. They immediately rushed off to rent an armored Mercedes with tinted windows, for the embassy limousine was not to Kovalev's liking. He saw the main outcome of the war in Chechnya as the signing of a presidential directive that supposedly established the legality of this crime. Another such notable was the director of Russia's Federal Migration Service Tatyana Regent, who impressed people with her total incompetence and indifference toward the issues she handled. I met other notable persons as well. My acquaintance with the human rights advocate Sergei Kovalev, for instance, turned into a genuine friendship.

As much as possible I tried not to sit behind a microphone during sessions of the UN in order to avoid situations where I would have to denounce someone for criticizing Russian military atrocities in Chechnya or the Baltic representatives, whom I liked. At one event a scandal developed over Latvia. I felt ashamed about Russian policy toward the Baltic states. After acknowledging during the late Soviet era the existence of secret protocols to the Molotov-Ribbentrop Pact that had enabled the USSR's occupation of the Baltic states, subsequently, with incredible offhandedness, Russia changed its position and denied that the takeover of Latvia, Lithuania, and Estonia in 1940 had been an occupation. Russia delayed the withdrawal of troops from these countries. The pretext—that is, the need to stay and defend the Russian-speaking population—was particularly rich. I found all of this extremely distasteful and tried to avoid an altercation.

Latvia's ambassador to the UN branch offices in Geneva, Sandra Kalniete—later the ambassador to Paris, the minister of foreign affairs, and a member of the European Parliament—is a very sharp-minded diplomat and a pleasant interlocutor. We agreed that neither of us wanted a battle of words and harmoniously compiled a list of critical points to which neither of us would react. As a result the public squabble ceased, and a dialogue began. My colleagues called me a Latvian spy.

A lack of professionalism leads to absolutism, peremptoriness, and mediocrity. Unfortunately, this was a common reality. For example, working in the Russian Security Council I practically had to conduct a campaign to eradicate ignorance regarding the Conference on Security and Cooperation in Europe at a meeting of second- and third-ranking officials in ministries and departments, including the intelligence agencies. They sincerely believed that the accords' "third basket" provided a basis for a military incursion into Chechnya "under the pretext of defending human rights." Such ignorance regarding international rights and politics became increasingly evident after the collapse of the USSR, although many of those who implemented policy in Soviet times were also hardly distinguished by their erudition. For example, I was literally shocked on one occasion when I was asked to review the suitability for publication of a scholarly monograph written by a retired colonel of the General Staff who had worked all his life on problems concerning NATO. I encountered striking evidence that this former intelligence officer was ignorant of the text of the North Atlantic Treaty's founding document and the principles and operational mechanism of NATO's military organization. I could extend this sorry list of glaring incompetence that I witnessed, but these two examples provide sufficient evidence of the level of qualifications and knowledge of those in power and the persons who worked for them.

When Putin came to power, he created an almost ideal mendacious and hypocritical regime that combined the demagoguery of Soviet totalitarianism that he was intimately familiar with, partly from his "undercover" work for the Soviet Embassy in the German Democratic Republic, and the dirty tricks and technological activities of the special services. Consequently, he succeeded in winning the trust not only of those of his fellow citizens who were susceptible to vacuous but beautiful words but also of many persons abroad. A KGB officer is accustomed to playing to his interlocutor and lying in order to ingratiate himself and not fail in his current mission. What sort of an agent would he be otherwise? If he makes a mistake, he immediately wriggles out of it; moreover, others always prepare the ground in advance to implement his plan. But if the plan fails, then he makes every effort to deny his own role in the unsuccessful provocation. This is hardly the mark of diplomacy.

As a staff member of the Security Council, I was well aware that Putin said exactly what each one of his foreign interlocutors wanted to hear. Putin was not in the least embarrassed that he said diametrically opposite things in conversation with his next interlocutor. There is a bit of Russian jargon meaning "to play the role of an agent." Thus, Putin, an old hand at putting on an act, does it with everyone in succession. As the saying goes, a fish rots from the head.

Unfortunately, my observations are very relevant to contemporary Russian diplomacy and political life as a whole. In sum, most of what transpired in the headquarters of the Russian Foreign Ministry and its missions abroad makes for a rather dismal picture.

There is a saying in Russian, "If you have power, you don't need intelligence." At some point in Russian history this became a virtual call for action, a kind of distillation of the absolute. The well-known result of the mindless buildup of military and other means of coercion was the defeat of the USSR in the Cold War and its subsequent collapse. While diplomacy is one of the key intellectual centers of any country, unfortunately, once again Russian diplomacy is not up to the current challenges.

Some Russians nurture a pathological hatred of European civilization. This hatred, which I personally abhor, derives from a morbid rejection of everything outside the parameters of the familiar rules and stereotypes drilled into their heads by the Bolsheviks and their miserable existence, according to which, for example, slavery and filth are natural. This hatred will prevent Russia from becoming a civilized country in the foreseeable future. It will continue to cringe before any supposedly elected authorities and to revel in its own abnormality until at least a third generation has grown to maturity in conditions of freedom, democracy, and, correspondingly, of self-respect. Incidentally, those who call themselves patriots consist predominantly of the xenophobic public.

Returning to the subject of the post-Soviet breakdown of the Foreign Ministry, one must give Yeltsin or his puppet masters their due. After numerous failures to fill the position of foreign minister of Russia when it was still part of the USSR, he appointed the young and talented diplomat Andrei Kozyrev to the post. However, Kozyrev lacked sufficient knowledge and experience to become a powerful and influential minister of foreign affairs of one of the greatest world powers during the nadir of its transformation. Most of all he lacked the trust and support of the president, who was being manipulated by the special services.

In the first half of the 1990s, Russian foreign policy was a rather strange amalgam of a progressive, pro-Western orientation on some issues along with the most utterly reactionary and vengeful approaches toward, for example, Latvia and Estonia, as well as support for the criminal activities of Slobodan Milošević in Serbia and Radovan Karadžić in Bosnia. Such dualism derived from the interests of players involved in intra-governmental conflict in which foreign policy often played the role of small change. Kozyrev himself was basically interested in the domestic situation. On his watch the diplomatic service lost its professionalism and creativity to a significant degree, but despite the massive exodus from the ministry of its most talented officials, the service nevertheless managed, barely, to survive.

Yevgeny Primakov, who replaced Kozyrev as foreign minister, was largely responsible for destroying the diplomatic service. He sharply changed the direction of Russian foreign policy, denied its humanitarian role, and "tightened the screws" inside the ministry. All this was done while Russia was diplomatically impotent. (Incidentally, when Primakov was appointed prime minister and was flying to the United States on a visit on March 24, 1999, he ordered the pilots to turn his plane around over the Atlantic and head to Moscow as a protest over the start of NATO's bombing of Yugoslavia. This act was enthusiastically welcomed by supporters of confrontation with the West, but it bore no resemblance whatsoever to the practice of diplomacy.) After Primakov's appointment as Russian foreign minister in January 1996, Russia's foreign policy almost instantly became anti-Western. NATO was proclaimed our prime enemy, just as during the Cold War, and our allies included Milošević; Alexander Lukashenko of Belarus, known in the West as "Europe's last dictator"; and Primakov's old friend Saddam Hussein. Russia began to consort with anti-Western regimes. Consequently, at that point many of the remaining creative and democratically inclined officials left the diplomatic service.

When he became prime minister, it seemed that Primakov made a good choice in naming Igor Ivanov as his successor. Ivanov knew the Foreign Ministry very well and had worked as deputy director of the foreign minister's secretariat. (He was effectively in charge of current and operational matters under Eduard Shevardnadze when the Soviet Ministry of Foreign Affairs was on an upswing.) But here, too, a misstep occurred. Ivanov did something unbelievable: he appointed his acquaintances from the secretariat to leading positions in the Foreign Ministry even though the scope of the secretariat's activity was very specific. To be sure, the secretariat did employ some natural talents who were willing to question their superiors' judgment, but they were the exceptions. The general rule in the secretariat was subservience. "What would you like me to do, sir?" It was precisely these kinds of persons whom Ivanov promoted. From then on Russian diplomacy became irrevocably the domain of lackeys. There is no other way to describe a service whose officials were devoid of any convictions or, if they had any, carefully concealed them. That was not how things were even in the bad, old Soviet times. Back then, professionalism, which demanded a thorough knowledge of problems as well as experience, had been the foundation on which one's positions were based.

Frequently diplomats could neither do what they thought was necessary nor act as they thought was correct. Of course, the desire to make a career is a normal phenomenon. But by what means? By knowledge, professionalism, mastering one's brief? Or by an automatic and mindless obsequiousness, servility, and intellectual and moral subservience? Unfortunately, right after the breakup of the USSR, the latter approach began to predominate in the Ministry of Foreign Affairs. Of course, there had always been ministry officials who made their careers via cringing, but their careers generally never got very far. The purge of the USSR Foreign Ministry after its merger with the Russian Foreign Ministry caused irreparable harm to the diplomatic service. Kozyrev's directive establishing white, gray, and blacklists for advancing further in the diplomatic service severely damaged the attitudes and esprit of diplomats at every level. Although it was not his intent, with this purge of the apparatus, Kozyrev provided a false moral reference point for the ministry. Under Primakov the liberals had to hide their convictions; everyone held their fingers to the wind. Then Ivanov made toadyism the law.

Starting with Ivanov, diplomatic work became meaningless as well as devoid of purpose and substance since toadyism is inconsistent with diplomacy. Under his sway, work consisted basically of drafting triumphant reports on the mythical achievements of our foreign policy. No one felt any need to amend previously staked-out positions.

Sergei Lavrov, who replaced Ivanov in 2004 and remains Russia's foreign minister at present, is the faithful executor of the most noxious directives from higher-level government authorities. He is even more reactionary than Yevgeny Primakov was.

The Russian Diplomatic Academy as it had existed earlier became a thing of the past. Many of those who considered themselves its supporters actually parodied it. The art of dialogue and finding mutually acceptable solutions ceased being integral parts of Russian diplomacy. Instead, it began to discharge functions that were not essential to this type of activity. Its distinguishing characteristics were provocation, demagoguery, disinformation, ignorance and misunderstanding of its subject matter, and a degree of dogmatism that was unprecedented even in Soviet times. (Parenthetically, it might be noted that the long-serving Soviet minister of foreign affairs during the Cold War Andrei Gromyko—known as "Mister No"—looks like a profound foreign policy thinker in comparison with some of the Russian Federation's ministers. On occasion, Gromyko exhibited both common sense and sparks of creativity in what he did. I am referring in the first instance to the policy of détente and agreements to reduce the danger of war.)

The pompous facade of the tall building housing the Russian Foreign Ministry hides the loathsomeness and desolation within. I am not referring to the swarms of cockroaches inside but to other "delights" unworthy of a self-respecting headquarters. The main problem is the wasteland inside the heads of those serving in it. A diplomatic service that proposed employing nuclear weapons in domestic conflicts such as that in Chechnya has no right to be called by that name. Diplomacy shorn of any sense—what could be sadder and more unnatural?

Postscript to an Epoch of Hope

In the process of dismantling Soviet totalitarianism, colleagues who shared my democratic ideals and I tried to get rid of sticky, omnipresent spiderwebs. At their center was an enormous, ideological law enforcement Spider that had earlier been called the leadership of the Communist Party and the KGB—in short, the TsK GB, or the Central Committee of State Security. After the breakup of the USSR, neither the CPSU nor the KGB existed any longer under their prior names, but the monster behind them survived essentially unchanged.

In totalitarian states the Spiders are rather different from those depicted in scholarly literature. This particular Spider does not kill all those who fall into its web. The basic poison it deploys is hypnosis, which it uses to manipulate the people of Russia. When the poison failed to work, the Lenin-Stalin era Spider dispatched its victims to the GULAG, the country's most important building sites, which were founded on slave labor. It also sent people there to meet the "needs of production"; moreover, the production demands continued into the post-Stalin period.

The Spider now has other means at its disposal as well—from shooting to depriving one's freedom to administering polonium-210 (which was used to kill Alexander Litvinenko in London in 2006). Punitive psychiatry, which worked for the totalitarian Spider and was terminated only toward the end of Gorbachev's perestroika, has been revived under Putin's "vertical of power."

Unlike in an ordinary spiderweb, the Alpha Spider in the totalitarian spiderweb coexisted with smaller spiders.

The threads of the totalitarian spiderweb entangled the entire country, including almost every single person. It snagged them organizationally via the Communist Party, the Soviet government, the professional organizations, and, of course, the law enforcement organs—namely, the KGB and the militia, which worked for this monster. It also ensnared the people psychologically and morally via the hypnosis of their upbringing and education; through the state means of mass information, intimidation, and punishment of dissidents; and through the powerful system of mythmaking that few could stand up to. Feeding on human flesh and human souls, the spiders acquired and maintained power and material benefits. The Alpha Spider could not have held out for long without the Beta, Gamma, and other smaller spiders: the leaders of ministries and departments, local bosses, bureau heads.

Twice the Spider loosened its grip on the totalitarian spiderweb. The first time was in the period of Khrushchev's thaw following Stalin's death. During Gorbachev's reforms of the late 1980s and in the early Yeltsin period, the spiderweb thinned out, and the weakened Spider sitting at its center became even more embittered and even more eager to catch its prey. Russia was at a crossroads after the breakup of the USSR. The future fate of the country depended on whether the Spider would succeed in restoring its spiderweb. Paradoxically the democratic reforms impregnated the totalitarian monster, and its young spread out all over Russia, even venturing beyond its borders.

After the failure of the attempted 1991 coup d'état, it seemed that the totalitarian web had been broken and the Spider had breathed its last. This widely shared delusion was caused when the communist totalitarian ideology seemingly had vanished in virtually an instant. In reality everything turned out otherwise. During Yeltsin's presidency, the mechanism of totalitarianism and the suppression of the individual already began to regain strength. The KGB was disbanded, but it was replaced by new special services, each of which encroached upon human rights in its own way and frequently interfered with the authority of the other special services. (For example, under Yeltsin the Presidential Guard Service along with the Federal Security Service substituted for the then supposedly nonexistent political police and intervened in politics and in the "sorting-out process" between businessmen and others.) The CPSU, the "ruling and guiding force of Soviet society," returned under Putin with the new name of United Russia; its program consisted solely of supporting him. Officials from the special services and the military occupied the leading positions in both foreign and domestic policy as well as the economy. There was no place in Russia for an ordinary citizen, nor any respect for his or her rights. Concepts of national security, grandeur, and geopolitics reigned. The old monster of totalitarianism was reborn and grew vigorously. Although it appeared in a different form than in the Soviet period, its spiderweb became unprecedentedly dense, solid, and suffocating.

Thus, all the attempts to destroy the spiderweb that had entangled Russia failed. Its strands were stronger and held the people in their grip. This occurred in large part because the masses blamed the disasters that overtook the country on the democratic changes from the late 1980s and early 1990s. For example, it was democracy rather than the bitter opposition to it that many people associated with the shootings in Tbilisi, Nagorno-Karabakh, and Vilnius. This misconception greatly strengthened the Spider's web, especially during Yeltsin's presidency when the special services, which had striven hard to discredit democracy, began crawling back to power.

The majority of the authentic Russian intellectual elite seems entangled by strands of fear or strands of money and material goods. Intellect is also a commodity, but the Russian word *intelligentsia* denotes intellectuals who are burdened with convictions and a conscience. By no means do I oppose or wish to denigrate either of the two concepts; I simply point out that in Russian the word *intellectual* has a somewhat different meaning than in the West, where, for example, it is not unusual for intellectuals to resign from the government when they disagree with its activities. As for Russian intellectuals, a category to which several members of the Putin government must be assigned, their moans of disagreement with what is going on, along with their zealous implementation of its most dubious missions, merely evoke feelings of squeamishness. This contrast is precisely why it is necessary to stipulate that membership in a particular elite is not defined either by the position one occupies or by one's social status. For example, it would be wrong to include in the category of "intellectual elite" the most successful persons of the Putin-Medvedev period, those occupying the most important government positions and boasting incalculable fortunes. Nor can those intellectuals who traded in their convictions for a variety of benefits be included within this "elite."

The condition of the Russian elite raises another point of concern since it is the quality of the elite that defines the level of society and its value. After the breakup of the USSR, the "political elite" appeared to change. In reality, however, it remained essentially the same and was headed by Yeltsin, who had been a staunch communist. Moreover, its quality deteriorated as its ranks swelled with officers and agents of the special services.

Members of the scientific and artistic elite were squeezed on one side by their fear of a return to the past and, on the other, by their own impoverishment and that of Russia as a whole. These twin pressures led members of the creative professions to trip over themselves to support President Yeltsin and the authorities. The natural consequence was their loss of internal freedom, one that subsequently accelerated with the state's takeover of the mass media. With the elimination of the Fourth Estate, a victory that Putin celebrated at the beginning of his administration, Russia reverted to the Soviet practice of unremitting mass hypnosis of the people.

The widespread diffusion of computers, the Internet, and mobile phones has significantly increased the sensitivity of the spiderweb to any sort of deviation from the Spider's needs. While comfortably sitting in an armchair, one may easily read others' correspondence and listen not only to their phone conversations but also to those conversations conducted close by when equipped with listening devices.

The evolution of the spiderweb in post-Soviet times is extremely paradoxical. The first and greatest paradox is that for a large majority of the population, the Russians' quest for freedom began to make significant progress with the reforms of Gorbachev and Yeltsin but was soon replaced by a nostalgia for the order of the Stalinist dictatorship or, at best, for the era of stagnation (1964–85). This shift occurred partly because the reforms were deliberately compromised by elements of the state apparatus, the Central Committee, the KGB, and the economic planners during Gorbachev's perestroika; by the active efforts of the special services under Yeltsin; and, after Putin's assumption of power, by all the state information and propaganda agencies. The fall in living standards and quality of life also inevitably had an impact, as many people associated the decline with the democratic reforms.

A second paradox lies in how the totalitarian Soviet regime, which ruthlessly uprooted any kind of nonconformism, itself greatly helped to strengthen the dissident movement in the USSR, in particular, by signing the Final Act of the Conference on Security and Cooperation in Europe. Of course, the movement arose earlier, but it changed significantly following the signing of the Helsinki Act, which included the third basket dedicated to human rights. Was this a mistake on the part of the regime? In reality, a fascinating chess match had played out between conservatives and proponents of liberalization in the USSR during the process whereby participating states of the CSCE reached accord on the Final Act.

The basic mission assigned to the Soviet delegation in Helsinki was to "confirm the results of the Second World War and postwar development," and that meant, in part, the division of Germany. Thus, the Soviets' main issue at the CSCE was gaining acceptance of the principle of the inviolability of borders in their current configuration. Naturally, the Western partners understood this very well and made every possible use of this Soviet concern to include provisions regarding human rights in the Final Act. Thanks in part to the efforts of Anatoly Kovalev, head of the Soviet delegation, the Soviet leadership found itself in a situation where it could achieve its goal only via compromise, ensuring the principle of the inviolability of borders in exchange for accepting the third basket. Since Soviet leader Brezhnev repeatedly said to his inner circle that he could die in peace after acceptance of the Final Act's "confirming the results of the war and postwar development," resolving the issue of the third basket was facilitated.[6]

The third paradox is that despite the efforts undertaken to establish democracy in Russia after Gorbachev's advent to power, democracy did not take root. After getting a taste of ersatz democracy and not realizing it was only an imitation of the real thing, the people spat it out. This made it possible for the Kremlin to destroy the multibillionaire oil magnate Mikhail Khodorkovsky in 2003 and openly exact its revenge upon him. The story of the government's seizure of his company YUKOS and the arrest of Khodorkovsky, the richest person in Russia, after he was suspected of having presidential ambitions vividly illustrated the status of freedom of entrepreneurship and of political and civil rights. Without delving into Khodorkovsky's activity per se, from a legal perspective the essence of the matter is that he became the *only "oligarch" punished for what everyone was doing; that is, it was a case of selective justice.* Many observers asserted that Khodorkovsky's first trial meant the end of an independent system of justice in Russia.

Corruption is another tsarina of justice in Russia. Lawyers say students at law school lectures are told the following anecdote: One side in a trial gave a bribe to the judge, and the other side gave a bribe that was twice as large. The judge, after thinking it over, accepted only half of the latter bribe, saying, "Now your chances in court are equal."

It is not only in court that corruption encroaches upon the rights of Russians. It is a phenomenon throughout Russia. Government and municipal officials are corrupt, as are the militia, doctors, and teachers. The most dangerous aspect is that the Kremlin and the Russian White House are corrupt. The halls of power have turned into a kind of closed joint-stock company where outsiders are not admitted. By its very nature the virtually blatant commercialization of power destroys human rights, democracy, and common sense. It seems that the Russian authorities have outstripped Napoleon's famous minister of foreign affairs Talleyrand, who sold and betrayed everyone and everything—except France itself. The authorities' looting of Russia indeed constitutes a form of betrayal.

Pervasive corruption is due to the people's extremely low wages. Massive poverty also engenders many other problems, among them prostitution, including of children, and an unprecedented number of cases of syphilis, tuberculosis, and other illnesses induced by social conditions. The exacerbation of social problems, together with the subservience to authority cultivated by the communists, renders political and civil rights of secondary importance, if not totally illusory.

This is especially so because from the moment he came to power, Putin strove to ensure that society received only the information that he approved. His first steps as head of state were directed toward extinguishing the freedom of the mass media. After liquidating Vladimir Gusinskii's influential independent media holding company Media-Most, Putin then subordinated TV's Channel One, previously controlled by Boris Berezovsky, to the Kremlin. Putin gradually pulled into his web other previously independent mass media. His reprimand to editor in chief Aleksei Venediktov of radio station Ekho Moskvy (Moscow echo) for Ekho's supposedly "incorrect" treatment of the war in Georgia demonstrates that the Russian authorities are even taking control of smaller media with extremely limited audiences. In this context particular attention should be paid to provincial media, which are often tightly controlled by the local authorities.

The suppression of freedom of opinion opened the floodgates for manipulating social awareness and for hypnotizing audiences with a force and effectiveness not at all inferior to, and perhaps even exceeding, the hypnosis of communist times. In Soviet times at least people believed in the possibility of something better—by which they meant democracy—but under Putin they have lost that faith. Against the protests of many people, Putin restored the music of the Soviet Union's anthem, to the strains of which Stalin carried out the genocide of his own people; made the communist red flag the banner of the Russian armed forces; erected a monument to Feliks Dzerzhinsky, the founding father of the Soviet secret police; and revived Stalin's popularity.

After the Orange Revolution in Ukraine, many young Russians began to cast aside their studies. In many Russian universities, rather than those who attended lectures and seminars, those students who joined the evocatively named Nashi (Ours)—the youth wing of Putin's party, United Russia—and took part in its activities were considered good students. Those who objected were bluntly informed there was no point in their continuing their studies. It also happened that students were taken from their studies to attend Russian Orthodox religious services.

Religious freedom in Russia has been imperiled since Soviet times, although the situation has changed since 1991. Russian authorities have used Russian Orthodoxy to fill the vacuum created by the collapse of communist ideology. The leaders of what the Constitution proclaims is a secular state do everything to show themselves as fervent Orthodox believers. To say the least, the authorities do not look favorably on other denominations and are particularly hostile toward Catholicism. The same people who in Soviet times shouted, "Glory to the CPSU," now with equal fervor shout, "Glory to God!"

Such a state of affairs is even more troubling, given the numerous publications that raise doubts about the moral profile of the top hierarchy of the Russian Orthodox Church. I am specifically referring to the fact that many of them, including the previous patriarch of Moscow and all of Russia, Aleksei II, were members of the KGB and to the financial and property manipulations of the Orthodox Church.

The authorities are also carefully nurturing aggressive nationalism and xenophobia. During Soviet times this was based on the need to frighten people with the specter of Russian Nazism. After the fall of the USSR the authorities intensified their efforts. News of interethnic differences and resulting related crimes became a part of everyday Russian life.

The spiderweb also entangled Western countries. Naturally, it would be naive to suppose that their governments did not see or understand what was going on in Russia. As far as I can judge, the move toward what might be called the "New Munich," in this case the appeasement of Russia, was due to very simple reasons. First was the West's fear of Russia's gigantic, destructive potential and of its unpredictable politics. Many Russians, including specialists in international relations, were convinced that the West hoped for all kinds of disasters to befall Russia. This delusion was the fruit of the psychology of the "defenders of the besieged fortress" who suffered from xenophobia and a persecution complex. The spider-web caught the West in another form as well—that is, the oil and gas that the West desired and that the infantile and vainglorious rulers of Russia turned from a national treasure into a weapon.

In a situation where the small number of oppositionists has been subjected to the Kremlin's manipulation and is suppressed by all possible means that are quickly written into law, to say nothing of political assassinations; when, to all appearances, a majority of the population supports Putin; and when the very word *democracy* has been turned into an imprecation, it seems that Russia has irrevocably become entangled in the spiderweb spun by the authorities and the people themselves. Is this so? Is there no hope? Yes, there is hope.

The Spider has imbibed so much blood and treasure that it is ready to burst, like the "model full-belly man" in the brilliant satire on Russian life by Arkady Strugatsky and Boris Strugatsky.[7] The answer to the question of when this will happen is very simple: it will happen when people stop mocking themselves, when they realize that they do not exist to serve as slaves for the authorities, and when they grasp that the authorities, who are no more than servants hired by the citizens of Russia to defend their rights and lawful interests, should work for them.

5

Inside the Secret Police State

"Order Number One for the complete seizure of power has been fulfilled. A group of FSB officers has successfully infiltrated the government." These words were pronounced in December 1999 in the headquarters of the KGB-FSB—the contemporary incarnation of the Cheka, the secret police force Lenin established in 1917— by the recently appointed head of state, Vladimir Putin. Apparently from his own experience, he confirmed that there's no such person as a "former" Chekist—that is, special service operative.

The advent to power in Russia of the special services is a unique phenomenon in world history, yet it seems fitting for Russia. The appropriate preconditions began to appear soon after the 1917 Bolshevik coup. Let us deduce these preconditions from the Bolshevik slogans that meant nothing in reality. We may recall the measures that the "revolutionaries" who came to power utilized in their "struggle against the autocracy"—namely, terrorist acts and robbery— and the measures they employed in ruling the country: the cynical abandonment of their own slogans; the massive terror campaigns to achieve their goals, including "suppressing counterrevolution" (often understood as nonconformism); the destruction of the peasantry including moderately well-off peasants with the proclamation of "collectivization" and "de-kulakization"; and the pursuit of industrialization via the hands of torturers in the GULAG. Setting demagogy aside, the only possible conclusion is that on November 7, 1917, terrorists and criminals seized power and then systematically transformed revolutionary terrorism into state terrorism.

Alexander Yakovlev, who is rightly considered the architect of perestroika as well as one of the most intelligent and honest persons of his time, wrote, "I came to the profound conviction that the October coup d'état was a counterrevolution that marked the beginning of a criminal-terrorist fascist-type state."[1]

Vladimir Bukovsky offered an interesting discussion of the nature of Soviet power:

> Sometimes . . . the self-destructive stubbornness of the authorities seemed simply unbelievable; however, we forget that terrorist power cannot be otherwise. The distinction between it and democratic power is that it is not a function of public opinion. In such a state people can have no rights—any inalienable right of the individual instantly deprives the state of an atom of its power. Every person is obliged to learn the axiom from childhood that never, under any circumstances, and by no means, will he ever be able to influence the authorities. Every decision comes only on initiative from above. Power is unshakable, infallible, and inexorable, and the only thing the whole world can do is to accommodate to it. One may beg mercy of it, but not make any demands. It has no use of conscientious citizens who demand legality; it needs only slaves. By the same token, it has no need of partners, only of satellites. Just like paranoids in the grip of their own fantasies, it cannot and does not want to recognize reality; it thrives on its delirium and imposes its own criteria on everyone.[2]

This kind of authority required a reliable and effective instrument to create an unprecedented form of slavery, including mental slavery, on the territory that it ruled. The Cheka, the All-Russia Emergency Commission, which ruthlessly uprooted all heresies, was such an instrument. Moreover, initially the activity of the Cheka was largely grounded in myths of its own devising. Just as the leadership of the "country of Soviets" viewed the USSR as a besieged fortress, a passion for spying became one of the favorite pastimes of the Russian authorities and an extremely important element of their politics. The period of greatest activity in this sphere was followed by a relative lull after the death of Stalin in 1953. It is hardly an accident that the leaders of the country's political police (for example, Feliks Dzerzhinsky, Nikolai Yezhov, Lavrenty Beriya, and Yury Andropov) were among its top leaders. But the special services remained *by the side of power* even when they were *in power*.

Yakovlev believed that a special form of rule developed in the USSR—that is, a dual power of the party and of the law enforcement organs.[3] "The Soviet state could not last for a single day without the punitive services," he wrote. "Such was its nature. And such being the case, the party had constantly to share power with the political police."[4] It may be that for all his wisdom and experience Yakovlev actually underestimated the power of the special services. Indeed, officials of the punitive services were necessarily members of the CPSU, but the special services were not controlled by the party. On the contrary, the authorities themselves were controlled by the special services at every level, from decision making on practically all matters, to listening in on telephone and other conversations of important officials and government leaders, to keeping tabs on them in other ways.

The monster created by Lenin, developed by Stalin, and, after the latter's death, nurtured by his successors up until the time of Gorbachev's reforms acquired unbelievable power. Its writ included ensuring the security of the regime and its leaders, conducting political investigations, performing the functions of intelligence and counterintelligence, preserving state secrets and maintaining the regime's confidentiality, protecting government communications, guarding the state borders, and dealing with virtually all the other questions that were even marginally connected with the concept of state security, a concept that had been boundlessly expanded to the point of utter madness. Almost every question came within its purview, in particular via the regime of secrecy, since during Soviet times almost everything was classified secret. Thus, the KGB was omnipresent even though not omniscient.

Overtly or covertly the KGB was everywhere. Every institution and many enterprises had a First Department, which comprised the official representatives of the security services. But this was a drop in the ocean compared to the covert activity of the KGB. The so-called active reserve, or officers of the special services who officially had nothing in common with the organs of state security, penetrated all of society. These employees of the Soviet special services were guaranteed a comfortable life. They could speak as they pleased and act as they pleased, while their interlocutors risked their future, their freedom, and even their lives at any moment. Moreover, employees of the "organs" were virtually guaranteed good career prospects and other perquisites in their official places of employment.

The special services were potentially able to become the ruling authorities on two occasions—after the death of Stalin in March 1953, when Lavrenty Beriya made a bid for power but was soon condemned for treason and executed that December, and after the "election" of former chief of the KGB Andropov as general secretary of the Central Committee of the CPSU in 1982. There are two basic versions of the Andropov story. One of them holds that Andropov was not without traces of liberalism and that he was a sufficiently wise politician not to transform the country into the patrimony of the political police. The other version is diametrically opposite. Its adherents contend that Andropov aimed for a dictatorship of the special services and did not succeed in doing so because during his tenure as chairman of the KGB he elevated its role higher than at any period since Stalinist times. Yakovlev asserts that Andropov's ascent signified that the dream of the special services to lead the country had been achieved and that only Andropov's rapidly failing health—he died in February 1984, barely fifteen months after his rise to power—saved the country from a new round of mass repressions.

Various arguments are adduced in support of both hypotheses. Obviously, it would be rather extravagant to suspect a communist leader of Andropov's age and experience of "excessive" liberalism. It is likewise obvious that it was under Andropov (basically when he headed the KGB) that a significant hardening of the regime took place, including the exaltation of the KGB and the intensification of the struggle against nonconformists and dissenters. That this occurred under Andropov, however, does not mean it was his doing. One should not forget that the leadership included a great variety of persons and that Andropov could have been subjected to strong pressure from reactionaries within the highest circle of leaders. There is reason to believe that the Hungarian revolution in 1956, where the future KGB chief and general secretary was then serving as ambassador in Budapest, exerted a strong influence on him. Several persons close to him thought that Andropov sympathized with the Hungarian path of development, which differed significantly from the Soviet one. Others referred to him as suffering from a "Hungarian syndrome."

During and after the time he headed the International Department of the Central Committee of the CPSU, Andropov drew into his circle quite a few persons whose thinking diverged from what was then the norm. Such persons might be characterized as "within-system dissidents" and included Georgy Arbatov, Anatoly Kovalev, Alexander Bovin, Fyodor Burlatsky, and others. It was Andropov who, contrary to then minister of foreign affairs Gromyko, approved the third basket of the Final Act of the CSCE.

None of this is meant to whitewash perhaps the most enigmatic of all Soviet leaders; my sole objective is to avoid simplifying and schematizing the tangled history of the USSR. We may suppose that Andropov basically fit the general mold of gray Soviet leaders, but he was smarter and better educated than the others. He was a creative person who drafted his own papers—a rare bird among the CPSU leadership—encouraged free discussion among his subordinates, wrote but never published poetry, treasured the Soviet avant-garde and collected their art, and loved Picasso. Did he believe in the false dogmas of the "Founding Fathers" without giving them much thought? This is entirely possible. In any case, in some ways he stood out from the generally accepted norm of top Soviet leaders. One should not dismiss the words of Igor Andropov, son of the former secretary-general and an extraordinary and undoubtedly honest man: "My father always hated communism!"[5]

Be that as it may, the KGB—a power *within* power and, in some ways, a power *above* power—was doing very well until Gorbachev's liberal reforms began to gain momentum in the late 1980s. It may be that precisely these reforms provoked the return of a situation in which, as Alexander Korzhakov wrote, agents of the special services ran the country. Incidentally, he illustrates this in a curious fashion, to be sure, not with the example of agents but in his own persona as the director of a powerful special service.

Korzhakov asserted—and to the best of my knowledge nobody ever took issue with him—that he planned the shelling of the Russian White House in 1993 and directly oversaw the assault, while President Yeltsin "rested" and during this terrible operation feasted with his cronies, celebrating the victory.[6] What a strange page of history! The decision that marked a turning point in the life of Russia was not taken by the president but by his security chief.

It is extremely telling that the fundamental paradox of Russia's post-Soviet development was the termination of the process of democratic reforms, the very goal that the conspirators of 1991 sought and undoubtedly achieved. This thesis requires some explanation since President Yeltsin initially achieved significant progress in creating democratic institutions in Russia. I have in mind the promulgation of a new constitution consolidating civil and political rights, the actions aimed at establishing parliamentarianism in Russia, the continuation of Gorbachev's policy of cooperation with Western countries, and the entry of Russia to the Council of Europe. But the key steps toward establishing democracy were taken when Gorbachev was governing. They included introducing freedom of speech, which was then called glasnost; removing punitive and psychiatric persecution of nonconformists; repealing political and religious statutes from the Criminal Code; establishing religious freedom; eliminating the diktat of the CPSU; and creating the foundations of parliamentarianism.

During President Yeltsin's term in office, with the exception of economic reforms, not only were none of the goals he declared achieved but also the authorities did absolutely nothing to try to achieve them. Although Yeltsin's obvious and well-known weaknesses clearly played a negative role, they alone cannot serve as an adequate explanation, especially since he wanted to go down in history as the first democratic president of a newly democratic Russia. Unfortunately, the fine-sounding democratic principles enunciated at the time were contradicted by the real actions taken by the nation's leaders.[7]

The perturbations of the era of perestroika and the breakup of the USSR and its consequences intensified the long-standing Russian nostalgia for a heavy hand. The people were pleased when Yevgeny Primakov, who demonstratively enhanced the role of the special services, occupied the Russian White House. It seems that the appointment of Primakov as prime minister marked the *critical moment in the seizure of power by the special services.*

The people were even happier when Yeltsin transferred power to Putin, a move that guaranteed the fusion of the state security organs with the highest state power. For the first time in Russian history and, for that matter, in all of world history, the special services and the authorities became one and the same.

How did this phenomenon occur? Was it the result of cunning and extremely clever intrigues, or was it by the will, thoughtlessness, irresponsibility, or shortsightedness of the electorate, which each time voted for and regularly supported a KGB lieutenant colonel with a very shady biography? Or could it just have happened by itself? I hope not.

As a result of the complete fusion of the higher-level state authorities with the special services, the anti-democratic goals of the August 1991 coup d'état were quickly and effectively achieved. From then on one could only wax nostalgic for the rudiments of a law-based state, democracy, civil society, and freedom of the mass media from the era of perestroika. The de facto restoration in Russia of a one-party system, the "counterterrorist operation" in Chechnya, the unparalleled contempt for the Constitution, and the methods employed in the political struggle would have earned the plaudits of one of the most famous predecessors of the permanent ruler of post-Yeltsin Russia—namely, Stalin himself. Putin's neologism "vertical of power" simply means the old Soviet administrative-command system. The new term *enemies of Russia* deserves commendation by those who earlier had employed the term *enemies of the people.*

Putin's initial actions as president-in-waiting and then as president of Russia clearly indicated his political direction and priorities. They included returning to the era of the Cold War, launching a second war in Chechnya, eliminating freedom of the mass media, and purposely reviving Soviet symbols—the Soviet anthem, albeit with different words, and the Soviet flag as the banner of the armed forces.

Thus, in the final analysis, despite the apparent failure of the August 1991 coup against Gorbachev, in reality the State Emergency Committee achieved its goals. Some observers hypothesized that during the period of perestroika the KGB conducted an enormous special operation of which the August 1991 coup d'état was only the visible tip of the iceberg. The KGB-FSB infiltrated its agents into Yeltsin's entourage, into parliament, into leading positions in government institutions and business, among the reformers, into the mass media, and in the Russian Orthodox Church; and they played a very active role in forming the new elite. The agents created a structure of influence that endured and brought great pressure to bear upon Yeltsin and on Russia as a whole.

It is possible that the members of the State Emergency Committee on their part sincerely achieved the goals they had proclaimed, and the new elite, including its second echelon, skillfully manipulated the situation in its own interests.

One may reasonably suppose that this second echelon of the State Emergency Committee, taking advantage of Yeltsin's peculiarities and poor health, something on which they could depend, was able to reverse directions in foreign policy, turn back the progress of reform, and achieve the unprecedented elevation of the special services into power. While they accomplished this, it was obvious that Yeltsin would not remain in power very long, so the successors and heirs of the KGB also mounted a brilliant operation to put forward their protégé for the post of president. I offer this as just a hypothesis, but it is a quite plausible one since it explains a great deal of what happened in Russia after the August 1991 coup.

But a simpler explanation is also possible: The monster created by Lenin, Stalin, and Brezhnev—the Central Committee of State Security—was simply doing its daily work of recruiting and infiltrating its agents everywhere it could. As the service did its work well, the agents' numbers reached a critical mass, and, as a result, *power simply fell into the hands of the special services*. Then everything took its accustomed course. The consequences of the August coup strengthened the influence of the special services and facilitated Putin's advent to power.

In essence, I categorically reject any "conspiracy theories." But in the given instance, I would prefer to think that this was a cunning multistage strategy of the special services rather than convince myself that this outcome was predetermined and natural.

The latter hypothesis would signify that the condition was incurable without a complicated surgical operation to excise the metastases of the special services and a subsequent complicated therapy to cure the ills of Russian society. But even if the assumption about some sort of long-standing, future-oriented KGB plan is incorrect, the result of the 1991 coup is that it was the KGB, by whatever name one calls it, that came to power in 2000.

This point is crucially important since it makes sense of many things. For example, Putin appears as a simple function of the activities of the Soviet-Russian special services, and the veil of liberalism is withdrawn from Medvedev. The forms, methods, and goals of Russian politics at home and abroad become clear, even predictable. Many things that are presently obscure become clear about supposedly liberal persons, well known both domestically and internationally, who, in reality, are collaborating with the Chekist regime. Possibly the main consequence of the revolution of the Chekists is that once in power the special services will never relinquish it *voluntarily*.

The Bolshevik version of Ivan the Terrible's *oprichnina*—his secret police—was weakened, but it did not disappear after Stalin's death in 1953. It operated under the euphemism of "developed socialism." That is what perestroika dismantled and that is what took its revenge in 1999–2000. Right after Putin came to power in the Kremlin, a foul, icy wind began to blow. This was partly caused by his worldview and membership in the secret services, and it was partly predestined by the preceding period. The credo that sums up the Russian president's worldview may be briefly stated: The state is all; the individual is nothing. There is a direct analogy with Stalin's speech at a reception in honor of participants in the Victory Parade of 1945: "I offer a toast to the plain, ordinary, and modest people, the 'cogs' who maintain our great mechanism in working condition."

Unfortunately, only a handful of persons noted the symptoms of Russia's return, as early as Yeltsin's presidency, to a policy of revanchism and reaction. Moreover, no one believed them. What they said contradicted not only the liberal image of the president and his advisers but also the expectations both of the West and of most Russians themselves.

It was also difficult for the public to accept that Yeltsin directly conferred power to the special services in the person of Putin. Therefore, a legend was cultivated and given credence about Putin's supposed democratic leanings. His collaborative work as deputy mayor to Anatoly Sobchak, the mayor of Saint Petersburg, played into this story. The image of an energetic, young judo expert imprinted itself in the minds of many persons.

Putin turned out to be an extremely successful ruler. Although he did nothing for the Russian economy, thanks to the high prices for oil and gas, a torrent of money literally flowed into Russia as payment for energy exports. This enabled Moscow to flex its muscles again not only with regard to energy but also on the path of rearmament, the inevitable precursor of revanchism. In their actions, the new *oprichnina* obviously made use of the war cry of their predecessors: The word and the deed!

The Word

Russians have a weakness for false prophets and false prophecy. Probably it is because the false prophets are not shy about their words or deeds; moreover, the latter are shamelessly masked in words. In Russia from time immemorial, words have played an incomparable role. For good reason from the time of Ivan the Terrible, Russian rulers have feared the word no less than the deed. But the main function of words in Russian politics is "hypnosis," which, as a form of manipulation, became the foundation of national politics after the Bolshevik coup d'état. It was precisely because of their effectiveness that philosophy, literature, science, and art became the most important areas of state regulation, and thus a system was established in the country that the philosopher Nikolai Berdyaev termed the "dictatorship of a systematic ideology."[8] He wrote that "a teaching that is the basis for totalitarian doctrine, which embraces every aspect of life—not only politics and economics, but also thought, consciousness, and all works of culture—can only be a matter of faith."[9] The Big Lie that the people all embraced socialism was enthroned. The essence of Gorbachev's reformation was to liquidate this dictatorship and this lie, a lie that was guarded by the entire punitive and law enforcement apparatus of the country headed by the KGB.

After Russia became a sovereign state, the tradition of the Big Lie returned to politics with full honors. Soon hypnosis returned as well. To work effectively, it was first necessary to conceal the actual state of affairs in Russia and next to create a distorted version of it that served the interests of the authorities.

The Ideological State

When people speak and write about the Soviet Union, they often limit themselves to asserting it was a totalitarian communist state. What they generally overlook is that the USSR was an ideological state; moreover, ideology was the weight-bearing structure. This observation is vital since under Putin, just as during the communist period, Russia has reverted to ideological dogmatism. Here we should remember that in 1985 Gorbachev rose to power and attempted to reform a country that not only was unique with respect to size, population, military potential, and other objective criteria but also was the only state with a secular ideology grounded in Stalin's uniquely correct interpretation of the dogmas formulated by Marx, Engels, and Lenin. All of Russia's domestic and foreign policies were traditionally rooted in myth-making. These myths arose partly as a reflexive defense against one or another real phenomenon, partly as a protest against it, and partly from ignorance or misunderstanding of the actual state of affairs and of history. One might also cite other reasons intrinsic to the Russian people, including Russia's historical peculiarities, the deficit of political culture that was nurtured by the authorities, and so forth. In the context of the present discussion, however, the most interesting myths are those devised and disseminated by the authorities along with the instruments employed for ensuring their effectiveness.

One of the Kremlin's propaganda points is that the predominant feature of contemporary Russia's foreign policy is the "restoration of national pride." But just what sort of national pride?

Many Russians, especially since Yevgeny Primakov became prime minister in 1998, finding themselves under the spell of the authorities, really did keenly feel the loss of the country's former power that resulted from the breakup of the USSR. Even during Soviet times, they were unable to forgive "betrayals of the country's interests" such as terminating the war in Afghanistan, withdrawing Soviet troops from the colonized countries of Central and Eastern Europe, allowing the reunification of Germany, ending the Cold War, taking steps toward real disarmament, and terminating support for terrorists abroad. In the first post-Soviet years Russia really was a very weak player in international affairs. And this was not simply a result of the acute economic crisis.

This myth is closely connected to another—that is, Russia was pursuing a "subtle foreign policy." Having participated in numerous political decisions from 1992 to 2004 as an official of the Russian Ministry of Foreign Affairs and as a staff member of the National Security Council, and later as an informed observer, I can confidently assert that from 1992 onward Russia had *nothing* that could really be called a foreign policy. The ill-considered actions of the Putin regime to destroy the postwar system of international relations—ones that threatened Russia itself most of all—may also not be called a policy. Moreover, things were no different under Putin than they were under Yeltsin.

Vladimir Putin, unlike Yeltsin, had undergone a certain kind of professional training and had some, though very restricted, experience in the realm of foreign policy. KGB officials like Putin looked upon the West as the enemy; indeed, many of them developed a visceral hatred of the West. In addition, the kind of work they were engaged in—the collection of intelligence, to say nothing of counterintelligence—is not an activity concerned with foreign policy planning and execution. The work consists of gathering information, playing dirty tricks on the "opponent," and recruiting agents. The service also ferrets out threats, often laying it on thick or simply inventing them. Nor should we forget that the KGB was a punitive organization that protected the authorities. Under Putin, intelligence officers, counterintelligence officers, and undercover agents took possession of the Kremlin, the government, the parliament, and all the conceivable and inconceivable floors, corridors, alleyways, and nooks of power.

This absence of a policy had lamentable consequences. Moreover, Soviet "military-patriotic education" was so effective that many Russians would not embrace a policy that forswore saber rattling. Putin revived the most dismal Soviet traditions, relying on images of domestic and foreign enemies in his policies.

Another object of national pride that was closely linked to Russia's "subtle" foreign policy was using oil and gas to blackmail foreign partners. Even during the depths of the Cold War, neither Brezhnev, nor Andropov, nor Chernenko considered it possible to resort to what in the West is called the "problem of the spigot." Of course, the rise in oil and gas prices was not something Moscow had caused.

Against this background, the widely disseminated and convenient myth of the democratic character of Russian power was particularly attractive. Unfortunately for Russians, Boris Yeltsin became a malicious parody of liberalism and democracy that alienated Russians from these concepts for a long time. His unforgivable shortcomings as head of state, his constant lies, and his distortion of the very foundations of democracy created a situation in which many saw the sober, cynical, and rather malicious Putin as a panacea for all the disasters besetting the country. The political and moral trajectory of Yeltsin's actions was evident from the start. But the myth of his supposed democratic inclinations, which took on a life of its own, suited the reactionaries who were striving to compromise the very notion of democracy.

Although Russia's national shame reached its acme under Yeltsin, it was still permissible to tolerate him, as became evident after he had exited the political scene. When Yeltsin finally sank into a condition that was strange for a head of state, as noted previously something entirely unimaginable occurred: he *appointed* as his successor an officer of the KGB under whom myth-making reached an incalculable height.

Another myth is that Putin had already retired from the KGB during the Soviet era. Anyone even the slightest bit acquainted with the work of the organs of state security during that time knows this was impossible. Only one possible conclusion follows: *Putin was infiltrated* into the close circle of one of the most outstanding, if complex, democratic leaders of the USSR, Anatoly Sobchak, the mayor of Saint Petersburg. Was Putin not one of the causes of the political downfall of this undoubtedly extraordinary man? An alternate version holds that Sobchak was, at the least, an alien presence in the democratic movement. This version likewise does nothing to paint Putin in flattering colors as it suggests that he was sent to assist Sobchak. In either case, Putin's collaboration with Sobchak worked to Putin's advantage. He presented himself as virtually the right-hand man of a leading democrat, a description that hardly fit Sobchak himself.

In fairness, I should emphasize that Putin merely inherited many of the Yeltsin myths; however, he improved upon some of them. Putin did not unleash the genocide of the Chechen nation, but he authored the false thesis that international terrorism was flourishing in Chechnya. Putin did not liquidate the emerging parliamentary democracy; he merely took this process to its logical conclusion. Putin did not initiate the persecution of an independent press . . . One could extend this list.

The myth of Yeltsin's democratic inclinations carried over to his successor. One must give Putin his due: He juggled the stereotypes so skillfully that for a long time he managed to avoid rejection by his Western partners, who perceived him as a fighter against terrorism and corruption and as a supporter of upholding Russia's Constitution. Invoking pretexts embraced by Russian, and part of international, public opinion, he succeeded in decisively compromising democracy and liberalism and in fully eliminating them as significant factors in Russian politics.

The Trials and Tribulations of Creating a National Idea

As a typical product of his time and his communist education, President Yeltsin was concerned about the need for establishing some sort of ideology. Considerable time and effort were spent by persons of various persuasions in and around the Kremlin to come up with one. Apparently, both Yeltsin and his successors remembered that in the beginning was the Word. During the period of stagnation from Brezhnev through Chernenko (1964–85), the communist leaders ruled the country with words. Those who devised

Yeltsin's ideology, pretentiously called the National Idea, thought that it would solve an entire range of problems. The new Kremlin masters could not live without an ideology and did not want to try. After wracking their brains vainly trying to think of something new, they settled on what they thought were the traditional foundations of Russian mentality—patriotism and Russian Orthodoxy. For many reasons this was unquestionably a mistaken choice.

Let us begin with patriotism. Love of one's motherland—one's village, city, country, people—is an innate human emotion. Although there are numerous aphorisms and sayings directed against patriotism, they usually evoke a sharp response from those who believe that *their* village, or *their* fellow tribesmen, or *their* country is always right no matter what and that others are guilty for any and all disasters. But there is also a different approach, succinctly expressed by the wise Charles de Montesquieu who wrote, "If I knew of something that would serve my nation but would ruin another, I would not propose it to my prince, for I am first a man and only then a Frenchman . . . because I am necessarily a man and only accidentally am I French." The nineteenth-century Russian essayist Nikolai Dobroliubov considered real patriotism a private expression of love for humanity that is incompatible with enmity toward particular nationalities. Moreover, Dobroliubov insisted that patriotism "excludes any sort of international enmity, and a person animated by such patriotism is prepared to work on behalf of all humankind."

Unfortunately, shortly after Russia acquired sovereignty, this expansive concept of patriotism as the foundation for international peace and cooperation was rejected in favor of jingoist or, more accurately, oleaginous patriotism, which in various forms became the prime cause of the country's numerous disasters. In this connection, the redistribution of the state property of the USSR occurred under patriotic slogans. In the loans-for-shares scheme of 1995 banks lent the nearly destitute government money in exchange for shares of enterprises, resulting in wholesale privatization that benefited the newly emergent oligarchic elite. This process, in which foreign capital was not allowed to participate, led to Russia's complete political as well as economic bankruptcy, the massive impoverishment of the people, and the consolidation of bandit capitalism. There are many similar examples of self-serving "patriotism."

Another foundation of the National Idea that crawled to the surface after the breakup of the USSR was Russian Orthodoxy. After the collapse of communist ideology, a large ideological vacuum occurred in Russia and with it an enormous, extremely promising market for some faith to fill that vacuum. Persons entirely lacking in convictions find there is nothing more profitable than commerce in convictions, including religious ones. They sell that which does not exist for themselves, converting what they consider mirages into power, influence, and money. Naturally, the originally Soviet part of the clergy and businessmen from the Russian Orthodox Church—in other words, those persons in the USSR who had been assigned to working with religions—rushed boldly into this market. It is not difficult to imagine who was entrusted by whom "to work in the field of religion." Religious publications and the press blossomed. From my own sources I knew for sure that some members of the Russian Orthodox hierarchy were also members or officers of the KGB, and with regard to certain others, I was able to guess what their original and basic place of work was.

After the adoption of the law on religious freedom, there was a leap from virtually universal aggressive atheism to an era of "candlesticks," as the leaders of the country, who posed before the cameras holding candles in their hands during church services, came to be called. (Let us note that the ostentatious Russian Orthodoxy of the country's leadership, while ignoring other religions, was a gross violation of the Constitution since it stipulates that the church is separate from the state and all religions are equal. Religiosity is a personal matter, not for display.) The Bible replaced the works of the "Founding Fathers" of Marxism-Leninism, whom none of the dignitaries, of course, had ever read. And why should they have since there were assorted professors, consultants, and other party-state retainers at hand? In the minds of the *nomenklatura* and its retainers, trained to accept without question various twists and turns, the firm conviction that God did not exist was replaced by a diametrically opposed and no less firm assurance. For much of the Russian population, it doesn't much matter what they believe; what is important is to believe in something . . .

Religion became fashionable for many people. This had nothing to do with faith. Fashion and faith belong to different orders. Of course, we all decide for ourselves whether to follow the fashion. For example, during perestroika, after a sumptuous meal accompanied by vodka, I declined to be christened by one of the highest officials of the Russian Orthodox Church in his private chapel. It is an understatement to say that I had more than a few questions about him. Chief among them: Why was he so delighted with the murder of Alexander Men?[10] Why did he think this had occurred so opportunely? Who had arranged the murder—was it he or his companions in arms and confederates? How could someone occupying one of the highest posts in the Russian Orthodox Church rejoice in a murder, especially the murder of a priest?

But let us return to the question of whether to follow the current fashion. In contemporary Russia it is not easy to resist the fashion for religion. For example, the blessing of his office was stipulated as a condition for confirming an official of my acquaintance in his new job. Those persons who pose as the most zealous Orthodox are employees of the special services and communists. (Incidentally, I am convinced with good reason that the overwhelming majority of our special service agents are dyed-in-the-wool communists.)

As with any other fashion, it is profitable and expedient to speculate on religion. After all, who would pass up the opportunity to take advantage of this market! Pseudo priests collect alms on the streets although it is forbidden by law. For substantial sums authentic priests bless whatever comes their way, from the launching pads of intercontinental missiles to the Mercedes of gangsters. Various kinds of pseudo- and quasi-religious agitators incite interdenominational, interethnic, and other kinds of discord. Priests with ruble signs in their eyes see the possibility of selling something at a better price by cozying up to the state.

In 1994 the Russian Orthodox Church declared that it was impoverished. The government could rescue it if it allowed the church's Office of Humanitarian Aid to import duty-free wine and cigarettes. Over a period of three years, ten thousand tons of cigarettes came to the Russian Orthodox Church's Office of Humanitarian Aid. According to various data, from this delivery of cigarettes the church would receive about a billion rubles every week in non-denominated currency. But this was not enough. The church, including the patriarch, played a very active role in the election campaign of 1996. It was rewarded by a government commission, which ruled that the church's wine, supplied gratis from Germany, was humanitarian assistance for the needs of the Russian Orthodox Church.

The patriarchy reached such a high degree of cynicism that it even extended its talons to military property: watercraft, naval docks, port equipment, airports, repair facilities, engineering technology, transportation equipment, and communications. It also grabbed hold of the medical-sanitary complex; cultural, sports, warehousing, production, and other investments; and parcels of land and other real estate that formerly belonged to the Ministry of Defense. According to rumors, the Russian Orthodox Church was also involved in the diamond trade, in the tourist business, and in the sale of real estate and material-technical equipment belonging to the former Soviet forces in Germany.

If one believes the laws in force in Russia, Orthodoxy is separate from and superior to mainstream Christianity. I will not dispute the notion that many of the highest clerics of the Russian Orthodox Church are indeed far removed from Christianity. Naturally, the question arises, were things better before? Of course not. But they were simpler. And there were no fewer genuine believers even though they were forced to conceal their religious convictions. One kind of hypocrisy and sanctimoniousness was replaced by others. Another thing: Russian Orthodoxy became a way of life. How convenient it was to invoke the name of God to cover up all kinds of disgraceful acts. This also became fashionable.

Be that as it may, whatever it was that replaced the "new historical community of people—the Soviet nation"—it inherited a complicated spiritual and philosophical legacy. The bankruptcy of the previous system was brought about by the gross errors and miscalculations of the authorities, who completely ignored the fact that the country was multi-confessional and multicultural.

Unfortunately, this was not limited to the unconstitutional and destructive state takeover of the Russian Orthodox Church while virtually ignoring all the other denominations. An enemy was required. And one was chosen. As noted previously, Islam was *picked out* as the enemy. It would be difficult to conceive of anything more harmful, dangerous, and unjust.

In Soviet times the party bureaucracy and the law enforcement machine purposely crushed the natural historic, cultural, and ethnoreligious pluralism of Russia (and the USSR as a whole). It was almost as if the regime had placed a bet upon Russian Orthodoxy as the sole religion acceptable to the communists as "the least of all evils" among the variegated religious life of the country. This, along with the role of Islam in national and cultural identity formation, significantly stimulated the upwelling of pro-Islamic sentiment in post-Soviet times.

After the end of the dictatorship of the CPSU and soon after the attainment of sovereignty by the states that had formed the USSR, however, Islam rushed into the philosophical and ideological vacuum, attracting a part of the population in the same way that Russians were drawn to Russian Orthodoxy. The First Chechen War, along with gross mistakes and miscalculations by the Russian leadership with respect to inter-confessional and nationality policies, has still further exacerbated the problem of Islam.

But one "enemy" was too few for the state-controlled Russian Orthodox Church. It declared a real holy crusade against all other confessions, groups, and faiths, and it branded all of the nontraditional religions as "totalitarian sects," although many of them had nothing in common with totalitarianism and the well-known destructive aspects of pseudo religions. The law enforcement agencies as well as thuggish church hangers-on served the Russian Orthodox Church. The diktat of religious and pseudo dogmas led to extremely dubious and unending disputes. The best example is the Moscow Patriarchate's blind fear of the Vatican and its pathological hatred of Catholicism.

In 2009 after Kirill, who was previously dubbed the "tobacco metropolitan" for the business ascribed to him, became the patriarch of Moscow and all Russia, the Moscow Patriarchate became an extremely strange organization. I made the acquaintance of the future patriarch Kirill soon after his appointment in November 1989 as chair of the synodal Department of External Church Relations of the Russian Orthodox Church, when I took part in a discussion with him and Deputy Minister Vladimir Petrovsky.

It was clear to which agency Kirill owed his allegiance. In Soviet times the directors of this department were always KGB agents. Although Kirill was appointed to this position at the height of Gorbachev's perestroika, and something might already have changed, it is doubtful that the KGB would have relinquished such a plum position. In addition, Kirill had been the representative of the Moscow Patriarchate at the World Council of Churches in Geneva in 1971–74. As confirmation of his secret allegiance, one may also point to the fact that he was joined at this meeting by a former official of the USSR Ministry of Foreign Affairs who was close to him at the time, Father Ioan Ekonomtsev. Kirill's KGB-FSB alias, Mikhailov, is also widely known. For many years Kirill had the reputation of a reformer and supporter of ecumenism. Soon after his enthronement, however, these illusions dissipated. Moreover, all the illusions regarding his humane qualities and his primary allegiance were also dispelled.

No matter how offensive they may have found it, people became used to the fact that the Russian Orthodox Church was headed by KGB agents. But they were indignant when this hierarch, an otherworldly white monk who loved to discuss asceticism, was seen wallowing in luxury and wearing an incredibly expensive Breguet watch on his wrist.

In Moscow there is a famous apartment house, the House on the Embankment or the First House of the Soviets. Initially it was inhabited by the Soviet "elite." Quite properly, Citizen Gundyaev, better known as Patriarch Kirill, lived there. Former minister of health Citizen Yuri Shevchenko was imprudent enough to live in the apartment above that of Citizen Gundyaev. As a result, the patriarch came to be identified not only with tobacco and Breguet watches but also with dust once Shevchenko undertook some repairs. It would seem like a worldly matter, but the repairs turned into an affair that nearly cost the ex-minister his apartment. The

construction dust supposedly so harmed the property of the patriarch, who had taken a vow of poverty, that Shevchenko's apartment
was seized on the complaint of a certain Citizeness Lidia Leonova
who, for some reason, was living in the patriarch's monastic apartment. In April 2012 the ex-minister paid out 20 million rubles to
the patriarch's tenant.

When a torrent of questions and criticisms poured down
upon the incumbent of the highest office in the Russian Orthodox Church, the Holy One's favorite, the sadist-maniac with ice-
cold eyes Vsevolod Chaplin, chairman of the Synod Department
for Church-Society Relations, provided explanations. They leaned
toward a conspiracy theory: the story about the apartment was
part of a larger campaign "to destabilize the situation in the country which is also aimed against the people, against the army, the
police, against the government. . . . At the core of this campaign is
a small group of pro-Western Muscovites, and residents of other
big cities, the pro-Western part of Russian financial circles, political establishment, and the media elite."[11]

At about the same time, members of the punk group Pussy
Riot dramatically exploded the situation prevailing in the Moscow Patriarchate when, wearing masks, they tried to perform a
punk prayer to the Virgin Mary in the Cathedral of Christ the
Savior on February 21, 2012, and called for the liberation of Russia from Putin. Naturally, their peculiar prayer was immediately
interrupted. Maria Alekhina, Nadezhda Tolokonnikova, and Ekaterina Samutsevich were arrested and handed two-year sentences
in a penal colony for hooliganism. Following an appeal, the court
commuted Samutsevich's punishment to a suspended sentence.

On April 3, 2012, the Supreme Church Council of the Russian
Orthodox Church adopted an extraordinarily powerful appeal
on such "antichurch forces." It is worth analyzing in some detail,
since the document enables us to understand more clearly what
is going on not only in the Russian Orthodox Church but also in
Russia as a whole.

According to this document by the "spiritual fathers," "antichurch forces fear the strengthening of Orthodoxy in the country
and are frightened by the renascence of national consciousness and

mass popular initiative." Bolshevism crawls out from every one of these words. From the appeal it follows that anyone who does not accept what is going on in the Moscow Patriarchate is taking an anti-Russian stance. Moreover, it seems that national consciousness did not exist in Russia before, and it is only now *reviving*. Just as in the times of Stalin and Brezhnev, what is emphasized is how few there are of "such people" (read—renegades). Further, there is a transparent hint about the influence of several among them and their willingness to "make use of their financial, informational, and administrative resources to discredit the hierarchy and the clerics in order to promote schisms and attract people away from the churches." In other words, a conspiracy! "Those who propagate the *false values of aggressive liberalism*" are uniting with these vile conspirators.[12]

One might subject these phrases to endless analysis. But the result would be the same—a lie. Nor would it be a sin if the "church fathers" glanced at a dictionary to understand that by its very nature liberalism cannot be aggressive.

Why, then, is this the view of the leadership of the Russian Orthodox Church? It turns out that the liberals do not embrace the Russian Orthodox Church because of its "inflexible position of opposition to such *anti-Christian* phenomena as *recognizing same-sex unions, the freedom to express all one's desires, unrestrained consumerism, and propaganda in favor of permissiveness and fornication*."[13] This passage is even more interesting in that the "holy fathers"—who, in the preamble to the law on religious freedom, insisted on distinguishing Orthodoxy from Christianity—now dare to pose as the most zealous defenders of that very same Christianity they previously disavowed. Let us recall that it was then metropolitan Kirill who was involved in drafting the law that enshrined this norm in its preamble. Deciphering the "holiness" of the Russian Orthodox Church hierarchy is no simple matter.

The appeal asserts that the "confrontation between the Church and anti-Christian forces" became even more obvious and sharper "during the campaign and post-election period, which *demonstrates their* [evil forces] *real political agenda, including their anti-Russia stance*."

Thus, the church authorities formulate the following postulate: The Russian Orthodox Church, the state, and Russia are one and the same. Moreover, any single element of the "three-tailed whip" may be omitted as being self-evident. In the context of this book, the falsity of such an assertion surely requires no explanation.

Let us return to the position of the Russian Orthodox Church, which claims that all its troubles, like those of its Patriarchate, are due to "planned and systematic efforts to discredit" it and not to its own internal problems. Moreover, "the clergy are drawn into provocations; the arch-priests and priesthood generally are the focus of unremitting attention on the part of malcontents looking for the smallest hook on which to distort everything via smear campaigns." It is difficult not to agree that the public has become witness to the undignified behavior of the Moscow Patriarchate and that the persons defended in the appeal, with a vigor worthy of a better cause, are themselves responsible for the "smear campaigns."

And, finally, as they say in diplomacy, let us go to the heart of the matter: "In this very context a libelous media attack on the Head of the Church is being mounted. All this converges into one campaign against Orthodoxy and the Russian Orthodox Church." The conclusion is quite striking: "We must all preserve unanimity of opinion."

The mask comes off. Patriarch Kirill was born in 1946 and thus is bound to understand the meaning of the words *unanimity of opinion*. He grew up and lived a large part of his life under the "unanimity of opinion" implanted by the communists.

This disproportionate response to the action of Pussy Riot and others can only evoke amazement. Somehow it was entirely forgotten that Russia is a secular country in which, according to the Constitution, the church should be separate from the state. Amnesty International recognized the participants in the group as prisoners of conscience and demanded their immediate release.

Then Sergei Gavrilov and Sergei Popov, deputies in the State Duma from the Communist Party and United Russia, respectively—with the approval of the hierarchy of the Russian Orthodox Church and the leadership of the lower house of parliament—hastened to establish an inter-factional group to "defend Christian values."

In Gavrilov's words, "Many deputies from various factions of the State Duma are united in recognizing the role and importance of the Russian Orthodox Church in the preservation of the spiritual, moral, cultural, and socio-political specificity of the Russian Federation as a unique Christian civilization." This passage evokes perplexity on two counts. First, the idea that Russia's originality equates with Orthodoxy is incorrect. The dominant religion undoubtedly did play an extremely important and far from one-sided role in its formation, but it was just one of many factors contributing to the national identity of the Russian people. Second, the thesis concerning the uniqueness of Christian civilization in Russia is surprising, as if other countries did not embrace Christianity. In addition, Gavrilov asserted that the deputies, along with the Russian Orthodox Church, intend to resist the "totalitarian and sectarian ideologies of *aggressive liberalism and secularism* and their unrestricted advocacy of hedonism, violence, consumption of narcotics and alcohol, and gambling."

Especially bewildering is the defense of Russian Orthodox hierarchs by communists who, according to their own founder, are supposed to be atheists. Gennady Zyuganov, the leader of the Communist Party of the Russian Federation, evidently either forgot this or did not know it. Condemning the "campaign of attacks" against the Russian Orthodox Church, he said, "The army and the Orthodox faith—these are the two pillars that after the liquidation of the accomplishments of Soviet power will be the first to be uprooted by those who hate the Russian people and Russia and whose main mission is the destruction of our spirituality and traditions. . . . Today we are observing a coordinated campaign of attacks on the Russian Orthodox Church by *representatives of aggressive liberal forces*."[14] In this connection, he did not fail to refer to "various kinds of Russophobic mud-slinging." And making allowances for the coefficient of mental development, the particular situation, and the passage of time, his words reek of something painfully familiar and Soviet: "*Sooner or later liberal crackpots will smash their own heads*," and "*aggressive liberalism is cave-man Russophobia,* [and] *blaspheming our religious values is the most refined and most vile extremism*." But Zyuganov has evidently developed a split personality, the result of which is that, in some unfathomable fashion, his essence as *Homo sovieticus* has been united with his alternate, essentially anticommunist essence. It is too obvious even to point out the servility of his utterances.

As a result of its extremely dubious leadership, the contemporary Russian Orthodox Church has been transformed into a simulacrum of an enormous totalitarian sect. It is not only the leaders who are guilty. The majority of priests are ill educated and coarse and think only of money. Their congregations accept this, and they become even more boorish and brutalized. Their lack of spirituality is sometimes reflected in proverbs and sayings—for example, "as lacking in spirituality as a priest," "greedy as a priest," "coarse as a priest."

Government officials and priests wax enthusiastically about the "rebirth of spirituality." It would be more accurate to speak of obscurantism and religious superstition, which the classics of Russian literature long ago stigmatized.

Since the emergence of religious freedom in Russia was one of the chief accomplishments I was involved in during Gorbachev's perestroika, I will take the liberty of departing from the chronological framework of this book to try and answer the following question: who among those, including myself, who secured religious freedom in the Soviet years bears responsibility for what happened in this sphere in contemporary Russia? Of course, in light of what happened, one cannot seriously argue that we were absolutely correct during Soviet times. Even giving us our due, we were unable to take into account all the hypothetical future dangers, especially such profound distortions of the very principle of freedom of conscience. We operated in a different historical context, when it was impossible to imagine that the Russian Orthodox would insult atheists and followers of different faiths. I think our chief mistake was in not anticipating the need for limits and responsibility in exercising the right of religious freedom.

What are the other elements of the National Idea? In other words, how, and with what means, does one hypnotize the people of Russia? The Kremlin provided a fairly distinct answer to this question for the first time after the hostage taking in a school in Beslan, North Ossetia, on September 1, 2004. What happened there was ascribed to the "weakness" of the state, and to avert such tragedies in the future, the Kremlin asserted the need to strengthen the authorities for its own sake, abolished the direct election of governors, and created a sham democratic supervisory institution called the Public Chamber. Further, as Putin said, we need to "*support citizens' initiatives in organizing volunteer structures in the area of maintaining public order. They are capable not only of *providing real assistance in gathering information and giving signals from the people* about the possible preparation of crimes, but can also become a real factor in the struggle against crime and terrorism."[15]

Are we going back to the past? Was this a call for denunciations and anonymous informers? Of course. The president was openly appealing for the revival of a mass stool pigeon movement, which was the fundamental basis of Soviet totalitarianism.

Naturally, such utterances demanded an explanation. Vladislav Surkov, the Kremlin's chief ideologist, rushed to the ramparts. According to what, in Soviet terminology, might be called a "guided interview," the most important thing that Putin said on September 4 and 13, 2004, was to call for the mobilization of the nation in the struggle against terrorism. "We must all recognize that the enemy is at the gates," cried this confidant of the president. "*The front passes through every city, every street, every house.* We need vigilance, solidarity, mutual assistance, uniting the strength of citizens and the state."[16]

Some sort of mysterious "interventionists," he maintains, are waging a "secret war" against Russia. There is a "fifth column of persons" even in Russia itself who will never be our real partners. However, why are they unknown? After all, it is not in some empty space but on the Kremlin's team in Russia that a spy mania has revived and flourished luxuriantly. Critics of those in power are called extremists and enemies of Russia.

Many persons approve of the clear impulse to equate the National Idea with the search for enemies. The hoary concept of an internal enemy has been revived in full force. Surkov includes liberals, along with terrorists, in the circle of enemies, but even his explanations appear insufficient. Authors such as Mikhail Yur'iev, who write either on Surkov's orders or simply from a desire to curry favor, are also involved.[17]

The fundamental premise underlying attempts to create the National Idea is that "Russia is and must be a great power." For some reason, however, authors writing in this vein often associate the idea of greatness with throngs of starving slaves who, inexplicably, willingly forfeit their rights and are ready to tighten their belts even more. Is this a direct allusion to the time of barracks socialism? This is hardly greatness but a parody of it.

The new ideologues truly believe that a universal fear of Russia is a necessary condition of Russia's greatness. They ignore the well-known fact that such fear existed earlier and resulted in the economic collapse and breakup of the USSR.

Contrary to the notions of those elaborating the National Idea, Russia is a multinational state in which the main criterion for belonging to the country is Russian citizenship and nothing more. The Russian nation and the Russian Orthodox faith are far from identical. Not only are many entirely respectable Russians not Orthodox, but there are also Old Believers, Catholics, and adherents of other faiths, as well as agnostics and atheists. If those aspiring to fashion the Russian National Idea consider themselves to be supporters of a strong Russian state, then they should realize that nothing would be more ruinous for Russia than to divide its people into Russians and non-Russians, Orthodox and non-Orthodox, or any other signs of distinction. In general, it is dangerous to divide. That path leads directly toward the breakup of the country.

Symbolically, the various types of supporters of a strong Russian state not only seek to be the authors of the National Idea—moreover in a very specific form—but also aspire to the role of Supreme Court. They blithely condemn as enemies almost everyone who disagrees with them. Those who are not considered enemies still are viewed at a minimum as second-class citizens. In their minds the National Idea is clearly a search for internal enemies. They are addicted to groping convulsively for the boundary between "enemies" and "near enemies."

It is quite touching, almost naive, how Mikhail Yur'iev let the cat out of the bag in grounding the need for the National Idea. To avoid any misunderstanding, I quote: "*One cannot introduce the concept of an internal enemy in the absence of an accepted national idea, because it is the national idea that defines what it is that must be considered an enemy.*"[18] In other words, the National Idea is needed exclusively to legitimize the concept of an internal enemy.

Democrats and, employing Yur'iev's vocabulary, "people in general [*obshchecheloveki*] must be cauterized." This is exactly what he wrote.

I think that Yur'iev played the same role for Putin and his ideologues as the notorious Nina Andreeva did for the reactionaries during Gorbachev's perestroika.[19] What happened on the ideological front in the later Yeltsin period and under Putin may largely be explained by the advent to power of people from the special services. They were taught not to make policy, to identify and formulate the national interests, and to defend them but something entirely different—that is, to maintain existing policies by specific and often quite unethical means. As a result in the minds of the ruling Cheka-KGB agents, the false idea that politics is a dirty business became firmly lodged. Once this happened, there could be no moral limitations whatsoever.

The saddest part is that so many people find such a way of thinking congenial. To a high degree, of course, this is due to such factors as suffering from an inferiority complex, striving to deflect onto others the responsibility for one's own mistakes and crimes, and, of course, continuing the age-old Russian habit of dividing people into "us" and "them."

Following the Leninist script, many efforts were undertaken in post-Soviet Russia to ensure that such ideas would become a material force possessed by the masses. Among these efforts were the removal of the opposition from the legal field, the de facto elimination of parliamentarianism, the creation of pro-Kremlin youth groups, and so forth. Nor was the Kremlin squeamish about employing "dirty tricks." It commissioned and published articles in the press, including the foreign press, thereby placing in circulation various myths supposedly bolstering or formulating the National Idea.

Secrecy

Starting with Lenin, policies that from the outset were grounded in crimes and lies to Russia and the world required a reliable defense in order to conceal the truth about the crimes and ensure the lies would pass for truth. This goal was served by secrecy, which was and remains the most important and indispensable component of Russian political tradition. It is an inalienable attribute of the rough and ready power game directed against the "enemies of the people" under Lenin and Stalin and the "enemies of Russia" under Putin. Thus, secrecy functions as the most vital element of the ideological state that actively employs hypnosis on its own people as well as on foreign public opinion.

The Soviet practice of classifying information on a broad range of issues embodied the boldest bureaucratic dream: do whatever you like, and let no one know about it. The ministries, the departments, and the censors perfected this practice to the nth degree. But all this paled in comparison to what transpired in the editorial offices and publishing houses that were virtually the undisputed masters of the materials presented to them for publication. That editors bore equal responsibility with authors for what was published, coupled with the editors' broad powers, led them to play it safe and act arbitrarily.

Almost everything was classified to one degree or another. One needed special passes to access the foreign periodicals and scholarly literature that were kept in special sections of the library. There, too, Russian "non-Marxist" philosophy languished. A striking situation arose after the Chernobyl tragedy. If one followed the letter and spirit of the law, merely announcing its occurrence was supposed to entail criminal responsibility since the locations of atomic power plants were classified. Such subjects as the USSR's failure to observe international law, the poverty of its people, and many others were all shielded in secrecy.

During Gorbachev's perestroika when, thanks to Shevardnadze and my immediate superiors, we liberated ourselves from the pernicious and unjustified classification of everything, I managed to launch an effort to review and mitigate the classification regime. I began with the secret office that compiled the index of issues constituting state secrets. What was there that was not enumerated in this extremely hefty brochure? The information that accompanied the memorandum to the minister turned out to be so sensitive that first a working group inside the Foreign Ministry was established and then an interdepartmental working group. Subsequently the notorious list was significantly shortened, time limits were established for how long information could be classified, and (along with work on other matters) the possibility of restricting the departure of persons possessing knowledge of secrets from the USSR had to be stipulated beforehand in work contracts. Other aspects of the classification system were also reviewed.

Secrecy serves several basic functions. The main one is the opportunity it affords to manipulate information to conceal outrages one has created. The notorious list also served this fundamental purpose. For example, information about the size of the mesh in fishing nets was classified if it was smaller than the generally accepted international standard.

But there were also politically significant and strategic issues. The main one was to deceive the people on any matter that the authorities desired. If something is classified, then no one knows about it; therefore, it does not exist. For example, almost everything concerning life outside the USSR was classified, including prices in the stores, salaries, and standards of living. However, in this area secrecy is effective only up to a certain point, after which censorship comes into force, whether officially, as in the USSR prior to perestroika, or unofficially, as was the case after Putin came to power. Yury Shchekochikhin wrote perceptively that "censorship is not censors, it is a state of society in which it is sometimes forced and sometimes desires to find itself. . . . Censorship is, most of all, a need of society itself at one or another stage of its development, one of the means of defending itself from the world outside that the authorities make use of, encouraging this instinct and supporting it by creating special state institutions."[20]

As for secrecy, at the level of everyday bureaucratic work, secrecy imparts a special quality to anything, even the most insignificant question. The lion's share of ciphered dispatches between Moscow and its diplomatic representatives abroad consists of completely open information: communications incoming from people on overseas assignments, summaries of articles published in the press, and similar trifles that could most certainly be sent by fax. But even though the faxes might not be read, and the summaries of articles might be of no interest to anyone, the mighty aura of secrecy comes into play. The cipher clerks were very surprised and asked for verification when they saw on many of my telegrams the notation "unclassified."

The most important function of the system of classification is that it facilitates the control of "bearers of state secrets," who are well aware that access (albeit formal) to classified material automatically implies the possibility of being shadowed by the special services. In addition, having access to state secrets also signifies the possibility of being barred from travel abroad, for a request for a passport to travel abroad is premised upon "approval" from the special services.

I can illustrate this with an example from my own experience. When I was given access to classified material at the Diplomatic Academy, I was summoned to the Special Department to review an encoded telegram that was of no interest to me whatsoever. The purpose was obvious: from the moment I signed that I had read it, I could be considered the bearer of a state secret, and the KGB had a formal basis to monitor my phone conversations and everything else in my life.

Here is another example. I was writing something at my desk in my office at the Security Council. Without knocking, the door was flung open, and in marched the chief security officer with a stern and severe look pasted on his face; behind him loomed two or three of his subordinates, checking procedures. Needless to say, there was trouble. "You're not following the rules! You're violating procedures! You must know what this will come to!" This is what it was all about. As someone who was actively engaged in work, I was simply unable to carry out the required demands. After receiving a classified document, officials were obligated to write down its number, its title, and a summary of its content in a special notebook (also classified, of course). When passing the document to anyone else, one had to make the appropriate notation and get the signature of the person who received it from you. There were mountains of such documents that flew back and forth among us officials, uncontrolled by the special services. Apparently, I had "rubbed so much salt" into someone's wounds that the person had decided to strike back in full force. In fact, the only officials who scrupulously entered into their notebooks all the papers they had received were good-for-nothings who had nothing better to occupy their time. However, my "well-wishers" miscalculated, for I was held in quite high esteem.

As noted previously, the regime of secrecy was firmly ensconced even in the Kremlin's medical establishment that initially served Soviet and, later, high-ranking Russian officials. In the First Polyclinic that treated the highest-ranking officials below the ministerial level, under no circumstances were patients ever given their medical records. According to the established rules in Russia, the pages of a medical record were supposed to be sewn together in order to avoid falsification. Not so in this clinic. Medical records were kept in loose-leaf binders from which at any time a page might be removed and another substituted in its place. Moreover, in the notorious Serbsky Institute of Forensic Psychiatry many medical records were also classified.

The Iron Curtain served the same purpose. Even for trips to "socialist" countries only the most reliable persons, from the perspective of the KGB, were selected. Foreign radio stations broadcasting to the Soviet Union were jammed. Even high-ranking diplomats were given foreign newspapers and magazines with articles and photographs cut out, and other articles were stamped with what, because of their shape, were called "screws," indicating the extreme sensitivity of this information. I remember from childhood such a photograph from the West German magazine *Der Spiegel* stamped with two such "screws" that showed five happy drunks sitting on an earthen berm around a Russian hut. Their faces were haggard; they looked stupefied, with vacant eyes and many missing teeth. They were terribly dressed and were singing something to the accompaniment of an accordion. Other poor huts were in the background with sheets drying on a clothesline. The caption underneath said, "If this is Heaven, then what is Hell?"

Hypnosis

After cutting off the flow of "harmful" information, what follows is hypnosis itself. Perfected during Soviet times, very few were able to resist it. Starting from kindergarten, one had drilled into one's head that the USSR was the best country in the world, where, due to the concern of the party and the government, the happiest people lived while all around were only enemies.

Membership in the Komsomol (the Communist Youth League) was a necessary condition for entry into many institutes and universities. The Komsomol conducted its hypnosis séances in the guise of regular and obligatory meetings and "volunteer work." In their institutes and universities, in the first instance, humanists, historians, philosophers, jurists, and journalists attended a practically continuous series of séances. Students in technical schools were not exempted, however. Everywhere the falsified history of the USSR, the history of the CPSU, and the philosophy of Marx and Lenin were required subjects of study. The great pianist Sviatoslav Richter said that his name was not engraved on the marble plaque honoring the best graduates of the Moscow State Conservatory because he had problems with the subject of scientific communism. Students who were Komsomol activists, to say nothing of those who were members of the CPSU, enjoyed special privileges with regard to taking exams and work assignments. Such was the upbringing of the so-called elite "builders of communism." Some elite they were!

Everyone without exception was continuously exposed to Soviet propaganda in the form of television, radio, newspapers, and magazines. Incidentally, it was no accident that the second-ranking person in the CPSU and, therefore, in the country was in overall charge of this propaganda. The propaganda mechanism was simple and well defined. The newspaper *Pravda* (Truth), which reflected the "general line of the party," provided guidance for the country's entire press. The television program *Vremya* (Time) played the role of auxiliary guide. More fundamental questions fell within the sphere of responsibility of the journal *Kommunist* (Communist). Other mass media had almost no chance of changing the interpretations of these publications and reports.

The duo of the CPSU and the KGB kept their eyes tirelessly fixed upon the "ideological purity of Soviet society." Moreover, in Soviet times there existed a very real vertical structure of power. In one way or another this duo existed almost everywhere throughout the country in the form of primary party, Komsomol, and trade union organizations in even the most remote and underpopulated villages. In the absence of other information, the endless repetition from daybreak to night of one and the same message over a period of years and decades throughout one's life compelled the overwhelming majority of the people to believe the reports, contrary to all the evidence.

During Gorbachev's reformation, the hypnosis initially weakened and then ceased entirely. But people who had become addicted, as to a narcotic, found doing without it difficult. Therefore, the revival of hypnosis under Putin, however deplorable, was objectively desired. In fact, it had already begun to reappear under Yeltsin. In brief, here is how the evolution of the hypnosis unfolded.

In the final years of the USSR, the system of secrecy assumed relatively normal dimensions. In the first post-Soviet years, it was in a shaky position. (There were many leaks of sensitive information.) But it later revived with new strength. Even the archives that had been opened after the breakup of the USSR were closed again. Instead of the Soviet censorship that had been done away with by perestroika, there came the telephone calls from on high, the intimidation and killing of journalists, and the elimination or transfer of the mass media to other more reliable owners.

A lot happened to freedom of speech under Yeltsin. The story of the rise and fall of the Media-Most Group and of the telecommunications company NTV are most revealing in this respect. Their chief Vladimir Gusinskii and his closest associate Igor Malashenko, making wide use of the telecommunications company NTV, played a significant role in Yeltsin's victory in the presidential election, after which NTV took off. At the same time, NTV sharply criticized the war in Chechnya and several of Yeltsin's closest associates, including the all-powerful Alexander Korzhakov, who then headed Yeltsin's personal security guards.

The thorough suppression of Media-Most and NTV occurred after they supported the electoral bloc headed by former prime minister Yevgeny Primakov and Moscow mayor Yury Luzhkov. Either one of them might have had a real chance of winning the 2000 presidential and 1999 parliamentary elections against the Unity Party whose electoral platform proclaimed unconditional support for Putin. The suppression of NTV and Media-Most was clearly the first step in smothering freedom of speech in Russia. Additional steps soon followed.

News of the direct involvement of Minister of the Press Mikhail Lesin provided supplementary evidence of the "impartiality" involved in the suppression of Media-Most. Specifically, he signed the document attesting that the deal to sell Media-Most was arranged in exchange for the freedom and security of Most Group chieftain Vladimir Gusinskii and his partners. According to Malashenko's testimony, during negotiations for the deal, Lesin repeatedly contacted Vladimir Ustinov, procurator-general of Russia, to coordinate the details and inquired especially how—according to which statute, for how long, and so on—criminal charges against Gusinskii would be deferred. Moreover, Lesin proposed that he receive a commission of 5 percent for arranging the deal.

The scandal concerning the liquidation of NTV is revealing but not unique. It suffices to recall that Boris Berezovsky, who was riding high during Yeltsin's presidency and who had done a lot to bring Putin to power, was soon deprived of his control of Russian television's Channel One with the Kremlin's active involvement. The "sixth channel," where a large part of the staff from NTV went in the summer of 2001, ceased to exist in its previous form, thereby signaling the final suppression of independent television and other mass media outside the Kremlin's control. From then on, as in the Soviet era, news, social, and political programs turned into apologias for the authorities. The mass audience no longer had access to an alternative point of view. Other media such as *Novaia gazeta* (New paper) and the radio station Ekho Moskvy, which appeared to maintain their independence from the Kremlin, had such small audiences—at least in 2001—that they could hardly hope to compete with pro-government sources of information.

In 2000 even prior to Putin's inauguration, the pro-Kremlin youth movement Idushchie vmeste (Going Together) was founded and became the forerunner of movements such as Nashi and Molodaia Gvardiia (Young Guard), established in 2005. These were not merely revivals of what, by comparison with them, was the inoffensive Komsomol but also the creation of an aggressive Putinjugend (Putin Youth), which was above the law. Everything was done to encourage membership in these movements. Moreover, students in a number of universities were compelled to participate in their projects, and those who refused were discredited and expelled.

Dragging youth into these political intrigues is extremely amoral per se, yet the amorality of the Russian authorities went much further. This was revealed in the winter of 2009 when Anna Bukovskaia, the former commissar of the movement Nashi, publicly acknowledged that this pro-Kremlin youth organization had created a network of paid agents to keep tabs on the opposition. She said that in 2007, on the orders of Nashi, a secret project was launched called Presidential Liaison that was aimed at infiltrating its paid agents into the opposition: first of all into Yabloko, then into the United Civic Front, Defense, and the National Bolshevik Party. The information collected went directly to the Presidential Administration.[21]

There is one more little-known but extremely important element of hypnosis. In the USSR there existed a phenomenon known as "active measures" (in professional jargon, *aktivka*), which was later renamed "purposefully conveyed information." This very specific phenomenon is critically important for understanding what is going on in Russia. It is a *set of top-secret measures worked out and implemented on instructions from the highest state authorities to achieve concrete political goals for which the participation of the special services is required.* A wide variety of persons and organizations, perhaps unable even to guess what this is all about, may be involved in achieving these goals. (For example, as part of the *aktivka*, a journalist may be deliberately fed information.)

This extremely sharp and effective means of conducting foreign and domestic policy is used to achieve the most important and delicate of goals. Everything connected with *aktivka* is a deep secret. Consequently, its planners and implementers can act with complete impunity.

Establishing political parties; discrediting or, on the contrary, praising someone or something; creating a mood in society that serves those in power—all this and much more may be the result of *aktivka*. When investigators encounter something in Russia that benefits the authorities but is difficult to explain from any perspective, they must ask, is this not *aktivka* in action?

For example, wasn't the murder of Alexander Litvinenko in London a case of active measures? On the one hand, too many absurdities characterize his killing. For example, traces of radioactive polonium-210 were left behind, and Andrei Lugovoi, the suspected killer of the former special services officer, was quickly elected to the Duma, which gave him immunity. On the other hand, it looked very much like a ritualistic murder, so one could not help but wonder whether it was planned and carried out as a way to get rid of an opponent of the regime. Particularly noteworthy is that Andrei Lugovoi was selected for the Liberal Democratic Party of Russia (LDPR) headed by Vladimir Zhirinovsky, who feigned madness but was really a cynical KGB officer.

The story of the founding of the LDPR clearly illustrates the meaning of active measures. According to the testimony of Anatoly Kovalev, who was present on the occasion, the "decision" to establish the LDPR "was adopted" during a dinner break at a meeting of the Soviet Communist Party Politburo. Vladimir Kriuchkov, the head of the KGB, took the floor and made the proposal. Gorbachev, who either did not understand or was confused about what was going on, had already lifted a spoonful of borscht to his mouth, paused, and then silently swallowed it. But by no means did his silence indicate approval.[22] Kriuchkov's proposal became the basis for a resolution of the Soviet Politburo. The result was that a multiparty system was proclaimed in the USSR, and a former officer of the KGB soon firmly settled in somewhat higher on the slope of the political Mount Olympus. It speaks volumes that such a party headed by such a leader took under its wing someone who was the prime suspect in a murder.

Responsible, if not necessarily clever, authorities were always very cautious with regard to active measures, even though they still committed unbelievable mistakes and allowed themselves to be deceived. As already noted, everything connected with active measures was highly classified and, therefore, hidden from view. But, for example, I can assert without fear of being contradicted that the revival of Nazi and fascist organizations in the USSR was the result of precisely such activities.[23]

We must draw a clear distinction between the active measures that are possible only with the approval of the highest authorities and those provocations carried out by the special services and other coercive agencies. For example, the clubbing and tear-gassing in Tbilisi and Vilnius of demonstrators who were also run over by tanks, as well as other crimes aimed at stopping Gorbachev's reforms, are examples of such provocations. No one can be sure, however, that orders to that effect were not issued by, for example, Yegor Ligachev, who was the second in command in the CPSU at the time and often in charge when Gorbachev traveled abroad or was on vacation.

Given the progressive seizure of power by, and final victory of, representatives of the special services, the following question arises: are not all of Putin's policies nothing other than purposefully conveyed information? In other words, has there not been an inversion between ends and means? Especially since under Putin an immense number of myths have arisen that are directly tied to purposefully conveyed information.

This is not the place to delve in detail into Soviet communist dogmas; however, those that resonated or were reanimated under Putin deserve attention—for example, the postulate of the unity of the party and the people under whose weight the Soviet people were crushed. Naturally, a return to Soviet communism in pure form was impossible and unnecessary. The pro-Putin party, United Russia, like the CPSU before it, literally occupied both houses of parliament, and membership in it was virtually obligatory for a successful career in government service. It was financed by businessmen, thus allowing it to be relatively secure from the state. Moreover, United Russia created its own Komsomol, or pro-

Kremlin youth movements. The proclamation that the parliamentary elections of 2007 were a "vote of confidence" in Putin not only made a farce of them, and demonstrated the effectiveness of the slogan "The people and the party are one," but also effectively eliminated parliamentary democracy in Russia.

To create his own cult, Stalin turned Lenin into a god. Putin took a different route, inciting others to proclaim him as the national leader. It took considerable effort to ensure that a majority of the population would accept this myth. Acting as Kremlin puppets, the mass media began to sing the praises of the incumbent president in every possible way. Meanwhile, Putin did everything possible to transform all his activities into media events. He turned every working session with a state official into a mini spectacle that was widely covered by television and other mass media. A large part of the population also lapped up the television shows in which Putin appeared in a variety of theatrical roles and costumes, mostly highlighting his patriotism and machismo.

The restoration of the dictatorship of ideology in Russia sometimes assumes grotesque forms. In February 2009 Minister of Emergency Situations Sergei Shoigu, absolutely outside his sphere of competence, asserted that persons who denied the victory of the USSR in the Great Patriotic War should be held criminally responsible. At first glance, this initiative is absolutely senseless, for the victory of the anti-Hitler coalition in the Second World War is a historical fact. But this attempt at verification conceals a dirty trick. From the time of Stalin, the role of the USSR's allies was invariably denigrated. Reflecting upon the tragic results of the war for the country's people now became subject to criminal penalties.

On May 15, 2009, President Medvedev, concerned about the "correct interpretation" of history, including the history of the Great Patriotic War, issued decree number 549 that established the "Presidential Commission to Counteract Attempts to Falsify History that Damage Russia's Interests." The title of the commission was revealing as it is impossible to falsify history exclusively to damage the interests of Russia. From the beginning apparently no consideration was paid to the fact that over a period of centuries and in Lenin–Stalin times as well as during the period of stagnation, history (including the history of the Second World War) was repeatedly falsified. It is typical, though not unexpected, that the composition of the commission copied Soviet ideological structures. It included representatives from the FSB, the General Staff, the Ministry of Foreign Affairs, the Foreign Intelligence Service, the State Duma, the Council of the Federation, the Ministries of Education and Science, the Ministry of Culture, the Russian Archives, the Federal Agency for Science and Innovations, and, for the sake of appearances, the Institutes of Russian and of World History of the Russian Academy of Sciences. The head of the Presidential Administration Sergei Naryshkin, a mechanical engineer by training and secondarily an economist, led the commission.

But this was not all. In the summer of 2009 a new scandal erupted. Radio Liberty obtained a scurrilous letter that had been sent by Academician V. A. Tishkov, the director of the History Section and the academic secretary of the Division of Historical and Philological Sciences of the Russian Academy of Sciences, to some of his colleagues. This letter made it clear that the bureau had adopted an official resolution, "On the Tasks of the Division of Historical and Philological Sciences of the Russian Academy of Sciences," in connection with the Russian Federation president's decree number 549 and the presidential commission. That such an official resolution exists is remarkable. The "scholars" had rushed to serve the powers that be.

But even this can be done in different ways. One can limit oneself to a formal reply, or one can prostrate oneself before power. The leadership of the Russian Academy of Sciences chose the second path. It arranged to provide an "annotated list of historical-cultural falsifications . . . (indicating the original sources, persons or organizations that created or disseminated the falsifications; and the potential danger of a given falsification to Russia's interests)." Moreover, the scholarly institutes are instructed to report on how they uncovered these concepts and provide a contact person or list of scholars to cooperate with the aforementioned commission of the Russian Academy of Sciences.[24] All of this is very reminiscent of both the methods by which Stalin destroyed Soviet science and the system of denunciation that existed in Soviet times.

Different things are permitted to persons with a different system of values and with a different degree of self-respect and of respect toward others. At a session of the parliamentary assembly of the Organization for Security and Cooperation in Europe in Vilnius on July 3, 2009, a resolution was adopted designating August 23, the date when the Molotov-Ribbentrop Pact was signed, a Europe-wide Day of Remembrance for Victims of Stalinism and Nazism. In addition to appeals to study history so as to avoid similar crimes in the future, the resolution called upon participating states, including the Russian government and parliament, "to ensure that any governmental structures and patterns of behaviour that resist full democratisation or perpetuate, or embellish, or seek a return to, or extend into the future, totalitarian rule are fully dismantled."

It was not difficult to predict Russia's reaction. The Federation Council and the State Duma called this resolution "an attempt to ruin the developing dialogue between Russia and the West." The Ministry of Foreign Affairs also took notice, drafting some sort of vague recommendations in response. What is the problem with historical truth? There was not a single negative word about Russia or its people in the resolution, only a condemnation of a criminal regime and of the Molotov-Ribbentrop Pact, which had already been censured in Soviet times.

All this forces one to remember that there has probably never been a country in the world where the discipline of history has been subjected to such prolonged and systematic outrages as in Russia. History not only fulfilled the "social demand" of preserving the existing order of things but also was widely used by everyone who could to advance his or her personal, narrowly egotistical goals. A rather narrow but powerful circle of ideologues vanquished history and established a monopoly over historical "truth" or, more accurately, "pseudo truth." They did not engage in scholarly research or value objectivity but indulged in dogmatism embellished with only two colors—black and white. As everyone knows, mixing these produces only the color gray, albeit in different shades. Many of these ideologues had no goal other than to conceal the truth and transform it into a lie.

This need to forget the truth in the name of immorality, lies, falsehoods, and justifications for intellectual and political weakness is characteristic of certain individuals and certain associations. Under Putin it revived in the form of a state policy directed, as the Russian historian Yury Afanasyev rightly noted, "toward cloaking one's rule in quasi-juridical form, to surrounding the self-reproduction of Putinism legally on the basis of preserving its immutability, relying, as has always been the case with the Russian authorities, on patriotic traditionalism and Russian archaism." The establishment of the commission is "only an episode in the sequence of well-thought out and logical actions of the Putinists to perpetuate their regime. However, these well-thought out actions are menacing and nonsensical."[25]

A glaring example of how hypnosis operates in practice came in the summer of 2010 when Russia was subjected to a siege of fire. Forests, villages, and vacation settlements burned, and the fire destroyed two military depots and came close to the nuclear centers in Sarov and Snezhinsk. According to data from the Global Fire Monitoring Center, from the start of 2010 through August 13 of that year, on the natural territories of Russia fires consumed an area of 60,575 square miles. These figures differ from the data provided by the Ministry of Emergency Situations (26,977 natural fire sites on a total area of 3,213 square miles) by an order of approximately nineteen times.[26]

The Russian and regional authorities must have known about the impending disaster. The weather forecasters had predicted a hot, dry summer; however, nothing was done to avert the disaster. The professional Chekist Putin was too distracted by the collapse of a Russian spy network in the United States and even found time to meet with the exposed agents and sing with them a popular Soviet song, "What Does Our Homeland Begin With?" Nor did he pass up the opportunity to appear at a gathering of rockers and talk about the feeling of freedom that riding motorcycles provide. The mayor of Moscow, a city that was choking on the heat and smoke from the burning forests and peat-bogs, safely waited out the fire by going on vacation.

The reaction to what was going on, although unofficial, was

wholly in the spirit of the Cold War: the Americans were said to be deploying a climate weapon, although more sober-minded specialists said that normal human activity was quite enough to provoke such a cataclysm.[27] The popular Russian "yellow journalism" paper *Komsomolskaia pravda* (Komsomol truth), citing the words of retired, former military, weather forecaster Capt. Second Class Nikolai Karaev, asserted that there was absolutely no doubt that the fires occurred as the result of intentional testing activity of what was supposedly a powerful new weapon at the High Frequency Active Auroral Research Program station located 250 miles northeast of Anchorage. By way of confirmation, it noted that "on the eve of the current weather cataclysm a new American pilot-less spaceship, the X-37B, capable of carrying a powerful laser weapon, was launched into space. The mission of the X-37B was highly classified."[28] This is a publication devoted to disseminating that kind of hypnosis.

It is true that in every joke there's a dollop of jest. When the head and co-owner of the company Your Financial Guardian, the Russian Orthodox entrepreneur Vasili Boiko, decided to put an end to confusion about his surname—many so surnamed were rather important people—and changed it to Boiko-Velikii (Boiko the Great), this action was viewed either as a joke or as a marker of his vainglory. How could one distinguish between them? There is as yet no answer to this question, but to make up for it Boiko-Velikii made the following demand of his employees.

1. In the course of the coming academic year all employees of all enterprises during work hours or after work must take the instructional course "Fundamentals of Orthodox Culture." . . .

3. All employees who undergo an abortion or who assist in performing one are subject to dismissal for cause;

4. All employees who are cohabiting, but not married, unless they become married by October 14, 2010—the Feast of the Protective Veil of the Holy Mother—will be subject to dismissal for cause;

5. Newly hired employees who are cohabiting, but not married, must get married within their probationary period (three months).

I appeal to you to pray more at home, away from home, and in places of worship for forgiveness of our sins and for sending down rains on the fields and our villages and pastures. And for God to bestow his grace upon our hearts.

I appeal to you to pray that the conflagrations subside and the fires cease.

I request that the enterprise accountants organize a collection of contributions from employees who wish to assist those suffering from the fires.

President OAO Russian Milk Vasili Boiko-Velikii.[29]

I think any commentary is superfluous, although I should note that there were enthusiastic responses. For example, speaking of this order, another entrepreneur, German Sterligov, in a broadcast on Ekho Moskvy, linked it to the fires: "Everyone says that the firemen are guilty, that the governors are guilty with respect to the fires, the heat, etc. Of course, this is due to our sins, and, ultimately, they are at least pointing in the right direction, so there is something to consider. Otherwise, it is utter nonsense."[30]

There's something for everyone. There are those who accuse the Americans; others say it is God's will, that the fires are punishment for sins. The main thing is to shift responsibility away from the authorities. Hypnosis has been elevated to a new and even higher level than it had attained under "socialism."

6

Strangling Democracy

A strange situation exists in Russia resulting largely from the nature of the Soviet period, the ideological character of the USSR, and the enhanced suggestibility of the Russian people: Beginning in 1917 the ruling authorities regularly and methodically committed improper acts. Concealing these acts required even more unacceptable practices, culminating in human disasters, tragedies, and limits on a wide spectrum of human rights. For the people to accept this as natural, the state had to possess additional means and instruments and to resort to indisputable and continuous lies. In 2000 Putin named this instrumentality the "vertical of power."

The Vertical of Power

It would be naive to assume that Putin and Company's lack of a formal program means that no such program exists. Of course it does. If it were openly proclaimed, however, both Russian and foreign public opinion would recoil in horror from the regime that has ruled Russia since 2000. Although this program is known only to the initiated, it can easily be deciphered by analyzing what the Russian authorities have done from the beginning of the present century. The program is one of reaction, reviving totalitarianism at home and expansion abroad.

When Putin became president, Russia was virtually ungovernable. Therefore, people accepted his deliberately neutral-sounding thesis about the need to establish a "vertical of power" in Russia as something natural, especially since the absence of a workable system of governance had produced negative consequences under both Gorbachev and Yeltsin. What that power represented, what its goals were, and what the means were for achieving them were quite another matter. Putin's vertical of power is nothing other than a new *oprichnina*—in other words, the creation of a group of Kremlin loyalists who enjoy special privileges and power.

I worked for many years with representatives of organizations that called themselves "the organs." Many of my colleagues and acquaintances belonged to these organizations. In the course of working with them, I acquired an in-depth understanding of their peculiar worldview. What, then, did those who took power in 2000 see as Russia's fundamental problems?

The first thing to understand is that a majority of employees of the Russian special services possess Bolshevik—that is, communist—convictions. Approaching the situation in Russia from this perspective, they trace the root of Russia's misfortunes to pluralism and the germs of democracy. Starting in 1997 when I was working in the Security Council, representatives of the special services "cultivated" the idea of the need to establish a two-party system in Russia rather than the multiplicity of parties that had sprung up in the first post-Soviet years. They spoke to me with such conviction about the harm of having a large number of parties that I realized they were parroting a line that had come down "from above." Under Yeltsin, however, this plan was not destined to be implemented.

The communist convictions of most officials in the special services and the military by no means signified their adherence to the ideas of Marx, Engels, and Lenin. They often had only the foggiest notion of such things. To them communism meant the organization of society, the way it functioned, and the relationship between the individual and the authorities. In other words, it was the Leninist-Stalinist model of state and society that inherently denied personal interests and enshrined public interests, which the authorities defined as the unity of thought and the domination of force in foreign and domestic policy.

When Gorbachev's opponents began to employ the vilest methods to stop his cascading reforms, the masses, with the help of the special services, naturally began to embrace the stereotype that politics is intrinsically a dirty business. Indeed, the KGB and the reactionary segment of the Soviet leadership proceeded from the false premise that all means were permissible to achieve their goals. Regrettably, from a short-term perspective, the extremely immoral Leninist-Stalinist approach to politics is justified. For this kind of politics to work, the tender shoots of democracy must be weeded out, the air holes through which fresh air flows must be sealed off, everything and everybody must be "arranged," and, above all, control must be established over the hitherto independent legislative and judicial powers as well as the mass media. As noted previously, Putin began his tenure as head of state by asserting his control over the Fourth Estate.

Intent on creating a new totalitarianism in Russia, Putin could not ignore the fact that the broad plenary powers of the president were partially limited by parliament. Under Yeltsin, the State Duma had been occasionally insubordinate and had even tried to impeach him. Moreover, not infrequently, opposition parties in the State Duma and the regional leaders seated in the upper house of parliament put the executive authorities in a difficult position. The new Russian autocrat could not abide such insubordination. Soon after assuming power he set about dismantling parliamentarianism in Russia; however, there was no special urgency with respect to the State Duma. Thanks to the efforts of the "patriots," a reliable pro-Putin majority had been established there.

In the summer of 2000 Putin changed the principle on which the Federation Council was based. Previously it comprised the heads of the constituent members of the federation; now it consisted of their appointed representatives. The upshot was that the Federation Council became wholly controlled by the Kremlin.

In September 2002 Putin administered a heavy blow to the very foundations of democracy. Changes were introduced into existing legislation that prohibited holding referenda in the last year of a presidential term or of the State Duma, as well as banning any initiative to hold a referendum during federal election campaigns. Thus, the prohibition covered the larger part of every election cycle, and the opportunity for citizens to initiate referenda was sharply constricted.

Beginning in December 2004, the highest officials (presidents and governors) of the constituent units of the Russian Federation began to be appointed by the respective regional parliaments on recommendations from the president of the federation. The people were deprived of the opportunity to elect the heads of the regions, who thus became wholly divorced from their constituents and completely dependent on the Kremlin. The governors had to please a single elector—namely, the president.

The year 2005 bade farewell to any hopes for fair parliamentary elections. New legislation stipulated that elections be conducted exclusively according to party lists, making it impossible to elect independent candidates, to create electoral blocs at every level of elections, and, for small parties, to unite and enter parliament through joint efforts. In addition, the threshold of unverified voters' signatures that would disqualify a party or a candidate from registering to run in elections was lowered from 25 percent to 10 percent. Since the verification of signatures is conducted by electoral commissions and law enforcement organs appointed by the vertical of power, this provides an opportunity to disqualify any party it so desires. But even this was not enough for the authorities. They also placed restrictions on election observers. As a result of these restrictions, only parties that have registered their lists for the election are permitted to send observers. This provision sharply limits the opportunity for independent oversight of the elections.

The Kremlin deemed these amendments to the legislation insufficient, and in July 2006 new changes were introduced that prohibited political parties from nominating members of other parties to stand in the elections. Thus, minor parties lost any chance whatsoever of combining their efforts, not by formally creating already prohibited electoral blocs, but by nominating candidates on some sort of single "basic" list. Moreover, political sympathies and party loyalty became the basis for limiting the passive voting rights of voters and the active rights of candidates aspiring to become deputies. At the same time, in elections at every level the choice of "none of the above" was removed. Russian citizens were thereby robbed of the opportunity to vote against all candidates as a way of expressing both their lack of faith in the candidates and the parties allowed to take part in the elections and their desire for new elections. Previously, if a majority of voters voted for "none of the above," the elections were considered invalid.

Finally, to avoid any election surprises, in November 2006 the requirement that a certain minimum number of voters must actually cast ballots to validate an election was abolished. Voters were thereby deprived of their final opportunity "to vote with their feet" as a way to force new elections with new candidates. It now became possible *to conduct elections without voters*.

By stretching the concept of "extremism" to the limit (more follows), the registration of candidates accused of "extremist activities" was forbidden. Thus, persons with uncleared convictions for various stipulated actions or those who had been handed administrative punishment for preparing and disseminating banned political symbols were excluded. This created supplementary mechanisms for barring the opposition from elections. It also introduced an extrajudicial limit on voting rights. Finally, electioneering through the media by certain candidates and parties against other candidates and parties was prohibited. Thus, the last elements of political competition were quashed, the opposition was unable to inform citizens of the mistakes committed by the authorities, and the citizens were deprived of the right to learn about them.

Not content with these legislative changes, Putin blatantly falsified election results on a broad scale. Technology was an important means for doing this.[1] Up until December 2011 when short-lived protest demonstrations occurred in Moscow, although well aware of these deceptions, people did not react to the familiar practice of rigging the election results, the pressure to vote for candidates indicated from "on high," the destruction of ballots, and the other forms of manipulating the elections. Thus, for the time being all future elections results were decided in advance. However, it cannot be denied that were honest elections held, their results would still tally with the Kremlin's needs. Yet the democratic opposition would be able to stay active in politics, thereby keeping alive hope for the emergence of civil society.

The concept of extremism was adapted for use in the struggle against dissenters. The law "On Counteracting Extremist Activity," adopted in 2002 and amended on July 27, 2006, includes the aforementioned vague notion of undermining the security of the Russian Federation. Moreover, it reenacts under a different name the notorious Article 11 of the Criminal Code, which replaced the explicitly political Articles 70 and 190 of the Soviet Criminal Code (referred to in chapter 1). In the same spirit, included in the definition of extremist activity is "the creation and/or dissemination of printed, audio, audio-visual or other materials (output) intended for public use and containing even one of the indicators stipulated in the present article."

However, progress continues on this front, and the Putinist lawmakers have improved upon Soviet penal legislation. With adoption of the amendments in 2006, the definition of extremism was further expanded to include "financing of the stipulated activity or other assistance in planning, organizing, preparing, and implementing the stipulated activity, including by means of financial resources, real estate, instructional, polygraphic and material-technological, telephonic, fax or other means of communication, information services, or other material-technical means." Moreover, any criticism of the authorities is defined as extremism. Anyone may be held responsible—for example, someone who rented out an apartment where extremist material was written, who lent money to an author, who allowed an author to use the telephone, fax, or email. One can hardly imagine all the possible interpretations of this notoriously illegitimate legislative norm.

So just what is this "extremist material"? It is "documents intended for publication or information for other bearers." But how does one determine if the materials are intended for publication? And where is freedom of speech? But this has no meaning for the legislator. The "author of print, audio, audio-visual and other materials (output) intended for public use and containing even one of the indicators stipulated in Article 1 of the present Federal law is considered to be a person engaged in extremist activity and bears responsibility in accordance with procedures established by the legislation of the Russian Federation." This responsibility is stipulated in Article 282 of the Criminal Code of the Russian Federation on "Inciting Hatred or Enmity as well as Humiliation of Human Dignity." The punishment is up to five years' deprivation of freedom.

No policies to encourage extremism exist in any civilized country, so this is a typical flourish of the current Russian hypocrites.

For the reader to develop a clearer picture of the goals and means of the vertical of power, we must again step outside the temporal limits of this book. Putin's third official presidential term has been marked by genuine legislative madness. (It is really his fourth term, as it is clear that the stuffed teddy bear Dmitry Medvedev took virtually no decisions during his term as president [2008–12] and simply warmed the presidential chair for his boss.) There is a good reason why Russian wits call the State Duma, or Russia's parliament, the State Dummy and the Runaway Printer. With unusual speed this strange machine has adopted draconian laws reinstating criminal responsibility for slander, the definition of which is vague in the Soviet tradition; prohibiting Americans from adopting Russian orphans; prohibiting foul language, which a large part of the population employs to one degree or another and which the overwhelming majority use at least occasionally; blacklisting websites, or censoring the Internet; tightening the rules for conducting meetings; outlining punishment for insulting the feelings of believers (the sensitivities of nonbelievers are ignored); passing a homophobic law; and prohibiting adoptions by same-sex couples.

Particularly noteworthy is the law that forces nongovernmental organizations (NGOs) receiving financial or other aid from abroad and "participating in political activities" to register as foreign agents. This is a sinister formulation in the Soviet Russian tradition, suggesting something extremely hostile to the country. By this means, the NGOs are made to condemn themselves as representatives of the interests of other countries and not of Russia. Moreover, in print as well as on the Internet, they must indicate that their publications were prepared by these same "foreign agents." Irrespective of their statutory goals and missions, any activity carried out on the territory of the Russian Federation—not only participation in political actions aimed at influencing policy but also in shaping public opinion—is considered political activity. Naturally, joint-stock companies with state participation and their branches are excluded from the scope of this law. This is a masterful trap. Many NGOs must either admit they are foreign agents and suffocate from lack of funds or immediately close up shop. Moreover, even after registering as foreign agents, the NGOs are subject to financial checks, supposedly aimed against money laundering of illegally obtained funds and against financing of terrorism. Their activities are scrutinized under a microscope. Further, the authorities can deny registration to any NGO on simple, unsubstantiated suspicions.

The overall result is the revival of repressive Soviet legislation but dressed up differently. In the absence of open persecution for political and religious convictions, even broader prohibitions—for example, of "extremism"—are required for the sake of appearances.

Toward this end Media-Most and NTV were destroyed, and then other independent mass media was as well. After suppressing freedom of speech, the guillotine for democracy was adjusted and perfected.

Pandora's Box

The blackest legacy of Soviet times was restored even prior to the seizure of power by the special services. This real Pandora's box was opened partly from mindlessness, partly from the incompetence of those in power and their inability to solve problems, and partly from a desire to deal with current issues. But there can be no doubt that from this Pandora's box burst forth terrorism, violence against one's own citizens, a spy scare, and heightened fears of both imagined and real dangers (which, of course, were sometimes specially concocted by the authorities). They were all deployed to create an atmosphere of general hysteria in the country to facilitate controlling the population. The reactionaries deliberately unleashed the genie of violence when they were still battling against Gorbachev's reformation. Under Yeltsin violence became a daily occurrence in Russian politics. It would take hundreds of pages to fully analyze the violence of the Russian state. Here I shall address only the most prominent manifestations. First, let us consider the role of violence itself in Russian politics over the past century.

Violence inflicted upon its own citizens is a trademark of twentieth- and twenty-first-century Russia. The Red Terror. The legendary Solovki Islands—the site of the first Soviet concentration camps where, beginning in 1921, Lenin exiled the nation's intellectual and spiritual elite—became the forerunner of the GULAG. The destruction of the nobility, the intelligentsia, the priesthood, the better-off peasantry, and other "enemies of the people" was the foundation of Bolshevik policy as were genocide and the forced internal deportation of people of various nationalities who were inhabiting the USSR. It is difficult even to enumerate the varieties of violence.

The USSR would not have survived long without violence against its own citizens. Mass repression was curtailed after the death of Stalin in 1953, but in 1962 the authorities decided to use the familiar methods "to restore order" in Novocherkassk.[2] However, this was the lone example of force being applied within Russia. Naturally, even after the demise of the USSR and during investigations conducted in 1993–94, the names of those responsible for the deaths were not revealed.

During perestroika, the provocative and disproportionate use of force occurred with beatings and teargassing in several regional capitals. Each was a disaster. In most cases the violence was provoked by neo-Stalinists for whom force was a political weapon. The lives and well-being of fellow humans were small change in the struggle to achieve political and other ambitions. The stakes were power.

Once Yeltsin became the undisputed head of state, he frequently resorted to outright violence. He first unleashed violence in October 1993, when he ordered tanks to shell the rebellious parliament. The state of emergency declared at that time led to massive violations of human rights, including attacks against passengers on public transport who included women, children, and the elderly.

One cannot reproach Putin for neglecting the coercive agencies. He loves to play with toy soldiers, not miniature lead ones, but live ones as he has done in Chechnya, in Georgia, in Ukraine, and in Syria. He views the officials of the law enforcement organs as his toy soldiers and the oppositionists as enemy toy soldiers. The rest of the population, which he considers the "electorate," are also toy soldiers. He would like them to be unthinking and submissive. Dressed in a flight suit he loves to pose in front of television cameras with his entourage in the cockpit of a jet fighter or a strategic missile bomber. He also loves to play with toy boats. As commander in chief he has this prerogative. This "leader of the nation" also does not hesitate to use force against his own people or against foreign countries.

This is not the place to attempt an exhaustive analysis, or even a full listing, of this phenomenon. Instead, I shall address a few of the more dangerous processes taking place in Russia.

Terrorism

Traditionally the Russian authorities required an enemy. In Soviet times prior to Gorbachev, "world imperialism" filled the bill. From the Kremlin's perspective, it brought in its train regional and local conflicts and "national-liberation struggles" (that in many cases were actually inspired by Moscow) and spawned international crises, some of which threatened a global nuclear missile confrontation. Undoubtedly, the Soviet Union's "anti-imperialist struggle" was one of the sources of international terrorism.[3] From the moment Russia began trying to "civilize" itself, the situation changed. Mikhail Gorbachev thought that having an enemy was not only unnecessary but even counterproductive. For Boris Yeltsin and his successors, however, an enemy was necessary. Why? To rationalize the breakdown of the country and its impoverishment. To hold onto power, to protect themselves.

Terror has a long history in Russia. Starting in the 1860s, terror was one of the basic means of revolutionary struggle. It was widely used to eliminate persons whom the revolutionaries deemed "harmful" and to destabilize society in order to obtain funding and other resources.[4] After achieving power, the revolutionaries did not dispense with this familiar and effective instrument for eliminating adversaries. In this respect, the USSR and Russia attained the very pinnacle of success.[5] De facto terror was the foundation of politics in the USSR. In twenty-three provinces of Russia from June 1918 through February 1919, 5,496 persons, of whom only 800 were ordinary criminals, were shot by Cheka organs.[6] In 1920, 6,541 persons were sentenced to death by revolutionary military tribunals.[7]

Naturally, the USSR employed terrorism in one form or another in its "anti-imperialist struggle." It is no coincidence that the bloodiest of pro-Soviet regimes, as well as leftist and extremist organizations, actively employed terrorism. Nor is it an accident that Ilyich Ramirez Sanchez, famous as Carlos the Jackal, was enrolled in a terrorist school in Cuba, a state friendly to the USSR. He also attended Moscow's former Patrice Lumumba Friendship University (since renamed), a school that trained revolutionaries and was known in the West as a global terrorist academy. Nor was it by chance that Abdullah Öcalan, founder of the Kurdistan Workers' Party, hid out in Russia, which he entered quite legally, although he was being pursued by police from many countries.

The first really notorious terrorist act in contemporary Russian history took place on June 14, 1994, in Budyonnovsk, where Chechen fighters seized hostages, including staff, at a two-thousand-bed hospital. Nevertheless, on June 16, during the crisis, Yeltsin flew to Halifax for a meeting of the Group of Seven. On his orders, on June 17, an assault on the hospital began, during which 166 persons were killed and more than 400 wounded. According to numerous witnesses, all the victims were killed or wounded by federal troops. The attack failed; the terrorists fled. Meanwhile, the public was shocked that Yeltsin was enjoying himself in Halifax. Then he attained one of his "high points," announcing, without any proof, that Turkey was prepared to provide sanctuary to the president of Chechnya, Dzhokhar Dudaev, and that Dudaev had accepted this proposal. The Russian president concluded his portentous announcement by asserting that Chechnya had become the center of global terrorism.

A series of meaningless, anonymous terrorist acts followed, without demands being made. Because of their specific characteristics, no historical analogies could be drawn with them. There was no answer to the question of why and by whom they were being committed, especially since the victims of the anonymous terrorists—terrorists who made no demands—were random persons, passengers on municipal transport, planes, trains. Right after each such crime a "Chechen footprint" was found but then quickly disappeared. People were terrified, especially in Moscow, where most of the terrorist acts occurred. Apparently the only goal of these terrorist acts was to create an atmosphere of fear, to incite hysteria. Strange as it may seem, one possible answer to the question of why lay right at hand: it is quite possible that the authorities were securing for themselves an ability to act freely against terrorists. One can also not discount that under Yeltsin the sharpest interclan struggles had developed.

What should we make of the claim that Chechens committed these terrorist acts? This version is totally logical when one considers how much grief the federal authorities have inflicted upon practically every Chechen family. However, the tradition of blood vengeance is hardly relevant here. It is always directed against specific offenders and does not entail revenge on the basis of nationality. Moreover, in Chechnya a code of honor still prevails that does not include anonymity, especially regarding revenge. In several instances Chechen leaders claimed responsibility for terrorist acts they were accused of committing even though, according to the Russian special services, these leaders actually had nothing to do with them. They claimed responsibility believing that such notorious terrorist acts would bolster their authority. Finally, one cannot discount the practice of kamikaze (suicide) attacks, like those in the Middle East, by persons who make no demands whatsoever. In sum, the truth about terrorist acts under Yeltsin is complicated and multidimensional.

In Russia the background of this series of terrorist acts was quite distinctive. A domestic political struggle was being waged between those who sought revenge for Russia's defeat in the war with Chechnya, on the one hand, and those who favored a peaceful resolution of the Chechen problem, on the other. Against this background, I could hardly ignore what someone from the Federal Security Service whispered to me: behind all these terrorist acts stood Minister of Internal Affairs Anatoly Kulikov, who had supposedly established a secret subunit for this purpose. This sounded quite plausible, since Kulikov was one of the leaders of the "war party," but the FSB was not exactly a trustworthy source of information. It is doubtful that, apart from those who never talk, anyone could say with assurance what the truth really was. Perhaps the whisper was intended to deflect attention away from the real guilty party and toward another agency? In any case, one sensed, at the very least, that behind several of the terrorist acts during Yeltsin's administration stood *someone in power who did not want to see a peaceful resolution of the problems Russia faced, including that of Chechnya.*

Of course, under Yeltsin the problem of terrorism was particularly acute and abnormal. After all, it was he who launched the First Chechen War, releasing the genie of terrorism from the bottle. It was on his watch that the special services began playing with terrorist acts. However, there is nothing more cynical than what Putin has been up to with respect to terrorism. His stance toward terrorism is simple: Terrorism benefits him, and he makes use of it. To do so he must lie systematically, which he does selflessly, ecstatically, mechanically, as the spy-president was taught to do.

Putin came to power on a wave of fear evoked by the explosions in apartment houses in Moscow on the night of September 9, 1999, on Guryanova Street and early in the morning of September 13, on Kashirskoye Boulevard.[8] In the absence of any evidence, responsibility for these terrorist acts was laid on Chechen separatists.

Who could believe the later assertion by the director of the FSB that employees of his organization had furtively placed hexogen, which had been used for the explosions in Moscow, in an apartment block in Ryazan supposedly to test the vigilance of citizens? Of course, no one believed this. And then they forgot about it. It would have been better not to forget, for the result was that the authorities got away with it. After all, the FSB had been caught red-handed.

Literally on the eve of Putin's appointment, the second incursion of Chechen fighters into Dagestan occurred and was immediately characterized as "international terrorism." (Since it was not on his watch, it means he was not guilty! Who recalls that he headed the FSB at the time? No one remembers.) His assertion about it being international terrorism appears to be gibberish or basic illiteracy. How could one speak of international terrorism within the boundaries of a single, albeit multinational, country? But it was neither gibberish nor illiteracy but a precise, far-reaching calculation. After the terrorist acts of September 11, 2001, in the United States, Putin found the bogeyman of international terrorism extremely helpful! It was this tragedy, along with his boldly stated declaration that terrorism in Russia was not homegrown but international, that helped Putin convince President George W. Bush to insist the European Union should reconcile with Russia and not allow any further cooling of relations. Thanks to this assertion, the West overlooked the Kremlin's outrages in Chechnya, the de facto elimination of freedom of the mass media, and all its other excesses.

Russians were enthusiastic that a decisive man was at the helm, a man who had launched an antiterrorist operation against Chechnya. Again almost no one noticed the bald lie. From the start it was hardly "antiterrorist operations"; rather, there were broad-scale military actions, skillfully managed politically, that led to a wave of terrorism. In any case, Putin's poll numbers shot up, which is what he wanted. According to what was long the official version, terrorism and Chechnya were indistinguishable. But the most terrible terrorist acts that occurred were so mysterious that one could not help wondering how they could take place and then end in the way they did.

That Putin also managed to turn these major terrorist acts to his advantage raises disturbing questions. Included among these acts was the surrealistic story of some 700 theatergoers who attended the popular Moscow musical *Nord-Ost* in the theatrical center in Dubrovka and were taken hostage on October 23, 2002. (This figure is an estimate; the actual number of hostages is unknown.) The terrorists demanded the withdrawal of troops from Chechnya and promised to blow up the building if it was stormed. Was this another confirmation of Putin's thesis never to negotiate with terrorists and not to withdraw troops from Chechnya? As far as he was concerned, the terrorists could just "go take a piss." This is just how most ordinary Russians reacted: They praised Putin for not negotiating with the terrorists. In effect, they applauded the authorities for killing so many people rather than leaving that to the terrorists. Meanwhile, the international community was horrified and expressed condolences but did not raise any inconvenient questions. A routine investigation followed that spared the Kremlin any embarrassment.

According to official figures, 129 people died as the tragic result of this hostage-taking and the subsequent storming of the theater by special forces. (On good evidence, independent experts consider this a low estimate.) Most of the victims died from an unknown and rather mysterious gas that the special services used before storming the building. Many obvious questions remain unanswered. How could such a large group of terrorists, who were armed to the teeth, enter the hall without hindrance? Where did they live and make preparations for the seizure of hostages? Where did they store their weapons and prepare their explosives? Who planned the operation? Why were all the terrorists, without exception, killed after they were helpless and unconscious following the use of the gas? Was the report about taking two terrorists prisoner—a man and a woman—true? If so, why was nothing more heard about them? Why did some of the special forces participate in the attack without an antidote (to the poison gas)? Why were the medics unprepared to receive the victims and not informed about the type of gas employed? In the final analysis, how many people died? To say the least, everyone knows that the official figures for the number of dead were far from accurate.

The mysterious gas responsible for the deaths during the "liberation" of the hostages deserves separate mention. Contrary to the official version and according to information in *Novaia gazeta*, what was employed in Dubrovka was not based on fentanyl, for which there is an antidote, but rather another inhalant anesthetic, phtorotan. (In the West it is called galotan.) It needs to be very carefully controlled since in its surgical state the drug quickly anesthetizes people and makes it very difficult for them to breathe, leading to asphyxiation and death. In the words of the newspaper's medical expert, "Apparently, those who decided to employ phtorotan were impressed by its virtues: it does not ignite, it does not burn, it does not explode, as it does in its gaseous state."[9]

Much is explained by the whispered information that it was Putin who supposedly personally directed the operation to "liberate" the hostages of *Nord-Ost*. Moreover, the investigative journalist Anna Politkovskaya published an article in *Novaia gazeta* that in any country other than Russia would most likely have led to the fall of those in power. Politkovskaya demonstrated the complicity of the authorities in the tragedy and their role in aiding and abetting the terrorists. She managed to find out that one of the terrorists who had seized the theater and was later killed, according to various sources, was working in the Information Division of President Putin's administration with spin doctor Sergei Yastrzhembskii and had associated with Vladislav Surkov.

Politkovskaya and the editors of *Novaia gazeta* believed that a certain Khanpash Terkibaev was an agent dispatched by the special services to manage the terrorist act from within. It was Terkibaev who secretly secured the passage of the Chechen terrorists through Moscow to the Dubrovka theater, which he entered as a member of the terrorist detachment and then left before the attack commenced. In Politkovskaya's words, "It was he who assured the terrorists that 'everything is under control,' 'it's full of scum,' that 'Russians have again taken money,' and all you need to do is to 'make a bit of a noise,' and what will come out of it is a 'second Budyonnovsk and that way we will secure peace, and then, after the assignment is fulfilled 'they will let us go'—not all of us, but they'll let us go."[10] It follows from this that *the seizure of hostages in the theater was initiated and organized by someone from the special services.*

After *Nord-Ost*, Terkibaev became a "companion in arms" in President Putin's administration and was supplied with "all the documents enabling him to travel freely everywhere he was needed," thereby giving him access to the Chechen leader Aslan Maskhadov and to Yastrzhembskii. He was even entrusted with engaging in negotiations, in the name of the Putin administration, with deputies of the Chechen parliament and escorting them, as the leader of the group, to the Council of Europe in Strasbourg, France.[11]

An even more terrible terrorist act was the seizure on September 1, 2004, of a school in Beslan in southern Russia, where, contrary to preliminary official information claiming there were 354 hostages, independent sources said there were actually 1,200. The preliminary official version stated that more than 390 persons died. Others claim the authorities did not include 350 unidentified body parts in the number of victims. According to official data, 700 former hostages were hospitalized. More than 200 persons (the figure of 260 is also given) were also said to be missing. Excuse me—how can they be missing?

Yet another cynical lie: tanks and flamethrowers were involved in storming the school. The preliminary official version failed to mention this. How can this action be called rescuing hostages? Who was saving them by employing inappropriate weapons? We should thank the people of Beslan who forced the authorities to acknowledge what would otherwise have been concealed. Yet something else has not been revealed—namely, who issued this criminal command. Most likely only an extremely cynical person endowed with enormous power could act so incompetently.

Putin took advantage of this terrorist act to further suppress democracy and escalate his cruel policies. He issued an extremely pointed statement asserting that "weakness" was the cause for what had happened. (The weak get beaten, the head of state explained, using the logic of common hooligans.) Most important, Putin characterized the seizure of the school in Beslan as "an attack against Russia." According to Putin, terrorism is an instrument for "tearing fat chunks" off of Russia. Russia was confronting a "total, cruel, and full-scale war." The logical conclusion was that it was necessary to strengthen the authorities. (Toward this end, during the Chechen campaigns, the president did away with the direct election of governors.)

Why then was it necessary to kill Aslan Maskhadov in March 2005? He was the most moderate and, at the time, the most legitimate Chechen leader. Was it so there would be no one with whom to sit down at the negotiating table? And why, for so many years after what was pronounced the victorious conclusion of the antiterrorist operation, did Shamil Basaev, the Chechen guerrilla leader, remain so elusive that the question arose as to whether he possessed some sort of safe conduct document? Later, according to a triumphal communiqué, he was supposedly killed by the FSB in July 2006, but no one was able to confirm this reliably.

Finally, why did Putin, who unthinkingly preferred to sacrifice the lives of hundreds of his "subjects" and would not "even sit down at the negotiation table with terrorists," *personally* and with evident pleasure, invite Hamas to Moscow in 2006, to the revulsion of the civilized world?

Eliminating Undesirables

One of the problems illegitimate states face is the frequent need to engage in cover-ups with respect both to specific individuals and to their own actions. Even so, sometimes what is secret becomes known. Another requisite is the need to deny actions and information that would harm the illegitimate entity and its officials.

A unique situation developed in post-perestroika Russia. The instruments for suppressing and punishing dissenters and for forcing the people into conformity had been disbanded. At the same time, after the breakup of the USSR, wide-scale looting, sharp and unrestrained political struggles, and many other factors logically facilitated the natural elimination, including physical elimination, of persons whom the state or individuals in power considered undesirable.

The journalist Dmitry Kholodov, who worked for the popular scandal sheet *Moskovskii komsomolets* (Moscow Komsomol member), was the first victim of a notorious political assassination. He died in an explosion in his office on October 17, 1994, when he opened an attaché case that supposedly contained important documents. According to the investigation, Kholodov was gathering materials for an article in which he intended to address corruption in Russia's Western army group. He was scheduled to appear soon at parliamentary hearings on this question.

If the elimination of Kholodov was likely intended to cover up the theft of military property and the involvement of various officials, the killing of opposition deputies in Russia's State Duma was quite a different matter. Gen. Lev Rokhlin, who sharply criticized the situation in Russia, especially in the army, and demanded the dismissal of President Boris Yeltsin, was killed on the night of June 3, 1998. His widow was accused of his murder but was later cleared.

Galina Starovoitova, one of Russia's leading democratic activists and rights defenders and a candidate for president of the Russian Federation in 1996, was shot in the doorway of her house in St. Petersburg on the night of November 20–21, 1998.

On August 21, 2002, Vladimir Golovlev was killed. He was one of five cochairmen of Liberal Russia, a party opposed to Putin that had been initially founded by Boris Berezovsky but later turned against him. In depositions he provided the Procuracy of the Chelyabinsk region regarding privatization in the district, Golovlev asserted that several well-known persons were involved in questionable dealings. Among them he named Anatoly Chubais and Viktor Khristenko, who held high posts in Russia. The mass media reported that in all about fifty persons had been named, including the entire leadership of the Chelyabinsk region in the 1990s and a number of high Kremlin officials.

Sergei Yushenkov, a friend and comrade in arms of the previously assassinated deputies Golovlev and Starovoitova, as well as of the leader of Russian human rights activists Sergei Kovalev, was shot four times on April 17, 2003. An investigation did not rule out the possibility that the killing of the two deputies to the State Duma and the leaders of Liberal Russia, Yushenkov and Golovlev, were linked. *The killing took place on the day that Liberal Russia, the party of which Yushenkov was a leader, officially announced it had completed registration with the Ministry of Justice and declared it was fully prepared for the elections.* Yushenkov had charged that Putin had come to power as the result of a coup d'état, and he accused the special services of being involved in the apartment house explosions in Moscow and Volgodonsk in the fall of 1999.

At least one more death fits the category of political murder. On July 3, 2003, Yury Shchekochikhin, deputy chairman of the State Duma's Committee on Security and deputy editor in chief of the opposition newspaper *Novaia gazeta*, died of a sudden and raging illness. According to the official version, the cause was a very rare acute allergic reaction, although Shchekochikhin had never suffered from allergies.

All these are widely known, if partially forgotten, facts. But no one knows how many undesirable politicians and journalists in the country were killed, maimed, beaten, terrorized, or intimidated. Few also were aware of, or paid any attention to, any cases concerning the leakage of information about several interesting documents.[12]

On February 13, 2004, the Kremlin executioners turned a new

page in their history when the former vice president of Chechnya Zelimkhan Yandarbiev was killed in Qatar. In Doha the Qatari special services quickly arrested three Russian citizens who were on assignment there and accused them of the premeditated murder of Yandarbiev. One of them, an official of the Russian Embassy, was subsequently released. The court in Qatar sentenced the two others, who did not enjoy diplomatic immunity, to life sentences.

Russian authorities were suspected of numerous attempts on the life of Georgian president Eduard Shevardnadze. Russia was also the main suspect in the attempt on the life of Ukrainian presidential candidate Viktor Yushchenko, who was hospitalized during the election campaign in September 2004. His doctors concluded that he had been poisoned with dioxin.

In the fall of 2006, there took place what can only be called an orgy of political killings committed for their shock effect. On October 7, the well-known opposition journalist Anna Politkovskaya was shot dead in the entryway to her house. Almost immediately, Putin cynically asserted that this murder would cause more harm than her activity as a journalist did. In Putin's view, the harm Politkovskaya had caused was mostly because she had openly and fearlessly criticized him.

Mystery cloaked the investigation of this crime. For example, security cameras captured the car in which the killers had arrived, as well as a view of the house itself, but the license plate numbers were not visible. They tried to determine the numbers from other cameras, but everything was obscured. Forensic expertise was of no help. Nevertheless, they managed to determine the car in which the killers had arrived. Later it turned out that some time before the death of the journalist, Lt. Col. Pavel Ryaguzov of the FSB had extracted Politkovskaya's address from an FSB database and immediately phoned his old acquaintance Shamil Buraev, the former head of the Achkhoi-Martanovskii district in Chechnya, who was loyal to the Russian Federation. When it turned out it was an old address, a police operation was mounted to discover the new one. Thus, two groups had Politkovskaya under observation: one was the killers; the other was responsible for surveillance and infiltration.

On November 23, 2006, former FSB officer, forty-four-year-old

Alexander Litvinenko, who had fled to Great Britain in 2000 and received a British passport in October 2006, died in the hospital of University College London. A significant amount of the radioactive element polonium-21—a rare substance that is strictly controlled in the few countries, including Russia, that produce it—was found in his body. The English doctors and police unsettled Moscow, because they had not only found polonium-210 in Litvinenko's body but also established where he had been poisoned and identified his suspected poisoners (former officers of the Russian special services Andrei Lugovoi and Dmitry Kovtun), and other victims, including the bartender who had served the poisoned tea. They also found traces of radioactive contamination in places Litvinenko, Lugovoi, and Kovtun had visited.

A rather striking illustration of what was going on was Russia's dissemination, in various forms, of all kinds of improbable versions of the murder—for example, that Litvinenko had traded in polonium and didn't know how to handle it, and that he had committed suicide ("to irritate Putin"). The poorly concealed disinclination of the Russian investigation organs to cooperate with the British and their categorical refusal to hand over to British justice the prime suspect Lugovoi were equally telling. (Lugovoi was transformed into virtually a national hero and elected a deputy to the Duma from the Liberal Democratic Party of Russia, which, as noted previously, had been created with the help of the Soviet KGB.)

Soon the situation became quite Kafkaesque. At a conference in Dublin on November 24—that is, the day after Litvinenko died—Yegor Gaidar, the head of the first Yeltsin government, suddenly felt very ill and was rushed to a hospital with signs of poisoning. An examination by Irish doctors established that the patient had undergone a radical deterioration in his main bodily functions over a short period. However, they were unable to determine the cause, nor were traces of radiation found in Gaidar's body or in places that he had visited. The doctors were also unable to give a diagnosis of the poisoning since there was no actual toxic substance in Gaidar's system. Irish and British police conducted an investigation of the incident. For good reason, Gaidar was obviously frightened by what had happened to him and accused "the explicit or covert opponents of the Russian authorities who wish to promote the further radical deterioration of relations between Russia and the West." That Gaidar's condition improved while he was in a Moscow hospital and that an unusual statement later was issued in his name, one that unexpectedly echoed the official position that Litvinenko had been poisoned by notorious "enemies of Russia," naturally raised serious questions. An author of political thrillers might depict the situation as resulting from the blackmail of a well-known Russian politician who had been given an antidote in exchange for issuing such a statement and stopping his criticism of Putin. The impunity of the killers and the anonymity of those who commissioned these crimes are the trademarks of political killings in Russia.

Nevertheless, occasionally the curtain of secrecy is raised, as happened with the murders of Litvinenko and Zelimkhan Yandarbiev, thanks to foreign special services and sometimes thanks to journalists. Thus, for example, a sensational article by Igor Korol'kov, published in *Novaia gazeta*, revealed that criminal gangs had been created in Russia that were working under the supervision of the special services and the Ministry of Internal Affairs.[13] Their mission was the extrajudicial elimination of undesirables. Investigations into their crimes were obstructed and criminal cases collapsed. Witnesses who were prepared to give depositions about the involvement of the GRU (military intelligence) in these activities were eliminated. One gang had been assembled from veteran criminals who had been released early from prison and provided with arms to assist in the redistribution of property.

An investigation of the murder of the journalist Kholodov pointed to these organizations. Officers of the GRU who had been involved in special operations in Abkhazia in Georgia, the Trans-Dniestr region of Moldova, and in Chechnya, where they physically eliminated persons who had been fingered to them, fell under suspicion. One of the accused officers had once placed a magnetic explosive device under the car of Russia's then deputy minister of finance Andrei Vavilov; fortunately, the deputy minister was not killed. While investigating the Kholodov case, apart from the GRU, the investigation also pointed to the organized crime division (GUBOP) of the Ministry of Internal Affairs.[14]

Let us revisit the series of terrorist acts in Moscow in the mid-1990s that took place during Yeltsin's presidency. The idea of a well-coordinated attack on Moscow by Chechen gunmen received wide currency. However, as an investigation and a court later proved, it was not Chechen fighters but a former KGB colonel who exploded the bus at the National Exhibition of Economic Achievements. It was also a former FSB officer who tried to blow up the railroad bridge across the Yauza River in Moscow. Both of these former employees of the special services were directly connected to Maxim Lazovsky's criminal gang.[15] At least eight active duty officers of the FSB worked in close contact with the gang. This was established by the chief of the Twelfth Section of the Moscow Criminal Investigation Department Vladimir Tskhai, a lieutenant colonel in the militia. As soon as it became clear that the Moscow militia headquarters would not relinquish its spoils, Lazovsky and his closest accomplices were eliminated, while the teetotaler Tskhai died from cirrhosis of the liver.

Novaia gazeta possesses a document that appears to be a set of secret instructions. It refers to the creation of a completely secret, illegal, special subdivision and of several regional operational fighting groups. The organizational form of this body took the form of a private detective and security enterprise, and its leadership and core employees appear to be persons released from the operational services of the *Ministry of the Interior, the FSB, the SVR, and the GRU*.[16] The plan is to establish a public organization—for example, the "Association of Veterans of Russian Special Services"—as a cover for its investigative and operational fighting activities. According to the plan, this organization will be utilized, in particular, in the creation of *permanently operating pseudo detachments* that will have strong operational contacts directly with the bandit wing of the OPGs and with the OPGs themselves, specializing in contract killings and terrorist acts.[17] What was envisaged was an organization of "*a fully equipped fictitious military unit both in the regions and in the center.*" Utilization of the special forces' extralegal reconnaissance "*to neutralize or physically eliminate the leaders and active members of terrorist and intelligence-sabotage groups waging war against federal authorities*" was not ruled out. Attention should be paid to the fact that murders would be committed *"with the goal of averting serious consequences."*[18]

Thus, in the view of *Novaia gazeta*, an integrated special services system has been created to carry out extrajudicial executions. According to *Novaia gazeta*'s sources, this document was signed by one of the then leaders of GUBOP, Colonel Seliverstov, and based on a secret resolution of the government. Yury Skokov, first deputy prime minister of Russia in the early 1990s, took part in drafting the resolution.

According to *Novaia gazeta*, this activity was coordinated by an FSB subunit, completely secret even by the organization's own standards, that was established in the early 1990s as the Directorate for Working with Criminal Organizations and was headed by Gen. Yevgeny Khokhol'kov. The mission of this subunit, consisting of 150 persons, was to infiltrate secret agents into the criminal world. This extremely secretive subunit was revealed at a press conference in 1998, at which five employees discussed its involvement in extrajudicial killings. Specifically, the employees asserted that the leadership of the directorate had hatched plans to physically eliminate Boris Berezovsky. After the press conference, the newspaper noted that the directorate was quickly disbanded, and Nikolai Kovalev, who was then the director of the FSB, retired.

According to *Novaia gazeta*, the technology of extrajudicial killings was perfected in Chechnya. Prisoners were interrogated under torture, then transported to an uninhabited place, where they were blown to pieces in groups of three to five.[19] As a result of such activity, criminality was elevated to what, in principle, was not only a new organizational but also political level.

On March 26, 2000, a tragedy occurred that was replicated on January 19, 2009. It started with Col. Yury Budanov. After getting thoroughly drunk while celebrating his daughter's birthday, he ordered Lt. Roman Bagreev to shoot up a peaceful Chechen village. The lieutenant did not obey. Then Budanov and his deputy, Lt. Col. Ivan Fedorov, beat up Bagreev. Afterward Budanov ordered the crew of his own infantry fighting vehicle to grab the eldest daughter of the Kungaevs, eighteen-year-old Elza, and take her to regimental headquarters. Unable to endure the "interrogation" that lasted for many hours,

Kungaeva died, and Budanov, who was later sentenced for kidnapping, rape, and murder, ordered that she be buried in the forest.

What happened subsequently is another mystery. Experts' conclusions differ on Budanov's responsibility. An examination "determined" that Budanov had not raped Kungaeva but that a certain soldier, Yegorov, had violated her corpse. Therefore, the charge of rape against Budanov was dismissed. Contrary to the findings of a court-ordered psychiatric examination, Budanov was sent for compulsory treatment. Then, under the influence of public opinion in Chechnya, the case was reexamined, and Budanov was sentenced to ten years in a hard labor penal colony, stripped of his state commendations, and denied the opportunity to hold leadership positions for three years after his release from confinement.

An overwhelming majority of the Russian public supported Budanov, and for many he became almost a national hero. After repeated requests for a pardon and conditional early release, in December 2008, the municipal court of Dimitrovgrad ruled that Budanov had repented of his crime and wholly absolved him of guilt. The authorities do not throw their own bastards to the wolves.

Then at a press conference in January 2009, in the Independent Press Center in Moscow, Stanislav Markelov, a well-known lawyer who had taken part in a series of high-profile cases and was an embarrassment to the authorities, announced his intention to dispute what he considered to be the illegal conditional early release of Budanov and, if necessary, to file a suit with the International Court for Human Rights in Strasbourg. After Markelov left the press conference, he was killed with a shot from a pistol fitted with a silencer. The *Novaia gazeta* journalist Anastasia Baburova, who left the press conference with him, threw herself on the killer, who then shot her.

Naturally, the Budanov case could be used as a cover for other objectives of the murder. For example, Markelov was connected with the *Nord-Ost* case, was a lawyer for Anna Politkovskaya, and represented the interests of those who suffered the mass slaughter by the Blagoveshchensk special-purpose militia unit in Bashkortostan in December 2004. Lawyers from the Institute for the Supremacy of Law, which he founded and directed, were actively engaged in the case of former GRU special forces Capt. Eduard

Ul'man, who confessed to the murder of six peaceful inhabitants of Chechnya as well as of Magomed Yevloev, owner of the website Ingushetiia.ru.[20] In other words, Markelov was punished for defending human rights and the independence of the judiciary.

After the murder of Stanislav Markelov, the assailant went into hiding. Moreover, for a long time *the investigation supposedly could not locate a single witness or a single clue.* Clearly, it is impossible to kill two people in broad daylight in central Moscow, not far from the Cathedral of Christ the Savior and a metro station, without being noticed.

These are only the most notorious cases. There are actually many, many more. I do not mean to imply that all the cases cited without exception are the result of actions by highly placed state authorities. It is another thing, however, to say that they have made the actions possible. Moreover, that people suspect their involvement itself speaks volumes. In sum, the orgy of killing "undesirables" began under Yeltsin and really took off during Putin's presidency.

Naturally, murder is the most efficacious and effective means of eliminating those who defy the authorities. But there are also other options—for example, making someone's life unbearable.

At the beginning of his administration, Putin was insufficiently skilled in the art of neutralizing those who stood in his way. Naive people interpreted his slogan of "Equidistance from the oligarchs" as a pledge not to make use of the oligarchs as his "money bags." It turned out that such an interpretation was quite wrong. Vladimir Gusinskii, who opposed him, was stripped of his media empire in Russia, and Boris Berezovsky, who helped bring Putin to power and was subsequently forced to flee to London for this fatal mistake, was also stripped of a large part of his fortune. *These* oligarchs were kept at a distance from influence in Russian politics; they were replaced by others. Gusinskii may have quieted down, but Putin miscalculated with respect to Berezovsky, who would not forgive his former fair-haired boy and became an active opponent of the Putin regime.

Yet another misfire of the early Putin period was the kidnapping by the special services of Radio Liberty journalist Andrei Babitskii, who had sharply critiqued Russian policy and its machinations in Chechnya. Babitskii was held by the Russian special forces supposedly for not having proper documents. The instantaneous exchange of the journalist, allegedly on his initiative, for three Russian soldiers supposedly taken prisoner by a nonexistent Chechen field commander was unpersuasive. Babitskii's release was secured solely due to the proactive stance taken by Russian and foreign journalists. There are grounds for suspecting that had the journalists been more passive, Babitskii would have been eliminated.

But Putin is educable. In February 2003 in a meeting with leading Russian businessmen in the Kremlin, the president of Russia asked, "Mr. Khodorkovsky, are you sure you're in compliance with the Tax Department?"

"Absolutely," replied the boss of the largest Russian oil company YUKOS and one of the richest men in Russia.

"Well, we'll see about that," Putin muttered ominously.

The result was that on October 25, 2003, the young oligarch, who had not concealed his presidential ambitions and who supported liberal political parties, was arrested. Prior to this, Chairman of the Board of Directors of the Menatep Interbank Association Platon Lebedev was arrested.[21] The core of the accusations against Khodorkovsky was that he had created an organized criminal group, by which, evidently, was meant his business partners, to evade taxes and engage in other improper activities.

Can anyone have the slightest doubt that YUKOS strove to maximize its profits or that the laws in force at the time these "crimes" were committed provided such an opportunity? The possibility that Khodorkovsky and some among his associates did something illegal cannot be ruled out. But something else is troubling: almost all Russian entrepreneurs were engaged in the same or similar activities, but only Khodorkovsky and YUKOS were punished. No unprejudiced observer could doubt that the underlying reason was the Kremlin's fear of Khodorkovsky's presidential ambitions. The selectivity of the judicial system in and of itself is testimony to its incompetence.

As ordered, the court sentenced Khodorkovsky to nine years in a camp. To discourage Khodorkovsky from aspiring for early release, he was regularly placed in a punitive isolation cell. But the authorities considered all this insufficient.

In the winter of 2007, a scandal erupted. On December 27, Vasily Aleksanian, the executive vice president of YUKOS who had served in his position for only five days and had been arrested on April 6, 2006, lodged an official complaint that accused the investigators of pressuring him by refusing to provide him with medical assistance. Yet the condition of the virtually blind Aleksanian, who was suffering from cancer and AIDS, was deemed "satisfactory," and he himself was judged "fit to undergo further inquiries." Just what were these further inquiries regarding a mortally ill and unspeakably suffering man? It was all very simple. Aleksanian was refused medical assistance because he did not agree to give testimony against Khodorkovsky and Lebedev in exchange for that medical assistance. Or, in Aleksanian's words, "in effect in exchange for my life." According to Aleksanian, when he said he knew of no crimes committed in YUKOS or by its employees and refused to give testimony, the conditions of his confinement deteriorated. He was denied pain medicines and held in a near-freezing cell that was so cold he had to sleep in his overcoat for an entire year.

Nevertheless, under the pressure of public opinion, on February 8, 2008, Aleksanian was transferred to a specialized clinic, and his trial was halted. But even then the authorities acted with extraordinary cynicism. Aleksanian was chained to his bed, not permitted to shower, and not allowed to say good-bye to his relatives.

Naturally, the Russian authorities never slackened their obsessive attention to journalists. According to what most likely is incomplete information from the Glasnost Defense Foundation, since Putin came to power the profession of journalism in Russia has become extremely dangerous. The following table, based on data the fund collected about journalists and editors, illustrates this point.

Year	Killed	Disappeared	Attacks on editors	Attacks on journalists
2001	17	3	102	
2002	20		99	
2003	10		96	29
2004	13		73	15
2005	6		63	12

2006	9		69	12
2007	8		75	11
2008	5	2	48	5
2009	9		58	10
2010	12		58	6
2011	6	1	80	
2012	3		91	4

Punitive psychiatry, that terrible instrument in the struggle against dissent, which had been eliminated with such difficulty under Gorbachev, was also revived. As in the past, there reportedly were numerous such cases.

Opposition politicians, rights defenders, political commentators, and journalists vanished from television screens and the mass print media. They were regularly replaced, to use Stalinist jargon, by small cogs in Putin's vertical power machine. The accusations against those who disappeared from public view were not always convincing. The result is that Russians think and vote as the Kremlin wants them to. The people are silent. Unfortunately, they no longer have any interest in these matters.

The Games That Spies Play

The revival of an obsession with espionage is always not merely a symptom that things are out of joint in Russia but also an indication that the leaders are beset by a complex of unseemly problems and improper schemes. Here we may recall the Lockhart Conspiracy that the Cheka had concocted as early as the summer of 1918, alleging that the English diplomat R. H. Bruce Lockhart intended to promote a coup d'état by suborning the Latvian riflemen who guarded the Kremlin. Naturally, the Chekist provocateurs "uncovered" the plot, thus averting the coup d'état they themselves had dreamed up. The history of the CPSU was a compulsory subject everywhere, so all students in higher educational institutions in the USSR learned this totally bogus story. It is revealing that the red terror began soon after the "discovery of the Lockhart plot," this far-fetched attempt on the life of Ulyanov (Lenin). By employing torture the Stalinist investigators and procurators beat the "enemies of the people" into "confessing" that they were working for foreign intelligence services.

The Leninist-Stalinist tradition of provocations slackened after the death of Stalin, the "Father of Nations," in 1953. Of course, the West was regularly accused of "terrible provocations." For example, the police or security service in some Western country might detain a Soviet diplomat or his wife in a store for attempted shoplifting. The Soviet side would immediately lodge a protest about another supposed provocation, although everyone knew that a petty thief had been seized. However, since they enjoyed diplomatic immunity, that was the end of it. Of course, Western special services were engaged in recruitment and the other work that agents do. Several of these cases became known, but as a rule, they didn't become big scandals. There were other scandals that involved the expulsion of Soviet spies hiding under the cover of Soviet diplomatic representatives and the tit-for-tat expulsion of Western diplomats. Under Gorbachev these scandals subsided and disappeared entirely after the disgrace of the August 1991 attempted coup. Moreover, in late 1991 the USSR informed the Americans about the system of listening devices that had been implanted in the U.S. Embassy in Moscow. For a long time the employees of Russia's secret services were distressed that, as a result, their secret agent network was exposed. The Chekists forgot that their service was merely an auxiliary instrument of politics; that political decisions were made by Gorbachev, Yeltsin, Soviet foreign minister Boris Pankin, and Chairman of the KGB Vadim Bakatin; and that all of these democratically inclined officials had decided this matter unanimously.

It cannot be denied that the USSR's intelligence presence in the West was disproportionate and obviously excessive. For example, in 1987 there were sixty-one diplomats in the Soviet Representative Office in Geneva, of whom only twenty were employees of the Ministry of Foreign Affairs of the USSR, Byelorussia, and Ukraine.[22] Moreover, many agents of the secret services were under deep cover as career diplomats, officials of other ministries and departments, scholars, and so forth.

Despite the break that occurred during perestroika and, especially, in the last months of the USSR, the soil cultivated to manipulate society by using the supposed threat of domestic and foreign enemies remained arable and productive. This was already evident in the 1990s. After Putin came to power even more elaborate games took place that focused on the spy mania and secrecy, obvious signs of a return to the bad old days. This phenomenon was inevitable under Yeltsin because of the struggle between the doves and the hawks who needed to demonstrate clearly the utter insidiousness of domestic and foreign enemies; under Putin it was to justify the hardening of the regime and the elimination of dissenters.

From Yeltsin's administration forward it was understandable why Russian counterintelligence despised ecologists, given the catastrophic condition of Russia's environment. For example, they did not appreciate the actions of the retired senior captain Alexander Nikitin, an expert for the Norwegian NGO Bellona Foundation who divulged the environmental hazards of nuclear contamination from aging Soviet nuclear submarines. Charges were filed against him in a local FSB case in Saint Petersburg in 1995. The authorities were likewise displeased with his publication of reports by ecologists about the contamination of northeastern Europe by nuclear waste from the Northern Fleet. This was the basis for accusing him of treason and divulging state secrets. He was tried and eventually acquitted, but it took him five years to clear his name.

Another spy scandal connected with ecology was the arrest in 1997 of Junior Capt. Grigory Pas'ko, an employee of the paper *Boevaia vakhta* (Battle station), for cooperating with the maritime bureau of the Japanese television company NHK as well as the Japanese newspaper *Asahi*. Pas'ko was accused of "high treason." In the winter of 1995, Japanese television broadcast his video showing the discharge of liquid radioactive waste into the Sea of Japan from the repair and dismantling of Russian atomic submarines. The video unleashed a storm in Japan. No well-informed, reasonable persons believed that Nikitin and Pas'ko were guilty of crimes.

Several Western countries believed that during Yeltsin's administration Russia had already significantly boosted its intelligence operations directed against them to Cold War levels. Official Moscow excused itself on the grounds that Russia was within its rights to use its intelligence services in defense of its national security. Moreover, in view of growing international cooperation among the special services, it was wrong to talk about a menacing Russian intelligence presence.

We must point out several features of the Russian authorities' espionage games. First is that after the downfall of the USSR, all the necessary material preconditions existed for them to play these games. With the exception of the most enterprising persons who were able to prosper in the new conditions, everyone else, including officials, scholars, and other professionals, became impoverished and were desperate to earn money by whatever means. In order to survive, everybody traded whatever they could: books, crockery, and their bodies, among other things. Information, opportunities, and influence were all for sale. In this context, officials behaved in the most improper fashion, thereby laying the foundation for total corruption. Scholars who were driven to the edge of physical survival had no other recourse since their work, experience, and knowledge were of no interest whatsoever to the new authorities.

Naturally, it would be the height of naïveté to suppose that foreign intelligence services were not engaged in recruiting Russian citizens. There is another, unquestionably vital side of the question—namely, industrial espionage. But some of the espionage scandals are beyond the bounds of reason.

As someone who worked for many years in the field of science and understands the research methodology of Russian scholars, the sources to which they have access, and the degree of information they possess, I was struck by the case of Igor Sutyagin, head of the U.S. Defense Technology and Defense Economy Policy section in the Department of Political-Military Studies of the Institute for U.S. and Canadian Studies, who was arrested in 1999 and given a sentence of over ten years. As a former employee of a department in this institute concerned with military matters, I was convinced from the outset that the charges against Sutyagin were baseless. The charges included passing information about missiles, military aircraft, the composition of the strategic nuclear forces, the Ministry of Defense's progress in implementing plans to achieve a unified state of preparedness, and the composition and status of an early warning system in case of a missile attack. Not a single employee of the institute could get anywhere near any documents dealing with these matters, even if he had access to secret materials. Sutyagin lacked such clearance. Moreover, even if, on his own initiative, anyone possessing the highest level of clearance expressed an interest in these or similar questions, he not only would have failed to receive the relevant documents but also would have aroused extreme suspicion on the part of the special services.

A terrible scandal erupted in the late 1970s when I worked in the Department of Military-Political Studies of the Institute for U.S. and Canadian Studies. In an article published in an unclassified scholarly journal, my senior colleague supposedly let slip a vital state secret by revealing the contents of highly classified directives addressed to the Soviet delegation to nuclear missile disarmament negotiations with the United States. How could he have gotten access to the holiest of holies of Soviet policy? He hadn't. As an honest professional whose job required him to publish articles, he had simply pondered the question of what position the Soviet representatives might take at the nuclear negotiations. His analysis was based on common sense and information from unclassified publications. Even the KGB could find no fault with him. There was raucous laughter in the Ministry of Foreign Affairs. What sort of directives were they if their contents could be figured out by an ordinary scholar?

In the case of Sutyagin, it was perfectly natural that he met, possibly not just on five occasions but many more times, with representatives of the special services of other countries. It is impossible for international specialists not to meet with their foreign counterparts, often with no way of knowing whether they belong to the special services. Another accusation against him was equally absurd: as a teacher at the Obninsk Training Center of the Russian Navy, he supposedly tried to ferret out secret information from the military cadres studying at the center to pass along to foreign agents.

Of course, it is difficult to say anything definitive when the subject is espionage. This is especially so when the accused is a rather highly placed diplomat who, unlike a researcher at the Institute for U.S. and Canadian Studies of the Russian Academy of Sciences, really may know a lot. However, doubts arose about the validity of the accusations of espionage against Valentin Moiseev, the former deputy director of the First Department of Asian Countries in the Russian Foreign Ministry, when a twelve-year sentence delivered by a Moscow municipal court handed down in December 1999 was commuted to four and a half years by another Moscow municipal court.

Another case that raises serious questions is that of Anatoly Babkin, the director of the Department of Missile Technology at the Bauman State Institute of Technology in Moscow, who was taken into custody in April 2000. It should be emphasized at once that the Bauman Institute is an extremely important organization that is involved in extraordinarily sensitive issues. The name of the department that Babkin headed speaks for itself.

This is a dark tale from beginning to end, since Babkin was initially the chief witness in the troubled case of the American citizen Edmond Pope and at first gave testimony confirming his espionage activities. Later Babkin recanted his testimony, saying it had been given under the pressure of the investigations and that he himself was on the verge of a heart attack.

The story of Edmond Pope, who was arrested in April 2000, handed a twenty-year sentence, and then pardoned by President Putin in February 2001, merits inclusion in a textbook for beginning provocateurs. But that is not our focus here. After Pope returned to the United States, an accusation was leveled against Professor Babkin. The sentence of the court in his case, delivered in February 2003, deserves a round of applause. The court found Babkin guilty of transmitting information to the American spy Pope on the technical specifications of the Shkval high-speed submarine torpedo and sentenced him, in accordance with the article on high treason in the Criminal Code, to an eight-year *suspended* sentence. A single comment is in order: *in Russia a suspended punishment for espionage happens only for espionage that never occurred*.

The list of pseudo spy scandals is extensive. For example, in January 2006, a spy scandal erupted around a stone. In brief, it was alleged that supposed agents for the United Kingdom, working under the cover of Great Britain's embassy in Moscow, secreted espionage equipment under a rock in one of Moscow's squares and then collected information from portable computers carried past it. No one had seen this rock, so a representative of the FSB triumphantly demonstrated a full-scale model of it. The FSB declared that it arrested the Russian agent and that he had started to confess. However, before long everyone, including the FSB, forgot about this. Moreover, the names of the four English evildoers, exposed through the heroic efforts of the FSB, were widely disseminated, but for some reason the "plotters" were not expelled from Russia. One of the main charges against the employees of the British Embassy was their participation in financing NGOs in Russia. This financial assistance also was presented as the main evidence of espionage activities on the part of the NGOs themselves.

The Russian special services traditionally take an extremely jaundiced view of NGOs, especially those with links abroad. Chekist paranoia contends that Georgian and Ukrainian NGOs, using foreign funds and acting on the orders of their foreign sponsors, were behind the Rose and Orange Revolutions, respectively, in 2003 and 2004. With considerable experience in falsifying election results in Russia and planning to do it again, the Putinocracy could not help being scared by their own invented fears regarding the "subversive character" of NGOs, especially those financed from abroad. As a result of this phobia, in April 2006 new legislation took effect that severely hampered the work of NGOs and virtually empowered the government to shut down any of them at its own discretion. In addition, the needlessly complicated system of overseeing NGOs mandated by this legislation grants authorities the right to veto the financial and work plans of the NGOs. The NGOs also face pressure from the law regarding the struggle against extremism, as discussed earlier. In other words, any activity, not only of NGOs but also of private persons engaged in the defense of human rights, immediately becomes actionable as a manifestation of extremism, just as it was in the period from Lenin through Chernenko.

Contrary to expectations, the new legislation did not become the pretext for the mass elimination of NGOs; they were simply shown their place. Russians, already accustomed to a lack of freedom, began to play by the new rules of the game that were actually the traditional rules for Russia. But as noted previously, the law requiring those NGOs receiving funds from abroad to register as foreign agents threatened their very existence.

In these ways, the Russian authorities applied themselves to uprooting the last shoots of a nonexistent civil society. Long before they reined in the Kremlin, the Chekists had achieved their goal of blocking the emergence of civil society. Their espionage games had succeeded.

In 1875 Nikolai Nekrasov, the liberal Russian writer and critic, wrote that there had been worse times but none so base as the present. Even an outline of the Stages of the Great Path that, since the downfall of the USSR, Russian authorities have followed in restoring control over the people and in establishing their absolute power demonstrates that Nekrasov's words apply even more to contemporary Russia than when they were written.

The opportunities available to the Kremlin gods have increased immeasurably compared to any time in the past. Many factors are responsible. First is that the authorities completely ignore the law. Second is the submissiveness of the people. Here the view of the psychologist Liubov Vinogradova, executive director of the Independent Psychiatric Association of Russia, is worth considering. She observes that *only around 15 percent of the Russian population engage in inquisitive behavior—that is, the ability to consider various options in order to improve one's position.* From this she concludes that, Russia "is a country of persons with 'ingrained powerlessness.'" It is very easy to provoke persons in a state of ingrained powerlessness to engage in any kind of aggression.[23] They are easily manipulated because they are not free. Finally, new technology enables the authorities to establish an unprecedented degree of control over persons and groups of interest to them.

Earlier in Russia there were great writers, philosophers, and poets who inspired their contemporaries by defining the great issues of the day. They set the parameters for thought. Now they have been replaced by those who repress thought and who traffic in thoughtlessness. They are manipulators who fear an informed and thoughtful public. There is an ugly feature of Pandora's box: it is easy to open, whether from curiosity or for other reasons, but it is much more difficult to recapture the disasters that have been let out of it. As it is said, he who sows discord in his own house will inherit the wind.

From the time of the great Spanish painter Francisco Goya comes yet another truth: the sleep of reason gives birth to monstrosities. There can be no doubt about the prolonged sleep of reason of the Russian state. The monsters stare us in the face.

7

The New Russian Imperialism

I referred earlier to the torment the Russian people and the elite suffered from their breaking with familiar habits. That same point fully applies to foreign policy. From the moment the USSR ended, many of those engaged in the foreign policy arena in Russia suffered likewise and experienced a total break similar to an inveterate narcotics addict going cold turkey. The Soviet imperial monster disintegrated into fifteen states, but several, to be sure, did not fundamentally change as a result of this collapse, at least not in their outlook.

One might think that after the end of the Cold War it would be possible to breathe a sigh of relief on both sides of the Iron Curtain that until recently had divided Europe. But that's not how it was. The death agony of what had seemed to be the unshakable foundations of the world order occurred at an excruciating pace. The reason was simple: the changes were so profound that they occurred only with difficulty. Unless one grasped the actual changes in the situation, this new reality clashed with prior conceptions of what it would be like, a state of affairs that could engender the most serious consequences. Moscow's corridors of power continued to echo with laments that "earlier they respected and feared us, but now they do not." Many officials were literally tormented by nostalgia for the Cold War, for saber rattling. The withdrawal symptoms from the phantoms of greatness and power led to the revival of an aggressive Russian foreign policy and to a new Russian imperialism.

I realized the gravity of the situation while I was still in the diplomatic service and when the Soviet empire had barely exited the stage of history. From the swivel chair of the chief of the Foreign Ministry's department responsible for human rights, cultural, and humanitarian questions that I temporarily occupied while the chief was on another assignment, and after his return when I worked as the deputy chief, I witnessed the beginning of extremely strange developments. Paradoxically, in essence the breakup of the USSR was marked by the rise of revanchist moods within the Russian political elite. These moods were particularly evident with respect to the Baltic states and Georgia, which did not join the Commonwealth of Independent States, Russia's stillborn ersatz imperium in the post-Soviet era.

In the Mirrors of the Yalta-Potsdam System

Regrettably, the history of Soviet international relations and foreign policy is often ignored in analyzing what occurred after the collapse of the USSR. However, it is precisely that history, reflected in the distorting mirrors of those Kremlin offices engaged in formulating and implementing Moscow's foreign policy, that plays such a vital role in their decision-making procedures. Therefore, let us briefly review the sources of post-Soviet foreign policy, those very same sources over which Russian reactionaries of every stripe wax nostalgic.

The foundation of post-Soviet revanchism is the indisputable fact that the USSR lost the Cold War. The cornerstones of the world order that existed from 1945 to 1992 were set in place by World War II's victorious powers during the Yalta and Potsdam Conferences. Let us review the basic features of the postwar world that were determined by the decisions made at these conferences.

The first divided Europe into spheres of influence for the USSR and its Western allies in the anti-Hitler coalition. The USSR received the opportunity to colonize the countries of Central and Eastern Europe. East Germany, Poland, Hungary, Czechoslovakia, Romania, and Bulgaria entered the Soviet empire. Initially, it also included Albania. To them may be added Latvia, Lithuania, and Estonia, which were annexed by the USSR in 1940 in line with the secret protocols of the Molotov-Ribbentrop Pact. Naturally, a personal factor played a significant role, since the achievement of these territorial acquisitions was directly linked to Stalin. Thus, the words *postwar world order* and the *Yalta-Potsdam system of international relations* are euphemisms for the *Stalinist model*.

The second vital feature of the Yalta-Potsdam system was that the victorious powers in the Second World War monopolized what might be called *the right to truth in international affairs*. This was expressed most clearly in the UN Charter, which secured the position of the United Kingdom, China, the USSR, the United States, and France as permanent members of the UN Security Council with the power of veto. Subsequently, the special role of these countries was reaffirmed when international law permitted only these five nations to possess nuclear weapons and their means of delivery.

Third, the Yalta-Potsdam system was characterized by a global confrontation between the USSR on the one side and the United States and other Western countries on the other. The fundamental struggle between the USSR and the West took place in Europe. In organizational terms the creation of the Warsaw Pact and NATO marked the division of Europe into two opposing blocs. There also developed a face-off between the two blocs in other regions of the world, sometimes leading to direct clashes involving military force.

Overall the Yalta-Potsdam system of international relations was marked by confrontation, the hegemony of ideology, and a neocolonial relationship between the USSR and the countries within its sphere of influence. Naturally, such a model could not long endure.

When Gorbachev came to power, the USSR was politically, economically, socially, and ideologically bankrupt. Nevertheless, it continued the full-scale confrontation with the West that was draining its last ounces of strength. Although Gorbachev may not have been fully conscious of just what he was doing, in reality dismantling the Yalta-Potsdam system was one of the foundations of his foreign policy and signified a complete break with Stalinism not only domestically but in international affairs as well. It must be borne in mind that the Yalta-Potsdam system, like any other forceful division of the world, could exist only under certain historical conditions and, thus, had objectively determined temporal limits.

Until the last moment, many Russian liberals, politicians, diplomats, and scholars refused to acknowledge that the USSR had lost the Cold War. There was a certain logic to this refusal. Under Gorbachev the USSR *itself* had renounced the Cold War; it had gotten over the Cold War *itself*. The liberals did not taste the bitterness of the vanquished; rather, they felt the pride of the victors. The reactionaries, for their part, asserted that the Cold War had been lost exclusively due to the policies of Gorbachev, Shevardnadze, and Yakovlev; the treachery of mythical "influential agents"; and other such absurdities.

The Russian public was inclined to identify the defeat of the Soviet Union in the Cold War with the fall of the Berlin Wall, a simple and obvious symbol. In fact, the Soviet Union's defeat in the Cold War had occurred long before the start of Gorbachev's perestroika. The pre-Gorbachev Soviet leaders, unable from the outset to understand in time that their foreign policy would inevitably fail and, later, to recognize that it already *had failed*, repeated the eternal mistake of having generals preparing to fight the last war. By hewing to a policy of isolation from the outside world and confrontation with the West, they accelerated the USSR's economic decline. Meanwhile, efforts to increase its military potential did not lead to strengthening but to undermining Soviet security. Such, for example, was the case with the development of the SS-20 missiles, which the United States responded to by stationing highly accurate Pershing and guided missiles in Western Europe. The Soviet economy did not survive the arms race. Orienting Soviet science and production toward military ends came at the cost of constantly growing scientific and technological backwardness in all other areas. A situation in which minerals were the chief export and grain the main import, while the economy was primarily directed toward satisfying constantly growing military demands, inevitably led toward catastrophe.

Some Soviet leaders realized that victory in a full-scale war was impossible, while the liberals among them grasped the ruinous character of existing Soviet foreign and domestic policy. This had made it possible for Moscow to accept the Final Act of the Conference on Security and Cooperation in Europe (1973–75) that asserted the willingness of the USSR and its allies to cooperate in the sphere of human rights and humanitarian affairs. Despite the marked reluctance of the Soviet leadership to fulfill the obligations it had assumed, that the Soviet Union signed the Final Act signaled the possibility of altering the country's human rights policies.[1] Consequently, this objectively contributed to the erosion of the ideological foundations of the Yalta-Potsdam system. The final chord in the funeral march about the greatness of the USSR was its aggression against Afghanistan in 1979.

Grasping the catastrophic situation, soon after he came to power, Gorbachev determined to jettison the very foundations of Soviet foreign policy—the Leninist "class approach" to international relations. Such an approach had entailed the confrontation with the West, the arms race, and the pursuit of security primarily through military means, as well as ideological warfare and a policy of colonialism. Gorbachev's new direction led to both anticipated and unanticipated results.

Among the anticipated results was the end of ideological warfare, the termination of the Soviet intervention in Afghanistan, the disappearance of the threat of all-out nuclear war, the end of the arms race, the provision of freedom of choice to the countries of Eastern Europe, and, finally, the end of the Cold War. The Velvet Revolution of 1989, the fall of the Berlin Wall, and the unification of Germany essentially spelled the end of the Yalta-Potsdam system dividing the world and, therefore, constituted the first steps in eliminating the Stalinist model of international relations.

However, such major changes inevitably brought about some unplanned results, although in part they were quite predictable. First was the voluntary dissolution of the Warsaw Pact and the Council of Mutual Economic Assistance (known as Comecon), which had been the foundation, respectively, of military cooperation and economic cooperation between the USSR and the East European countries. The withdrawal of Latvia, Lithuania, and Estonia from the USSR was a natural result, although it was unanticipated for some reason by the Soviet leadership. Of course, the major unanticipated consequence of perestroika was the collapse of the USSR.[2]

Naturally, it would have been easy for Gorbachev to continue the policies of his predecessors. Both the Soviet Union's "allies" and the West would have accepted that as a matter of course. According to the logic of the Cold War, international tension would have increased. Significantly greater upheavals than those that resulted from the fall of the USSR would inevitably have occurred at the international and domestic levels.

Although Gorbachev's change of course in Soviet foreign policy was objectively necessary, the overwhelming majority of the Soviet leadership, foreign affairs specialists, and the politically active part of the population did not see it that way. After all, Moscow retained the instruments needed to continue its diktat vis-à-vis the states of Eastern and Central Europe and the "socialist-oriented" developing countries elsewhere. The illusions regarding the military-political and economic potential of the USSR remained in place. Thus, Gorbachev's decision to provide freedom of choice to the "people's democracies," to employ the terminology of that time, was voluntary. It would be unfair to underestimate the intellectual and moral feat that Gorbachev and his associates accomplished.

Missed Opportunities

The collapse of the Soviet empire created an opportunity for the further, profound transformation of Russia, of its foreign policy, and, consequently, of the entire system of international relations. However, this did not happen. The imprint of the Yalta-Potsdam system was too deeply embedded in the consciousness of Russian politicians, who were too accustomed to living by the old rules and to perceiving Russia as a besieged fortress. If it seemed from the sidelines that Russian foreign policy was evolving in a more commonsense direction, then something very different was visible from the inside—that is, the influence on Russian diplomacy of subjective and objective as well as external factors.

Subjective factors are listed first since they played the determining role in Yeltsin's foreign policy. He took power completely unprepared in the foreign policy arena, and he did not even understand the consequences of the Belovezhe Accords, which dissolved the USSR and established the CIS, that he himself signed. As was evident from the outset, Yeltsin surrounded himself with a weak team dominated by reactionaries. Naturally, there was a struggle between the reactionaries and the liberals within his retinue. Yeltsin often found the old, pre-perestroika approaches more congenial because he could understand them more easily.

The members of the political elite either did not want, or were unable, to come to terms with the relative weakening of the country's foreign policy potential compared to the period prior to 1992, the loss of familiar allies and the Soviet sphere of influence in Europe and beyond, and the illusory nature of the Commonwealth of Independent States. They felt keenly Russia's loss of status in the international arena. Their discomfort was exacerbated by changes in the agreements for guaranteeing international security that they were unable to control.

The fact of the matter was that the multilateral arrangements for guaranteeing international security that Russia had entered into had lost much of their efficacy. The world situation had fundamentally changed, and the international organizations created during the Cold War were either unable or unwilling to adapt to the new conditions. Conflicts, particularly in the former Yugoslavia and on the territory of the Commonwealth of Independent States, starkly demonstrated the complete incapacity of existing international law and multilateral international organizations to respond adequately to situations of that kind.

Despite its democratic facade, the United Nations was one of the basic components of the Yalta-Potsdam system. While proclaiming that the General Assembly was its highest organ, the founders of the organization gave real power to the Security Council, whose permanent members were the victorious states in the Second World War and had the right of veto, and this arrangement predetermined its ineffectiveness. The General Assembly became an ideological arena that decided nothing; the work of the UN was blocked by the conflicting interests of its members.

As for the Organization for Security and Cooperation in Europe (OSCE)—known as the Conference on Security and Cooperation in Europe up to 1994—it played an important role in reducing the level of confrontation during the Cold War. But in its present guise, the OSCE has fulfilled its mission and has exhausted the resources invested in it at the time it was established. In this situation, NATO, which possesses the necessary means, including powerful military forces, to resolve problems confronting it, then acquired a key role. Naturally, NATO became the main attraction for the former allies of the USSR, now freed from Soviet domination, in keeping with their national interests and historical experience.

But I cannot fail to mention Moscow's response to the expansion of the European Union: it was viewed as the next threat to Russia's national security. The Kremlin and the Ministry of Foreign Affairs seriously believed that the expansion of the EU would lead to Russia's being in opposition to a unified European stance on a wide range of international issues. In this connection, Russian officials and observers emphasized various "NATO-centrist tendencies" that were supposedly capable of seriously weakening Russian diplomatic positions. Russian thinkers were simply unable to understand that the United States was the natural ally of the EU. Moscow was seriously disturbed that Russia had only an insignificant share of EU foreign trade and that the European Union could supposedly apply pressure on Russia at virtually no cost.

The populism of Yeltsin and the opposition compounded these mistakes given their professional incompetence. They failed to understand and come to terms with the new situation in which Russia found itself. From the outset the incompetence of Russian foreign policy, beginning in 1992, landed the country on the sidelines of international relations.

The inutility of the Belovezhe Accords of 1991, the precipitous collapse of the USSR, the inattention to foreign policy issues, and the lack of qualifications of Yeltsin's advisers—all played a significant role in ensuring that for a long time Moscow was basically focused on problems of the Commonwealth of Independent States. Problems of the post-bipolar world order entirely escaped the view of the Kremlin and the Ministry of Foreign Affairs.

Yet despite its frequent inconsistency, in the initial post-Soviet period, as far as possible Moscow pursued a course oriented toward democratic values through the efforts of Andrei Kozyrev, the first foreign minister of the Russian Federation, and his rather small number of liberal professionals. In reality, however, this was merely the semblance of a democratically oriented policy that, therefore, discredited itself. There was actually no such policy. To the extremely weak professional credentials of Yeltsin's team in the sphere of international affairs must be added Yeltsin's superficial understanding of democratic values; perhaps it was unsurprising for one who until recently had been a communist big shot. Instead of devising an intelligent foreign policy aimed at securing Russia's long-term interests both at home and abroad, Moscow made a partial move toward several Western countries while simultaneously denying that the very essence of Serbian president Milošević's politics was antidemocratic. Russia's support of the dictatorial regimes of Milošević in Serbia, Saddam Hussein in Iraq, and Alexander Lukashenko in Belarus clearly illustrated this. Kozyrev made concessions to the reactionary parliament in order not to further complicate Yeltsin's position in the sharp domestic political struggle. The result, as previously noted, was that foreign policy was reduced to a matter of small change whose value regularly diminished. What seemed at the time to be merely tactical concessions smoothed the path for Russia's slide toward revanchism and new confrontations both with its neighboring post-Soviet states and with the West.

The situation fundamentally changed when Russia's diplomacy was headed by the revanchist Yevgeny Primakov, who succeeded, with startling rapidity, in turning Russians against the West and especially against NATO and in broadly instilling in them anti-Western sentiments. Russia's foreign policy acquired an unmistakably anti-Western cast. Kozyrev's concessions to the reactionaries were now transformed into a consistent policy. Russia's opportunity to achieve democracy was irretrievably lost. For a short time, its politics had changed direction, but under Yeltsin they remained essentially Bolshevik. Nevertheless, despite Yeltsin's fecklessness with regard to international affairs, during his presidency he managed to partially neutralize the intrigues of the hawks.

The difficulties Russian foreign policy encountered during that period were caused not only by domestic political haggling and dilettantism but also by the objective situation. Russia's economic and social problems were relegated to the back burner during the struggle for power between Yeltsin and the opposition. With an economy still dominated by the state, weakened by the arms race, focused on military and ideological security rather than on common sense, and engaged in an absurd degree of paternalism toward a population accustomed to being treated that way, Russia seemed ungovernable either because that is what the rulers desired or because of their inability to think straight. One of the inevitable consequences of the Belovezhe Accords was that Russian industry faced a crisis given that the economic specialization of various Soviet regions had resulted in the mutual economic interdependence of the former Soviet republics. The only existing, if poorly functioning, economic mechanism had been thoughtlessly destroyed, with all sorts of pernicious consequences.

These factors contributed to a lack of vision on the part of Russia's leadership regarding foreign policy interests and objectives, to diplomatic inconsistency and aimless blundering during Yeltsin's presidency, and, in the following period, to the cultivation domestically of fertile soil for what seemed almost a natural return to imperialism. The sum total of these deficiencies significantly facilitated the carnival trick of propagating the thesis about Russia's loss of its role as a superpower and the further weakening of its international position.

The intellectual sluggishness of Moscow's top leaders engendered an almost constant deterioration in Russia's foreign policy positions. Russia's leaders and diplomats stubbornly failed to take note of the changes occurring around them. While the European Union was opening its borders among its member countries, shifting to a single currency, taking measures to work out a unified foreign policy, and ensuring its security, Russian foreign policy was convulsively clinging to the inexorably vanishing shades of the past. The profound transformation taking place in the world order was passing it by.

To be fair, not only Moscow but also Washington and other capitals failed to recognize the new political realities. Instead of taking advantage of the end of the Cold War to bring about a fundamental and widely acceptable restructuring of the world, the United States, as if on auto pilot, continued to assert its own unilateral leadership in world affairs. Several West European leaders also failed to act in the common good. These factors virtually guaranteed the emergence of a new Russian revanchism founded on the Big Lie, whose roots reach deep into history and psychology. This multilayered and diverse but holistic lie constitutes the foundation for the worldview of a large number of Russians and their rulers. The heart of this lie is the belief that the regime founded by Lenin and Stalin was a great and glorious empire. This view ignores both the criminality of those who created and maintained this regime and the fact that the USSR was driven to extinction by its own sins and mistakes as well by the defects of its intellectual and moral development. Given this delusion, the USSR's imperial policy, its confrontation with the West, and the Cold War are extolled. Moreover, as I have already noted, ever since the demise of the USSR, a core article of faith of Russia's hawks is the contention that the Soviet Union collapsed as the result of its democratic reforms.

Russian revanchism also feeds upon the absurd theory that the USSR ceased to exist as a result of the policies of Western countries. This theory brings to mind the concept familiar to psychiatrists about a lack of critical self-awareness. Anyone with even the slightest knowledge of Russian history knows the theory is wrong. Of their own accord, the presidents of Russia, Ukraine, and Byelorussia signed the decision to terminate the USSR. That decision was instantaneously and almost unanimously ratified by the parliaments of what had been three constituent Soviet republics.

Russian revanchism is rooted in incompetence and fabrications that are entirely divorced from reality. At its foundation is an assertion equating a country's greatness with its military might and the consequent fear and confrontation. Another component is the capacity to hold one's own and other peoples in slavery.

Déjà Vu

After Putin came to power, the hitherto contradictory character and inconsistency of Russian foreign policy were replaced by a pronounced anti-Western thrust. A return to the epoch of the Cold War was clearly observable. Russia emphasized its relations with China, North Korea, Cuba, Iran, and Iraq even as significant cooling occurred in relations with Western Europe and the United States. The aforementioned scandal involving Edmund Pope, who was accused of espionage and then freed by Putin, was a well-understood signal.[3] Another indicator of Moscow's mood was that

Azerbaijan occupied one of the privileged positions in the Commonwealth of Independent States. It was headed by the former KGB chief of the republic Gaidar Aliev, a shady and odious character even in Soviet times. In the conflict in Moscow's corridors of power, the Slavophiles, or nativists, who stood for savagery and lawlessness, triumphed unconditionally over the Westernizers, as partisans of universal values were called in Russia. As a staff member of the Russian Security Council, I saw clearly that inveterate but cunning and hypocritical reactionaries had come to power.

Meanwhile, the new autocrat was only just hitting his stride. His visit to Havana in December 2000, and other openly anti-American and anti-Western acts, did not produce the desired result. Relations with the West deteriorated sharply but yielded nothing in return. This tough pragmatist, brought up in the KGB, faced a dilemma. Should he continue and further develop his neo-Stalinist convictions, or should he try to extract the maximum benefit from his position as the leader of the largest, and one of the best-endowed, countries in the contemporary world? It was not an easy choice, but nothing is impossible for unprincipled, cynical politicians. Initially he could pose with the leaders of the democratic world as if he were "one of them," and later he could execute a 180-degree turn.

In his effort to appear as one of them, nothing could have been more timely for Putin than the 9/11 tragedy in the United States. If it had not occurred, Putin would have had to invent something like it. This tragedy became the turning point in Russia's relations with the West and served as justification for present and future outrages in Chechnya and other post-Soviet territories. Moscow wagered everything in its diplomatic game on the card of joint struggle against international terrorism, a bet that succeeded with the help of President George W. Bush at the EU-Russia summit in Brussels in 2001.

After establishing the vertical of power, seizing control of the minds of Russians, and utilizing the torrent of petrodollars, Putin employed a broad range of means and created opportunities to confront Western and other countries he disliked. Such conduct was typical of the Cold War. Russia began using energy blackmail and invoked terrorist acts carried out by others as levers to pressure other countries—in particular, Georgia—as well as engaging in provocations and demonstrations of force against individual members of NATO and their armed forces. Moscow had not engaged in such behavior since before Gorbachev took power. Meanwhile, inside Russia a mood of xenophobic hysteria gathered strength.

Putin, the KGB protégé, eliminated all moral, ideological, and political constraints in his rigid confrontation with the West. This had been impossible under Yeltsin, partly because of the collapse of Russia's economy and military establishment. Putin himself was lucky, for he inherited the country's reins on the threshold of its emergence from financial crisis.

A distinctive intellectual and ideological mustiness emanated from almost all of the papers and resolutions addressed to the new president. Putin never concealed his negative view of the West or of democracy. He made his position crystal clear even while making buffoonish bows in the direction of Western politicians who were satisfied with his performance. From the moment Putin came to power, although he was still restricted by his prime minister, Russia again began ratcheting up international tension. Yet when Putin began confronting the West, an indispensable component of a full-scale Cold War was lacking—that is, the existence of comparable capabilities on the opposing sides that makes the outcome of the contest as a whole, as well as any particular episode within it, impossible to predict.

There are other key differences between Putin's confrontation with the West and those of the Cold War decades. First is that the Cold War developed at a time when the USSR and the Western countries had clearly divided Europe into their respective spheres of influence. Their struggle was often in the form of conflicts that usually did not involve direct confrontation; rather, they occurred at the periphery. Now, after losing its allies among the developing countries, Russia no longer possessed what might be called its strategic depth in confrontation with the West. Nevertheless, Moscow declared that the post-Soviet republics constituted its sphere of vital interests and asserted its right to order them about. It thereby assumed the role of a regional power.

There is an additional, perhaps decisive, difference. From the Cuban missile crisis to the end of the Cold War, nuclear restraint was the bedrock foundation of the Cold War. After 1992 it seemed partially to have lost its efficacy. A paradoxical situation developed. In terms of military potential, Russia could not really depend on anything but nuclear weapons. At the same time, Russia was certain that Western and other nuclear powers would never use their nuclear weapons against it. In effect the policy of restraint turned into a one-way street that provided Moscow assurance that it could engage in adventurism with impunity.

Another important element to consider is the indisputable fact that the Russian pseudo elite keeps its capital in Western banks, in real estate, and in other forms of property. This not only makes the Russian elite very vulnerable and cautious but also inspires hope that Moscow will not cross the extremely dangerous line that it has drawn.

By 2004 the signs of Moscow's return to Cold War policies were visible even to the naked eye. Unprejudiced observers clearly observed the symptoms even prior to the Orange Revolution in Ukraine. Moscow's complaints that the OSCE was too concerned about human rights—as it was bound to be in accordance with the Final Act signed during the Cold War—is a striking example of this. Something that even Brezhnev had swallowed ceased being palatable under Yeltsin, to say nothing of Putin's distaste.

The motivation for Russia's confrontational policy is very simple: it is nostalgia for a phantom of past greatness. Unfortunately, not only the public but also the overwhelming majority of the political elite associate this supposed greatness with the Cold War, saber rattling, and the "monolithic unity of society." They are blind to the fact that precisely this pseudo greatness, consisting of a militarily powerful and economically underdeveloped country, was what brought the Soviet Union to ruin. The Russian authorities' distorted understanding of national greatness and well-being, shared by an easily swayed public, psychologically serves the purpose of revanchism and a one-sided revival of the Cold War.

Another equally important factor is that the Kremlin needs an alibi to divest itself of responsibility for the existing socioeconomic and political situation in Russia. For a rather long time, Yeltsin's, and then Putin's, "escape route" from domestic and foreign policy problems was to manipulate references to an "internal enemy." Initially it was the struggle against the "red-brown threat"—the communist-fascist threat—that gave Yeltsin a free pass with the West; then it was the struggle against the oligarchs and Chechen terrorism, which Moscow neatly transformed into "international" terrorism.

The Kremlin also benefited from ratcheting up tension with the West. Inducing a state of public hysteria made it easy to manipulate the Russian people. The revanchists succeeded in doing this from the outset, and this hysteria became one of the foundations of Putin's domestic policy from the moment he came to power.

Putin's anti-Western proclivities and aggressiveness grew in well-cultivated soil. As far as I could judge from my office in Moscow and from Russian representatives at European meetings in Brussels, for a long time Western colleagues did not reject Putin's policies, especially since he invoked familiar causes to justify his tough policies at home and abroad. For example, Putin effectively turned to his advantage the tragedy of the hostage taking on September 1, 2004, in Beslan and characterized it as "an attack on our country." He used it both to ratchet up tension inside Russia and in international affairs and to launch a further assault on democracy. "We are dealing," he declared, "with the direct intervention of foreign terrorism against Russia. With total, brutal, and full-scale war."

I was just then leaving the diplomatic service and knew very well that although there was not the slightest foundation for such statements, a critical turning point had occurred in Russia's foreign and domestic policy. Nor was there any doubt that this turning point had been prepared in advance. By then a real or imaginary remilitarization of Russia was under way, and Russia publicly proclaimed itself a revanchist country; however, these declarations made no impression upon the West. Although the Kremlin and the Foreign Ministry were doing almost everything possible to increase tension with the West, for some reason the West was giving Moscow a free pass.

Putin's message to the Council of the Russian Federation Assembly on May 10, 2006, contained an open proclamation of confrontation with the West. "The main lesson of the Great Patriotic War is the need to maintain the battle readiness of the Armed Forces," the president pronounced. But Russia, it seemed, was spending very little on this. Putin formulated very clearly the meaning of his foreign and defense policies: "We must make our house . . . sturdy, reliable, because we can see what is going on in the world. . . . As the saying goes, 'Comrade Wolf knows whom to eat.' He eats, but listens to no one. And, it's clear, he has no intention of listening." ("Comrade Wolf" is a pure Stalinist expression. Although the United States was not named directly, it was perfectly clear the United States was the country he had in mind.) Putin then asked bombastically, "What's all this fuss about the need to struggle for human rights and democracy when what's really important is to achieve our own interests? Here, it seems, everything is possible, and there are no limits whatsoever." To stand up to Comrade Wolf and other foes, according to Putin, "present-day Russia needs an army possessing all the means to respond adequately to current threats. We must have Armed Forces capable of *simultaneously fighting in global, regional, and, if necessary, in several local conflicts.*"[4] In essence he asserted that Russia should be prepared to take on the whole world at the same time. This message might be called the doctrine of an unlimited number of wars. Due attention has not been paid to it.

No wonder. Nothing like it was possible since the Cold War; moreover, even communist leaders such as Brezhnev, Chernenko, and Andropov did not speak like that. This message was also a barely disguised declaration of a willingness to return to the bad times of confrontation between Russia and the West.

The most obvious sign of Russia's return to Cold War policies was Putin's signature in July 2007 on a decree announcing Russia's withdrawal from the Treaty on Conventional Armed Forces in Europe (CFE) and the associated international agreements. This treaty had been signed in Paris in 1990 and adapted to new conditions in 1999 at a summit of the OSCE in Istanbul. It restricted the number of tanks, armored vehicles, large-caliber artillery, warplanes, and helicopters. Putin cynically justified his decision by arguing that the modified treaty had been ratified only by Russia, Belarus, Kazakhstan, and Ukraine. The other countries had weighty reasons for not ratifying the modified treaty since Russia had not implemented the original treaty, having failed to withdraw its troops from the territory of Georgia (about which more follows) and Moldova. They refused to ratify the CFE, and naturally, the NATO countries expressed solidarity with them. The West's refusal to fast-track ratification of the agreement to modify the CFE served as Moscow's main argument. Withdrawal from the CFE was a rather infantile reaction to the changing relationship of forces in Europe following the demise of the USSR and the diminution of Moscow's power in world and European affairs. Moscow was irritated by the expansion of NATO, which then supposedly significantly exceeded the quantitative limits on weapons established by the treaty. This was a phony argument as the modified CFE calculated weapons not according to military-political alliances, as previously, but according to each separate member state. Moscow refused to accept the U.S. intention to station "essential military forces" at bases in the former Soviet colonies of Bulgaria and Romania, which had joined NATO. Russia added that Latvia, Lithuania, and Estonia had not participated in the modified CFE.

Another chronic, acute disarmament problem was the Anti-Ballistic Missile (ABM) Treaty, signed by the United States and the Soviet Union in 1972, that provided one of the main foundations of strategic stability. After the Republicans came to power in 2001, Washington declared its intention to withdraw from this treaty, calling it obsolete. At the end of 2001 the United States officially announced its withdrawal from the treaty, which lapsed in the summer of 2002. In December Washington began to create a national ABM system. Moscow viewed Washington's actions as intentionally aimed against Russia, ignoring the fact that nuclear missile weapons had proliferated to additional countries since the treaty had been signed thirty years earlier. Russia was especially perturbed by the U.S. intention to deploy elements of the ABM system in Europe. The Kremlin declared that if the American ABM system was implemented, then Moscow would prepare an "asymmetrical response." This streamlined formula masked the utter mental vacuity of Russia's politicians and military on this question. The asymmetrical Russian reaction was taken to the point that, in the words of Lt. Gen. Vladimir Popovkin, commander of the space forces, the Russians were studying the question of placing on Russian Embassy grounds in various countries radio-location surveillance stations to monitor outer space. Popovkin asserted that this would enable them to pinpoint the launch point of missiles that could not be seen from Russian territory and to target the Russian ABMs on them. Rattling its weapons, Moscow publicly announced its intention of targeting its missiles on countries that agreed to take part in implementing the Americans' plans.

Some countries are fortunate. Russia, for example, is extremely fortunate to possess an abundance of useful minerals, especially oil and gas; a large population; and a favorable geographical location. Yet combined with the mentality of the vertical of power that emerged right after the Bolshevik coup of 1917, these natural riches, a veritable "gift of the gods," turned into a curse.

During Putin's first term, a flood of petrodollars inundated Russia. Unfortunately, the authorities were absolutely irresponsible with regard to this bonanza. Obviously, the funds should have been invested in modernizing the country, above all in revitalizing the collapsing economy, in diversifying it, in improving the catastrophic social safety net—in sum, in what Alexander Solzhenitsyn called "preserving the nation." Instead, Russia became merely a supplier of energy and other useful minerals to other countries. Russia's rulers were pumping Russia's natural resources abroad, like a primitive pump, and were unable even to consider the possibility of using the revenues to address long-festering internal problems.

But it was not simply that nothing was done. Paradoxically, the increase in revenues even worsened the situation in Russia. The aggressiveness of the hawks, until then restrained by their penury, was unleashed by the influx of petrodollars, which facilitated the remilitarization of the country or, more accurately, enabled the hawks to flex the remnants of their atrophied military muscles. (Moreover, given the universal corruption, the funds allocated to this sector could be used for purposes other than those intended and, with varying degrees of cynicism, diverted into the pockets of those in power.) In addition, the rise in oil and gas prices stimulated a division of property that made free enterprise in Russia completely impossible. Finally, the rulers in Moscow now had additional opportunities to blackmail Western and post-Soviet countries that the Kremlin disliked and had a heightened interest in doing so. Putin immediately placed his bets on gas as Russia's main instrument in international politics, for the post-Soviet states depend upon Russian liquid fuel for 60–80 percent of their needs. Moreover, Russia supplies about 25 percent of the EU's needs.

The year 2006 could have been a banner year for Russian diplomacy as for the first time Russia was chairing the Group of Eight (G8). And though 2006 did become such a year, Russian politicians and Russian businesspersons, who by this time had become synonymous, began to saw off the branch on which they were sitting. On January 1, Russia cut off supplies of natural gas to Ukraine and reduced the amount of fuel it was pumping into the European pipeline system. Thus, from the very beginning of its chairmanship of the G8, Russia did everything possible to ensure its failure in that role and to undermine the trust that is the basis of political and economic cooperation. By this action Russia was seeking to punish Yushchenko's Ukrainian government, which it disliked, and to intimidate the West or, at least, to keep it on starvation rations. Moscow also wanted to gain control of Ukraine's gas pipeline system by obtaining for Russia's own Gazprom a 51 percent share of the company that operated it. Starting with this conflict, the Putinocracy probably took a final decision to construct a vertical of power in its relations with adjacent countries. It would be able "to rise from its knees" again by administering blows to Georgia and Ukraine and by emphasizing Western Europe's dependency on Russian gas and, consequently, on the Kremlin's beneficence.

Russia inherited from the USSR not only gas, oil, and other useful minerals but also an enormous, collapsing military establishment that resisted essential reforms. It exhibited all of the defects that had proved fatal to the Soviet empire, including stereotypical modes of thinking and an acute inferiority complex, as well as old and newly acquired weaknesses. The enormous size of Russia's military establishment greatly increased the likelihood of its being deployed, and that is precisely what happened: first in Chechnya, then in Georgia, and most recently in eastern Ukraine.

An obvious stimulus for hardening Moscow's policy toward the post-Soviet republics were the "color revolutions." But if, as a result of the Rose Revolution in Georgia in 2003, one leader whom Putin disliked was replaced by another whom he liked no better, then it was quite another thing with regard to the Orange Revolution in Ukraine the next year; that really frightened him. Moscow asserted that the Orange Revolution was a Western, basically American, creation that had been engineered by Western-financed NGOs.

The Kremlin had decided to bet on its favorite, the incumbent, acting Ukrainian prime minister Viktor Yanukovich. No one in the Kremlin realized that openly supporting one of the candidates on the eve of the elections would be seen as anything other than gross intervention into the domestic affairs of a sovereign nation. But that wasn't enough. The Kremlin launched a campaign against presidential candidates Viktor Yushchenko and Yulia Timoshenko, apparently blithely ignoring the high probability that they would wind up as the leaders of Ukraine.

Of course, many governments try, with varying success, to exert influence not only on foreign governments but also on foreign public opinion, including with respect to elections. However, they try to act without publicity so as not to spoil relations with other candidates. Moscow did everything crudely and openly.

As noted earlier, Russian diplomacy ceased being a science and an art, the application of mind and tact. None of these components could be observed in the Kremlin, in the Russian government, in the Foreign Ministry, or in Russia's overseas embassies. The leaders and officials stopped trying to identify and study problems of international relations and to look for possible, mutually beneficial solutions. Instead, they endlessly repeated the same prefabricated positions without any preliminary probing or even genuine, deep analysis. These positions, moreover, were hastily slapped together when it was already too late to do anything.

After Yushchenko's victory, Moscow's irritation with Ukraine, and toward him personally, escalated. Yushchenko did not hide his sympathies with Georgia. His effort to free Ukraine from the obtrusive and menacing presence of Russia's Black Sea fleet in Crimea and to place limits on its activities and his desire for Ukraine to join NATO infuriated Moscow.

Russian diplomacy actively and cynically exploits the existence of so-called overseas compatriots and the Russian-speaking population of post-Soviet republics to pursue its foreign policy objectives. This conjures up distressing allusions to the transfer to Hitler's Germany of the Sudeten district of Czechoslovakia on the supposed grounds that the Czechoslovak authorities were constantly violating the rights of the solid bloc of ethnic Germans living there. The project of employing "overseas compatriots" for geopolitical objectives began almost immediately after the breakup of the USSR when the Russian Foreign Ministry, acting on orders from on high, raised the question of defending Russian-speaking populations in post-Soviet states. Here I must emphasize the international legal and political impropriety of posing the question, not as a matter of protecting Russian citizens, but as one of protecting "Russian-speaking" persons and "ethnic Russians." This was particularly strange since the Russian authorities were unwilling to offer Russian citizenship to those they were supposedly defending. Moreover, Moscow did not pursue routine diplomatic work to secure human rights in post-Soviet countries. Instead, it engaged in patently ineffective, provocative, loud-mouthed démarches. Thus, from the beginning, the defense of compatriots abroad was marked by virtually undisguised double standards and blatant hypocrisy.

Yet there really were human rights problems in post-Soviet countries. According to estimates used by the Russian authorities, more than twenty million Russian compatriots were living in the post-Soviet states.[5] Moscow asserted that in the majority of post-Soviet states, with the exception of Belarus—despite their formal proclamation of the equality of citizens irrespective of ethnicity, faith, and language—ethnic Russians were inadequately represented in the organs of power at all levels. By this statement Moscow, in effect, made perfectly clear that its main concern was power.

Veiled discrimination existing in the sphere of work and employment and limitations on rights in the fields of education, culture, and language took a variety of forms. The problem was that these Russian-speaking former citizens of the USSR, who had remained in place after the collapse of the Soviet Union and had done nothing to provoke hostility, had suddenly come to be viewed as a dubious and undesirable element even though Russian remained one of the official languages in these former Soviet republics. Naturally, elementary courtesy requires at least a modest knowledge of the national language of the country in which those who speak another official, but non-native, language are living. In Soviet times, however, this was not encouraged. On the contrary, attempts were made to suppress the national languages in favor of Russian. This effort was accompanied by a deliberate policy of settling Russians in the union republics, often at the initiative of the local authorities.

It was natural for the new authorities to take every possible advantage of a situation where the former Soviet republics were acquiring sovereignty. Among the steps they took were establishing their national languages as the official languages; sharply constricting Russian-language cultural, informational, and educational spaces; and squeezing the Russian language out of official records and daily use. These actions were consistent with the introduction of the languages of the indigenous-majority peoples as the official languages. For example, the language problem and the policy of compulsory "Kazakhification" were some of the main reasons for the exodus of Russian speakers from Kazakhstan that was dubbed the Great Flight. (Over two million Russians left Kazakhstan after its independence.)

By the beginning of the twenty-first century, the process of reducing the Russian component from the cultural life of Ukraine had led to a decline in the number of Russian theaters from forty to nine, the removal of Russian cultural monuments, and the renaming of Russian street names. In Russian-speaking Kiev, the number of schools teaching in the Russian language was reduced by a factor of ten. In the Ternopol, Rovno, and Kiev regions, Russian-language schools were closed, and only three remained open in eight other regions.

In Latvia and Estonia, which the USSR annexed in 1940 as a result of the Molotov-Ribbentrop Pact, the situation was exacerbated by mass deprivation of citizenship. Moscow rejected the option of bringing these problems up directly with the member states of the CIS, fearing, in the language of the Russian Foreign Ministry, their "unhealthy and sometimes even inadequate reaction." It chose to pursue "quiet diplomacy" (as it was referred to in Foreign Ministry documents), but that turned out to be quite ineffective in this case. Meanwhile, Moscow "took everything out on Latvia and Estonia." This occurred because of the orientation of the Baltic states, which joined NATO and the European Union. However, even here Moscow's words—even the harshest words— were not backed up by any measures aimed at actually supporting the ethnic Russians. Clearly they were merely being used as a political card.

Russians in the Baltic states repeatedly asked the ministry (including me, personally) not to defend them since such expressions of "concern" only made things worse for them. But the Kremlin and the Foreign Ministry ignored these requests. Nothing was done for the people who really needed help. Apart from their propaganda value, the authorities had no use for them and, therefore, were uninterested.

At the very least, the Kremlin's efforts to establish its dominion over the Slavic part of the former USSR, Russia's dependence on happenings in the CIS, and the clumsiness of Moscow's pseudo diplomacy inevitably alienated the post-Soviet states. Nowhere did Moscow's attempts to transform this interstate quasi union of the CIS into a decent cloak for the increasing contradictions evoke any understanding. By the time Putin came to power, considerable efforts had already been made to whip up hysteria among the Russian public over their so-called compatriots.

Moscow had an opportunity in the spring of 2007 to confront Estonia in the spirit of the Kremlin's xenophobic imperial policy. The authorities in Tallinn decided to move the *Bronze Soldier*, a monument to Soviet servicemen who had died in Estonia during the Second World War, as well as their graves while fully observing all military honors and traditions. A majority of Estonians viewed this monument, which stood in the center of their capital, as a symbol of the Soviet occupation. On September 22, 1944, the Soviet army had "liberated" Tallinn from the lawful authorities of Estonia since by then almost no German troops remained there. Estonian flags were removed from government buildings, and members of the Estonian government were arrested, with later some being shot and others sent to the GULAG. Therefore, the monument to the "soldier-liberator" was known to Estonians as the "monument to an unknown aggressor."

Behaving in an openly provocative manner, Russia declared that it had received no information about the transfer of the monument and the graves, and it organized pro-Russian demonstrations in Estonia that escalated into riots. In Moscow a "shock brigade" literally besieged the Estonian Embassy, while representatives of the pro-Putin youth organizations Nashi and Molodaia Gvardiia held demonstrations both in Moscow and in Estonia. The Russian ambassador to Estonia refused to attend the solemn ceremony of reinterring the remains. The mayor of Moscow called upon Russian consumers to boycott Estonian goods, and activists set up a camp on the Estonian border in an attempt to block automobile traffic between the two countries. Russian deliveries of oil, which were usually shipped to Estonian ports by rail, abruptly stopped supposedly because of repairs to the railbed. Passenger rail service between Moscow and Tallinn suddenly became unprofitable and likewise ceased. On May 9, the day when Russia marks its victory over the Nazis, the Russian side unexpectedly closed the main highway linking the two countries to heavy truck traffic.

Russian mass media also misinformed the Russian people. It alleged that hundreds of ethnic Russian arrestees had been savagely beaten in the terminal of Tallinn's port and that a Russian who died in the course of the disturbances was supposedly beaten to death by police when he actually was the victim of an ordinary knife fight. Additional disinformation was thrown in for good measure that the *Bronze Soldier* had been sawed into pieces. These false reports accompanied provocative calls for a Bronze Revolution in Estonia and for an insurrection on May 9, in which the entire Russian-speaking community of Estonia should take part.

At the same time this hysteria was mounting, in the suburban Moscow town of Khimki a monument to fallen warriors was quietly moved, and other military graves were cynically destroyed. Not a peep was heard about this from either the authorities or the public. There is no doubt that Moscow, counting on the support of a large number of Russian-speaking people in Estonia, was trying to escalate the situation there from within while assisting this effort in every way possible by actions in Russia as well.

The imperial syndrome, combined with political incompetence and irresponsibility, led to obscene Russian behavior with respect to the principle of the inviolability of borders. While verbally declaring its adherence to this principle, in the post-Soviet period and as early as the presidency of Yeltsin, the Kremlin pursued a policy aimed at supporting separatists who wanted to split Trans-Dniestr from Moldova and to break up Georgia by splitting off South Ossetia and Abkhazia. The majority of the area's people, contrary to international law, were given Russian passports.

Russian policy on these questions became particularly vociferous after the proclamation of Kosovo's independence and its recognition by a number of Western countries. Russian diplomacy outwardly opposed such recognition. Meanwhile, with poorly disguised satisfaction, Russia embraced it as a precedent that untied its hands with regard to recognizing the independence of Abkhazia and South Ossetia.

There is no doubt that extremely serious problems exist in Georgia, among them Abkhazia. The problem of Abkhazia was created in the first years of Bolshevik rule. Ever since then the Abkhazy have sought independence from Georgia; however, the region's status in international law is unambiguous. From the time the USSR broke up, Abkhazia has been considered part of Georgia, but Abkhazian separatists have received military as well as moral and political support from Moscow.

Georgia's other sore point—South Ossetia—is also a legacy of the Soviet era. After the demise of the USSR, Ossetia, like the Ossetian people, found itself divided between different states. South Ossetia became part of Georgia, while North Ossetia remained part of Russia. In the Soviet period this hardly mattered since the internal boundaries of the USSR were purely administrative and did not affect people. The situation changed drastically after the collapse of the USSR. The third, subjective, problem was the personality of Georgian leader Zviad Gamsakhurdia, who came to power in 1991 and brought his country to the edge of catastrophe.

The Russian authorities believed—or pretended to believe—that Georgia was actively helping the Chechen fighters. This was a rather doubtful proposition, considering the active role of the Chechens in the Georgian-Abkhazian armed conflict on the side of the Abkhazian separatists. Yet this assertion was extremely useful to Moscow since it facilitated the immediate solution of two problems: it enabled the Kremlin to call terrorism on Russian territory an international issue and to intensify pressure on Georgia.

Moscow nudged Abkhazia and South Ossetia toward separatism in every way possible with the goal of incorporating them into Russia. "We will never leave Abkhazia," declared Sergei Shoigu, then the minister of emergency situations—that is, de facto head of the coercive apparatus, an alternative to the Ministry of Defense and the Ministry of the Interior—at a meeting of the diplomatic staff when I worked at the Russian Mission to the UN in Geneva in 1992–96. The conflict between Tbilisi and Abkhazia forced Georgian president Eduard Shevardnadze to make Georgia a member of the CIS in the hope of somehow neutralizing Russian aggression vis-à-vis Tbilisi.

In December 2000 under the patently concocted pretext of Georgia's unwillingness to enter into a mutually acceptable agreement on the means of securing the Russian-Georgian border, Russia unilaterally introduced a visa system governing the trips back and forth of Russian and Georgian citizens. One of the main arguments was that Georgia was supposedly supporting Chechen international terrorism. It also maintained that criminal elements, including Chechen extremists, were congregating in the Pankisi Gorge and several other parts of the Akhmetskii District; that training centers for fighters were located there along with hospitals to treat them; and that organizations that hated the special services, and were providing material, technical, and financial assistance to the terrorists, were operating there under the guise of humanitarian missions.

Pro-Russia inhabitants of Abkhazia and South Ossetia, however, were accorded a special status and exempted from the visa regime. The politicians in Moscow knew that an overwhelming majority of the inhabitants of Abkhazia and South Ossetia lacked Georgian documents and that traveling to Tbilisi, the location of the lone Russian consulate in Georgia, to obtain visas would supposedly pose a real threat to their safety. According to imperial logic, instituting a visa regime on the Abkhazian and South Ossetian portions of the border constituted a de facto "blockade" of these regions of Georgia. No attempt was made to conceal that hindering the earnings and provisioning of the population of these regions that were directly connected with Russia, and depriving them of the opportunity of crossing the Russian border, would certainly turn into a humanitarian catastrophe for the people living there. The Georgian government correctly deemed the maintenance of a visa-free regime along the Abkhazian and South Ossetian portions of the Russian-Georgian border as Russia's de facto annexation of these regions. Moreover, starting from the early 2000s, Russia began issuing Russian passports to inhabitants of Abkhazia and South Ossetia, thereby transforming the population of these separatist republics into its own citizens, whom they were not only able but also now obligated to defend. Preparations for the division of Georgia entered what was, in principle, a new phase with obvious historical analogies.

The advent to power of pro-Western president Mikheil Saakashvili in Georgia as a result of the Rose Revolution of 2003 produced a sharply negative reaction in Moscow. The very fact of a broad popular movement, one that led to a change of government, did not sit well with the architects and builders of the vertical of power. The Russian authorities looked askance on Saakashvili's policies, which aimed at bringing Georgia closer to the West in all respects and at its entering NATO.

An extremely revealing event, particularly in light of subsequent developments, as well as improbable from a diplomatic perspective, occurred during preparations for Russian foreign minister Sergei Lavrov's visit to Tbilisi in February 2005. He refused to visit the memorial in Tbilisi to Georgian soldiers who had died fighting for Georgia's territorial integrity in the early 1990s.

In March 2006 Russia prohibited the transit through Georgia of agricultural products from third countries, asserting that frequently they came with false certification. Soon Russia banned the importation of Georgian wine and Borzhomi mineral water on the specious grounds that they were of poor quality. Russia refused to evacuate Georgian citizens, including children, from Lebanon during the conflict there in July 2006, prompting indignant responses.

In September 2006 Moscow interpreted the spy scandal involving five Russian servicemen arrested on charges of espionage in Tbilisi as an anti-Russian provocation. Putin also took note of this occasion, characterizing what was happening as an "indication of the reinstatement of the policies of Lavrenty Beriya [Stalin's secret police chief] both domestically and in the international arena." This is a case of a thief crying, "Stop thief!" On September 30 the Georgian Ministry of Internal Affairs distributed videos and transcripts of phone conversations regarding the activity of the Russian servicemen detained on charges of espionage. According to the ministry's information, in addition to espionage they were engaged in sabotage and terrorist activities. Specifically, according to the Georgian authorities, those arrested were implicated in a terrorist act in Gori in 2005 and in blowing up the Liakhvi and Kartli-2 power lines; the railroad in Kaspi on October 9, 2004; and the oil pipeline in Khashuri on November 17, 2004. Moscow's whining that the Georgians specially whipped up this scandal is entirely groundless.

Moscow's response was harsh and unprecedented. In October 2006 Russia cut off air links with Georgia and terminated postal and transportation communications between the two countries. Russia recalled its ambassador and other diplomats from Tbilisi and stopped issuing visas to citizens of Georgia. Georgian restaurants and casinos in Moscow were shut down. Schools compiled lists of ethnic Georgian pupils. An anti-Georgian propaganda campaign was launched, and Georgian businesspersons in Russia began to encounter particular difficulties.

Previously, in June 2006 while responding to Western demands that Russian troops be withdrawn from parts of Moldova and Georgia, the Russian Foreign Ministry officially and publicly declared that the unrecognized post-Soviet republics had the right of self-determination. In other words, Russia announced its readiness to recognize the separatist regimes in Trans-Dniestr, Abkhazia, and South Ossetia. This was "punishment" for the actions of Moldova and Georgia in strengthening their ties with the West and asserting their European orientation.

The watchword of the *oprichniks* was that actions must follow words, and this translated into trade and natural gas wars against Georgia and Moldova. But even that was not enough. Moscow began openly to establish bilateral relations with the authorities in the unrecognized republics. The presidents of Trans-Dniestr, South Ossetia, and Abkhazia were demonstratively received by the Foreign Ministry, which concluded bilateral agreements with them on economic cooperation and financial assistance.

In November 2007 the Russian special services were again implicated in anti-Georgian activities in connection with a days-long antigovernment meeting in Tbilisi. At a special briefing, Givi Targamadze, the chairman of Georgia's parliamentary committee on defense and security, revealed transcripts of telephone conversations between several leaders of the opposition and officials of the Russian special services. "These people openly coordinated their actions with the plans of Russian intelligence. This cooperation . . . has a long history. We didn't speak about it earlier, but now we publicly declare that what is currently going on in Tbilisi is nothing other than a direct and massive Russian attack on Georgia," he declared. For Georgians news that the list of Russian agents included the leader of the Labor Party, Shalva Natelashvili; a member of the leadership of the Republican Party, Levan Berdzenishvili; the former minister of state Georgy Khindrava; and Konstantin Gamsakhurdia, the leader of the Freedom Party and son of the first president of Georgia, was an earthshaking revelation. The transcripts of their phone conversations with Russian intelligence officers were broadcast on Georgian television.[6]

In August 2008 Russia launched a broad-scale war against Georgia, hypocritically cloaking it in its duty to protect Russian "peace-makers" and other Russian citizens. (Recall in this connection that Russia had issued Russian passports to Georgian citizens.) Naturally, Moscow prepared this ideological cover poorly. Also naturally, Russia easily won this war in the pro-Russia parts of Georgia. This was not a war against the people, unlike the wars in Afghanistan and Chechnya. Thus, Russian politicians succeeded in the plans that they had formulated in the early 1990s, saying, "We will never leave Abkhazia."

Of course, the Russian-Georgian war inevitably produced reverberations in Moldova, which, like Georgia, had become an independent republic following the collapse of the USSR. (Parenthetically, the inhabitants of Trans-Dniestr, the region of Moldova that Russia targeted, were also issued Russian passports.) Meeting at the end of August 2008 with Moldovan president Vladimir Voronin, Russian president Dmitry Medvedev, Putin's stunt man, drew a direct analogy between what was going on in Georgia and what might happen in Moldova.

Several aspects of this conflict must be highlighted. First, Bessarabia, a part of the Moldavian Soviet Socialist Republic, was arbitrarily attached to the Soviet Union in 1940 by the notorious Molotov-Ribbentrop Pact. Thus, it is hardly surprising that many Romanian-speaking Moldavians favor uniting their country with Romania. The Russian-speaking inhabitants of Trans-Dniestr, the separatist left bank of the Dniestr River, categorically oppose it.

The Trans-Dniestr region, which occupies 12 percent of the territory of Moldova, constitutes a vital interest for Russia. It contains 28 percent of Moldova's industrial production, the foundation of which is heavy industry, and was part of the USSR's former defense complex. Moreover, 90 percent of the country's electrical energy is generated on the left bank. A gas pipeline passes through the Trans-Dniestr and carries Russian gas, via Ukraine, to Romania and Bulgaria. Russia's interest in economic cooperation with the Trans-Dniestr region centers on the area's developed agro-industrial complex as well as the output of light industry, electronics, radio technology, and the defense industry; machine building; and metallurgy. As its main foreign economic partner, Moscow maintains a policy toward Trans-Dniestr that is very similar to its policy toward Abkhazia and South Ossetia. There, too, the aim is to split up Moldova, again by making use of the Russian-speaking population.

At this point we must step outside the chronological framework to grasp the logic of events. As a historian and international relations specialist, not even in my worst dreams, especially after the end of the Cold War, could I imagine that Russian foreign policy would assume the mantle of Hitler's foreign policy. Did this happen, like so much else, from ineptitude? I don't think so. Soon after the breakup of the USSR, the theme of "compatriots" and "Russian-language speakers" emerged and fit in very well with the imperial moods of the majority of the Russian elite, especially those weighed down with epaulets.

I don't know specifically who planned and began implementing the criminal plan right after Yeltsin became the master of the country. I only know that it existed from the start. (I myself took part in drafting the initial papers on this matter without realizing where it was heading, since I had not the least conception of the authorities' schemes.) It was probably not Putin, who was then just a small fry, although he knew Germany firsthand. It was probably not any of those who then occupied center stage in Russian politics. Most likely it was someone from among the Soviet "dinosaurs," if not by age—though that, too, is possible—then by his view of the world. It was obviously someone familiar with the history of international relations. A person (or a group of persons) with imperial and totalitarian convictions. In addition, a consummate manipulator. It seems it was someone from the security services, or *siloviki*, although I can't rule out persons working in the Foreign Ministry, where many nasty things were going on.

But that is not the crux of the matter. The main point is that starting in 1992, Moscow's revanchist, imperial policy became one of the dominant motifs of domestic politics and an important factor in international relations.

The West played an extremely significant role in the revival of the Cold War and Russia's recoil from democracy, thereby letting slip a historic opportunity to move Russia in the direction of real democracy. The chain of mistakes began in Gorbachev's time when the leaders, politicians, and diplomats of democratic countries were unable or unwilling to believe in the sincerity of the new Soviet leader's reformist intentions and of his diplomacy. For good reason one of the key phrases in Gorbachev's Nobel lecture in Oslo on June 5, 1991, was this appeal: "We wish to be understood." But in response to the unprecedented openness and readiness to compromise of Gorbachev's foreign policy, the West continued to pursue its traditional diplomacy of pressure on its longtime potential adversary. Western leaders came around to believing Gorbachev when it was already too late in the game.

Then, in the framework of Realpolitik, the West, particularly the United States, supported Yeltsin, the winner, who was incapable of rising above the level of a provincial party boss. A series of glaring mistakes was made regarding Yeltsin. For example, when the semiliterate leader of this great power declared that the country he headed wanted to join NATO, the West responded immediately but did not invite Russia in. It could have been wiser. The ultrasensitive Yeltsin was deeply offended, and the reactionaries in his retinue were handed a powerful argument against cooperation with the West.

What followed—namely, the 1993 coup pitting Yeltsin against Russia's parliament—was a nightmare both for Russia and the West. Naturally, the West bet on Yeltsin, but it also conferred its de facto blessings on any actions of the more democratically inclined authorities of the moment. By the time of the 1996 presidential election, the West was so frightened of the quite real possibility that the communists might return to power that it supported Yeltsin unconditionally. Against this background, notwithstanding public concern, Western politicians kept mum about the First Chechen War, giving President Yeltsin a free pass. The West not only facilitated but also guaranteed the massive and flagrant violations of human rights in Russia, the genocide of Russia's own people in Chechnya, and the *appointment* of KGB officer Putin to the position of president.

During the era of perestroika under Gorbachev, ideals are what really drove Soviet politics. Unintentionally, the politics of ideals sometimes sounds as if it were divorced from reality. Such an approach, however, is far from the case. To be sure, Gorbachev put forward what may have seemed unrealizable goals as, indeed, not a few of them turned out to be so. Among them were reducing the danger of war; establishing a common European home; creating a nuclear-free, nonviolent world in the realm of foreign policy; building socialism with a human face via democratization in the USSR; and providing its citizens with a full spectrum of human rights at home. Pursuing these goals, he was forced, on the one hand, to maneuver within the upper leadership of the USSR that was then mostly hostile to reforms and, on the other hand, metaphorically to breach the wall of mistrust and misunderstanding of his Western partners who doubted the sincerity of the new Soviet leader.

Gorbachev's policy of ideals was pursued in the real world, which was largely hostile to such ideals. Skeptics argue that if politics does not reckon with reality and is not the art of the possible, it can hardly be called politics at all. That begs the question of what is possible and what is not. A politics of ideals expands the limits of the possible. Gorbachev's political experiment clearly illustrates the absence of contradictions between the politics of ideals and that of reality.

Unfortunately, the West was either unable or unwilling to step outside the framework of its traditional approaches. Despite obvious Soviet progress by 1988 to secure human rights and the success of Soviet-American negotiations in this sphere, even someone inclined to stimulate democratic changes in the USSR such as U.S. assistant secretary of state Richard Schifter indirectly acknowledged that he and others like him were not ready to try unconventional, breakthrough approaches. For example, the U.S. State Department demanded certain confirmations of Soviet sincerity in this sphere before agreeing to the final document of the Vienna conference of the CSCE. Members of the outgoing administration of President Ronald Reagan, and Secretary of State George Shultz in particular, were invested in the success of the Vienna conference as they wanted to open the door to negotiations on conventional forces in Europe. For its part, as noted in chapter 1, Soviet diplomacy conditioned its acceptance of the Vienna document on an agreement to convene a conference on human rights in Moscow. The Americans had a hard time making up their minds and insisted upon various conditions before condescending to agree.

During a three-hour conversation with Anatoly Kovalev, then the second-ranking person in the Soviet Foreign Ministry, Schifter identified the question of allowing exit visas for refuseniks as the key issue for the Americans, emphasizing that the number of fast-tracked cases had to be significant. He explained his thinking as follows. The Reagan administration had approximately six weeks remaining in its term to explain to the American people whether an agreement in Vienna was possible. Schifter believed it would be risky to name too high a figure, for the Soviet foreign policy establishment might not be able to manage it. However, during a five-day workweek it was possible to review 2 cases before lunch and 2 after lunch; so in Schifter's opinion, in the course of a week, the Soviet bureaucracy could review 20 cases. On this basis, Schifter came up with a figure of 120 and the following day handed the Soviet side a list with that number of refuseniks. In essence, this signified agreement to the Soviet proposal to host the CSCE human rights meeting in Moscow.[7]

On the one hand, this looked like a splendid example of cooperation in pursuit of common and noble goals. On the other hand, despite the obvious evidence of fresh and positive approaches, Schifter still lacked sufficient trust in his Soviet interlocutors and did not fully understand that in the Foreign Ministry only through such démarches were his Soviet interlocutors able to solve long-festering problems in the interest of their own country. In a confidential conversation, Anatoly Kovalev told me of his disappointment that Schifter had not asked for more.

Meanwhile, many Western politicians were taking advantage of the developing situation in the USSR, especially after the August 1991 coup, to extract the maximum benefit for themselves without giving much thought to the long-term consequences. During Gorbachev's perestroika a positive interaction generally existed between Realpolitik and the politics of the idealists—Gorbachev,

Shevardnadze, and Yakovlev—but after President George H. W. Bush changed American policy in the direction of greater "pragmatism," this positive sum game collapsed.

With the breakup of the USSR, Realpolitik became an even stronger trend in international politics. To a large extent this was the paradoxical result of the West's no longer having to face the critical question of how to coexist with an unpredictable Soviet giant armed to the teeth. During the periods of international détente, Western leaders behaved more decorously than they did after the breakup of the USSR. For objective reasons they had to enter into dialogue with the USSR, but they neither bowed and scraped before its leadership nor evinced friendly feelings. After the breakup of the USSR, Western leaders pursued a policy of political expediency, a derivative of Realpolitik. In this context political expediency was a poisonous byproduct of cynicism, fear, hypocrisy, and political shortsightedness. Such a policy alone allows one to support those whom, in a normal system of contacts, it would be impossible to support. Most likely one should look for the roots of political expediency in 1938 in Munich, where, to put it mildly, the shortsighted leaders of Great Britain and France demonstrated political expediency toward Hitler, who wanted to receive the Sudetenland from Czechoslovakia. Everyone knows what happened afterward.

Munich—it is precisely this shameful label that best describes the Russia policies of several Western countries. It applies to a wide range of issues, from their virtually silent acquiescence to the partition of Georgia, crimes in Chechnya, and political assassinations to their unwillingness to discuss questions of human rights and democracy with the Russian authorities. The West's politically expedient policy of Realpolitik has already come back to haunt both it and Russia, which should not under any circumstances be confused with its rulers.

Ironically, no matter how paradoxical it may seem, the Soviet masters behaved more decorously, too, during the Cold War than did their successors in the Kremlin. Starting with Brezhnev, the leaders during the period of stagnation, looking at the West, understood that if they behaved otherwise, that would be the end of détente.

Unfortunately, neither history nor historians are currently very popular among politicians or voters. What is valued are technocrats and so-called pragmatists who often not only are unversed in the past and its lessons but also believe they have no need for advice from experts in those fields. The result is that what they do is grounded in myths and incompetence rather than in realities, and it cannot be considered politics.

Conclusion

In 2007 I left government service. As I had predicted, the situation in Russia had worsened. After Putin came to power, it became impossible to influence what was going on. I was not surprised. My political career with its peaks and valleys of activity and effectiveness stretching over four periods of national history—the period of stagnation, the changes of Gorbachev's perestroika, the Yeltsin years, and the rise of Putinism—had prepared me for this. My family's upheavals and historical education sharpened my intuition regarding events in Russia.

Much had happened in that time, but everything pointed in one direction: the Putin regime's attempts to do everything possible to return the country to the past had already resulted in a complete fiasco. Let us not forget that even the crumbling USSR was objectively much stronger than contemporary Russia, which has been weakened not only by the fatal errors of the past but also by the complete madness of Putin's policies.

The political lunacy had already begun under Yeltsin. It was then that the foundation was laid for the unprecedented power of the special services. It was then that preparations began to revive the imperial monster. It was then that the dictatorship of a systematic ideology again crawled out into the open. It was then that undesirables began to be eliminated, both physically and morally.

It was under Yeltsin that the foundations for a new Russian imperialism were constructed. As noted previously, one of the main instruments for this was the so-called policy of "defending Russian-speaking people." The partition of Georgia was in preparation long before it actually occurred. The same operation took place with respect to Ukraine, Moldova, and other post-Soviet countries.

The rebirth of the reactionary ideology of Nicholas I's era—namely, Russian Orthodoxy, autocracy, and *narodnost'*—also occurred under Yeltsin. The last of these concepts, which is essentially untranslatable into other languages, requires some explanation because its meaning is especially political in this context. From the very beginning to the present, it has meant the rejection of anything foreign; a sort of "special Russian path"; and some sort of mystical and, even more, mythical unity of power, religion, and the people on the basis that the Russians—"God's chosen people"—have the only "true" religion, traditions, and customs and, therefore, stand above all other peoples. In other words, it represents a dense xenophobia that rejects the value of human individuality, rights, and freedoms, as well as other universal values. It was precisely *narodnost'*, sometimes glorified by politicians as a "collective mentality [*sobornost'*]," that served in Rus' as the rationalization for crimes committed by those in power against the individual, including, for example, Stalinist collectivization. It also serves as justification for the phony populist demagogy on which the semblance of democracy is based. *Narodnost'* has become especially popular under Putin, although the special services prepared the ground for this starting from the time of Gorbachev's perestroika. The other elements of this triad are much simpler. After the collapse of the USSR, Russian Orthodoxy became the de facto state religion, and the president became an autocrat.

It is doubtful that Yeltsin himself was aware of much of what was happening on his watch. One may suppose with a high degree of probability that during his presidency the links between cause and effect were largely broken.

The situation was exacerbated by the fact that Russians, unfortunately, suffer from defective vision, including historical vision, as well as infantilism.[1] This is precisely why they accepted, and many even welcomed, the loss of their own rights and freedoms. Is it not revealing that during the May Day celebrations in 2014, many marchers carried portraits of Stalin and Beriya? Is it not a national catastrophe that the overwhelming majority of Russia's people was overjoyed by the dismemberment of Georgia and especially of Ukraine? Russia again fell victim to the situation Alexander Herzen, the great nineteenth-century Russian writer and critic, described: the entire society seemed to be infected by the disease of imperial patriotic syphilis. In Herzen's day this was a reaction to Russia's brutal suppression of the Polish uprising of 1863 in which the people demanded reforms, democratization, and independence.

The symptoms of the chronic illness of the Russian people and its rulers became much more acute following the start of Russia's undeclared war against Ukraine, including its annexation of Crimea in 2014. The concrete actions of the Russian authorities in pursuing an opportunity to conduct their insane foreign and domestic policy are merely details. The main thing is that Russians accepted it uncomplainingly and even enthusiastically.

Until recently to say and, even more, to write that the Cold War is again gaining strength after a brief intermission would have been almost indecent, since this would have contradicted generally accepted views. It makes sense only now, when Russia has demolished de facto the entire system of international security. Having failed to take note of Russia's Cold War–inspired policies—policies that Moscow itself spoke of quite openly but about which the West did not want to hear—the West, to its own surprise, finds itself at a red line, a line that the Putin regime has long since crossed.

The same situation exists when attempting to explain that Russia is now experiencing a new period of stagnation. It has become clear that this neo-stagnation has already transmogrified into a dictatorship of a systematic ideology to which the overwhelming majority of Russians have submitted. As an omnipresent mindset, this national catastrophe is worse than all the preceding ones. After getting a taste of freedom, Russia has renounced it of its own free will and opted instead to establish a new satrapy.

As soon as Putin was appointed the "successor," I realized the futility of hoping for a democratic path of Russian development. My intuitive perception of this badly brought up, poorly educated, dull Chekist with the demeanor of an underworld thug tallied with information I possessed as an official on Russia's Security Council. He habitually lied, took decisions that made no sense, and did everything he could to crush the buds of democracy. Naturally I considered it impossible to take part in what was going on. Although I consciously distanced myself step by step from real power in Russia starting in 2001, it was only in 2007, by emigrating, that I was finally able to complete this process.

The reasons for this probably can be understood from what I have already written, but they may be summed up as the crushing defeat of the ideals and values—hopefully a temporary defeat—to which more than one generation of my family, including this writer, was devoted. To a high degree this defeat was concisely expressed in Putin's speech of February 10, 2007, at the Forty-Third Munich Security Conference; however, his speech was simply *just another routine* Cold War declaration. His choice of Munich as the venue for delivering this extremely confrontational speech imparted an especially sinister meaning to the phrase *New Munich*. Was this choice of venue dictated by Putin's idiosyncratic sense of humor?

In any case, I remember that in Munich, Putin expressed terrible sadness about the dominating factor of force in international relations and about the disregard for international law. He also decried the fact that "in international relations more and more frequently one encounters the striving to resolve one or another question, arising from so-called political expediency, grounded in current political competition"; that "no one feels secure any longer"; and that NATO and the United States, in the first place, threaten Russia's security. And he raised one more extremely important factor: *according to Putin it is becoming impossible to resolve conflicts through political means.* As the saying goes, "It takes a thief to know a thief," as this factor became fully evident with Russia's aggression first against Georgia and then against Ukraine.

In Munich, in language that everyone understood, Putin yet again enunciated a policy of revanchism and Cold War. Those who did not want to hear his words have only themselves to blame.

Russian history is full of bad and even criminal rulers. But as Pyotr Chaadaev wrote, nations are moral beings just like individual persons. In the first half of the nineteenth century, he complained that "among the saddest features of our distinctive civilization, . . . we still only discover truths that others find trite," and that "standing as it were outside of time, we are untouched by the worldwide education of the human race." Naturally he could not have foreseen that his conclusions would come true in Russia almost two hundred years later. Alas, the age-old slavishness of the Russian people, or their submission to power—many love to praise it, calling it long suffering—has brought on another catastrophe. The overwhelming majority of Russians dare not even think of challenging the authorities, let alone overthrowing them. The most they hope for is to weasel something out of them. This fully applies to many of the "leaders of the opposition." It is precisely such passivity on the part of the people that makes the situation so hopeless.

As a result of the symbiosis between the openly criminal authorities and the subservience of a people hypnotized by the power of the contemporary mass media, Russia again presents an indisputable danger to itself and to those around it. Apart from imperialism and revanchism, the greatest risks stem from the mentality of most of the inhabitants of the country.

But let us return to Chaadaev's diagnosis of infantilism. Among the characteristics of infantilism is a striving to receive something desired without making any effort, a confidence in one's impunity, an unshakable conviction of one's own rightness, a disinclination and inability to get along with others and to take their interests into account, an unwarranted cruelty, and an aggressiveness raised to the level of absolute egocentrism. All of these characterize the content and style of contemporary Russian domestic and foreign policy. Its xenophobia not only refers to its fear or hatred of other countries, peoples, cultures, and religions but often also perceives as inimical everything that is not "ours"—that is, even persons from other towns, to say nothing of persons holding other political views. Regrettably, the concept of tolerance is alien to contemporary Russia.

The combination of a slavish psychology, infantilism, and xenophobia is already a danger in itself. But its danger grows immeasurably from the age-old messianism that has been inculcated into many generations and has grown particularly acute from the time of the Bolshevik coup. These factors all became the main ingredients of the explosive mix of the new Russian imperialism. The lack of any popular check on the authorities, on the one hand, and the people's heightened suggestibility, on the other, enable Moscow's sovereigns to engage in any kind of adventures they please.

As a result of massive impoverishment, demagogic juggling of democratic slogans, and concentrated lies from the authorities, a large majority of the population developed a strong allergy to democracy. Growing nostalgia for the "good old days" guaranteed the popularity of tough approaches and actions, including the use of force, both domestically and abroad. In the absence since then of any influential independent mass media, the authorities have enjoyed an unchallenged ideological monopoly. In these conditions, the likelihood of a democratic evolution in Russia was so slight that it could not even be seriously considered for the foreseeable future.

Speaking of the will-o'-the-wisp of democratic prospects for Russia in the foreseeable future, it is appropriate to turn to an article by Yury Afanasyev, one of the leaders of the democratic movement in Russia in the perestroika period.[2] He believes that "as before, our people have not become a people that is a subject of history, but have remained a people that is a mass, a crowd in history." In this connection, Afanasyev notes "contemporary Russia's reversion to its old ways, its return to the Russian and Soviet rut," which he characterizes as "repetition, unchangeability, centuries-old structural stability—this constantly changing immutability." Integral components of this rut are "Russian Orthodoxy, messianism and expansionism, people's habits, and their world view." These "components, constantly interweaving, mutually interacting, changing (sometimes to the point of becoming unrecognizable) created that very same 'Russian rut' which we seem to have fallen into today." Here Afanasyev clarifies his point: "Actually, if one takes a closer look, for us 'to return' really means to wind up at a place from which we never departed."

The gloomy picture Afanasyev paints points to the impossibility of a truly democratic evolution of Russia in the foreseeable future, one not "bestowed from above." What would be needed is some sort of break from continuity, from constructing the "Third Rome," and from messianism and other attributes that, unfortunately, are inherent in Russia.

The pas de deux of many oppositionists with the Russian authorities, along with several other aspects of their conduct, raises the question as to whether any democratic opposition as such really exists in Russia. Under the name of "opposition," haven't the special services been taking active measures since the time of Gorbachev? One cannot exclude this possibility especially since, to put it mildly, many of the "opposition leaders" seem unconvincing. I am referring to the obvious, or thinly disguised, agents of the special services. But there are more serious grounds for considering such an assumption about the opposition as a serious working hypothesis. None of the so-called opposition leaders aspires to presidential power. Moreover, none of them has even the hint of a program; the slogan "Russia without Putin" is not a program. A slogan is just a slogan, not something that entails any concrete action. I will stick my neck out and conjecture that for a long time the opposition politicians have only been playing at opposition, and some among them have been doing this from the beginning in order to create the appearance of a political struggle in Russia.

In contemporary Russia not even the germs of a civil society exist, thanks to the efforts of its rulers. The within-system dissidents who really made a decisive contribution to hopes for the democratic development of the country have been replaced by a mediocre semblance, a sort of ersatz "within-system opposition," that seeks neither power nor any serious changes in domestic and foreign policy.

It would be wrong to overlook or to disparage the actions of those people who are motivated by notions of conscience, honor, dignity, justice, and the interests of the nation and its inhabitants. Among all age groups and members of various professions, more than a few people act according to the famous motto "Do what must be done, and let the chips fall as they may." It is unfortunate that acting with the means available to them, they rarely attract any attention. The martyrology of victims of the Russian authorities is far from complete and by no means limited to well-known persons, however, especially because in contemporary Russia even elementary personal and professional decency frequently stands out as a meritorious deed.

Such deeds are always performed by those whom Putin and his gang label as "traitors to the nation" and "fifth columnists." For now the protest movement itself has misfired. But moral-ethical protest has survived, if only among a very small part of the population. However paradoxical it may seem, one cannot dismiss the possibility that it is precisely the moral-ethical character of protest that may hold some promise for the future. Naturally, there are risks involved. A similar protest in the late nineteenth and early twentieth centuries was infiltrated in the end by unscrupulous political adventurers whom Fyodor Dostoevsky prophetically called devils, and it led to the collapse of the country.

Speaking of the extremely unlikely possibility that Russia may take the path of democracy, it should not be forgotten that during the era of the moribund Brezhnev, Andropov, and Chernenko, almost nobody could foresee that the end point of the trajectory of the communist dictatorship would be the democratization of the USSR followed by regime collapse. This reminder leads me to another observation.

The situation unfolding in contemporary Russia is not new. Russia found itself, if with certain important reservations, in a similar situation, usually called stagnation, during the period when Brezhnev, Andropov, and Chernenko ruled the USSR. Stagnation possessed several distinct features: the unlimited power of a narrow circle of rulers unconstrained by the people, the disregard of domestic and international law, the Cold War, the arms race, the global opposition to democratic countries, the suppression of dissent, the constant mass hypnosis of the people regarding "successes achieved" and "hostile encirclement," and the breakdown of civilian industry along with the buildup of military industry. The period of classical stagnation also had additional features that it shares with the current situation.

In essence, considering developments in Russia since Putin came to power—his success in establishing "stability" and constructing a "vertical of power," on the one hand, and the sad historical experience, several aspects of which have been delineated previously, on the other—one may confidently refer to the contemporary neo-stagnation as a core element of Putinocracy. How long it will last is another question.

Although neo-stagnation is significantly different from the Brezhnev–Chernenko stagnation, the two do share many common features. This is evidenced above all by the dysfunctionality of the rulers involved, even though the two cases differ. The latter's case of gerontocracy manifesting itself in senile indisposition, including dementia, is completely different in character from the former's case of infantilism, which is characterized by an incomprehension of even the basics of governance and an inability and unwillingness to work. However, the consequences of both cases for Russia, its inhabitants, and the world are entirely comparable. The present authorities' penchant for playing with power is no better than the beastly seriousness of the communist leaders.[3]

Another common feature of Putinocracy and classical stagnation is their ramping up of ideology; however, even here there are also profound differences. The rulers of the stagnating USSR, who mistook their dreams for reality, thought they possessed certain lofty goals and ideals. (Such people are easily and conveniently susceptible to self-deception.) While they did not even read the "holy books" of their anti-religion, they were mired in propagandist clichés and stereotypes, which, in any case, were based on their own convictions, their own experiences, their knowledge, and their lives.

The situation is fundamentally different with regard to those responsible for neo-stagnation. They have no personal experience or knowledge of what they advocate. Like little children they play at soldiers, toying with the fate of Russia and other countries. But they have an unshakable faith in the myth of the greatness of the USSR that, for them, is symbolized by Stalin, Dzerzhinsky, and their ilk. They ignore the fact that the ascent of the human spirit, the victory in the Second World War, and other achievements were possible not because of the authorities but despite them. The mythology about the "accomplishments" of the Communist Party and the Soviet government turned out to be too firmly instilled in a population rendered hapless by heterodoxy. It turns out that the current cynical authorities—a criminal class that has acquired state power and turned the Kremlin, the Russian White House, the ministries, and the federal agencies into their own property— find this mythology convenient and to their liking.

The principal warriors against the ideals of democracy and human rights—the dyed-in-the-wool xenophobes, the anti-Semites, those who hate the humanity of human beings, the morally and intellectually limited creators and products of reality who are leading Russia to political, economic, and moral ruin—did not, and do not, understand that they are the blind leading the blind along a path that ends in the abyss.

The creeping rehabilitation of the Soviet authorities' crimes against their own and other peoples that began under Yeltsin is much more amoral and cynical than what the "true Leninists" did. After the fall of the USSR, it was more difficult *not* to know what had transpired than it was to know the truth.

Naturally one may explain the return to stagnation by pointing to diverse reasons, ranging from the almost total historical illiteracy of its initiators and inspirers to their deeply hidden and perverted pro-Soviet convictions. The latter version looks even more convincing in that Putin's United Russia party in essence mimics the CPSU and that the "warriors of the invisible front"—namely, Putin and his colleagues from the "Soviet overflow" who came to power—are simply committed Bolsheviks. We should not fail to recall the professional training they underwent in Soviet times. (I say this confidently as someone who belongs to that generation.) That the authorities found the Soviet model convenient has played a large role in recent developments.

Another common feature of both classical stagnation and Putin-esque neo-stagnation is the absence of a dialogue not only between society and the authorities but also among the authorities themselves. Under Putin and his puppet Medvedev, the absence of a dialogue among the authorities is much more serious than it was in Soviet times. In his diaries, Anatoly Chernyaev writes of his horror that in what was then the highest organ of power, the Politburo, there was no discussion of the most complex and critical issues. However, leaders at every level were not averse to consulting with their subordinates, who considered it normal to express their disagreements and take issue with them, defending their own points of view and not infrequently succeeding in persuading their superiors to change their minds. The same thing happened under Yeltsin, although in a different form: they simply manipulated him.

With Putin's ascension to the throne, dialogue with the authorities ceased. "Putin never alters his decisions," I was told by one of his former KGB colleagues in response to an attempt to correct a glaringly mistaken decision by the then acting president. Soon another thing became clear: he also didn't need the advice of experts. As president, he didn't spend more than fifteen minutes a day reading documents.[4] According to the journal *Russkii newsweek* (Russian newsweek), after Putin became prime minister, "they said that in the [Russian] White House there was simply no such format: Putin, the chairman of the Council of Ministers, i.e. the prime minister, worked on the documents by himself. He came to a meeting for 15–20 minutes, met with [Vice Premiers Igor] Shuvalov, and [Aleksei] Kudrin, chaired the meeting, and left. . . . A swimming pool and two banquet halls were constructed on the fifth floor [the prime minister's floor]," one of the prime minister's subordinates confirmed, "and there the flies flew about." At the time the report was published, apart from President Medvedev, the only persons with direct access to Putin were Vice Premiers Igor Sechin and Kudrin.[5]

During Yeltsin's presidency, chaos reigned in the practice of personnel appointments. Chernyaev was indignant about the insecurity of personnel appointed to positions during the Brezhnev era. Appointments and tenure in office were a "function of the supreme leader's personal sympathy or antipathy."[6] This practice returned under Yeltsin. Putin succeeded in extending this instability to other spheres, including business, and even to the possibility of engaging in oppositional activity. This is the most vivid confirmation of neo-stagnation in Russia. As in classical stagnation, neo-stagnation has fostered maximum growth in the role of the punitive organs, although under Putin this growth has been incommensurately larger than it was under Brezhnev, Andropov, and Chernenko.

This is how the authorities have negotiated the next formidable series of hairpin turns. Having just escaped the Leninist-Stalinist rut, they returned to it, lightly disguising this fact with the semblance of democracy. It is purely out of Yevgeny Schwartz's *The Naked King*, but for now no one in Russia or abroad dares say that the king is naked.[7]

Neo-stagnation will last longer than the stagnation of the

Brezhnev–Chernenko era. Back then people were hoping for something better; they waited for and searched for it. Now most of them are nostalgic for the past of Stalin and Brezhnev. This neo-stagnation may be the most prolonged period of mediocrity and will last until people finally tire of it and realize the terrible destructiveness of such an existence. Neo-stagnation will inevitably be accompanied by the further brutalization of domestic politics and conflict abroad. Just how far can the Russian authorities go?

Russia has long been heading toward renewed confrontation with the West. After the breakup of the USSR, clear-thinking politicians initially neutralized this tendency. Gradually their influence declined, and many of them left the political stage. Although it began much earlier, this shift became particularly clear to me when I was working in the Security Council. The rise to power of the special services made the brutalization of Russian politics inevitable. From my own experience I know just how much one's profession, and one's specialization within that profession, influences a person's worldview. Even if one speaks of Russia's diplomatic service then, for example, the Americanists, as a rule, were distinguished by their greater toughness and the Europeanists, on the contrary, by their flexibility and their inclination to seek compromises. What can one say about persons who thought in terms of threats, enemies, and confrontations? It was impossible for them to execute a sharp turn while preserving face or wearing perhaps just a mask. They needed a long period of preparation to engage the Western leaders, among other things. After winning over President George W. Bush and Italian prime minister Silvio Berlusconi and engaging the services of Germany's ex-chancellor Gerhard Schröder, Putin felt the moment had come for him to change his political mask.

After proclaiming its readiness to renew the Cold War, which had been overcome with such great effort, through the lips of pseudo-president Medvedev the Kremlin risked its cooperation with the European Union and NATO by playing the card of imperial ambition. In other words, it returned to the fallacious foreign policy that had led to the economic and political collapse of the Soviet Union and, ultimately, to its disintegration. Unfortunately, the Kremlin's political calculation turned out to be right. Western leaders did not consider the dismemberment of Georgia sufficient reason to spoil their relations with Moscow. This irresponsible approach echoed in Ukraine, initiating the worst crisis in the system of international security since the Cold War.

There are several possible explanations. One is a fear of what else this enormous, enraged state, with an impaired memory and intellectually and morally underdeveloped rulers, might do. Another is the West's dependence on Russian energy supplies. Even if these two most plausible hypotheses are true, from a moral perspective the policies of several Western states still look very dubious. Not only are their positions vis-à-vis Russia, Georgia, Ukraine, and international law at stake, but their own security and long-term interests are as well.

The stance of Western leaders who ignored the willingness of Russian authorities to destroy in an instant their normal relations with democratic countries that had been achieved through more than forty years of painstaking labor led to the crushing victory of the hawks over the doves in the eternal struggle within Russia. As has occurred repeatedly in Russian history, this was a victory over itself, over its own people, over common sense.

The West's pusillanimous behavior toward Russia only exacerbated the situation and gave the Kremlin a feeling of impunity. Meeting no rebuff for actions that deserved to be punished by the international community, Putin came to believe he could get away with anything. His massive persecution of oppositionists and his repressive legislation failed to provoke an adequate reaction. But the trial and conviction of the female punk rock band Pussy Riot in 2012 and, especially, Russia's homophobic law of 2013 could not remain unnoticed. Directly or indirectly they impacted very broad circles of public opinion in the West.

Further, no one doubts that it was on the direct orders of Putin that Mikhail Khodorkovsky spent almost ten years in captivity. The tragedy of Vasily Aleksanian, denied indispensable medical assistance when he refused to give false testimony on Khodorkovsky's trial (see chapter 6), is the acme of meanness and sadism! A similar case was that of the accountant Sergei Magnitsky, driven to his death in the notorious Moscow pretrial isolation facility Matrosskaya Tishina in November 2009. He too was refused cancer treatment; moreover, there were several indications that he had been tortured. Magnitsky's "crime" consisted of having disclosed a scheme to embezzle funds from the state budget. U.S. senator Benjamin Cardin (D-MD) very properly proposed that those responsible for Magnitsky's death be punished. In 2011 the U.S. Department of State prohibited the entry of sixty Russian officials connected with Magnitsky's death. In December 2012 the United States passed a law imposing personal sanctions on persons responsible for violating human rights and the principle of the supremacy of law, among them officials of the Russian Ministry of Internal Affairs, the Federal Security Service, the Federal Tax Service, the Arbitration Court, the Procurator General's Office, and the Federal Service for Implementation of Punishment. The "Magnitsky list" was implemented in Great Britain. too. However, this action was obviously insufficient to teach Moscow a lesson.

Moscow's reaction to even the mildest of Western criticism is difficult to describe. Within the framework of its own pseudo diplomacy, it then decided to deny its own orphans the right to be adopted by Americans in 2013. In other words, unfortunate Russian children paid a hundredfold for the utterly absurd patriotism of unscrupulous Russian politicians who turned them into hostages.

On February 27, 2015, the charismatic, *truly democratic*, and *fearless oppositionist* leader Boris Nemtsov was killed beneath the walls of the Kremlin. This area is under the intensive, round-the-clock control of the Russian special services—above all, the Federal Guard Service—consequently, nothing is possible there without their knowledge. Considering that both the Federal Guard Service and other special services report directly to the president of the Russian Federation, there cannot be the slightest doubt about who gave the order; an executioner merely carried it out. As a result of what moreover was the ritual murder of Nemtsov (Putin and his gang love infantile demonstrations!), Russia lost the most outstanding, uncompromising, authoritative, and experienced opponent of the Putin regime. (Nemtsov had held the posts of governor, minister, and first deputy premier.)

On January 21, 2016, retired High Court judge Sir Robert Owen announced the results of a public inquest by the High Court of London into the matter of Alexander Litvinenko's death, which has been discussed earlier. On the basis of painstaking work, including secret documents from the British special services, Owen stated that the FSB was probably responsible for the murder of Litvinenko, and the operation to eliminate him was likely executed with the approval of the then director of the FSB Nikolai Patrushev and President Vladimir Putin.[8] In this context one should not be confused by the word *probably*. The court issued a definitive decision.

Why does Russian diplomacy block the ending of bloodletting in Syria? The answer has been rather simple from the start: it does so out of the infantile fear of setting a precedent that would allow taking analogous measures with respect to Russia. President Medvedev spoke about this on February 22, 2011, when referring to the revolutions in Tunisia and Egypt. "Earlier they prepared such a scenario for us, and now they will try even harder to implement it," he said. "In any case, this scenario will not take place. But everything happening there will have a direct influence on our situation, moreover we are talking about a rather long perspective, a perspective of decades." To this, of course, is added the striving to demonstrate Russia's weight in international affairs. (In this connection, Western comments about Russia's return to the role of a world power are particularly bizarre.) Naturally, both economic and geopolitical considerations also play a role. In any case, largely as a result of Russia's senseless and irresponsible power plays, according to UN statistics from March 15, 2011, to December 10, 2013, there were 128,000 Syrians killed and more than 2 million wounded, and the whereabouts of 16,000 persons arrested by the Syrian authorities are unknown.

Invoking the pretext of the struggle against terrorism, but in reality to support the regime of Bashar al-Assad, Russia commenced the bombing of Syria on September 30, 2015. Russia refused to distinguish between the opposition to the regime and the terrorists operating on Syrian territory. The result of Russian bombing, according to the Syrian Observatory for Human Rights, was that by September 30, 2016, no fewer than 9,364 persons had been killed, among which 3,804 were civilians, including 906 children and 561 women.

The destruction by Russian warplanes on September 19, 2016, of a humanitarian convoy some six miles from Aleppo and the bombing of rebel-controlled living quarters and of hospitals located in that city must certainly be considered war crimes. Overall Russian policy in Syria should be recognized as a crime against peace and humanity.

During the Cold War, the leaders of both camps, divided by the Iron Curtain, understood very well the danger of incorrectly interpreting the intentions of the other side and, to a greater degree, even the most insignificant unpremeditated military incident between the USSR and the United States. In that context, the current deployment in Syria of S-300 and S-400 antiballistic missile systems intended to prevent U.S. strikes against Syrian objectives appears to be a flagrant provocation directed toward further, possibly uncontrolled escalation of tension in Russian-American relations. The fanning of war hysteria by the Russian authorities, their announcement guaranteeing daily bread rations in Saint Petersburg in time of war, and their assurances that all residents of Moscow will be provided underground shelters together raise questions about the intentions of the Russian authorities and their competence.

Until the recent past, extremely distressing references circulated regarding pre-perestroika Soviet foreign policy. Against the background of what is going on in Ukraine and in Syria, the exacerbation of relations with the West, unprecedented since 1966, Soviet policy during the Cold War looks comparatively rational.

The situation became significantly more complicated after the start of Russia's intervention in Syria in September 2015. And it would seem that the sudden declaration in March 2016 about cutting back the scale of this intervention provoked many questions and conjectures about why Putinocracy considered this necessary.

It is possible, of course, that Putin wanted to end Russia's isolation and, moreover, enter the international antiterrorist coalition as an equal member. But in that case, he did it in a very strange way—by primarily striking blows against the moderate opposition and by killing peaceful citizens, women, children. Moreover, the question arises: by doing so, isn't Russia sustaining the Islamic State?

The results of what is taking place in Syria are tragic. And without Putin's active support of Bashar al-Assad, the bloodletting in this country might have ended. In the five years from the start of the civil war in Syria about 470,000 people have died and about 1.9 million have been wounded. About 13.8 million Syrians have been deprived of their livelihoods. All in all, 45 percent of the population have had to leave their homes, with 4 million having left the country and 6.4 million having become internally displaced persons.

If anyone speaks of Russia's return to the role of a world power, it is worth looking at the Syrian tragedy in a broader context. As noted, the Putin regime does not accept freedom and democracy. It despises the very possibility that a nation might freely choose its rulers or, even worse, overthrow them, especially if Putin considers them his allies. Here one may draw a parallel between Putin's policies in Syria and Ukraine.

Moreover, Putinocracy considers the EU a hostile organization and that the best thing to do is to destroy it. Everything else is no more than hypocrisy and intrigues. This I already knew from the time I worked on the staff of the Russian Security Council, and what I have seen later on basically comports with that given inclination. In saying this, I am by no means asserting that there were not persons who initially took opposing positions as a matter of principle. Among them I can name Igor Ivanov, who was then minister of foreign affairs of Russia and opposed seeing the EU as a threat.

And now let us look at how Russia's policy toward Syria played out in the EU.

Europe was overwhelmed by a wave of terrorism. The most notorious acts of terror took place in Paris on January 7, 2015. Twelve persons, including two policemen, were killed and 11 wounded in the offices of the satirical weekly *Charlie Hebdo*. On January 9 a terrorist seized a kosher grocery at the Vincennes Gates in Paris and took 15 persons hostage. Four people died. The largest-scale series of terrorist acts in Paris took place on November 13, 2015. In those acts, 130 persons died and more than 350 were wounded. On July 14, 2016, Bastille Day, a nineteen-ton truck killed 86 persons and wounded 308 by driving through a crowd that had assembled on the English embankment in Nice to observe France's national day.

There can be no doubt that the terrorist acts in Brussels on March 22, 2016—killing 31 and wounding 340—were closely connected to those in Paris. But why Brussels? The argument that many Arabs and many Muslims live there both clearly reveals racial and religious intolerance and is incompatible with a civilized worldview. The hypothesis about a conflict or even a war of civilizations looks more than doubtful in this context. We know that for a conflict to flare up, especially between cultures that until then had lived amicably together, someone had to have organized this conflict. After all these attacks are not part of a family quarrel that arose simply from a misunderstanding or the bad mood of some family member. Let us focus on the fact that, summing up, these terrorist acts were directed against democracy, freedom of speech, and religious freedom, which, incidentally, Muslims living in Europe fully enjoy. To this list, however, one must unfortunately add the issue of still extant anti-Semitism, as evidenced by the shooting at the Jewish Museum in Brussels in May 2014 and another at the Grand Synagogue in Copenhagen in February 2015.

But let us return to the facts.

As a result of the fighting in Syria, for which Russia bears considerable blame, a wave of a million refugees overwhelmed Europe in 2015. In this connection many EU countries experienced both domestic as well as inter-state problems. A split appeared in the solidarity of EU countries. And England voted to leave the EU in June 2016. The very foundations of European civilization, including humanism and the observance of international law, also came into question.

When working on the staff of the Russian Security Council, in 1997 I encountered schemes by the special services to direct Islamic extremism and Islamic terrorism against Europe and the United States under the pretext that these phenomena were supposedly purposefully created by them and aimed against Russia. Are we perhaps not witnesses to the successful implementation of these schemes? But this is just one among a number of possible and rather vague conjectures.

In any case, we possess the facts concerning Russia's disruption of the attempt to end the civil war in Syria through diplomacy, then its military support of the Assad regime, and its deliberate or unintentional provocation of the most dangerous challenges and threats to European civilization. By taking the path of Cold War, revanchism, and high-handed rule, Russia has once more chosen a road that leads to self-destruction—to organizational self-destruction, since it is by no means a homogeneous empire, and to moral self-destruction, since the denial of what is humane in people and in politics signifies none other than the complete contempt for people on the part of Putin and his gang, as well as their dullness, their cruelty, and their greed.

As demonstrated, contemporary Russia manifests all the symptoms of slipping into a thinly disguised form of totalitarianism, which, to a high degree for that country, is a synonym for terror. Most of all it takes the form of periodic actions against persons and organizations the authorities dislike. The Russian authorities cannot permit themselves to indulge in massive repressions; but in any case, they have no need to when it suffices to intimidate those who step out of line.

Neo-stagnation may have extremely dangerous foreign policy consequences. Russia's imperial ambitions will be further developed. Fortunately, Latvia, Lithuania, and Estonia, which are the objects of the Kremlin's special hatred, are protected by membership in NATO and the European Union, but other post-Soviet countries are in a more vulnerable situation. The West, too, is under threat. By underestimating Moscow's aggressiveness, Western leaders greatly assisted in strengthening the position of the hawks and their preparations for initiating a new Cold War. If the leaders of Western countries continue to take a relaxed view regarding Russian politics, then the consequences may turn out to be unfortunate. Russia's aggression against Ukraine in 2014, however, may have finally taken the scales from their eyes.

With regard to Russia's domestic politics, ultimately, neo-stagnation may either lead to a new wave of reforms and to a new perestroika, but in a new guise, or it may lead to an upheaval, the result of which may be the establishment of a genuine democracy, one not bestowed from above but seized from below. In case of an upheaval, regrettably, violence will be unavoidable, for those in power will not retreat without engaging in bitter resistance. However, for all of this, neo-stagnation will inevitably progress through certain stages of development that may take quite some time and require the passage of at least three generations.

The most dangerous, and entirely probable, outcome of stagnation in Russia is disintegration. It is fraught with extremely serious consequences. Russia is a country saturated with nuclear and other weapons, potential Chernobyls, and discarded debris from the chemical industry. It is a country with a collapsing monoculture economy oriented to the export of oil and gas. It has been intellectually bled white from a brain drain and the authorities' inadequate attention to science, art, education, and culture. It has promoted antagonisms throughout its own territories and among its own people along ethnic, religious, property-holding, and other lines. Apart from Moscow, too few components of the Russian Federation have a strong enough interest in preserving the country's unity.

In the event of a breakup of Russia, a number of new nuclear powers with serious disputes with other post-Russia states might arise on Russia's present territory. Grave problems would inevitably arise over the disintegration of the armed forces and their infrastructure. (This was one of the arguments Russia used in annexing Crimea.) Moreover, the majority of post-Russia states would be headed by persons insufficiently schooled in military-political issues, and that situation might seriously elevate the threat of deploying weapons of mass destruction, to say nothing of the high risk of armed conflicts using conventional weapons. At the same time, it is very likely that the breakup of Russia would decrease the level of confrontation between the post-Russia states and their neighbors as well as with Western countries.

The economy of the country would collapse once and for all. However, in the event the enormous territory breaks up into small states, under certain conditions their economies might revive for a historically brief period. The West would almost certainly be engulfed by a wave of refugees.

The vertical of power that Putin created, and that serves as his insurance against democracy, is incapable of overcoming the breakup of the country. However, it guarantees the virtually universal accession to power of the *siloviki* and other corrupt officials with their characteristic mentality in the post-Russia states.

In any case, environmental pollution will continue to present a serious danger. By the late 1990s, the ecology of Russia was already disastrous. For a long time Russian authorities did not want to devote sufficient attention to preserving the environment, and post-Russia authorities, even if they desired to do so, would be unable to address it. This enormous territory is turning into a constant source of global environmental pollution.

Unfortunately, a pessimistic prognosis regarding Russia's future may be altered only in the event of some sort of extreme situation occurring—for example, if those in power are overthrown due to a social upheaval during which the internal security forces and the army remain at least neutral. But who would come to power then? They could be rabid nationalists and "faithful Leninists," but they could also be democratically inclined persons. This scenario has one indisputable advantage—the probable loss of power of the special services and other *siloviki*.

There are additional reasons why Russia's immediate future looks bleak. For example, the collapse of Russian science and primary through secondary education, as well as higher education, inevitably impacts the entire country. From the early Yeltsin period on, for some reason education has been considered almost unnecessary. The main goal now is to make money, preferably without having to work too hard. The miserable salaries of school and university teachers have produced a situation in which people simply purchase graduation certificates and diplomas, to say nothing of buying admission to institutes of higher learning. Furthermore, there has been a significant decline in the quality of professional teachers. The consequences are lamentable.

The decline in the general level of education has been accelerated by attempts to compel all young men without exception to serve in the army. If these efforts succeed, this will surely lead to not only an intellectual but also a demographic disaster, considering that the army even recruits persons who are unfit for military service due to health reasons. There are not enough eligible others to sustain Russia's enormous military organization.

Scientific work has ceased to be prestigious. Therefore, young people are not attracted to it. There can be no science without a fundamental change of direction that averts its extinction, with all the ensuing fatal consequences for Russia and for world science.

Considering that many Russian misfortunes are rooted in politics, both contemporary and past, it is appropriate to mention that in place of real politics, which Russia has not had for a long time, "political technological fixes" have been substituted that aim at achieving instantaneous results via any means. What kind of future awaits a country whose leaders for many years have given no thought to its relatively distant future; for whom people do not exist, only voters; and who substitute their personal interests and ambitions in place of the national interest?

Can Russia escape a catastrophe? Yes. But for it to happen, there must be a miracle—that is, Russia's genuine intellectual and moral elite must come to power. By "elite" I have in mind a new generation of persons of the caliber of Academician Andrei Sakharov, leading rights defender Sergei Kovalev, Anna Politkovskaya, Alexander Yakovlev, and other such honest, brave, and unselfish people. Several points should be noted here. First, contemporary Russian leaders and prominent politicians do not belong to this intellectual and moral elite. In reference to this particular *political* elite, one can only say they regularly and systematically violate all written and unwritten laws. Second, the ruling pseudo elite has driven the genuine elite out of the political arena as well as the arena of public opinion. Third, as far as it is able, the ruling pseudo elite denies the genuine elite access to the mass media and other sources of influence.

In 1851 Alexander Herzen, the outstanding oppositionist to the tsarist regime, wrote, "Just one more century of despotism such as we have now, and all the good qualities of the Russian people will disappear. It is doubtful whether without a principle of active individuality, the people will preserve their national character, and the civilized classes their education." For all the pessimism inherent in this pronouncement, Herzen did not envision the possibility of an incomparably more savage despotism. He could not even imagine such a thing. It is interesting that the Bolshevik dictatorship was aimed precisely at extirpating the principle of active individuality. But despite the mental devastation wreaked by the authorities, this very same principle of individuality remained intact, at least among some talented children, fleeing from the prevailing dullness, who chose paths that did not depend on the authorities—for example, music and chess, as well as activities to defend rights, and so forth. There were also exceptions among those in government service, including the most highly placed, even if they were considered "party loyalists." The most outstanding examples are found in the splendid trio from the era of reformation: Gorbachev, Shevardnadze, and Yakovlev.

But Herzen was mostly right. In one guise or another, the dystopias of Yevgeny Zamyatin, George Orwell, and Aldous Huxley came into being on Russian soil and included the mass hypnosis of the people, the establishment of a "ministry of truth" and its reconstitution under Putin, the predicted substitution of "we" for "I," the happiness in slavery, and the welding together of the lower classes of society. Moreover, under Putin, *stability*—part of the main slogan of Huxley's *Brave New World*—became the foundation of Russian politics.

The main reason why Russia once again, as in Soviet times, has been caught in a maelstrom of violence, lies, and fear is because the people have been crippled by the authorities for generations. This very same maelstrom also has tried to swallow countries that were in geographic, economic, or political proximity to Russia itself.

What could be more dangerous than the Russian authorities taking revenge for nonexistent threats and supposed insults? Especially when they live in an imaginary world light years from reality.

Somewhere a hundred years ago, Russians lost such concepts as *soul* and *conscience*. There were eccentrics who wrote about this, such as Dostoevsky, for example. Now one of his books—namely, *The Devils*—especially pertains to the Russian authorities, for in it he calls the "right to dishonor" the most important and dangerous component of the revolutionary movement.

On Russian soil *the right to dishonor* is not an empty phrase.

It is just like the aforementioned mental devastation produced by hypnosis and manipulation. Precisely this combination led to the incalculable sufferings of the Soviet empire "from Moscow to the farthest borders," as a popular song of Soviet times went. It is this degradation of national consciousness that is fraught with the greatest risks for everyone.

Will Russia escape from the spiral of destroying itself and other countries? The repetitiveness of events in Russian history is fascinating, especially since every loop in this spiral leads to an ever-increasingly inhuman level.

In the twenty-first century, Russia as never before has become a danger to itself and to those around it. I am not even referring to nuclear weapons; what is truly dangerous are elementary thoughtlessness, thriftlessness, and irresponsibility. They are dangerous in any industrially developed, well-armed, or simply densely populated country. Any one of these factors is capable, at a minimum, of producing serious consequences for its neighbors. Russia is a disintegrating ecological and chemical time bomb in which—under the influence of moral senility and the material disintegration of the state and its infrastructure—the incapacity and fecklessness of those responsible for its deployment and the security of themselves and those around them may have already armed the detonator.

I can repeat under oath: even without using any weapons of mass destruction, Russia is capable simply from carelessness of destroying itself and even other states that are not among its closest neighbors. For this crime, extenuating circumstances could not be found.

In conclusion, I again quote Chaadaev, who wrote, "By your leave, in the face of our misfortunes I do not want to share the striving for unbridled patriotism which has brought the country to the brink of the abyss, which wants to disentangle itself while persisting in its illusions, not wishing to acknowledge the desperate position it has itself created."[9]

CAST OF CHARACTERS

Identification is based on relevance to this book. Entries are in alphabetical order by last name.

Adamishin, Anatoly L. (1934–)
Liberal pro-perestroika deputy foreign minister of USSR under Mikhail S. Gorbachev, later minister for cooperation with member states of the Commonwealth of Independent States (CIS) (1997–98).

Adamov, Yevgeny O. (1939–)
Head of Russia's Ministry of Atomic Energy (1998–2001) arrested in Switzerland (2005) on U.S. warrant accusing him of misappropriating $9 million that it provided Russia to upgrade security of nuclear facilities; extradited to Russia and sentenced to five and a half years of imprisonment, which a higher court overturned for political reasons.

Afanasyev, Yury N. (1934–2015)
Political and public figure, historian, people's deputy of the USSR (1989–91) and of Russia (1991–93).

Akhromeyev, Sergei F. (1923–91)
Marshal of the USSR, military adviser to Mikhail S. Gorbachev, and supporter of anti-Gorbachev coup in August 1991 who in all probability committed suicide after it collapsed.

Andropov, Yury V. (1914–84)
Head of KGB (1967–82), general secretary of the Central Committee of the Communist Party of the Soviet Union (CC CPSU) (1982–84).

Beriya, Lavrenty P. (1899–1953)
Head of People's Commissariat for Internal Affairs (NKVD) (1938–46), loyal subordinate of Stalin.

Boldin, Valery I. (1935–)
Mikhail S. Gorbachev's chief of staff, one of the backstage leaders of the anti-Gorbachev coup d'état (August 1991).

Bordiuzha, Nikolai N. (1949–)
Secretary of Security Council of Russian Federation (1998–99).

Brezhnev, Leonid I. (1906–82)
General secretary of the CPSU (1964–82), presided over period of "classical" stagnation (*zastoi*).

Bukovsky, Vladimir K. (1942–)
Leading Soviet dissident, political prisoner, and critic of punitive psychiatry in USSR.

Chaadaev, Pyotr Y. (1794–1856)
Russian philosopher and critic, advocate of Westernization to end Russia's isolation and stagnation.

Chernenko, Konstantin U. (1911–85)
General secretary of the CC CPSU (1984–85).

Chernyaev, Anatoly S. (1921–2017)
Foreign policy adviser to Mikhail S. Gorbachev.

Churkin, Alexander A.
Chief psychiatrist, USSR Ministry of Health.

Diachenko, Tatiana B. (1960–)
Younger daughter of and influential adviser to Boris N. Yeltsin. She remarried in 2001 and is now surnamed Yumasheva.

Fradkov, Mikhail Y. (1950–)
Russian representative to the European Union (2003), prime minister (2004–7), director of the Foreign Intelligence Service (SVR) (October 2007–October 2016).

Glukhov, Alexei I. (1935–)
Acting director, Office of Humanitarian and Cultural Cooperation, Ministry of Foreign Affairs, USSR (1986–89).

Gorbachev, Mikhail S. (1931–)
President of USSR (1990–91), general secretary of the CC CPSU (1985–91).

Gromyko, Andrei A. (1909–89)
Foreign minister of the USSR (1957–85), known in the West as "Mister No."

Herzen, Alexander I. (1812–70)
Russian public and political figure, writer, philosopher, and liberal critic of tsarism.

Ivanov, Igor S. (1945–)
De facto senior assistant to Eduard Shevardnadze (1986–91), minister of foreign affairs of Russia (1988–2004), secretary of Security Council of Russia (2004–7).

Khrushchev, Nikita S. (1894–1971)
Post–Stalin leader of the USSR (1953–64), eased Stalinist repression and criticized some of Stalin's crimes and cult of personality in "Secret Speech" (February 1956).

Kirill, Patriarch (Vladimir M. Gundyaev) (1946–)
High official in Russian Orthodox Church involved in foreign policy matters and secular affairs, including importing alcohol and tobacco into Russia. In all probability a KGB agent, alias "Mikhailov."

Kokoshin, Andrei A. (1945–)
Secretary of Security Council of Russian Federation (1998).

Korzhakov, Alexander V. (1950–)
Bodyguard and close adviser to Boris N. Yeltsin, head of Presidential Security Service (1993–96).

Kovalev, Anatoly G. (1923–2002)
First deputy foreign minister of USSR (1986–91), trusted adviser to Mikhail S. Gorbachev, father of the author.

Kovalev, Sergei A. (1930–)
Political and public figure, one of the leaders of the Soviet and Russian dissident and human rights defenders' movement.

Kovalev, Valentin A. (1944–)
Minister of justice, Russian Federation (1995–97).

Kozyrev, Andrei V. (1951–)
Minister of foreign affairs, Russian Federation (1991–96).

Kriuchkov, Vladimir A. (1924–2007)
Chairman of the KGB (1988–91), one of the main organizers of the August 1991 putsch.

Lenin, Vladimir I. (1870–1924)
Primary leader of the Bolshevik seizure of power (October 1917), founder of the USSR.

Ligachev, Yegor K. (1920–)
Second-ranking member of the Politburo of the CC CPSU (1985–90), leading critic of perestroika.

Litvinenko, Alexander V (1962–2006)
Former FSB agent, while living in exile in the United Kingdom, poisoned with radioactive polonium-210 by FSB agents (November 2006), probably on orders from Vladimir Putin.

Medvedev, Dmitry A. (1965–)
Vladimir Putin's proxy, president of Russian Federation (2008–12), prime minister (2012–).

Nemtsov, Boris Y. (1959–2015)
Russian democratic politician, leading liberal critic of Vladimir Putin, assassinated in Moscow near the Kremlin.

Pasternak, Boris L. (1890–1960)
Great Russian poet, writer, Nobel Laureate in Literature (1958) but was compelled to decline the prize due to persecution by Soviet authorities.

Petrovsky, Vladimir F. (1933–2014)
Liberal deputy foreign minister of USSR under Mikhail S. Gorbachev, later United Nations undersecretary-general.

Pitirim, Metropolitan (Nechaev, Konstantin V.) (1926–2003)
Head of publishing division of the Russian Orthodox Church (1963–94), very influential, and in all probability a KGB agent, alias "Abbat."

Politkovskaya, Anna (1958–2006)
Investigative journalist and leading critic of Vladimir Putin; assassinated in Moscow (October 2006).

Prikhodko, Sergei E. (1957–)
Responsible for the foreign policy activity of the president as a director of the Presidential Executive Office, as first deputy director, then as first deputy chief, Government Staff (1993–2013); deputy prime minister (2013–).

Primakov, Yevgeny M. (1929–2015)
Russian politician, foreign minister of Russian Federation (1996–98), prime minister (1998–99).

Pugo, Boris K. (1937–91)
Minister of the interior for the USSR, plotter in August 1991 coup d'état against Mikhail S. Gorbachev, and may have committed suicide after its collapse.

Putin, Vladimir V. (1952–)
KGB agent, president of the Russian Federation (1999–2008, 2012–).

Roth, Dr. Loren (1939–)
American psychiatrist, part of U.S. delegation to investigate Soviet psychiatric abuse (1989).

Rushailo, Vladimir B. (1953–)
Secretary of Security Council of Russian Federation (2001–4); executive secretary of CIS (2004–7).

Rybkin, Ivan P. (1946–)
Russian politician, secretary of Security Council of the Russian Federation (1996–98).

Sakharov, Andrei D. (1921–89)
Soviet nuclear physicist, leading dissident and critic of Soviet communism.

Schifter, Richard (1923–)
U.S. assistant secretary of state for human rights and humanitarian affairs (1985–92).

Shchekochikhin, Yury P. (1950–2003)
Investigative journalist for *Novaia gazeta*; member of the Duma, Russia's parliament; victim of unproven political assassination via poisoning (July 2003).

Shevardnadze, Eduard A. (1928–2014)
Minister of foreign affairs, USSR (1985–91), a leader of the democratic reforms in the USSR.

Shoigu, Sergei K. (1955–)
Minister of emergency situations, Russian Federation (1991–2012); minister of defense (2012–).

Solzhenitsyn, Alexander I. (1918–2008)
Leading Russian writer, critic of the Soviet system, Nobel Laureate in Literature (1970).

Stalin (Jughashvili), Josef V. (1879–1953)
Member of the top Soviet leadership after the Bolshevik coup of 1917, general secretary of the CC CPSU (1922–53), Soviet dictator from the second half of the 1920s until his death.

Surkov, Vladislav Y. (1964–)
Chief Kremlin ideologist, in particular of Russian nationalism, under Vladimir Putin (1999–2011); adviser to Putin.

Yakovlev, Alexander N. (1923–2005)
Ideologist of perestroika, close adviser to Mikhail S. Gorbachev.

Yanaev, Gennady I. (1937–2010)
Soviet politician, vice president of USSR (1990–91), appointed president during the anti-Gorbachev coup d'état (August 1991).

Yeltsin, Boris N. (1931–2007)
President of the Russian Federation (1991–99).

Yuvenaly, Metropolitan (Poyarkov, Vladimir K.) (1935–)
One of the most influential officials of the Russian Orthodox Church and in all probability a KGB agent, alias "Adamant."

Zhirinovsky, Vladimir V. (1946–)
Russian politician, ultranationalist leader of far-right Liberal Democratic Party.

CHRONOLOGY

March 11, 1985 Mikhail Gorbachev becomes the general secretary of the Central Committee of the Communist Party of the Soviet Union (CPSU).

February 25–March 6, 1986 First attempt at a thorough reexamination of the foreign and domestic policies of the USSR, undertaken by Gorbachev at the Twenty-Seventh Congress of the CPSU. Humanitarian problems and human rights included among the key problems of international security.

April 26, 1986 Accident at the Chernobyl nuclear power plant.

May 15, 1988–February 15, 1989 Withdrawal of Soviet forces from Afghanistan.

June 28–July 1, 1988 Nineteenth Party Conference of the CPSU adopts a resolution to transfer supreme state power to a Congress of People's Deputies of the USSR.

October 1, 1988 Gorbachev becomes chairman of the Presidium of the Supreme Soviet of the USSR.

1988–91 "Parade of sovereignties"—anti-constitutional declarations asserting the superiority of laws of the constituent republics of the USSR over the laws of the USSR itself.

January 15, 1989 Adoption of the final document of the Vienna meeting of members of the Conference on Security and Cooperation in Europe, including important obligations in the realm of human rights essential for democratic reforms in the USSR. By a decision of the Politburo of the CPSU, the Vienna document was put into effect throughout the territories of the USSR and its implementation made mandatory for all ministries and departments.

March 26–May 21, 1989 Elections for people's deputies of the USSR (the first free elections in the USSR).

May 25, 1989 Convening of the First Congress of People's Deputies of the USSR; Gorbachev elected chairman of the Supreme Soviet of the USSR (parliament).

1989–91 Creation of an "underground" of Soviet special services by means of creating secret associations of militarized detachments from former or active employees of the special and militarized services of Russia and the Commonwealth of Independent States; transfer of funds from the CPSU to trusted persons.

February 26–March 12, 1989 Visit of American psychiatrists to the USSR, one of the key events in the liquidation of punitive psychiatry in the USSR.

March 4, 1990 Election of people's deputies of the Russian Soviet Federated Socialist Republic (RSFSR).

March 14, 1990 Adoption of "On the Establishment of the Presidency of the USSR and Introduction of Changes and Addenda to the Constitution of the USSR," a law that abolishes the CPSU's monopoly on power.

March 15, 1990 At the Third Extraordinary Congress of People's Deputies of the USSR, Gorbachev is elected president of the USSR.

May 29, 1990 Congress of People's Deputies of the RSFSR convenes and chooses Boris Yeltsin as the chairman of the Supreme Soviet.

June 12, 1990 The First Congress of People's Deputies of the RSFSR adopts a resolution declaring the RSFSR a sovereign state.

October 1, 1990 The USSR passes a law on freedom of conscience and of religious organizations.

May 20, 1991 Supreme Soviet of USSR adopts a law "On Procedures for Citizens of the USSR Regarding Departure from and Entry into the USSR."

June 12, 1991 Yeltsin is elected president of Russia.

1990–91 Parade of sovereignties of subjects of the RSFSR.

August 18–21, 1991 Attempted coup d'état led by the KGB and the reactionary wing of the CPSU.

December 8, 1991 Signing of the Belovezh Accords by the head of the RSFSR (Yeltsin), Byelorussia (S. Shushkevich), and Ukraine (L. Kravchuk) on terminating the existence of the USSR.

September 21–October 4, 1993 President Yeltsin signs Decree No. 1400, dissolving the Congress of People's Deputies and the Supreme Soviet of Russia, leading to armed clashes and the shelling of the parliament building by tanks. Estimates suggest that 300–400 people were killed.

December 2, 1994 Operation Muzzle in the Snow carried out by the presidential security service, dissatisfied with Channel One's television coverage of the First Chechen War, against NTV owner Vladimir Gusinskii; beginning of the establishment of broad control over the mass media.

December 11, 1994 President Yeltsin signs Decree No. 2169; and military operations in Chechnya by units of the Ministry of Defense and domestic troops of the Ministry of Internal Affairs begins.

July 3, 1996 Yeltsin, although very unpopular, is reelected to a second term as president in a ruthlessly rigged election.

August 31, 1996 Alexander Lebed, secretary of the Security Council of the Russian Federation, and Aslan Maskhadov, chief of staff of Chechnya, sign the Khasavyurt armistice agreement. Russian forces are fully withdrawn from Chechnya, but a decision on the status of the republic is put off until December 31, 2001.

August 17, 1998 A technical default on basic types of government debts is declared; rejection of maintaining a stable ruble-dollar exchange rate, artificially inflated by massive intervention by the Central Bank of Russia.

September 11, 1998 The State Duma confirms Yevgeny Primakov as prime minister of Russia; the special services commence the decisive seizure of key posts throughout the state apparatus of Russia.

August 9, 1999 On the same day, Vladimir Putin is appointed first deputy chairman and acting chairman of the government.

President Yeltsin proclaims Putin, having headed the FSB since 1998 and served as the prime minister for the previous few days, as his successor.

September 4–16, 1999 A series of explosions occurs in apartment houses, almost certainly carried out by the regime, in Buinaksk, Moscow and Volgodonsk; 307 people are killed.

September 23, 1999 Russian troops begin massive bombardment of Grozny and its environs, starting the Second Chechen War.

December 31, 1999 President Yeltsin announces his early retirement and appoints Putin acting president of Russia.

Night of April 13–14, 2001 Concluding the political conflict between the Kremlin and NTV, due in particular to the war in Chechnya and the telecommunication company's refusal to support pro-Kremlin candidates in the parliamentary elections of 1999, Gazprom representatives replaced the security guards at NTV headquarters and annulled the journalists' passes; beginning of wholesale liquidation of freedom of the media.

October 25, 2003 Arrest of Mikhail Khodorkovsky, who was later sentenced to nine years of forced labor. This marks the start of complete executive power and control over all the activities of large-scale Russian businesses.

March 2, 2008 Dmitry Medvedev is chosen as president of Russia. Putin becomes prime minister.

August 8–12, 2008 Russia's war against Georgia results in Georgia completely losing control over the territories of Abkhazia and South Ossetia.

December 4, 2011–March 4, 2012 Protest movement, known as the "Snow Revolution," against the official results of elections to the Sixth State Duma and election of Putin to a third term.

March 4, 2012 In the first round, having secured 63.6 percent of the vote according to official figures, Putin is elected to a third presidential term.

February 2014 Russia annexes Crimea.

April 2014 The beginning of armed conflict in eastern Ukraine to link it to Russia, at a minimum, utilizing armed support from the Kremlin; establishment of the Donetsk People's Republic and the Luhansk People's Republic, separatist enclaves in eastern Ukraine.

July 17, 2014 A Russian-made Buk surface-to-air missile, which is not in the arsenal of the Ukrainian armed forces, brings down Malaysian Airlines flight MH 17, a Boeing 777, on a flight from Amsterdam to Kuala Lumpur over the eastern Donetsk region of Ukraine. Fifteen crew members and 283 passengers die.

March 2014 The United States, the EU, Canada, Australia, and New Zealand, as well as a number of international organizations, including the European Commission, NATO, the European Council, and others, introduce the first set of sanctions after Russian aggression against Ukraine. Russia adopts countermeasures. Beginning of the collapse of the Russian economy.

September 2015 Responding to a request from Syrian president Bashar al-Assad, whom the Kremlin has supported from the start of the conflict in Syria, the Federation Council approves sending Russian military forces to Syria in the struggle against terrorism. Russia begins air strikes in Syria.

NOTES

Notes from the translator are indicated by —Trans. at the end of the note.

Foreword

1. See P. Reddaway, "Should World Psychiatry Readmit the Soviets?," *New York Review of Books*, October 12, 1989, 54–58; and for a detailed analysis of the abuse system, see P. Reddaway and the psychiatrist Sidney Bloch, *Russia's Political Hospitals: The Abuse of Psychiatry in the Soviet Union* (London: V. Gollancz, 1977); and their *Soviet Psychiatric Abuse: The Shadow over World Psychiatry* (London: V. Gollancz, 1984). The U.S. government published a 117-page account of the U.S. delegation's visit.

Preface

1. Ivan A. Bunin (1870–1953) was a Russian writer who was awarded the Nobel Prize for Literature in 1933.

2. Literally, the word *perestroika* means "reconstruction" (of the entire economic and political system).

3. This book was originally published in Russian: Andrei A. Kovalev, *Svidetel'stvo iz-za kulis rossiiskoi politiki I: Mozhno li delat' dobra iz zla?* [Witness from behind the scenes of Russian politics, vol. 1, Can one make good from evil?] and *Svidetel'stvo iz-za kulis rossiiskoi politiki II: Ugroza dlia sebia i okruzhaiushchikh* [Witness from behind the scenes of Russian politics, vol. 2, A menace to oneself and those nearby] (Stuttgart: Ibidem-Verlag, 2012).

4. MGIMO represents Moscow State Institute of International Relations. —*Trans.*

5. The Soviets referred to the Cuban missile crisis of October 1962 as the Caribbean crisis. —*Trans.*

6. Shurik is a diminutive of Alexander. —*Trans.*

7. Yury Andropov (1914–84) was then head of the KGB. —*Trans.*

8. This reference is to the workers' uprising against the communist regime in East Germany in mid-June 1953 that was suppressed by Soviet military force. —*Trans.*

9. Fyodor I. Tyutchev (1803–73) was a Russian writer. The quotation is from "Silentium!," a poem published in 1830. —*Trans.*

Introduction

1. Liudmila Alekseeva, one of the old veterans of the dissident movement in the USSR, writes in her unflinchingly honest book *The Generation of the Thaw*, "I did not know a single opponent of socialism in our country, although we were troubled by the inhumanity of

our society. We adopted the slogans of the Czechoslovak reformers [in the Prague Spring of 1968] who fought against Stalinism. We shared the idea that was dear to our hearts of 'socialism with a human face.'" Liudmila Mikhailovna Alekseeva and Paul Goldberg, *The Generation of the Thaw* [in Russian] (Moscow: Izdatel' Zakharov, 2006), 14–15.

2. See Transparency International, "Corruption Perceptions Index, 2015," January 27, 2016, www.transparency.org.

3. This phrase is borrowed from *The Doomed City* (1989) by Arkady Strugatsky and Boris Strugatsky, well-known Russian science fiction writers.

1. Diplomacy and Democratic Reforms

1. Born in 1935 Glukhov became a career diplomat and was later Russia's ambassador to Estonia.

2. Meaning sent to a correctional colony. —*Trans.*

3. The term applies to the Eastern Catholic Church, which is affiliated with Rome but has its own liturgy and rites. —*Trans.*

4. Murashkovites are a sect with Protestant, Judaic, and pagan features, formed by ex-Pentecostal I. P. Murashko in 1920 in the western USSR.

5. Only one doctor had to agree to detain the person—by force if necessary.

6. The *oprichnina* is the name of the secret police established by Ivan the Terrible. —*Trans.*

7. In early January 1991 Soviet troops shot and killed several Lithuanians among the thousands besieging the TV and Radio Building in Vilnius.

8. Nikolai I. Bukharin (1888–1938) was a top Bolshevik leader and opponent of Stalin's who was executed on spurious charges of treason after a show trial, which outraged much of world public opinion.

9. The State Emergency Committee was the group of plotters who sought to overthrow Gorbachev in the August 1991 coup and seize power in Moscow.

2. The August 1991 Coup

1. Otto Skorzeny was a colonel in the Nazi Waffen SS who was skilled in sabotage and special operations. In September 1943 he led a successful German operation to free Benito Mussolini from Allied captivity. —*Trans.*

2. Yevgeny Dolmatovsky (1915–94) was a minor Soviet poet and lyricist. —*Trans.*

3. Yury Shchekochikhin, "Odnazhdy ya vstretilsia s chelovekom, kotoryi perevozil 'zoloto partii'" [I once met a man who was transporting the "party's gold"], in *S liubov'y: Proizvedeniia Yu. Shchekochikhina; vospomonaniia i ocherki o nem* [With love: The works of Yu. Shchekochikhin; reminiscences and sketches of him] (Saint Petersburg: Inapress, 2004), 142–43.

4. Sergei Sokolov and Sergei Pluzhnikov, "Zoloto KPSS—desiat' let spustia: Pochemu 'novye russkie' kapitalisty finansiruiut kommunistov" [The CPSU's gold—ten years later: Why the 'new Russian' capitalists are financing the communists], *Moskovskie novosti* (Moscow news), August 5, 2001.

5. Sokolov and Pluzhnikov, "Zoloto KPSS."

6. "Zhestkii kurs" [A tough policy], Analisticheskaia zapiska Leningradskoi assotsiatsii sotsial'no-ekonomicheskikh nauk [Analytic notes of the Leningrad Association of Social and Economic Sciences], *Vek XX i mir* [Twentieth century and the world] 6 (1990): 15–19; and Vladimir Gel'man, *Tupik avtoritarnoi modernizatsii* [The cul-de-sac of authoritarian modernization], February 23, 2010, http://www.polit.ru/article/2010/02/23/gelman.

7. Vadim Medvedev was a cautious colleague of Gorbachev's from the CPSU Politburo.

8. V. I. Boldin, *Krushenie p'edestala: Shtrikhi k portretu M. S. Gorbacheva* [Collapse of the pedestal: Brush strokes for a portrait of M. S. Gorbachev] (Moscow: Izdatel'stvo Respublika, 1995).

1. A. N. Yakovlev, *Omut pamiati* [Whirlpool of memory] (Moscow: Vagrius, 2000), 461.

2. Vladimir Bukovsky, *To Build a Castle: My Life as a Dissenter*, trans. Michael Scammel (New York: Viking Press, 1979), 247–48.

3. The OGPU was the Soviet secret police (the Joint State Political Directorate). The quoted material is from Yakovlev, *Omut pamiati*, 90–91.

4. P. Ya. Chaadaev, *Polnoe sobranie sochinenii i izbrannye pis'ma* [Complete works and selected letters] (Moscow: Nauka, 1991), 347.

5. See V. D. Topolyanskii, *Skvozniak iz proshlogo* [A draft from the past] (Moscow: Prava cheloveka, 2009), 182–83.

6. Topolyanskii, *Skvozniak iz proshlogo*, 190.

7. This decision was taken well before the election of Gorbachev. According to my information, Yegor Ligachev and Mikhail Solomentsev made Gorbachev's support of this adventure a condition of their support for his candidacy as general secretary of the CPSU.

8. Alexander Korzhakov, *Boris Yel'tsin: Ot rassveta do zakata* [Boris Yeltsin: From daybreak to sunset] (Moscow: Interbuk, 1997), 209.

9. This budget-cutting policy entailed nonpayment of salaries and pensions and the impoverishment of the people.

10. According to official data, inflation was lowered from 2,600 percent in 1992 to 11 percent in 1997 and to 4.1 percent in the first half of 1998. In July 1998 inflation was 0.02 percent. The federal budget in 1997 was fulfilled with a deficit of 3.2 percent of GDP as against 3.5 percent in the approved budget.

11. In this connection, Moscow did nothing to preserve its positions in these countries.

12. I was working at the time on the staff of the president of the USSR, was one of the two initiators of the Soviet proposals, and played the role of "battering ram" as we pushed for acceptance of the decision to attend and expand relations. Evgeny Gusarov of the Ministry of Foreign Affairs was the other initiator of this foreign policy initiative, which came to nothing.

13. Shevardnadze's failure to attend the Rome session of the NATO Council made it impossible to adopt an official resolution regarding the start of a new stage of relations between the USSR and NATO and had serious consequences for the subsequent development of relations between Russia and the North Atlantic alliance and the West as a whole.

14. As far as the author knows, this statement was not prepared in advance, and Yeltsin's press secretary had to "correct" the head of state.

15. It was irrational because Moscow was unable to influence the decisions that were taken. NATO's role in stabilizing the international situation was not taken into account at all. It was illogical because not a single one of the architects or implementers of Russian foreign policy, as well as the pundits who supported this policy, could answer the question of how states that were partners of Russia's could be united in an alliance that was hostile toward it.

16. Regarding the priority of republic legislation over federal laws, in the constitutions of Sakha (Yakutia) Republic and the Republic of Ingushetia, procedures were included for the ratification of federal laws by the republics' organs of state power.

17. For example, see those of the Republic of Adygeia, the Kabardino-Balkar Republic, the Karachaevo-Cherkessia Republic, the Krasnodarskii and Stavropolskii territories, and the Voronezh, Moscow, and Rostov regions. In the republics of Sakha (Yakutia), Bashkortostan, Dagestan, Komi, and Tuva, voting rights were accorded only to the citizens of these republics. The right to be elected head of state or of the legislature was likewise restricted exclusively to citizens of these areas.

18. As far as I know—I took part in behind-the-scenes efforts at a peaceful resolution of

the Chechen problem in 1997–98—the Chechens themselves, including their chief negotiator Movladi Udugov, had a very imprecise notion of Chechen sovereignty. According to participants in the negotiations, the Chechens did not envision for themselves any sort of sovereignty except within Russia. They did not grasp that the concept of sovereignty meant something else. Thus, without understanding its actual content, the Chechens' clumsy use of a term that Yeltsin had uttered was far from being the least of the reasons for the discord between Moscow and Grozny. This, in turn, obviously demonstrates that Russian politicians ascribe much more meaning to words than to actions.

19. Violations of the rights of Russians living in Chechnya, an allegation that the Russian authorities love to point to as the main reason for launching the war, cannot be taken seriously.

20. This agreement was signed on August 30, 1996, by Secretary of the Security Council Alexander Lebed and Chief of Staff of the Armed Forces of Chechnya Aslan Maskhadov. What was envisioned was a cessation of military hostilities and the holding of a democratic general election in Chechnya. Resolving the question of the status of Chechnya was put off for five years, until 2001.

21. I was a supporter of granting Chechnya the right to self-determination, including the right to secede from membership in the Russian Federation, combined with the unconditional restoration of the educational and health care systems and the industry of the republic. In my opinion, this not only was a moral imperative but also was dictated by the purely pragmatic consideration of strengthening the Russian state system even in the event that Chechnya proclaimed its independence and actually seceded from Russia. Without question, such an option had to be provided. This was especially necessary because the actual rebuilding of the republic, not just in words, would have been the surest way to keep Chechnya in the Russian Federation.

22. According to the estimates of specialists, constructing one kilometer of border fencing would cost about $400,000 and one entry and exit point about $4 million. Further, to all appearances, this option must have been understood in the Kremlin, in the presidential administration, and in the government when the decision was taken to begin the Second Chechen War, but I cannot bear witness to this as I was hospitalized at the time.

23. The leading human rights defender Sergei Kovalev told me he had established the facts for certain that Russian troops had committed atrocities that were ascribed to the Chechens. For example, in his words, to raise the "fighting spirit of the troops," the successors of the red commissars placed mutilated corpses and genitals severed by the Special Forces on the armored troop carriers but asserted that it was the work of the Chechens. Generally Moscow cultivated hatred toward the Chechens and toward residents of the Caucasus as a whole.

24. Many believe that these incursions were operations by the special services with the goal of legalizing the start of the Second Chechen War. This is indirectly confirmed by Sergei Stepashin's pronouncement that the Kremlin began planning the military operations in Chechnya in March 1999. Additional evidence is the close link between Shamil Basaev and Boris Berezovsky. See, for example, J.-M. Balencie and A. de la Grange, *Mondes rebelles: Guérillas, milices, groupes terroristes* (Paris: Éditions Michalon, 2002), 1444.

25. During his presentation at the Kennan Institute in Washington on April 24, 2002, Sergei Yushenkov emphasized "the virtual lack of any system of civilian control over the activities of the special services in Russia" and "the absolute unwillingness of Russian authorities to pay attention to this and to carry out a truly objective, independent investigation" of the explosions in the apartment houses in Moscow and Volgodonsk, as well as of the events in Ryazan. According to the official version, the FSB was conducting exercises in Ryazan, but according to a widely disseminated view, shared by Yushenkov, a terrorist act was averted. He presented a version of events according to which a coup d'état took place in Russia on Sep-

tember 23. Here is why: On September 23, a group of governors of twenty-four persons, with the initiator of the group being the governor of the Belgorod region, Yevgeny Savchenko, demanded that the president of the Russian Federation turn over all power to Prime Minister Putin. And that same day, September 23, the president issued a secret decree that was the basis for the start of military actions in Chechnya, the beginning of the Second Chechen War. These actions and steps were taken precisely because of the view in Russian society that the explosions in Volgodonsk, Moscow, and of the house in Ryazan had been perpetrated by Chechen fighters. On September 24, Putin gave the order to the troops to commence military operations in Chechnya. Incidentally, this was the prerogative of the president. Moreover, in accordance with our constitution, armed force could be utilized only in three situations, none of which was present.

26. The exact number of wounded was not provided. Some observers believe the terrorist acts in the fall of 1999 that, without evidence, were ascribed to the Chechens were actually the work of the Russian special services.

27. Putin called for finishing off "the terrorists in the john." The staff of the Security Council devised its own glossary according to which the Chechen fighters were called bandits. Banditry, according to the Criminal Code of the Russian Federation, is considered a criminal offense; thus someone may be labeled a bandit only by a court of law.

28. Speaking of Wahhabism, although I am using Moscow's official terminology, I am fully aware that the definition is extremely controversial.

29. According to approximate data, there were more than twelve million Muslims in the North Caucasus, Tatarstan, Bashkortostan, Udmurtia, Chuvashia, and the Mari-El Republics; in Siberia; in Ulyanovsk, Samara, Astrakhan, Perm, Nizhny Novgorod, and Ryazan regions; and in Moscow, Saint Petersburg, and elsewhere. At the time, there were 2,739 registered Islamic religious associations (24 percent of religious associations registered in the country). Moreover, the actual number of functioning Islamic organizations was significantly higher, since in a number of regions they arose spontaneously and were not registered.

4. How the System Really Works

1. Andrei Illarionov, "Reformy 90-kh v Rossii proveli vo blago nomenklatury!" [The reforms of the 1990s in Russia were carried out for the benefit of the nomenklatura!] *Komsomolskaia pravda*, February 9, 2012.

2. The ministry that Adamov then headed was (and is) located near the Kremlin on Ordynka Street.

3. Sergei Dovlatov (1941–90) was a Russian writer who achieved success as an exile in the United States. —*Trans.*

4. One wise chief, the target of many denunciations owing to his position, would store accounts in a specially designated file without reading them and take them outside of town and burn them.

5. See, for example, chapter 5, p. 211.

6. Anatoly Kovalev, *Iskusstvo vozmozhnogo: Vospominaniia* [The art of the possible], (Moscow: Novyi Kronograf, 2016), 202–3.

7. This is a reference to their novel *Monday Begins on Saturday* (1965). —*Trans.*

5. Inside the Secret Police State

1. Yakovlev, *Omut pamiati*, 8.

2. Bukovsky, *To Build a Castle*, 247–48.

3. Yakovlev, *Omut pamiati*, 11–12.

4. Yakovlev, *Omut pamiati*, 358.

5. Hélène Blanc and Renata Lesnik, *Les prédateurs du Kremlin, 1917–2009* (Paris: Édition du Seuil, 2009), 127.

6. Korzhakov, *Boris Yel'tsin*, 166–99.

7. Academician Georgy Arbatov was in his day an intimate of Brezhnev, Andropov, Gorbachev, and Yeltsin; his is a record for political longevity among intimates of top leaders in the USSR and Russia. Arbatov wrote, "If we still possess in some form democratic procedures and institutions, elections, transparency, the rudiments of a lawful state, then for these we must thank not the 'liberal economy' connected with [Yegor] Gaidar's 'shock therapy,' nor Yeltsin's actions as president. This is what remains from the Gorbachev Era, that his successors have been unable to weed out or stamp out entirely." G. A. Arbatov, *Yastreby i golubi kholodnoi voiny* [Cold War hawks and doves] (Moscow: Algoritm & Eksmo, 2009), 104.

8. N. A. Berdyaev, *Istoki i smysl russkogo kommunizma* [Sources and meaning of Russian communism] (Moscow: Nauka, 1990), 99.

9. Berdyaev, *Istoki i smysl russkogo kommunizma*, 100.

10. Alexander Men (1935–90) was a prominent Russian Orthodox theologian and author who was murdered on September 9, 1990, by an unknown assailant under conditions that raised suspicions of the KGB's involvement in his death. —*Trans.*

11. Sergei L. Loiko, "Russian Orthodox Church Is in Spiritual Crisis, Critics Say," *Los Angeles Times*, April 22, 2012.

12. Italics mine.

13. Italics mine.

14. Here and further the italics are mine.

15. Italics mine.

16. Italics mine.

17. Mikhail Yur'iev, "Vnutrennii vrag i natsional'naia ideia" [The internal enemy and the national idea], *Komsomolskaia pravda* [Komsomol truth], June 11, 2004.

18. Yur'iev, "Vnutrennii vrag." Italics mine.

19. Nina Andreeva, a Soviet chemistry teacher and political activist, published an open letter in the newspaper *Sovetskaya Rossiya* [Soviet Russia] in March 1988, denouncing Gorbachev and perestroika and giving heart to the old guard communists. —*Trans.*

20. Shchekochikhin, "Odnazhdy ya stal deputatom" [I once became a deputy], in *S liubovyu*, 39.

21. Nina Petlyanova, "Shpionashi" [The Nashi spies], *Novaia gazeta* [New paper]), no. 16 (February 16, 2009).

22. A similar story about this episode can be found in the book by A. N. Yakovlev: "I recall that during a break in one of our regular meetings, we sat down to eat. Mikhail Sergeevich was sullen, silently eating borscht. Suddenly Kriuchkov stood up and said roughly the following: 'Mikhail Sergeevich, carrying out your instructions, we have begun to found a party; we will give it a contemporary name. We have selected several candidates to lead it.' Kriuchkov did not give specific names. Gorbachev was silent. It was as if he hadn't been listening and had really withdrawn into himself." Yakovlev, *Omut pamiati*, 382.

23. Yakovlev also writes that, during Soviet times, the Russian Communist Party engendered "various sorts of nationalist and pro-fascist groups under the supervision of and with the help of the KGB." Yakovlev, *Omut pamiati*, 383.

24. Vladimir Tol'ts, "Fal'sifikatsii: Spiski podozrevaemykh i podozrevaiushchikh" [Falsifications: Lists of suspects and those identifying suspects], *Svoboda Russian News*, July 1, 2009, http://www.svobodanews.ru/content/article/1766749.html.

25. Yury Afanasyev, "Ya khotel by uvidet' Rossiyu raskoldovannoi" [I would like to see Russia released from its spell], *Novaia gazeta*, no. 55 (May 27, 2009).

26. Greenpeace Russia, "Data of the World Center for Monitoring Fires," Forest Forum, August 13, 2010, http://www.forestforum.ru/viewtopic.php?f=9&t=7613&view=unread&sid =828475e4f49dd9ad8ff4c6ef3ce14bc#unread, http://www.fire.uni-frieburg.de/GFMCnew /2010/08/13/20100813_ru_htm.

27. Dmitry Pisarenko, "Klimat prevrashchaetia v moshchnoe oruzhie: V chem prichina zhary?" [Climate turns into a powerful weapon: What is the cause of the fires?], *Argumenty i fakty* [Arguments and facts] no. 29 (July 21, 2010).

28. Svetlana Kuzina, "Zhara v Rossii—rezultat ispytaniia klimaticheskogo oruzhiia v SShA?" [Are the fires in Russia the result of an American climate weapon test?], *Komsomolskaia pravda*, July 29, 2010.

29. Vasily Boiko-Velikii, "For facilitating repentance in our people," address to employees of Russian Milk and all companies in the group Your Financial Guardian, August 9, 2010, http:/rusk.ru/st.php?idar=43371.

30. "Orthodox enterprise: Life by their own rules?," Discussion, Culture Shock, August 14, 2010, http://echo.msk.ru/programs/kulshok/703023-echo/.

6. Strangling Democracy

1. On March 19, 2003, material was posted on the site for wps–Russian Media Monitoring Agency that said the decision to strengthen the fsb was adopted in the first instance to "enhance management of the election process." As a result of the reform of the coercive agencies, the Russian Federation Automatized State Election System (rfases) passed from the Central Elections Commission (cec) to the fsb. According to information from Deputy Director of the Center for Political Technologies Dmitry Orlov, even before this the cec was only the corporative user of this system. A special subunit of the Federal Agency of Government Communications and Information exercised control over receiving and supplying data from the very beginning of the system's operation. The work of the rfases was wholly closed to outside observers. It was impossible to verify the reliability of information provided for open access— for example, accusations that were posted on the Internet. For precisely this reason, in the view of the authors of the publication, the capable hands of the rfases had many means of rigging the data as 99 percent of the observers only received copies of the final results. This facilitated, for example, not only routine alterations to ballots and the "throwing in" of additional ballots (ballot stuffing) but even the creation of virtual voting precincts on the computer network. In general, the rfases was something like a "black box"; you put in the ingredients (information) and out came the results (the name of a deputy). The publication summed it up as follows: "Control over the process of transformation lies in the hands of the increasingly powerful fsb."

2. In June 1962 Soviet troops forcefully suppressed worker demonstrations in the southern Russian city of Novocherkassk, resulting in dozens of killed and wounded. See Samuel H. Baron, *Bloody Saturday in the Soviet Union: Novocherkassk, 1962* (Stanford: Stanford University Press, 2001). —*Trans.*

3. In saying this, I am not in the least absolving other countries of their share of responsibility, but here I am speaking of Russia.

4. In the period between 1901 and 1911, about 17,000 persons became victims of terrorist acts.

5. According to several estimates, more than 25 million people were exterminated in the course of intra-party struggle, civil war, collectivization, and industrialization.

6. Nikolai Berdiaev et al., *Smertnaia kazn': Za i protiv* [The death penalty: For and against] (Moscow: Iuridicheskaia Literatura, 1989), 104.

7. Berdiaev et al., *Smertnaia kazn'*, 110.

8. It was reported that 94 persons died in the first incident, and 121 died in the second.

9. Vyacheslav Izmailov, "Ne vosplamenyaetsia, ne gorit, ne vzryvaetsia" [It does not ignite, doesn't burn, doesn't explode], *Novaia gazeta*, no. 82 (October 30, 2006).

10. Anna Politkovskaya, "Polgoda posle 'Nord-Osta': Odin iz gruppy terroristov utselel. My ego nashli" [Six months after "Nord-Ost" one of the terrorists has survived. We found him], *Novaia gazeta*, no. 30 (April 28, 2003).

11. Politkovskaya, "Polgoda posle 'Nord-Osta.'"

12. For example, in August 2000, Order No. 130, signed earlier by Minister of Communications Leonid Reiman, was registered in the Ministry of Justice and went into force. This was "An Order to Introduce a System of Technical Means to Secure Operational-Search Measures on Telephonic, Mobile, and Wireless Communications and Publicly Used Personal Communication Devices." Publishing this notice, the newspaper *Segodnia* [Today] asserted that in line with this document all Internet providers as well as operators of telephonic, network, and paging services were obliged to draw up and coordinate with the FSB a plan to establish listening devices, initially providing the special services with all passwords, and then at their own expense install the listening devices on their networks, inform the FSB on how to employ them, and train agents in their use. It was specially stipulated that this work be kept secret.

According to *Segodnia*'s August 22, 2000, report, the order said, "Information about the subscribers who were being subjected to surveillance as well as the decisions on the basis of which surveillance was being conducted would not be provided to the network operators." Such a formulation gave the special services practically unlimited opportunity to listen in to everyone and everything.

13. Igor Korol'kov, "Zapasnye organy: Spetssluzhby sozdali parallel'nye struktury dlia ispolneniia vnesudebnykh prigovorov" [Reserve organs: The special services created parallel structures to carry out extrajudicial sentences], *Novaia gazeta*, January 11, 2007.

14. The acronym GUBOP stands for Glavnoe upravlenie po bor'be s organizovannoi prestupnost'iu (Main Administration for the Struggle against Organized Crime). —*Trans.*

15. Maxim Lazovsky (1965–2000) headed a criminal gang whose members were implicated in various domestic acts of terrorism. He was shot to death in April 2000. —*Trans.*

16. The acronym SVR stands for Sluzhba vneshnei razvedki (Foreign Intelligence Service). —*Trans.*

17. The acronym OPG stands for Organizovannaia prestupnaia gruppirovka (organized criminal gang). —*Trans.*

18. Italics mine.

19. I am following the previously cited Korol'kov, "Zapasnye organy."

20. This is another example of how they take care of their own. Ul'man vanished into thin air without a trace. Another instance speaks for itself: the jury found the murderer innocent.

21. The arrest of Aleksei Pichugin, an employee of the Internal Security Department of YUKOS, was somewhat unique in this story; therefore, it is put into this footnote.

22. "Tezisy vystupleniia pervogo zamestitelia ministra inostrannykh del SSSR A. G. Kovalev na zasedanii Politburo, 13 August 1987" [Bullet points of the speech by First Deputy Foreign Minister of the USSR A. G. Kovalev at the meeting of the Politburo, August 13, 1987], from the author's private archive.

23. Galina Mursalieva, "Mezhdu strakhom i nenavist'yu" [Between fear and hatred], *Novaia gazeta*, no. 130 (November 19, 2010).

7. The New Russian Imperialism

1. USSR minister of foreign affairs Andrei Gromyko never tired of saying, "We need to cut the bottom off the Third Basket." [He was referring to the section of the Final Act dealing with human rights. —*Trans.*]

2. Needless to say, the collapse of the USSR was the result of the coup of August 1991, but the coup was also an attempt to put an end to perestroika.

3. Although I stood at the periphery of this scandal, I knew, first, that everything connected with it was personally controlled by Putin; and, second, from the very start it was clear to me that the Pope affair was groundless and the result of a provocation.

4. Italics mine.

5. In Azerbaijan there were 340,000 ethnic Russians (including immigrants from the republics of the North Caucasus), 15,000 in Armenia, 1.2 million in Belarus, 400,000 in Estonia, 200,000 in Georgia, 4.5 million in Kazakhstan, 685,000 in Kyrgyzstan, 900,000 in Latvia, 307,000 in Lithuania, 600,000 in Moldova, 65,000 in Tajikistan, 200,000 in Turkmenistan, 11.5 million in Ukraine, and1.2 million in Uzbekistan.

6. Zurab Imnaishvili and Yury Roks, "Poboishche v tsentre Tbilisi: V popytke noiabrskogo perevorota Gruziia obviniaet Rossiyu" [Carnage in the center of Tbilisi: Russia is accused in the November coup attempt in Georgia], *Novaia gazeta*, August 11, 2007.

7. Anatoly Adamishin and Richard Schifter, *Human Rights, Perestroika, and the End of the Cold War* (Washington DC: United States Institute of Peace Press, 2009), 170–71.

Conclusion

1. Andrei Volnov, "Nostalgiia po pesochnitsa: Psikhonevrologicheskoe issledovanie povedeniia rossiskoi vlasti" [Nostalgia for the sandbox: A psycho-neurological study of the conduct of Russian power], *Novaia gazeta*, February 7, 2007. [Andrei Volnov is a nom de plume of the author.]

2. Yury Afanasyev, "My ne raby? Istoricheskii beg na meste: 'Osoby put' Rossii" [Are we not slaves? Historical running in place: Russia's "special path"], *Novaia gazeta*, Tsvetnoi vypusk ot [color edition], no. 47 (December 5, 2008).

3. According to Daniil Granin, this is how the outstanding biologist and geneticist N. V. Timofeev-Resovskii (1900–81) characterized the reason for many disasters.

4. I knew this from working on the staff of the Russian Security Council.

5. Konstantin Gaaze and Mikhail Fishman, "Sluzhili dva tovarishcha" [Two comrades served], *Russkii Newsweek* [Russian newsweek], December 22, 2008.

6. Anatoly Chernyaev, *Sovmestnyi iskhod: Dnevnik dvukh epoch, 1972–1991* [Combined outcome: A diary of two epochs, 1972–19910] (Moscow: ROSSPEN, 2008), 280–81.

7. Yevgeny Schwartz (1896–1958) was a Russian playwright and author of *The Naked King* (1934), which is partly based on Hans Christian Andersen's *The Emperor's New Clothes*. —*Trans.*

8. Telegraph Video and AP, "Watch: Vladimir Putin 'Probably' Ordered Alexander Litvinenko's Murder, Concludes Chairman Sir Robert Owen," *The Telegraph*, January 21, 2016, www.telegraph.co/uk/news/uknews/law-and-order/12112046/Watch-Vladimir-Putin-probably-ordered-Alexander-Litvinenkos-murder-concludes-Chairman-Sir-Robert-Owen.html.

9. Chaadaev, *Polnoe sobranie*, 478.

INDEX

Abkhazia, 121, 238, 279–81, 283, 284–85
"active measures" (*aktivka*), 208–10
Adamishin, Anatoly, xiv, 18, 20, 24, 51, 61, 68
Adamov, Yevgeny, xviii, 147–48
Adygeia, Republic of, 329n17
Afanasyev, Yury, 214, 296
Afghanistan, 3, 12, 132, 184, 259, 284
Akhmatova, Anna, 85
Akhromeyev, Sergei, 71
Alekhina, Maria, 193
Aleksanian, Vasily, 244, 303
Alekseeva, Liudmila, 327n1
Aleksei II, 45, 171
Alexander II, xxv–xxvi
Alexander III, xxvi
Andreeva, Nina, 200, 322n9
Andropov, Igor, 177
Andropov, Yuri, xx, 99, 176, 185, 270, 298;
    Anatoly Kovalev and, xxxiv–xxxv; char-
    acter and personality, 177; special services
    and, 174, 176–77
antialcohol campaign, 109, 329n7
Anti-Ballistic Missile (ABM) Treaty (1972),
    271–72
anti-Semitism, 63, 299–300, 308
"Anti-Soviet Agitation and Propaganda"
    criminal code, 32–33
Arbatov, Georgy, xx, 177, 332n7
Arctic region, in Yeltsin era, 133–35
Armenia, 36, 121, 335n5
Asahi newspaper, 247
Assad, Bashar al-, 305, 307, 309
assassination. *See* political assassinations
assembly, freedom of, 34–35
August 1991 coup against Gorbachev, 67–95,
    328n9, 335n2; Anatoly Kovalev's health after,
    72–77; atmosphere after, 71–72, 85–91; doubts

about true failure of, 68–71; economic and
political context of, 67–68; Gorbachev's loss
of power after, 91–95; outcomes of, generally,
77–79; redistribution of property and power
after, 80–85; special services and, 142, 179–
80, 181; the West and, 288
Azerbaijan, 36, 121, 266, 335n5

Babitskii, Andrei, 242–43
Babkin, Anatoly, 250
Baburova, Anastasia, 241
Bagreev, Roman, 240
Bakatin, Vadim, 69, 76, 90, 246
Bakhmin, Vyacheslav, 62
Baklanov, Oleg, 70
Basaev, Shamil, 130, 233, 330n24
Bashkortostan, 125, 126, 132, 241, 329n17
Bekhtereva, Natalia, 75
Belarus, 162, 263, 271, 275, 335n5
Bellona Foundation, 247
Belovezhe Accords (1991), 120, 260, 262, 264
Berdyaev, Nikolai, 182
Berdzenishvili, Levan, 283
Berezovsky, Boris, 170, 207, 235, 242, 330n24
Beriya, Lavrenty, 174, 176, 282
Berlusconi, Silvio, 302
Beslan school seizure and hostage-taking,
    xxiii, 198, 232–33, 269
Bessarabia, 284
Bessmertnykh, Alexander, 61
Bogoraz, Larisa, 62
Boiko-Velikii, Vasili, 215–16
Boldin, Valery, 92, 93
Bolshevik coup, 3, 225; diplomatic services
    after, 151; policies leading to, xxvi; totalitarian
    system established after, 98, 104–5, 182; used
    by special services to gain power, 173–74, 218

Bordiuzha, Nikolai, xviii–xix, 149, 150
Bosnia, 161
Bovin, Alexander, 177
Brezhnev, Leonid, xiv, xxiii, 7, 32, 168, 180, 268, 270; Anatoly Kovalev and, xxxii, xxxiv, xxxvi–xxxvii; gas and oil and, 185; nostalgia for, 302; stagnation under, 19, 99, 186, 289, 298–99, 301–2
Bronze Soldier monument, in Estonia, 277–78
Brutents, Karen, 85–86, 88
Budanov, Yury, 240–41
Bukharin, Nikolai, 62, 328n8
Bukovskaia, Anna, 208
Bukovsky, Vladimir, 101–2, 174
Bulgakov, Mikhail, 113
Bulgaria, 256, 271
Bunin, Ivan, xxv
Buraev, Shamil, 236
Burbulis, Gennady, 153
Buriatia, 125
Burlatsky, Fyodor, xx, 177
Bush, George H. W., 289
Bush, George W., 230, 266, 302

Cardin, Benjamin, 304
Central Committee of the CPSU, xxix–xxx, 11, 22–23, 39–40, 51, 57–58, 164–66, 176–77; August 1991 coup and, 77–79, 80–84, 92, 180; hatred of Gorbachev, 79; perestroika and, 38–39, 108–9; Pope John Paul's visit and, 23; psychiatry and, 51, 57–58; religious freedom and, 39, 40; special services in Yeltsin era and, 98
Chaadaev, Pyotr, xii, xxiv, 104, 294–95, 314
Channel One (television), 170, 207
Chaplin, Vsevolod, 193
Charlie Hebdo attack, 307–8
Chazov, Yevgeny, 55, 59
Chebrikov, Viktor, 58
Chechnya: First Chechen War, 112, 128–30, 191, 229, 286; Putin and, xvi, 179, 186, 269, 274, 280; Second Chechen War, 130–33, 139, 179, 330n24; terrorism and need for enemy of Russia, xxii, 225, 227–34, 236, 266; in Yeltsin era, 123, 124, 127–33, 138, 149–50, 329n18, 330–31nn19–27
Cheka, 173, 174, 200, 226, 245–46

Chernenko, Konstantin, 7, 99, 185, 186, 251, 270, 298–99, 301–2
Chernobyl nuclear catastrophe (1986), 18, 33, 118, 201
Chernyaev, Anatoly, 64, 300, 301; August 1991 coup and, 68–69, 71, 72, 87, 88, 93
China: migrants to Russian territories in Yeltsin era, 121–22, 124, 135; Russia's post–Cold War foreign policy and, 257, 265
Chubais, Anatoly, 83, 235
Churkin, Alexander, Soviet psychiatry and, xiv–xv, 25, 48, 53, 57
Cold War: end of, and new realities for Russian foreign policy, 255–56; end of, and nostalgia for phantom greatness of past, 265–90
Collapse of the Pedestal (Boldin), 92
Committee of State Security. *See* KGB
Commonwealth of Independent States (CIS), xxiii, 120–21, 260–62, 277
Communist Party of the Russian Federation (CPRF), 83–84
Communist Party of the Soviet Union (CPSU), xxx, 178; "hypnosis" and, 206; Lockhart plot and, 245; redistribution of property and power after August 1991 coup, 142–43; special services and, 175, 176
"Comrade Wolf," 270
Conference on Security and Cooperation in Europe (CSCE). *See* Final Act of the Conference on Security and Cooperation in Europe (CSCE); Organization for Security and Cooperation in Europe (OSCE)
Congress of People's Deputies of the USSR (1989), 33, 38, 79
conscience, freedom of, 23, 27, 35, 36, 40, 42, 44, 58, 197
conservatism, concept of, xxvi
Constitution of the USSR, 27, 33
Council of Mutual Economic Assistance (Comecon), 259
Council of the Russian Federation Assembly, 269–70
Council on Religious Affairs, 24–25, 40–43
Crimea, xv, xl, 12, 16, 121, 275, 293, 310
Criminal Code of the Russian Soviet Federated Socialist Republic (RSFSR): perestroika and, 31–36, 60, 178; Putin era controls and, 222–23

Gorbachev, Mikhail (*continued*)
Communist Party, xvi; hatred for, 78, 79; John Paul II and, 44; on LDPR, 209; loss of power, 91–95; speech at United Nations, 22–23, 61; "world imperialism" as enemy of, 226. *See also* Gorbachev era; perestroika

Gorbachev era: absence of system of governance and, 217; August 1991 coup and outcomes of, xvi, 64, 67–72, 78, 79, 86–87, 88; diplomatic services and, 152–64; dismantling of Yalta-Potsdam system and end of Stalinist model of international relations, 257, 259–60; espionage and, 246; religious freedom and, 39; special services and, 218–19; West's mistakes during, 286–90

Grachev, Pavel, 128

Grishin, Viktor, xxxvii

Gromyko, Andrei, xxxvii, 17, 18, 163–64, 177, 335n1; Anatoly Kovalev and, xxxiv–xxxv

Group of Eight (G8), 273

GRU (military intelligence), 238–39, 241–42, 334n17

GUBOP, 238, 240, 331n14

GULAG (Main Directorate for Corrective Labor Camps), 11, 23; creation of "Soviet person" and, 101–5; forerunner of, 225; slave labor and, 107–8, 164; special services power and, 173

The Gulag Archipelago (Solzhenitsyn), xxxiv–xxxv, 102

Gusarov, Evgeny, 329n12

Gusinskii, Vladimir, 170, 206, 207, 242

Helsinki Act. *See* Final Act of the Conference on Security and Cooperation in Europe (CSCE)

Herzen, Alexander, 292–93, 312–13

homophobic law (2013), 303

Hungarian revolution, xx, 176–77

Hussein, Saddam, 162, 263

Huxley, Aldous, dystopia of, 313

"hypnosis" of Russian people: "active measures" (*aktivka*) and, 208–10; falsified current events, 214–16; falsified history, 211–14; as foundation of Russian politics, 182–83; propaganda and, 205–6; suppression of freedom of speech, 206–8

ideological state, Soviet myths and national pride and, 183–86

Idushchie vmeste (Going Together) youth movement, 208

Ignatenko, Vitaly, 69, 94

Iliumzhinov, Kirsan, 127

Illarionov, Andrei, 142–43

illegal arms sales, xxii, 145

imperialism, "new" Russia, 255–90; nostalgia for Cold War and new realities for Russian foreign policy, 255–56; Putin and post-Soviet republics, 272–85; Putin's anti-Western policies, 265–72; West's mistakes and, 285–90; Yalta-Potsdam system and, 256–60; Yeltsin's policies and missed opportunities, 260–65

infantilizm (childish willfulness), xxiii, 7–8, 172, 292, 295, 299, 304–5

Ingushetia, Republic of, 126, 329n16

intellectual freedom, perestroika and, 35–36

intelligentsia versus intellectuals, in Yeltsin era, 166–67

internal enemies, National Idea and search for, 197–200

International Bill of Human Rights, 26, 27

International Helsinki Federation for Human Rights, 62

International Treaty on Civil and Political Rights, 64

Internet providers, surveillance and, 334n12

Invitation to a Beheading (Nabokov), 9

Iraq, 4, 109, 263

Iskander, Fazil, 28

Islam: filling of religious void left by National Idea, 191; fundamentalism of, 131–33, 308, 331n29

Israeli visas, 29

Ivanov, Igor, 52, 162–63, 307

Ivanov, Sergei, xix, 149, 150

Ivan the Terrible, 145, 181, 328n6

Izvestiia, 41, 50

Japan, 124, 127, 138, 247

John Paul II, Pope: Gorbachev and, 44; visit to USSR, 23, 39

journalism and journalists, Putin's attacks on, 234–45

Kabardino-Balkar Republic, 126, 329n17

Lukyanov, Anatoly, 93
Luzhkov, Yury, 207

Magnitsky, Sergei, 303–4
Malashenko, Igor, 206, 207
Malkevich, V., 148
Manzhosin, Alexander, 146–47
Markelov, Stanislav, 241–42
Marx, Karl, 2–3, 24, 183, 205, 208
Marxism-Leninism, 2, 4, 15, 40, 108, 188
Maskhadov, Aslan, 232, 233, 330n20
media, Putin era control of, 167, 170, 211, 221
Media-Most Group, 170, 206–7, 224
medical information, secrecy and, 204
Medvedev, Dmitry, xxi, 7, 9, 167, 181, 211, 223,
    284, 300, 301, 302, 305
Medvedev, Vadim, 89, 328n7
Men, Alexander, xvi, 189, 322n10
Milëkhin, Gennady, 56
military: decline of power in Yeltsin era,
    122–25, 142–43; dedovshchina ("systematic
    bullying") in, xxii; remilitarization under
    Putin, xx, 4, 10, 270–74
Milošević, Slobodan, 161, 162, 263
Ministry of Health, psychiatry and, xiv–xv,
    25, 34, 48, 50, 53–56, 58, 59, 76
Moiseev, Valentin, 250
Moldova, 121, 271; ethnic Russians in, 335n5;
    Putin's policy toward, 279, 283, 284–85, 291
Molodaia Gvardiia (Young Guard), 208, 278
Molotov-Ribbentrop Pact (1939), xxi, 65,
    158, 213, 256, 277, 284
Montesquieu, Charles de, xxxix, 187
Moscow, terrorist acts in, 229, 239, 334n8
Moscow Conference on the Human Dimen-
    sion of the CSCE, 20, 22, 59–65, 88
Moscow Patriarchate, 43–44, 191–95
Moskovskie novosti, 82
"Munich," as shameful label, 289
Murashkovites, 42, 328n4

Nabokov, Vladimir, 9
Nagorno-Karabakh, 36–37, 62, 121, 166
The Naked King (Schwartz), 301, 335n7
narodnost' (dense xenophobia), 292. See also
    xenophobia
Naryshkin, Sergei, 212
Nashi (Ours) party, 170–71, 208, 278
Natelashvili, Shalva, 283

National Bolshevik Party, 208
National Idea, 171, 186–87; search for inter-
    nal enemies and, 197–200; suppression of
    religion and, 188–97
nationality, as ethnicity in Russia,
    xxxviii–xxxix
Nazarbaev, Nursultan, 79
Nazism, in Russia today, 11
Nekrasov, Nikolai, xx, 252
Nemtsov, Boris, 304
NHK television, 247
Nicholas I, xii, 292
Nicholas II, xxvi
Nikitin, Alexander, 247
nomenklatura (privileged elite): benefits of
    being, 107–8; coup's outcomes and, 67, 83–
    85, 142–43; religion and, 188–89
nongovernmental organizations (NGOs):
    espionage and, 251–52; laws controlling,
    223–24
Nord-Ost musical, terror attacks, 230, 231–
    32, 241
North Atlantic Treaty Organization (NATO),
    xxviii; former socialist republics and
    expansion of, 120–24, 261–62, 271, 277,
    329n13, 329n15; in Gorbachev era, 87; in
    Yeltsin era, 158, 161–62
North Caucasus, 127, 132–33, 138–39, 331n29,
    335n5
North Ossetia, 126, 280
nostalgia: for Cold War, 255–56; for phan-
    tom greatness of past, 265–90; for stag-
    nation, 168; for totalitarianism, 167–68,
    302
Novaia gazeta (New paper), 207–8, 231–32,
    235, 238, 239–41
Novocherkassk, restoring of order in, 225,
    333n2
NTV, 206–7, 224
nuclear submarines, espionage and, 247
nuclear weapons: Anti-Ballistic Missile
    (ABM) Treaty (1972), 271–72; dangers of
    Russian state disintegration and, 310; mis-
    sile disarmament, 249; nonproliferation
    treaties, 146–48; restraint of use as foun-
    dation of Cold War, 268

Öcalan, Abdullah, 227
Ogata, Sadako, 156–57

Putin, Vladimir (*continued*)

xx; Litvinenko's murder and, 305; 1999 parliamentary elections and, 139–40; Patriots ss and, 81; special services and rise to power of, 98, 178–82. *See also* Putin era; "vertical of power" of Putin

Putin era: anti-Western foreign policy and, 265–72; control of elections and, 221–24; domestic policies and, xix–xxi; espionage and, 247; failure of policies of, 291–95; foreign policy and, xxii–xxiv, 159–60, 184; foreign policy likened to Hitler's, 285; former SSRs and, 272–85; National Idea and search for internal enemies, 175, 198, 269–70, 295; neo-stagnation during, 298–302, 309–10; "overseas compatriots" and Russian language speakers and, 275–76, 285, 291; political assassinations during, 13, 234–45; revival of national pride, 184–86; Soviet dogma and, 210; suppression of freedoms, 170; Syria and, 305–9; terrorism and need for enemy of Russia, 229–34; violence against Russian citizens, 225–26; weak protests against policies of, 295–98. *See also* Russia, today

Putinjugend (Putin Youth), xxi, 208

Radio Liberty, 212, 242
Reagan, Ronald, 1
Reagan administration, 287–88
Realpolitik, of West, xxiii, 286–90
refuseniks and right of return: conditions regarding, 20, 23, 25–29, 288; draft law to improve conditions, 29–31, 63–64
Regent, Tatyana, 158
Reiman, Leonid, 334n12
religious freedom: National Idea and, 188–97; perestroika and, xiv, xv–xvi, 24, 36, 39–45, 60, 189, Putin's suppression of, 171
Reshetov, Yury, 29, 41, 51, 54, 57
revanchism. *See* Yeltsin era, revanchism and rejections of democracy during
Richter, Sviatoslav, 205
Rokhlin, Lev, 234
Roman Catholic Church. *See* Vatican
Romania, 271
Rose revolution, in Georgia, 251, 274, 281
Roth, Dr. Loren, 53, 56
Rushailo, Vladimir, xix, 149

Russia, today: dangers of disintegration of, 4, 12–13, 295, 310–14; Nazism in, 11; psychological rejection of freedoms, 7–15; renewed conflicts with West, 302–5; suppression of information on living conditions outside, 202, 204–5
Russian Academy of Sciences, 212
Russian Federal Service on Currency and Export Control (vek), 148
Russian Federation, sovereign rights and, 125–27, 329nn16–17
Russian Federation Automatized State Election System (rfases), 333n1
Russian Orthodox Church: de facto state religion and, 292; kgb and, 39, 171, 180, 188, 192; National Idea and suppression of true religion, 187–97, 199; perestroika and, xv–xvi, 39–41, 43, 44–45; Pope John Paul's visit and, 23; in Putin era, 171; Soviets' use of, 105
Russkii newsweek (Russian newsweek), 301
Rutskoi, Alexander, 70
Ryaguzov, Pavel, 236
Rybkin, Ivan, xvii–xviii, xxviii, 149–50
Ryzhkov, Nikolai, 47

Saakashvili, Mikheil, 281
Sakha (Yakutia) Republic, 125, 126, 134–35, 329nn16–17
Sakhalin, 127
Sakharov, Andrei, 35–36, 38, 87, 312
Samutsevich, Ekaterina, 193
Sanchez, Ilyich Ramirez (Carlos the Jackal), 227
Savchenko, Yevgeny, 330–31n25
Schifter, Richard, 21, 54, 287–88
Schröder, Gerhard, 302
Schwartz, Yevgeny, 301, 335n7
"screws," and sensitive information, 204–5
Sebentsov, A., 58
Sechin, Igor, 301
Second Chechen War, 130–33, 139, 179, 330n24
Seliverstov (gubop colonel), 240
Semenov, Vladimir, xxxviii
September 11, 2001 attacks, Putin's reactions to, 229–30, 266
Serbia, 161, 263
Serbsky Institute of Forensic Psychiatry, 54–55, 56, 204

Trans-Dniestr, 238, 279, 283–85

travel restrictions: under Leninism-Stalinism, 106–7; relaxed under perestroika, 20, 23, 25–31

Treaty on Conventional Armed Forces in Europe (CFE), 270–71

Tsepov, Roman, xxi

Tskhai, Vladimir, 239

Turkmenistan, 335n5

Tuva, 125, 126

Twenty-Seventh Congress of the Communist Party of the Soviet Union (CPSU), 18, 20, 67

Tyutchev, Fyodor, xxxviii

Udugov, Movladi, 329–30n18

Ukraine, xxiii, 78, 121, 225; ethnic Russians in, 335n5; Orange Revolution in, 170–71, 251, 268, 274; Putin's policy toward, 273–77, 291, 292, 293, 294, 303, 309; U.S. rabbis' wish to visit, 24–25

Ukrainian Autocephalous Orthodox Church, xv, 43

Ukrainian Greek Catholics (Uniates), 41, 44

Ukrainian Orthodox Church, 43

Ul'man, Eduard, 241–42, 334n20

United Civic Front, 208

United Nations: Gorbachev's speech at, 22–23, 61; Optional Protocol to the International Treaty on Civil and Political Rights, 63; Security Council, 257, 261; Universal Declaration of Human Rights of, 21

United Russia party, of Putin, 157, 166, 170–71, 210, 300

United States: human rights violations of USSR and, 21; Magnitsky's death and, 304; mistakes made after end of Cold War, 286–90; psychiatrists' visit to USSR, 52–57; rabbis' wish to visit Ukraine, 24–25; Russia's post–Cold War foreign policy and, 264–65; Russia's role in Syria and, 305; Yeltsin era and, xviii

Universal Declaration of Human Rights, of United Nations, 21

USSR: breakup of, 79–80; economic policies and arms race, 258; as "evil empire," 1–2. See also Russia, today

Ustinov, Vladimir, 207

Uzbekistan, 335n5

Vartanian Mental Health Center, 56

Vatican, xxxiii, 39, 43–44, 91, 191. See also John Paul II, Pope

Vavilov, Andrei, 238

Venediktov, Aleksei, 170

"vertical of power," of Putin, 164, 179, 273; future and, 138–39; as means to destroy democracy in Russia, 217–24

Veselovskii, Leonid, 82, 83

Vienna conference, of CSCE (1986–1989), 22, 28, 29, 60, 63

Vilnius tragedy, 60, 61, 62, 93, 166, 210, 328n7

Vinogradova, Liubov, 252

Vol'sky, Arkady, 69

Voronin, Vladimir, 284

Vorontsov, Yuly, 18

Voznesenskii, Andrei, xxx

Vremya (Time) television program, 205

Vysotsky, Vladimir, 10

Wahhabism, 131–33, 331n28

Warsaw Pact, 122, 257, 259

West: Putin's anti-Western policies, 171–72, 265–72, 302–5; Russian hatred of European civilization, 160–61; weak responses to Russia's renewed confrontations, 302–5; Yeltsin's lack of understanding of values of, 110

within-system dissidents, xx, 2–3, 177, 297

World Psychiatric Association, xv, 46, 48, 52, 57

World War II, 211–14

xenophobia, xxii, xxxii, 14, 161, 171–72, 267, 277–78, 292, 295, 299–300. See also National Idea

Yabloko, 208

Yakovlev, Alexander, xiii, xvi, 93, 258, 313, 332nn22–23; Anatoly Kovalev and, xxxv, 76; August 1991 coup and, 69, 89; perestroika and, 3, 12, 17, 19, 23, 98–99; psychiatry and, 48, 51; Realpolitik and, 289; special services and, 173–74, 175, 176

Yalta-Potsdam system, and foundations of post-Soviet revanchism, 256–60

Yanaev, Gennady, 70

Yandarbiev, Zelimkhan, 236, 238

Yanukovich, Viktor, 274
Yastrzhembskii, Sergei, 232
Yazov, Dmitry, 92, 93
Year 2000 problem, 139–40
Yegorov, Vladimir, 55, 241
Yeltsin, Boris, xxi, 1, 234; anti-Russian sentiments in the CIS and, 121; appoints Putin as
president, 185, 286; August 1991 coup and,
69; character and personality of, 144; health
of, 128, 180; inadequate preparation for
challenges of democratization, 109–13; seizure of power, 78, 91, 93. *See also* Yeltsin era
Yeltsin era: absence of system of governance
and, 217; Arctic and Siberia and, 133–35,
139; Chechnya and, 123, 124, 127–33, 138,
329n18, 330–31nn19–27; corruption and,
145, 169–70; diplomatic services and, 152–
64; disintegration of military and political
power during, 122–25, 142–43; espionage
and, 246, 247–48; financial and ecological
policies and suffering of citizens, 4–5, 114–
20, 127, 133–35, 329nn9–10; foreign policy
of, 146–52, 260–63, 285; former socialist
republics, NATO, and claiming of sovereign rights, 120–27, 329nn16–17; "hypnosis" and, 206–7; institutionalized practices
and, 141–42, 144–46, 164–72; Kaliningrad
region and, 124, 135–38; lack of accomplishments, 178, 185; Leninism-Stalinism
and minds of citizens, 98–113; national
idea in, 186–87; powers limited by legislature, 219–26; revanchism and rejections
of democracy during, 3–7, 11–12, 97–172,
300; special services, 178, 180, 181–82, 291;
terrorism and need for enemy of Russia,
226–34; two-party system and, 218; violence and, 224, 225; Year 2000 problem
and, 139–40
Yevloev, Magomed, 242
Yezhov, Nikolai, 174
Young Communist League (YCL), 99, 100
Yugoslavia, 3, 157, 161, 261
yukos, 169, 243–44
Yur'iev, Mikhail, 199, 200
Yushchenko, Viktor, 236, 273, 274, 275
Yushenkov, Sergei, 235, 330n25
Yuvenaly, Metropolitan (Vladimir K. Poyarkov), 41–42

Zamyatin, Yevgeny, dystopia of, 313
zastoi. See stagnation
Zavalishin, Nikolai, xxxviii
Zhirinovsky, Vladimir, 11, 90–91, 139, 209
Zyuganov, Gennady, 84, 196–97

CPSIA information can be obtained
at www.ICGtesting.com
Printed in the USA
LVHW041820230819
628749LV00001B/26/P